Views of Berlin

Views
of
Berlin

From a Boston Symposium

**Edited by
Gerhard Kirchhoff**

Birkhäuser
Boston • Basel • Berlin

Gerhard Kirchhoff
Director, Goethe Institute Toulouse
F-31000 Toulouse
France

On the cover is the Europa Center in West Berlin on Breitscheid Platz with Kaiser Wilhelm Memorial Church, April 1985. Reproduced with permission of the Landesbildstelle Berlin.

Library of Congress Cataloging-in-Publication Data
Views of Berlin: from a Boston symposium/edited by Gerhard Kirchhoff.
   p. cm.
   Bibliography: p.
   ISBN 0-8176-3380-4
   1. Berlin (Germany)   I. Kirchhoff, Gerhard, 1924– .
DD860.V54   1988
943.1'55—dc19   88-14509

Printed on acid-free paper.

ISBN 0-8176-3380-4
ISBN 3-7643-3380-4

Typeset by Asco Trade Typesetting Ltd., Hong Kong.
Printed and bound by Edwards Brothers, Inc., Ann Arbor, Michigan.
Printed in the U.S.A.

9 8 7 6 5 4 3 2 1

These "Views of Berlin" are dedicated to all those who want to know more about the reality, the history, and the somehow absurd present of this unique city. Berlin, divided since 1945, continues to be alive and creative in all fields of human life and endeavor. The city has become the intersection of East and West, the "seismograph" of contemporary developments, both cultural and political. This book is meant also to pay homage to the spirit and courage of Berliners, who celebrated the 750th anniversary of their city in 1987 and lived up to the challenge of having been chosen the "Cultural City of Europe, 1988."

Acknowledgments

It is with great pleasure and sincere gratitude that I thank the many Bostonians, Berliners, and others who contributed to the Boston–Berlin Symposium. The Symposium was mainly co-sponsored by the Boston Public Library and the Goethe Institute, but also by the Berlin Economic Development Corporation of New York, Boston Musica Viva, Lufthansa German Airlines, Massachusetts Institute of Technology, the Museum of Fine Arts, the Senate of Berlin, and Technical University Berlin. The Symposium could not have been realized without the creative cooperation between its contributors nor without the extraordinary interest and financial engagement of its American and German sponsors. Thanks to all of them, and to all of those whose names I never learned as well as to Hans Aarsleff, Sigrid Bauschinger, The Boston Musica Viva, The Boston Public Library, The Boston Sänger Chor, Jenny Bowers, Heinrich G. Brugsch, The Busch-Reisinger Museum, Center Screen Cambridge, Gretchen Cromwell, Cynthia Cole, Peter Demetz, Karl W. Deutsch, Deutsche Sonnabend Schule Boston, Meinolf Dierkes, The Dinosaur Annex Music Ensemble, Ulrike Dorda, Ingeborg Drewitz, Baron Friedrich von Dungern, Eva J. Engel, Ilse Fang, Leon A. Feldman, Wolfe J. Frankl, Eckhart Gillen, Sol Gittleman, Louis Golden, Walter Gose, Thomas Hansen, Anneliese Harding, Dana K. Harmon, Charles W. Haxthausen, Kathleen B. Hegarty, Dick Higgins, Robert Hilliard, Walter Höllerer, Julian Crandall Hollick, Ronald Holloway, Peter Iden, Independent Broadcasting Associates, Lotte Jacobi, Peter Jelavich, Veronica Jochum, Alfred Keil, Immo von Kessel, Wilhelm A. Kewenig, Ekkehard Klausa, Jonathan B. Knudsen, Dieter Koch-Weser, Richard Kostelanetz, Gustave A. Laurenzi, The O'Leary Library (University of Lowell), Wolf Lepenies, The Longy School of Music, Louis Lowy, Philipp McNiff, Richard Merritt, Wilhelm V. von Moltke, The Museum of Fine Arts, National Public Radio Station WBUR, Orson Welles Cinema Cambridge, Peter Jan Pahl, Walter Picard, Otto Piene, Richard Pittman, Werner Preuss, Paul Raabe, Ulrich Rastemborski, Henry Ries, Barbara Rosenkrantz, Harry Seelig, The Helen Shliehn Gallery, Kenneth Smith, Susan Southworth, Marylou Speaker-Churchill, Jürgen Starnick, Manfred Stassen, Dietrich Stobbe, Shepard Stone, Peter Storkersen, Wolfgang Stresemann, Manfred

Stürzbecher, Maria Tatar, Edith Toegel, Edith Waldstein, Wilhelm Weise, Richard von Weizsäcker, Kevin White, and A. Leslie Willson.

Now there is this book that, to a large extent, makes the Boston–Berlin Symposium accessible to readers. It would not have been possible to publish it without the support of the Senate of Berlin, Inter-Nationes, and Siemens Capital Corporation, New York. The Senate of Berlin contributed to the production costs and placed at the publisher's disposal most of the photographs chosen for this book. Of course, it was through people that these institutions worked. And so, I also want to thank Wolfgang G. Oergel of Traffic Office Berlin, Thomas Frieske of the Landesbildstelle Berlin, Hans Joachim Wulschner of Inter-Nationes, Hans W. Decker of Siemens Capital Corporation, and their coworkers for their valuable help.

My colleagues in Boston and in Munich who supported the Symposium also receive my thanks, especially Elmar Brandt (now in Sao Paulo), Jürgen Drews, Horst Harnischfeger, Peter Hebel (now in Rome), Fritjof Korn (now in Casablanca), Jürgen Uwe Ohlau (now in New York), Anneliese Harding, Diane Kent, Christine Kodis, and Ulrike Dorda. After my transfer to the Goethe Institute in Toulouse, France, Hans Winterberg, now Director of the Goethe Institute Boston, along with Jürgen Kalkbrenner and Hartmut Lang of the German Consulate General, helped to carry the publishing project over some hurdles that would have been insurmountable without their aid.

It took the effort and enthusiasm of many people to arrive at this stage. Now, having achieved this objective, cordial thanks to all who contributed, particularly to Philipp McNiff, then Director of the Boston Public Library, with whom I drew up the outlines of the project, to Kathleen Hegarty, his assistant, and to my colleagues in the production of the Symposium.

Toulouse   G.K.
December 1988

Contents

Contributors

Karl W. Deutsch	Stanfield Professor of International Peace, Emeritus, Harvard University, Cambridge, MA 02138, USA
Ingeborg Drewitz	Writer, Professor h.c. (deceased)
Leon A. Feldman	Professor of Hebraic Studies, Faculty of Arts and Science, Rutgers—The State University of New Jersey, New Brunswick, NJ 08903, USA
Wolfe J. Frankl	Former Director, North America Berlin Economic Development Corporation, New York, NY 10017-2079, USA
Eckhart Gillen	Mitarbeiter des Museumspädagogischen Dienstes Berlin, D-1000 Berlin 45, Federal Republic of Germany
Thomas S. Hansen	Professor of Literature, Department of German, Wellesley College, Wellesley, MA 02181, USA
Walter Höllerer	Professor of Literature, Berlin Technical University, Institut für Deutsche Philologie, Allgemeine und Vergleichende Literaturwissenschaft, D-1000 Berlin 19, Federal Republic of Germany
Ronald Holloway	Writer and film critic, Helgoländer Ufer 6, D-1000 Berlin 21, Federal Republic of Germany
Peter Jelavich	Professor of History, Department of History, University of Texas at Austin, Austin, TX 78712-1163, USA
Wilhelm A. Kewenig	Senator für Inneres, Land Berlin, D-1000 Berlin 31, Federal Republic of Germany
Gerhard Kirchhoff	Director of the Goethe Institute Toulouse, F-31000 Toulouse, France
Ekkehard Klausa	Privatdozent, Regierungsdirektor, Senatskanzlei Berlin, D-1000 Berlin 62, Federal Republic of Germany

Richard Kostelanetz	Writer and artist, 141 Wooster Street, New York, NY 10012-3112, USA
Wolf Lepenies	Rektor Wissenschaftskolleg zu Berlin, D-1000 Berlin 33, Federal Republic of Germany
Louis Lowy	Professor Emeritus, School of Social Work, Boston University, Boston, MA 02215, USA
Richard L. Merritt	Professor, Department of Political Science, University of Illinois at Urbana–Champaign, Urbana, IL 61801-3696, USA
Wilhelm V. von Moltke	Professor of Urban Design, Emeritus, Harvard University, Cambridge, MA 02138, USA (deceased, 1988)
Walter Picard	Former Member of the German Bundestag, Visiting Professor at American Universities, Nieder-Roden, D-6054 Rodgau, Federal Republic of Germany
Joachim Werner Preuss	Editor and theater critic, Sender Freies Berlin, D-1000 Berlin 19, Federal Republic of Germany
Jürgen Starnick	Senator für Stadtentwicklung und Umweltschutz, D-1000 Berlin 61, Federal Republic of Germany
Dietrich Stobbe	Former Governing Mayor of Berlin, Member of the German Bundestag, D-5300 Bonn 1, Federal Republic of Germany
Wolfgang Stresemann	Former Indendant of the Berliner Philharmonic Orchestra, D-1000 Berlin 33, Federal Republic of Germany
Maria Tatar	Professor, Department of Germanic Languages and Literatures, Harvard University, Cambridge, MA 02138, USA
A. Leslie Willson	Professor, Department of Germanic Languages, University of Texas at Austin, Austin, TX 78712-1126, USA

Introduction

Since the blockade of 1948/49, the divided city of Berlin has been the mirror that reflects the tensions between the East and West. West Berlin became and still remains the symbol of Western democracy, of its strength and its credibility. It has come to stand for the alliance and cooperation between a Europe in the process of rebuilding and the United States. There have been and will continue to be ups and downs in these transatlantic relations, caused by differing interests and opinions; and in any alliance of democracies where freedom of expression is taken seriously, these ups and downs are to be expected, even at times welcomed, as a reaffirmation of democratic freedom. So, despite the occasional quarrels and misunderstandings, there has remained on both sides of the ocean the basic conviction that the future of the United States as well as that of Europe depends on mutual respect and understanding, and these must be based on full and complete knowledge about one another. A continuing American–European dialogue that covers all questions of common concern is essential to this understanding. And the lessons learned in Berlin, particularly in West Berlin, the intersection between East and West, will help insure this understanding.

Because of the many connections—intellectual, philosophical, spiritual—between Berlin and Boston, the Goethe Institute and the Boston Public Library joined together to make Berlin the focus for a number of special cultural events starting in 1982. The fact that Berlin would be celebrating its 750th anniversary in 1987 gave special meaning to these events. The then mayors of Berlin and Boston joined together to open officially these activities and welcomed the participants in joint statements in which Bostonians and Berliners were invited to celebrate the cultural rapport of these two great cities.

Many scholars, artists, musicians, writers, and statesmen contributed to the German–American symposia from which this book was developed. The living past as well as the present were treated; and the emphasis was on the exchange of experience and research, knowledge and ideas, based, as far as possible, on communication in person between German and American citizens. The Boston–Berlin Symposium covered many aspects of Berlin's reality "then and now," but it was not intended to become an exhaustive "encyclopedia" on Berlin. Among the many Bostonians involved were former Berliners and others; they used their special interests and fields of work and included as well various Boston events with a Berlin connection. It was assumed that the actual program would include art exhibits, concerts, and film series, and that the lecture series would elucidate features of Berlin's past and present. But its details developed step by step, each stage evolving from the stage before it.

Most contributions to the various symposia have found their place in chapters in this book. A few could not be included. For example, the symposium "Berlin in the Age of Enlightenment" was withdrawn for separate publication. But the symposium "Berlin Society and Art Between the Wars" became part of Section II. Most of the symposium "Portraits of Berlin" appear in various chapters of the book. The symposium "Aims, Work, Relevancy of Centers for Advanced Study" is represented by Wolf Lepenies' contribution in Section IV. The aim was to collect from these symposia a "Berlin mosaic," a variegated, lively account that provides insight into Berlin's past as well as its present and reflects the challenge and encouragement that the world can derive from this divided but still dynamic and creative metropolitan city.

Among the many highlights that cannot be recreated for this volume was the "Berlin Evening," a multimedia show; another was "The Wild Stage Cabaret," modelled after a Berlin cabaret of the early 1930s. Both involved satirical songs of protest against the Nazis and their suppression of free thought, drastically symbolized by the burning of books in front of the University of Berlin on May 10, 1933.

Concerts of piano and orchestral music were presented at the Museum of Fine Arts and the Longy School of Music. National Public Radio aired a series of 13 concerts by the Berlin Philharmonic Orchestra and the Berlin Radio Symphony Orchestra as well as special documentary features on Berlin.

Nine exhibitions were mounted at the Goethe Institute, the Boston Public Library, the University of Lowell, and Harvard University's Busch–Reisinger Museum. These involved the photographic works of Heinrich Zille, Alfred Eisenstaedt, Henry Ries, Lotte Jacobi, and Moholy-Nagy, as well as (at the Busch–Reisinger) an exhibit of "Berlin and Berlin Artists of the 20th Century"; and (at the Boston Public Library) "Ex Libris: Publications and Photographs of the Literarisches Colloquium Berlin." The Library also presented "Berlin—A City in Search of its Future," an exhibit of pictures, models, and audiovisual elements dramatizing the cultural, scientific, and industrial developments that have taken Berlin from rubble to rebirth, from a World War II wasteland to one of the world's great cultural and scientific centers.

For various reasons, collecting the symposia papers and compiling this book were very time consuming. We regret that publication is so much later than we had planned. But in a sense the message of the book is timeless. The Boston–Berlin events were staged to help strengthen relations between Americans and Germans. The scholars, writers, and artists—Americans and Germans—who were involved in this vital dialogue were all dedicated to the goal of furthering understanding through their special knowledge of particular aspects of the city's activities. Relations improve and continue to improve. These papers will help. As different as they are, with all their critical as well as enthusiastic observations, they all have one quality in common: They all pay tribute to Berlin and are a convincing argument for its continuing, flourishing existence.

Toulouse   Gerhard Kirchhoff
December 1988

A Political Focus of East and West

CHAPTER 1

Berlin, A Center of German– American Relations— A Solid Friendship Despite Ups and Downs

Ekkehard Klausa

What is going on in German–American relations? A specter is haunting the United States—the specter of anti-Americanism in Germany. Should German anti-Americanism be more than a mere apparition, it would certainly be an ugly reality. It may seem not only strange but morally shocking to see people bite the hand that fed them so faithfully after World War II through CARE packages and Marshall Plan funds; that during the blockade of West Berlin in 1948/49 installed an airlift in order to literally keep this city alive; a hand that still today provides Germans with strong protection. Let us take a tough look at some German–American grievances and then try to understand the underlying facts.

In 1963, President Kennedy was welcomed in West Berlin by enthusiastic crowds, including students who, only one and a half years later, were to launch the "Free Speech Movement" that developed into the "APO" (*Ausserparlamentarische Opposition*), the extraparliamentary opposition with its fierce criticism of the state, capitalist society, and above all, the Vietnam War. In 1963, President Kennedy clearly was the darling of the Berliners, and he is reported to have remarked on his triumphant motorcade: "What a shame they aren't American voters."

Exactly nineteen years later, President Reagan came to visit Berlin. The streets seemed to belong to anti-Reagan demonstrations, one big and peaceful and one small and violent in which police officers were injured and police vans set afire. The president and 300,000 Berliners eager to greet him and to cheer his country had to be locked away into the park of Charlottenburg Palace, which was easy to seal off and to defend against Reagan haters. I deeply resented the precautions that I knew were necessary and the security checks that I had to undergo like everybody else.

Some years before, I had attended a mass rally for Soviet leader Leonid Breshnev in East Berlin. There were no security measures comparable to those taken for President Reagan. Breshnev could be presented to the unscreened masses. Of course, there were lots of policemen in uniform as well as in plain clothes around, but they seemed to have little or nothing to do. No popular resentment was visible against which they would have had to protect President Breshnev. In a Soviet-type dictatorship, there is no need for special precautions to deter a majority from voicing their desire to send the Russians home. They know all too well what would happen if they did. So they just shrug their shoulders and may even to some extent enjoy the pompous show of their supreme master's state visit. The chief oppressor may take a bath in the crowd with impunity.

In a democracy, on the other hand, a very small minority wanting to snip at the heels of an important state visitor can easily make the streets unsafe. They know that they have almost nothing to fear from their provocation of the majority feeling. After all, they live in a *Rechtsstaat*, i.e., in a political system that guarantees them the full protection of the law when they exercise their right to express their opinion freely. Nevertheless, the different experiences of two American presidents, visiting Berlin, show that a significant change in political climate had taken place between 1963 and 1982. In 1963, not even a minority hated the Americans. Had there been such a minority then, it would have simply been swept away by the public mood. Today, however, anti-Americanism has a psychological chance to articulate itself in public. It even seems to be on the offensive. In 1981, a new political party, the "Greens" or, in the Berlin case, the "Alternative list," entered the Berlin House of Representatives and, more recently, the *Bundestag* in Bonn—a party associated with heated and fundamental criticism of the United States. Some analysts have attributed this change in the climate of public opinion to the Reagan administration and its rather belligerent talk on very sensitive matters of atomic strategy during its early months. However, there is evidence that this change started much earlier. In 1980, Americans as well as the majority of the Germans were shocked by an open letter written by the prominent German poet Günter Grass and three of his fellow writers to Chancellor Helmut Schmidt. A significant passage reads as follows:

> Do not let yourselves be dragged by an American government, which since Vietnam, at the very latest, has lost all right to make moral appeals, into policies which could have as a result the destruction of life on this planet. We Germans cannot act as though we did not know what blood baths can be carried out in the name of "national honor." Every means, every utopian fantasy, every compromise must be acceptable to us Germans, if it serves to maintain and secure peace. Nobody is attacking us, nobody threatens us. In our land, loyalty to any alliance finds its limit as soon as the peace is threatened, whether by commission or omission.

This letter was written when the resident of the White House was a soft-spoken man from Georgia. Only four months had elapsed since the Soviets had invaded Afghanistan. The American hostages were still being held in Iran, and the United States had not yet attempted to liberate them by military force. Nevertheless, these writers held that the American government was trying to "drag" the Germans into policies that could destroy life on the planet. According to these writers, Germany was threatened by nobody—with the obvious exception of the United States.

The open letter by Grass and his colleagues clearly never represented even a significant minority view. It was sharply rejected by government and press alike. But writers are sometimes a sensitive seismograph for changes of mood. Not the mood of the majority but a small, yet influential elite. There is no doubt that today more, though still not many, Germans would sub-scribe to the anti-American views uttered by Günter Grass and others in 1980.

David Kramer, an American social scientist teaching in Berlin, did an in-depth analysis of survey research data and personal interviews and came to the conclusion that, while the vast majority of Germans continues to believe in German–American friendship and in America's responsible leadership for Western democracy and security, there is a small but growing and significant section of the German public that tends to be distant if not hostile. This new mood can be localized above all in the "successor generation," as opposed to the founder generation of German–American cooperation after the war. More disturbingly, it can be found in particular among highly educated members of that younger generation. The editor of *Die Zeit*, Theo Sommer, perceives an "elitist critique" of America within this minority made up of teenagers, academics, church people, and ecologists. There are, according to Sommer, three strands of motivation that come together in this anti-American syndrome. The first one is anti-modernism, opposition to what is known as the "American way of life." The second one is opposition to nu-clear power, both for civilian and military purposes. The third is pacifism. Sommer's analysis, it should be noted, was made under the presidency of Jimmy Carter.

In order to look into that matter, I did a little unsystematic research. I asked a selection of people from all strands of life to just give me some of the connotations that the United States as a country and the Americans as a people evoke in them. One of my interviewees was a bearded young church musician, a man whose lifestyle would be called "alternative" in Berlin: eco-logist, natural-food freak, vigorous opponent of nuclear-power plants, let alone nuclear missiles. I drew a fierce answer: "The Soviets are destroying other peoples from the outside with their imperialism, as in Afghanistan; the Americans are destroying them from the inside with capitalism." "But," I retorted, "don't you think we are, all of us, somehow deeply influenced by American culture?" "American CULTURE?" he sneered. "There is no such thing." He will hardly have realized that he was voicing a very old-fashioned, conservative if not reactionary, prejudice of long standing in Ger-man history.

Another of my interviewees was a young business executive who is moon-lighting as a local politician, being a *Bezirksverordneter*—a city district councilman for the Christian Democratic Party. Hence, he is a very active member of Chancellor Kohl's party which keeps emphasizing the indispen-sability and viability of German–American friendship. When I asked him for his views on America and American culture, he said that his picture was shaped by Vance Packard's *Hidden Persuaders*, which he had read as a boy. He professed a deep ambivalence about the kind of mass-consumer soci-ety that tends to level individuality by mass sales of mass goods and, con-sequently, by prefabricated mass ideas.

What do these statements reveal?

The criticism of the young Christian Democratic politician of American advertising and consumerism should definitely not be taken as thorough-going anti-Americanism. His simplistic Vance-Packard image of the United

States is distorted by cultural prejudice. He appears to be one of those young people who, according to Arthur Burns, former U.S. Ambassador to Bonn, would profit from a prejudice-shattering personal acquaintance with America and the Americans. This young man is, of course, a stout supporter of the U.S.–German political and military alliance. He has deep confidence in and gratitude for America's willingness and ability to defend the liberty of Western Europe in general and of Berlin in particular. Moreover, his line of cultural criticism, it should be noted, would be shared by many Americans, inadequate though it is as a comprehensive picture of the United States. The true meaning of this criticism is not a German condemnation of America but a self-criticism of capitalist society in general. Many things denounced as American devices for eroding traditional culture, such as fast food, TV commercials, and the like, are not exclusively American but aspects of capitalist or mass-consumer or post-industrial society in general. Being the most advanced post-industrial country, America merely leads the way and arrives at certain crossroads earlier than the rest of us. This, however, does not make a general cultural development a feature of the American national character.

Here lies the basic fallacy in the allegation of the young church musician who holds that "the Americans are destroying other peoples from the inside with their capitalism." It is not *their* capitalism: it is *ours*; and, of course, it need not be destructive. Rather, it is the best method to safeguard liberty in a society, though it does have a price and may harm traditional cultural values. The fallacy of the church musician, who must certainly be called anti-American, is something like a "projection" in the psychological sense. The real or imagined shortcomings of modern times are dumped at America's door as if she were personally responsible. This is *America used as a metaphor*—a brand of anti-Americanism that is little more than antimodernism.

The irony in this is that the anti-Americans cannot escape America. Even their intended anti-Americanism is an American import. David Kramer points out quite correctly that the "Alternative Movement," which is supposed to be the hotbed of anti-Americanism, is really an American invention to the bone. Nearly every one of its currents and components made an organized appearance in the American "counter-cultural" movement before coming to Germany:

— the community groups or *Bürgerinitiativen*,
— the ecology movement,
— alternative life-styles,
— youth movements and senior movements,
— land communes and regionalism,
— women's and homosexual movements,
— the psycho-sensitivity movement,
— religious sectarianism and spiritualism,
— the peace movement and Third-World initiatives,
— undogmatic left and spontaneity groups, called *Spontis* in Germany.

The *Hausbesetzer* or squatter movement—young people illegally occupying and often repairing run-down empty houses—which sprang to life in

West Berlin in 1980 and in Great Britain and the Netherlands much earlier, is probably the only independent European current.

Thus, the question is really not whether a German is pro- or anti-American but whether he is in favor of President Reagan, or of Senator Kennedy, or, in the extreme case, of Angela Davis. The peace movement may have grown into a mass phenomenon in Germany somewhat earlier than in the United States. However, it reached its high tide in America only months later and even swept Catholic bishops to an extent unthinkable so far in West Germany.

Such a trans-Atlantic coincidence makes it impossible, I think, to label the German peace movement anti-American. Rather, it is anti-Reagan and anti-Weinberger—no less and not much more than it is anti-Kohl and even anti-Schmidt. Not much more, either, than the American peace movement is against its own administration.

The coincidence of counter-cultural movements in Germany and America—yes, even the American copyright to virtually all of them— highlights two analytical points which, I think, suggest an explanation for German criticism of America that has little to do with fundamental anti-Americanism.

My hypothesis is:

a. Germany and the Germans are today deeply imbued with American political and cultural values and influences. The two countries are closer than ever. This is at least as true of alternative sub-culture as it is of the cultural mainstream in business, academia, the culture industry, and everyday life-styles.

b. Hence, German–American relations are no longer just international in character but must partly be understood in terms of *interior politics* of a community that includes both countries. The lines of conflict and of consensus are not frontiers between the two nations but cut across both of them. The same political types are going to cheer and hiss President Reagan in either country.

Moreover, we are so deeply imbued with American values and American dreams that we tend to react much more emotionally to what happens in the United States than in England and France. What the CIA (Central Intelligence Agency) does or is supposed to have done in Chile, El Salvador, and

---

Photographs on p. 8

Town Hall Schöneberg, office of the Governing Mayor of West Berlin with the Assembly Hall of the Land government.—May 18, 1982. Reproduced with permission of the Landesbildstelle Berlin (above).

Rally in front of the Town Hall Schöneberg, Rudolph-Wilde-Platz (later: John F. Kennedy Platz) on June 26, 1963. From right to left: John F. Kennedy, President of the United States; President of the Parliament, Otto Bach; Governing Mayor of Berlin, Willy Brandt.—June 26, 1963. Reproduced with permission of the Landesbildstelle Berlin (below).

Nicaragua arouses more feelings than what the British Secret Service or the French Deuxième Bureau could possibly do anywhere.

An FDP (Freie Demokratische Partei) member in the Berlin House of Representatives whom David Kramer interviewed about anti-Americanism made this statement:

> Here in Berlin it was the case that from 1945 until 1967, when the student demonstrations began against . . . the war in Vietnam . . . , a *very exalted*, an *idealistic image of America* existed. It was an accepted fact that America was not only the leading political and military power . . . not only the country with the most progressive civilization . . . , but American culture was taken as a model in all possible areas of life.

In a way, the Germans have so much adopted the American view that they agree with the traditional American conviction that the United States will not or should not act like a normal big power but should always be guided by idealism alone. In that sense, Vietnam and Watergate dealt a blow to an exalted image—may I say: it dealt a blow in Germany and in America alike? The exaggerated critique deriving from this disappointment may be called somewhat cheap and out of proportion, but it also testifies to an unusual closeness, a deep-reaching community of values, between our two nations.

I know a number of Americans in Berlin, and I understand that they are a little angry that young Germans are more likely to manifest their protest against American politics in El Salvador than against Soviet politics in Poland or even against the inhuman Berlin Wall just a few yards away. On the surface, this situation may indeed look like a blindness in one eye, like a bias against America. However, the truth of the matter is that it only expresses a great political and emotional closeness with the United States. What our brother seems to do wrong will arouse us more deeply than much dirtier acts committed by a stranger of whom we disapprove anyway. With the Americans, we share a belief in and a responsibility for a set of democratic values and their consequences in world politics. With the Russians, we don't. In that sense, much of the ill feeling that a German minority harbors against America is really a family syndrome. It is what we call *Hassliebe*—the hatred born out of love, a frequent situation between people who are emotionally close. We may think of the bittersweet feelings of a couple married, as our two nations happen to be, for more than thirty years. The conduct of those "oldlyweds" toward each other contrasts unfavorably with that of radiant fiancees. Nevertheless, they need each other and would not dream of a divorce. Another fitting psychological simile would be that of a growing-up son who feels compelled to affront his dad from time to time.

Photographs on p. 9

Riots near Nollendorfplatz (Schöneberg) after an unauthorized demonstration on the occasion of the visit of Ronald Reagan, President of the United States.—June 11, 1982. Reproduced with permission of the Landesbildstelle Berlin. (above)

Berliners observing a landing transport aircraft during the blockade of the Western Sectors in 1948/49.—1948. Reproduced with permission of the Landesbildstelle Berlin. (below)

This latter metaphor takes me to my last point: the question posed by some concerned American observers whether a *revived German nationalism* is using America as a punching bag for its self-assertion. There may be something in that. However, I hasten to add that we are talking of an unusually mild brand of nationalism.

You know that the British, for instance, fought heroic wars against the dangerous idea that some nation was superior to all the rest—without ever being vexed by the slightest doubt which nation was *really* superior. Similar propositions, I think, could be made about the nationalism of the *Grande Nation* or even about that of the United States. All of these three nationalisms are essentially nonmalignant forms of ethnocentrism, nothing to compare with the ferocious chauvinism that was sometimes known and feared under the name of nationalism and carried to the extreme by the Nazis.

What remains of German nationalism—or rather, what is right now enjoying a modest comeback after a long banishment—is even much milder than that of the Americans, the British, or the French. The Germans certainly no longer feel superior to other nations. After 1945, they had little to look back to. Every glance at their historic past—and, thus, at their national identity—seemed barred by the horrible twelve years of Nazi rule. Many Germans chose to forget that their history had lasted much longer than that. I believe that in those post-war years the *emulation of America* helped to fill the gap. The Cold War and American support allowed West Germany to find a new anti-communist identity and justification without first coming to terms with their immediate Nazi past—what we call *Bewältigung der Vergangenheit*. I have the impression that many Germans of that generation jumped with relief into a new identification with the United States in order to be left alone by their own history and by the painful need to search for a new national identity.

There lies, in my opinion, part of the explanation for the Americanization of German everyday life, of culture and language. To understand a modern German newspaper, you need an English dictionary. The good old *Bäckerei* or *Brotladen* is giving way, in many cases, to a neo-German *Brotshop*. In a German disco, you will hardly hear a German word. It's too noisy for conversation anyway, and what comes out of the loudspeaker is made in America.

In this situation, I think a modest comeback of patriotism or a response to the need for a national identity was inevitable and normal, even healthy. Of the more dangerous forms of nationalism we are, I trust, cured for a long time to come. But a new identification with German history is blossoming in all political camps. To the extent that it was a gap-filler, identification with America will be replaced by a modest national renaissance. I have the impression that some Germans are so heatedly criticizing America because they realize that German culture and they themselves have proceeded on the road of Americanization beyond the point of no return. If Americans today tend to be more irritated by criticism from Germany than from France or other countries, I take this as another proof of German–American family closeness. American friends have often told me that they feel more at home in Germany than in other European countries. So do many Germans in the United States. This kind of *Wesensverwandtschaft* (of kinship of the innermost self), or whatever it is, makes a rebuff more painful. But the *Wesensver-wandtschaft* or family similarity is there and remains strong. Even those 20 percent of the young Germans who today profess a political preference for the counter-cultural "Green Movement" will not be young and green forever. Growing up will lead most of them to a new recognition of the German–American community of values and of interests.

A person as outspoken against American world politics as novelist Günter Grass, whose pretty mean criticism I quoted earlier, would seem to present a clear case of anti-Americanism. However, he insists that he loves America. These are his own words:

> Nevertheless, as amazing as it sounds, I am often in America and love America and see the Americans as our allies. However, I think that in this situation criticism is the best sign of loyalty.

I feel that Günter Grass gives us a clue here as to what makes the difference between liking and disliking America: Grass is "often in America and love[s] America." I hardly met a single young German who set foot on American soil without losing at least a corner of his or her heart there. Hence, I think we would do a lot of good to our trans-Atlantic family relations in increasing exchange programs for young Germans and Americans on various social levels—not only students but also young employees.

A close American friend of mine who lives in Berlin admits that she sometimes feels hurt by what she perceives as malignant criticism of her country. But recently she reported a gratifying experience. She took her favorite sandals to a local shoemaker. The sandals were so ragged that she thought they couldn't be brought back to life, but they were. When she wanted to pay the shoemaker, he refused to accept any money on the ground "that you Americans did SO MUCH for us people in Berlin." Personally, I am confident that this shoemaker's emotion is shared by the vast majority of the Germans and that it will prevail. There are ups and downs in our relations. There are problem areas that are unavoidable in close relations, but they are not as alarming as they appear at first glance. What prevails is a solid friendship despite ups and downs.

CHAPTER 2

Postwar Berlin: Divided City*

Richard L. Merritt

Greater Berlin, one of the world's largest cities spatially and boasting almost 4.5 million inhabitants in 1943, during the next half-decade suffered three successive waves of disruption that left its population staggered, divided, but far from broken.

The first disruptive wave came with aerial bombardments and, in April 1945 when the Red Army stormed the city, savage streetfighting. It reduced greater parts of the city to piles of rubble. The U.S. Strategic Bombing Survey, for instance, estimated that 42 percent of Berlin's 1.5 million dwelling units were destroyed, and another 31 percent damaged to a lesser or greater extent; German sources estimated that they removed 98 million cubic yards of rubble from the city.[1][†] Evacuations reduced its population by a third from the peak of 1943. The destruction also crippled Berlin's communications and transportation facilities no less than its capacity to provide such normal municipal services as electricity, gas, water, and sewage removal.

The bombing and streetfighting nonetheless had a random effect as far as the eastern and western halves of the city were concerned. East Berlin—that is, the part that is now occupied by the Soviets—lost 24 percent of its population and 23 percent of its industrial capacity, whereas the three future Western sectors lost 27 percent of their population and 24 percent of their industrial capacity. East Berlin, with 37 percent of prewar Berlin's dwelling units, accounted for 26 percent of the bombing losses and 40 percent of the rubble.[2]

The effects of the second disruptive wave were distributed less equitably. Berlin fell to the Red Army on May 2, 1945; but not until July 1 did the Western Allies take over their occupation sectors in the city. During these two months, Soviet occupation authorities extensively dismantled the city's remaining industrial capacity to ship off to the USSR as reparations.[3] Possibly because of the unsettled nature of the reparations agreements, possibly because of the critical importance to the Soviet Union of western Berlin's

---

*Reprinted with permission from Ronald A. Francisco and Richard L. Merritt, editors, *Berlin Between Two Worlds* (Boulder, CO: Westview Press, 1986).
[†]See Notes section at the end of this chapter.

Ruins (Kreuzberg) 1945. Street right up from below: Alexandrinenstraße; above: intersection Oranienstraße with Waldeckpark; on its right: St. Jacobi Church.—1945. Reproduced with permission of the Landesbildstelle Berlin.

industry, possibly (as Western writers have charged) because of the realization that the Red Army would eventually have to yield the Western sectors to U.S., British, and French contingents, possibly (as Eastern writers have explained) because of concern that the West would fail to live up to the wartime Allies' tacit agreements on reparations—whatever the cause, the effect was that the dismantling during these two months cost West Berlin twice as much of its total industrial capacity (with the loss estimated variously at between 53 and 67 percent) as East Berlin had suffered (25–33 percent).[4]

The third disruptive wave constituted the division of the city itself. Soon after Berlin's joint occupation by the Four Powers, cooperation broke down along East–West lines.[5] The underlying issues were global in scope, but it was in Berlin that their practical effects were felt. These effects had to do with the provision of electricity and other municipal services; arrests and other forms of harassment; control over records and historical documents; and midnight confiscations of garbage cans, trucks, and building material. By March 1948, the four-power Kommandatura split. Three months later, after the Western currency reform and the Soviet currency reform in response, came the blockade of the Western sectors of Berlin and the West's

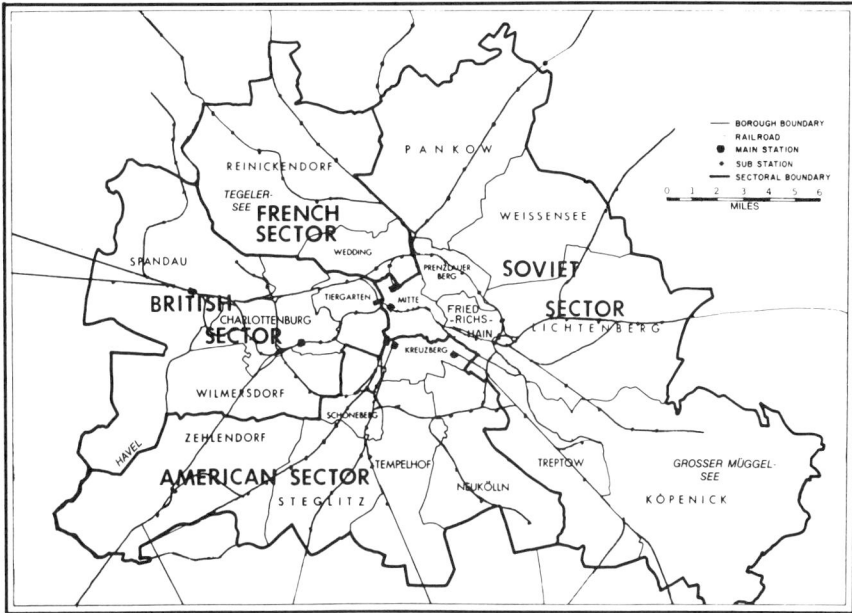

FIGURE 1. *Borough and sectoral boundaries of Greater Berlin, 1945.*

counterblockade of those areas of Germany and Berlin under Soviet control. The processes of quasi-unified municipal government broke down in August 1948, to be replaced by separate governments in East and West Berlin. A Soviet–American agreement in May 1949 ended the blockade and counter-blockade. It failed, however, to resolve the underlying issues spawned by the cold war, and left Berlin a divided city.

The question I shall address is how Berliners and their governments learned to cope with their divided city. The focus will be less on high-level diplomacy and intergovernmental relations than on the people living in the city. After all, whether or not a population learns to consider itself a single political community—sharing major values, responding to each other's concerns, identifying with one another, and all the rest—and whether or not the members of a formerly unified political community learn to accept its division into separate political communities depends less on official decrees than on the sentiments and behaviors of human beings carrying out their everyday lives. After surveying the political development of Berlin since 1945, I shall look at infrastructural, organizational, and behavioral changes in the city, before turning to the question of the future of divided Berlin.

Berlin in the Vortex of World Politics

The political division of Berlin was a direct consequence of the breakdown of the anti-Axis alliance of World War II. The architects of peace during the wartime period had had a daring vision: that any resolution of the global problem of peace would necessarily rely on full cooperation between East and West. They were at best reluctant to plan for the eventuality that this cooperation would collapse. When the reality of conflict replaced the vision of cooperation, many unanticipated issues rose to the surface—not the least of which was the anomaly of Western troops in charge of part of a city lying deep inside the Soviet zone of occupation without guaranteed rights of overland access.

The political division brought by the blockade was, no doubt, not the Soviet goal when its troops stopped all highway, railroad, and canal traffic between the Western sectors of Berlin and Western zones of Germany. The Soviet Union evidently expected that this pressure would force the West to relinquish its hold on the island-city. The West responded instead by setting up an airlift that could provision both the occupying forces and the 2.25 million West Berliners in their charge. Faced by the success of the airlift, the Soviets then tried to take over the city's government. Massive efforts to intimidate West Berlin's representatives, who comprised a strong majority of the assembly, forced them to remove their offices to the American sector, where they set up shop again. Meanwhile, those remaining in the East quickly reorganized and, in November 1949, proclaimed a new government. Berlin thus had two governments, each proclaiming jurisdiction over the entire city, but each, in fact, limited to areas controlled by its protective occupation forces.

What ensued was close to a dozen years during which the status of Berlin was cloudy. On the one hand, the governments in East and West Berlin acted increasingly independently of each other in a formal sense; and, by the mid-1950s, even the broad range of unofficial contacts which had continued were broken off. Officials in the West indicated that what they knew about the actions of their counterparts in the East came almost exclusively from newspaper reports. The principle of four-power occupation, on the other hand, remained intact, and with it the notion that, legally at least, Berlin remained a single city. There was relatively free mobility across the line separating the two halves of the city. A small number of people even lived in one half while working in the other. Then, too, the citizens of neither were granted full rights of participation in the national parliaments created in the Federal Republic of Germany (FRG) in the West and the German Democratic Republic (GDR) in the East.

The GDR's decision in August 1961 to build a wall around West Berlin radically transformed the city's political context and expectations. Viewed from the perspective of Walter Ulbricht and his colleagues in the East German government, the step was certainly understandable. The open border in Berlin since 1949 had contributed significantly to the flight of over 3 million GDR citizens—about a sixth of its total population, over half of them young men just entering the labor market, and including very large numbers of doctors, engineers, and other trained technicians. It had also provided East Germans with ready access to the glitter of West Berlin, to a very public display of what their life might be like were they not saddled with their Communist system. By building the wall, the GDR made clear its intention to stabilize the status quo. It dashed any hopes that may have

Barrier at the Soviet Sector (August 13, 1961); U.S. soldier at the sector boundary Friedrichstraße (Kreuzberg); behind him a water gun of the GDRs people's police.— August 24, 1961. Reproduced with permission of the Landesbildstelle Berlin.

remained in East or West that Germany or Berlin would be reunited in the near future.

The tension caused by the wall—and it was intense during the first months after it was built—eventually gave way to a more moderate attitude that legitimized the new status quo. At the outset, of course, there was great cause for concern. Propagandistic fusillades were fired across the wall in both directions; and by October 1961, Soviet and American tanks faced each other a few meters apart at Checkpoint Charlie. As late as the following spring, Soviet MIGs were still buzzing downtown West Berlin at dangerously low altitudes. The Cuban missile crisis of October 1962, however, brought mutual accommodations; and the simple passage of time accustomed people to the wall's existence even if they did not like it. By 1969 the political climate had changed to such an extent that West Germany's new Social Democratic chancellor, Willy Brandt, could initiate a policy of relaxation that ultimately included, among other things, a four-power agreement on Berlin in 1971 and subsequent intra-German agreements that eased the lot of West Berliners and permitted them once again to cross the border into the East. Later moves by the German Democratic Republic tied East Berlin ever closer to that country's political and constitutional structure.

Elaborate interpretations of its underlying meanings notwithstanding, the Quadripartite and other agreements of 1971/73 had the effect of giving the status quo of divided Berlin a seal of acceptance (albeit not, at least in Western eyes, approval). Thus it has remained in the years since then. But, while it may be a relatively simple matter to draw a political boundary and enforce it with immigration officers and, if necessary, bayonets and barbed wire, to divide a city and political community which act as an organic unity is quite a different matter.

Infrastructural Division

The political boundary between East and West Berlin, although based on borough boundaries that had long existed, is artificial in every other sense. Spatially, for example, the development of Greater Berlin was not unlike that of most other metropolises of its time. It had a core area comprising the central business district, government buildings, and cultural institutions such as theaters and the university; an inner ring of densely populated apartment buildings and an outer ring of suburban growth; and an integrated network of subway lines, sewers, water pipes, and the like that served the city as a whole. The long-term success of any political division not based on popular wishes would necessarily rest upon the disruption of that integrated infrastructure.

Municipal Services

That change could not come overnight can be seen in the example of Berlin's municipal utilities.[6] Geographic circumstances had played a role in the reconstruction of these services following the wartime damage and postwar dismantling. In contrast to the gas and water companies, which had their main offices in the Western sectors, the electricity company was located in the Soviet sector and, since the Red Army had shipped off over 90 percent of the power-generating facilities outside their own sector, the Western sectors of the city were almost totally reliant on decisions made in the East. The sewage system, which interlaced the entire city, poured about 98 percent of its raw sewage into leach fields and treatment centers located in the Soviet sector or zone.

The experience of the blockade made West Berliners insist on complete independence from the East with respect to most of these municipal services. During the blockade months, Soviet authorities had simply shut off the flow of electricity to the Western sectors, presumably as a means of bringing pressure to bear upon them. Even in the winter months of 1948/49, the average household in West Berlin received only two hours of electricity per day—and then at sometimes unpredictable hours. The Western Allies responded by flying into the city whole generators, part by part, to rebuild the Western Power Plant dismantled by the Soviets; and they provided economic assistance after the blockade to spur the development of West Berlin's power-generating capacity. By early 1955, West Berlin produced all its own electricity.

Separation, wherever it was feasible, became the rule for the other utilities as well. This process was completed for the gas company by 1950 and for the waterworks a decade later. West Berlin aimed at independence in rubbish disposal by constructing enormous incinerators. The increase in rubbish that accompanies prosperity, however, outstripped the increase in capacities to handle it, with the consequence that West Berlin ultimately had to negotiate with the GDR to dispose of it effectively. The city also continues to pay the GDR substantial sums every year to accept its untreated sewage (which the GDR, in turn, uses for fertilizing and other profitable purposes); both sides realize that a disruption of this service would produce unwanted consequences, such as the pollution of waterways flowing through Berlin and the GDR.

Spatial Organization

Buildings and streets, we might think, are even more resistant to change dictated by political circumstances than are municipal utilities.[7] An examination of spatial developments in Berlin since the war, nevertheless, reveals that political demands, at least when implemented unrelentingly, can have a significant impact in these regards as well.

Not the least of these developments stemmed from West Berlin's loss of the core-area functions it shared with the eastern part when Greater Berlin was still Germany's capital city. The division of Germany into separate and mutually antagonistic countries, West Berlin's exposed location deep inside the GDR, and the ever present possibility of yet another blockade conspired to push West Berlin to the periphery of West German life. Bonn took over the function of political capital, Hamburg became the center of commerce, and Frankfurt is the FRG's financial center. Nor do the country's major cultural impulses come almost exclusively from Berlin anymore, as was true in the 1920s. By contrast, the East German leadership, perhaps unwisely from some perspectives, chose to build up "Democratic Berlin" as the country's capital and locate there its main core-area functions.

What is happening is a process of adjustment: West Berlin is reducing the scope of its political and economic activity to bring it into balance with its current capabilities. In the short run, this process can turn West Berlin into a self-sufficient, viable political entity, besides making life in the city even more pleasantly bearable. Its long-run effect, however, is to reinforce the consequences of the city's division: the encapsulation and withdrawal of West Berlin from its traditional hinterland, and the acceptance by West Berlin of a peripheral position in West German life, in contrast to the centrality enjoyed by Greater Berlin before 1945 and by East Berlin in the German Democratic Republic today.

Just as Greater Berlin was the core area of prewar Germany, so too the borough of Mitte, or City Center, was the heart of Berlin. It contained the Reich's most important administrative offices, the city hall, and key embassies. Streets such as Unter den Linden and monuments such as the Brandenburg Gate (Brandenburger Tor) were known to the world. Mitte had the university, state library, world-famous museums, state opera, cathedral, national theater, and a host of other cultural establishments. It was the center of Germany's newspaper and book trade. Two-thirds of Berlin's insurance firms, three-quarters of its banks, and half of its ladies' garment manufacturers were located within a few blocks of each other. Mitte, no more than 4.1 square miles in size, clearly set prewar Germany's political, economic, and cultural patterns.

The political division of 1948 sharply reduced Mitte's practical importance and even its symbolic value. Wartime destruction, of course, had all but wiped out Mitte. After the fighting stopped and the occupation began, however, it once again became the focal point of Berlin life—under the aegis of the Soviet Union, in whose sector of occupation it lay. The city hall and other municipal offices began operations, often in provisional quarters, to be sure; and eventually theaters, the university, and the opera opened their doors again. The borough was prepared to resume its rightful role as the core area of one of the world's largest cities.

With the split came the realization for West Berliners that they would have to look elsewhere for a core area, at least until the city should be reunified. Least problematic was the search for a new central business district. Even before the war, writers and statisticians had noticed certain movements away from Mitte. The most important one was the emergence of a fashionable shopping center near the Berlin zoo and the Kaiser Wilhelm Memorial Church (Kaiser-Wilhelm-Gedächtniskirche) in the borough of Charlottenburg, about two miles southwest of the Brandenburg Gate. The availability of less-damaged buildings had led to a small scale revival before the blockade; political division and the economic recovery of West Berlin in the ensuing years merely enhanced this trend.

Before the 1950s were over, the Zooviertel (or Zoo Quarter) had firmly established itself as West Berlin's new core area (Figure 2). It housed the major businesses and the stock exchange. With its leading restaurants, first-

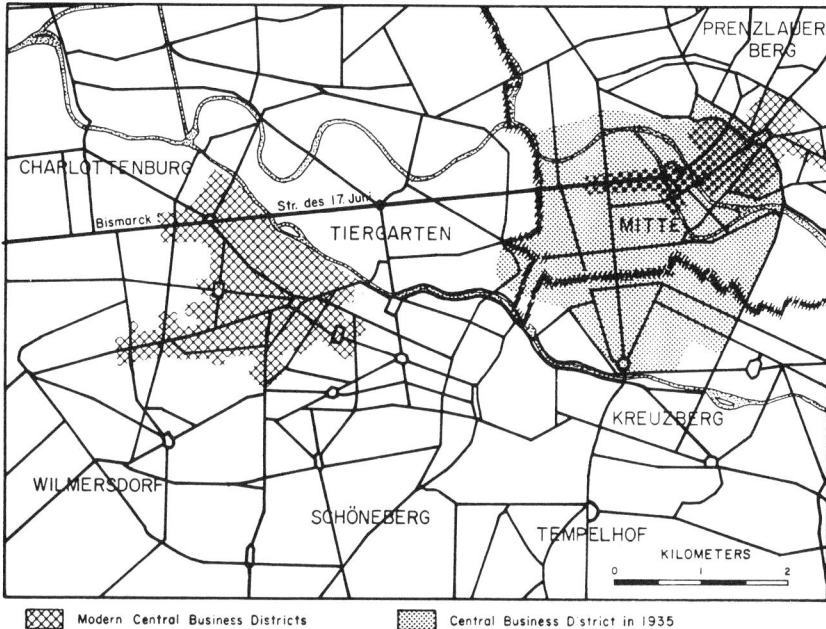

FIGURE 2. *Shift of Berlin's central business district, 1945–1985.*

run movie houses, and exclusive shops it became the focal point of tourists and West Berliners alike. Traffic patterns, which once had Mitte as their nodal point, now had the Zoo Quarter. Gradually, too, government offices drifted from their temporary quarters to a belt just to the south of this core area; and residential patterns began to accommodate themselves to the changing structure of West Berlin. In many ways, the brightly lit Kurfürstendamm, which runs through the center of the Zoo Quarter, has come to symbolize postwar Berlin in the popular mind just as the magnificent Unter den Linden did for old Berlin.

Meanwhile, East Berlin's core area was moving eastwards. Rebuilding in the immediate postwar period had concentrated on buildings in the western half of Mitte, not far from the intersection of Unter den Linden and Friedrichstrasse and fairly close to the West Berlin boroughs of Tiergarten and Kreuzberg. After 1949, city planners began to rebuild residential areas in the inner boroughs of Prenzlauer Berg and Friedrichshain (including a gigantic residential and shopping complex on the latter's main artery, then Stalinallee, but since 1961 Karl-Marx-Allee). The politburo of the Communist party's central committee decided in September 1964 to focus new construction around Alexanderplatz, a square 1.7 miles east of the Brandenburg Gate and near the point where the boroughs of Mitte, Prenzlauer Berg, and Friedrichshain meet. Since then, "Alex," as Berliners fondly call it, has become to East Berlin what the Zoo Quarter is to West Berlin.

The infrastructural aspects of a political community, as suggested earlier, exhibit remarkable durability and tenacity in resisting change. The very tenacity of the infrastructure, however, suggests that, once change is initiated, its reversal will be very difficult. The developments briefly summarized here thus portend an ever growing divergence of West and East Berlin, respectively, from the old center of Greater Berlin, and increased solidification of each around its own new core area.

Organizational Division

To some measure, people organize their lives around the voluntary associations in which they participate. Accordingly, if we want to fully understand people's perspectives and behaviors, we must look at their organizational ties. The division of Germany and Berlin in 1948/49 forced most associations previously unified across the new boundaries to follow suit. Even informal interaction among the branches in East and West became subject to political considerations. In Berlin, for example, politicization went so far that the East German regime forbade intracity athletic competition. Such pressures notwithstanding, three voluntary associations of major political significance sought to retain intact their organizational structure across the territories of the two Berlins: the Social Democratic party and the Protestant and Catholic churches.

Social Democracy

Politics in Berlin has long leaned to the left.[8] Although neither the home of the party itself nor the birthplace of its early leaders, imperial Berlin was the arena in which the Social Democratic Party of Germany (SPD) came to national prominence; and it is quite understandable that Social Democrats anticipated regaining political power in the city once Nazism had been defeated. Indeed, they were well on their way to doing so, and in the process all but eclipsing the Communist Party of Germany (KPD), when in April 1946 the Soviets engineered in the territories they controlled a merger of the two parties into the Socialist Unity Party of Germany (SED). The Four-power status of Berlin, nonetheless, gave both parties—the SPD and the SED—the right to operate freely throughout the entire city.

Freedom in principle, though, did not mean freedom in practice. For the SPD-East to have participated fully in the political process in East Berlin would have meant subordinating itself and its principles to the all-encompassing, SED-dominated National Front. The party's leaders would rather have dissolved the SPD-East than agree to such a proposition. They thus assumed the role of symbolic rather than active opposition to the SED's regime. Joining the party was not a way to influence the course of political events. It meant taking a stance that rejected the entire East German political system.

Not surprisingly, the SPD-East atrophied. Young people were reluctant to associate with it; and many of all ages who were members withdrew in the face of police harassment or else fled to the West. The membership roster, with approximately 25,000 dues-paying members in March 1946, declined to 8,330 in December 1950 and to 5,327 in June 1961, six weeks before the wall went up.[9] Those who remained became increasingly isolated. The party itself evolved from an open parliamentary system into a closed group with conspiratorial aspects. Finally, in August 1961, realizing that the construction of the wall had rendered the SPD-East untenable, the parent body in West Berlin dissolved it.

Churches

The place of organized religion in Berlin after 1945 presents a more complex picture. In the case of the more numerous Protestants, the territorial basis of their provincial church reaches back into the sixteenth century for its origin. Greater Berlin was but one of four dioceses comprising the Evangelical church in Berlin-Brandenburg (EKBB), which had its seat in the western borough of Charlottenburg. The other three dioceses were in the Soviet zone of occupation. What is more, its first postwar bishop, Otto Dibelius, also chaired the council of the federation of Germany's twenty-eight provincial churches, the Evangelical Church in Germany (EKD), created in July 1948. The Catholic diocese, too, extended beyond Berlin's borders to include a substantial portion of what is now the German Democratic Republic.

With the division of Germany and Berlin came pressure from the GDR, which was not friendly to religion in the first place, to make state boundaries those of the churches as well. Both the EKD and EKBB resisted this pressure. Church leaders argued that no state had the right to interfere in the church's internal affairs, including its organizational framework. Some, such as Bishop Dibelius, even questioned the very legitimacy of the East German regime, and seemed to be pushing East German Protestantism into the kind of underground battle against that regime that many Protestant leaders had conducted against Hitler's totalitarianism.[10] The effect was to hamper churches in East Germany and East Berlin in both their organizational tasks and their efforts to take Christianity to the individual.

Eventually the Protestants had to make concessions to the East German state. In 1969 the country's eight provincial churches formally broke off from the EKD to form a League of Evangelical Churches in the German Democratic Republic (BEK). Symbolic unity was nonetheless retained. The BEK's constitution not only committed the league to be part of a "special community" comprising the "whole of Evangelical Christianity in Germany," but it went on to assert the BEK's preparedness, "in the freedom born of partnership," to act accordingly on "issues which affect in common all Evangelical churches in the German Democratic Republic and in the Federal Republic of Germany." The EKBB struggled against division until the end of 1972. At that time, instead of formally breaking up its organizational structure, provincial church leaders in both East and West agreed to the establishment of a second bishopric to be responsible for the dioceses in East Berlin and Brandenburg, and adopted language that permitted each region to act as autonomously as was required. Since then, widespread cooperation and coordination have characterized the relationship between the two bishoprics in Berlin-Brandenburg as well as that between the EKD and BEK.

The Catholic church's willingness to make needed adjustments early gave it substantially more breathing space to develop its response to the state. Even before the wall went up, the church had made plans to install an East Berliner as bishop (although he was not enthroned until afterwards); and six years later, Bishop Alfred Bengsch wore a cardinal's hat. At a time when other East Berliners were not permitted to go to the West, Bishop Bengsch was free to visit his parishioners in West Berlin.[11] This *modus vivendi* is challenged from time to time, of course, but more to secure specific concessions than to open up the question of splitting West Berlin off from the Berlin bishopric.

What is less clear than the tactics pursued by the churches is the impact that their organizational structure had on members of their congregations. The impression obtained from interviews with Protestant officials in West Berlin is that most citizens who consider themselves religious are more concerned with personal than structural matters, and have a rather abstract notion of what the actual relationship between the churches in East and West actually is. The pastor of a parish that was split in 1961 by the wall, a parish once quite active in maintaining contacts with its sister church on the other side, notes that his parishioners nowadays are paying attention to other things, such as assistance to developing countries and nuclear disarmament. A quantitative analysis of the distribution of news in the EKBB's weekly newspaper, *Die Kirche* (The Church), bears out this impression. News from parishes in East Berlin has virtually disappeared from its columns.

Insisting on formal structural unity within Berlin's churches ultimately served the same purposes as keeping the SPD as a functioning body throughout the city. Both performed the symbolic function of defiance. They demonstrated to the East German regime that some groups would not buckle before its political demands; and they provided a beacon light of hope to individual citizens who needed to know that they were not alone in opposing that regime. Both also supported those whom the regime had crushed or was placing under pressure. At the level of the individual prepared to be a Christian in a socialist state or wanting to exert political influence in society, however, the value of such functions soon wore thin. Then, too, younger generations who grew up in a divided city have been less than impressed by the causes that inspired their elders. The task for most people is learning to live with the status quo, not changing it.

Behavioral Separation

Well, then, what about the Berliners? How did they respond to the measures aimed at tearing apart the political community they had shared? Various kinds of public-opinion data, although not specific to this theme, strongly suggest that most Berliners would favor the reunification of their city, but are aware that the prospects for this outcome are dim in the near future. Political community rests on more than sentimental attachments, however.

It also depends on people behaving in a fashion consistent with those sentiments. This raises the question: Have Berliners utilized the opportunities
available to them after 1949 to maintain contacts with the other side of the
city? In the absence of data on the behavior of individuals as such, data
which either do not exist or have not been made publicly available, we must
rely on indicators of behavior at the aggregate level to answer such a question.

The results of such a survey are discouraging as far as the maintenance of
ties between East and West Berlin is concerned. Even after the division of
1948, for instance, the border between the two parts of the city remained
open, at least in principle. Citizens of one side merely had to board a subway
or elevated railway to get to the other side, or else simply walk across at any
of eighty-six border stations. Any risk that such a step entailed remained
fairly constant from the end of the blockade in 1949 to the construction
twelve years later of a wall that ended virtually all Berliners' travel to the
other side of their city. Yet indicators based on a wide variety of interpersonal transactions—Eastern visitors to the theater and other events in
West Berlin, letters and packages sent between West Berlin and the East, sub-
scriptions to a West Berlin newspaper held by Easterners, and the like—all
dropped markedly between 1949 and 1961.[12] A composite index summa-
rizing these indicators (Figure 3) suggests that the rate of declining contacts
was greatest at the outset of the 1950s and then, by about 1958, flattened
out considerably.

If the 1950s, years in which the border between East and West Berlin was

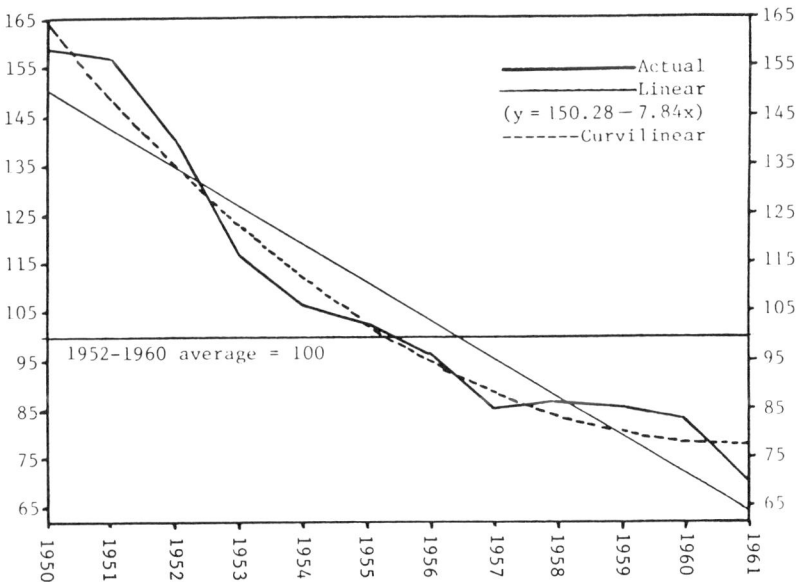

FIGURE 3. *Interactions between East and West Berliners, 1950–1961 (index figures, average of 1952–1960 = 100).*

relatively open, were an era of declining interaction, what would the closing of that border in 1961 bring? We might expect—and East German authorities doubtlessly hoped—that virtually complete separation would whittle down the last vestiges of community. Alternatively, given the strong West German emphasis on maintaining contacts with relatives and friends "over there," we might expect a surge in the forms of interaction that remained possible.

The reality, as indicated by available data, did not conform completely to either expectation.[13] Opportunities for interpersonal contacts between East and West Berliners were few and far between. In the mid-1960s, when visits to East Berlin during holiday periods were permitted, a substantial number of West Berliners obtained entry passes. The number of permits ranged from approximately one for every two Berliners during the Christmas and New Year's holidays in 1963/64—the first opening of the wall after August 1961—to less than half that number during the Easter and Whitsuntide holidays in 1966. Insofar as such a brief time period reveals trends in interpersonal contacts, they were downward. The distribution of emergency visiting permits because of pressing family matters also hints at a declining trend, even though the criteria for giving them to West Berliners were liberalized as the East German authorities discovered that such traffic was financially profitable. The number of packages shipped to or received from the East as well as attention patterns in West Berlin's weekly Protestant newspaper strengthen the impression that the trend of declining interest in the East among West Berliners was real and not the artifact of any particular analytic approach.

The Quadripartite Agreement of September 1971 laid the groundwork for at least a partial opening of the borders. Later that year, the West Berlin Senate and the GDR agreed, among other things, to permit West Berliners to visit East Berlin and the GDR for up to thirty days per year (even more in some cases, such as illness in the family), and to create offices in West Berlin to process applications. Although the traffic would be for the most part one-way, that is, for West Berliners only, the prospects nevertheless existed to reestablish ties severed or weakened during the 1960s. The significant question is how these West Berliners actually responded to the opportunity to reassert their sense of community across the wall.

Figures on the actual number of visits that West Berliners made to the East are striking in a couple of respects. First, the number of visits per year declined over the last dozen years, from 3.72 million between June 4, 1972, and May 31, 1973, to 1.56 million between June 1, 1981, and May 31, 1984 (Figure 4). A linear regression characterizing the shifts in year-to-year figures indicates that the average number of visits declined by 177,600 per year. (If this trend were to continue unabated into the future, then by 1994 *no* West Berliners would be crossing the border!) Second, there are remarkable dips in the curve from 1973 to 1975 and then again from 1980 to 1982. In part this is due to the extraordinarily high figure for 1972/73, when people may have been rushing to take advantage of the agreement before it should be cancelled, or to visit friends and relatives they may have not seen since 1966. In larger part, though, the dips coincide with the periods in which the GDR both raised the amount of hard currency which any visitor to the East was obligated to exchange and also expanded the number of individuals affected

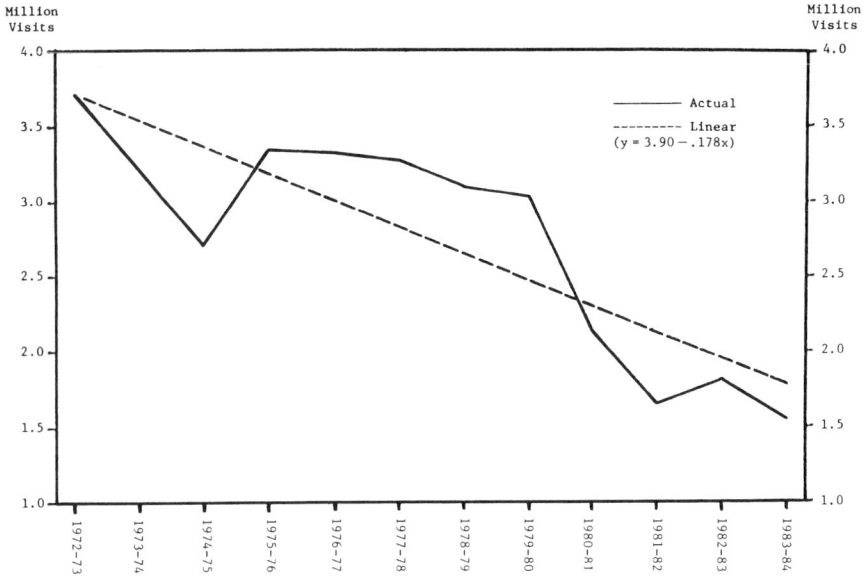

FIGURE 4. *Number of visits by West Berliners to East Berlin and the GDR, 1972–84.*

by the regulations. Visits lasting more than a single day seem to be less affected by the changes in fees than are those of shorter duration.

In a sense, the use of telephones may be replacing the mails as the chief means of communication between East and West Berliners. Packages shipped to the East continued to decline in the 1970s—from 7.41 million in 1971 to about two-fifths of that number (3.18 million) in 1977. As a result of the agreements of 1971–73, telephone service between the two halves of the city, broken off in the early 1950s, was restored, and the number of available lines was increased from year to year (from 40 in October 1971 to 609 in December 1981). In 1972–73 the daily traffic was roughly 8,200 calls to East Berlin; by 1981 the figure was 23,849 (down from 25,787 in the previous year).[14] The importance of these telephone calls as a means of sustaining a sense of community, nonetheless, remains to be seen. Not until a sufficient number of lines has been available for some time to handle desired conversations will it be possible to assess any trend. The most reasonable prediction to make is that when ample lines are available for all who wish to telephone between East and West Berlin (and quite possibly before then, if the decline from 1980 to 1981 is a valid indicator), the number of calls actually made will begin to diminish.

The partial reopening of the border in 1971 thus has not reversed the longstanding drop-off of interpersonal ties between East and West Berliners. With the exception of telephone traffic, where we may already have seen a peaking, every indicator available for the past three decades—for the 1950s when the border was fully open, for the 1960s when it was closed, and for the 1970s when it was partially open again—shows a pattern of decreasing communication. East and West Berliners are increasingly leading lives that are separate from each other.

Border of East Berlin; Brandenburg Gate with frontier barricade, Mitte, East Berlin.—Photograph taken from Tiergarten, West Berlin, May 1979. Reproduced with permission of the Landesbildstelle Berlin.

The Future of Divided Berlin

The evidence summarized here on the infrastructural basis of Berlin's political community, the organizations that sought to retain their unity across the border, and the actual behavior of people in interacting with Berliners from the other side of the city points fairly consistently to a single conclusion: the decline of political community in postwar Berlin. Where once there was a single city, now there are two. And, in concrete terms, the two cities have precious little to do with each other.

All this does not necessarily mean that political community is dead in Berlin. In this regard, several facts are important to note. First, although the level of contacts is declining, the contacts have not disappeared. It is likely that most of the decline is attributable to superficial ties, such as tourism or visits to casual acquaintances, and that it will continue until only the firmest of familial ties or those of friendship continue to exist. In addition, there are signs that younger Berliners are interested in setting up new contacts with their age-cohorts on the other side of the city or in the GDR. Although such contacts are likely to be of the sort that exist between the youth (and other groups) in any two neighboring countries whose residents speak a common language, it is also possible that such relationships can add substantially to the bedrock of sentimental community.

Second, we would be unwise to dismiss out of hand the significance of the linkages that remain. That they have a political impact can be inferred from the decision of the GDR in summer 1980 to raise once again the financial costs for West Berliners and others crossing the border into the East. The East German regime, while encouraging tourism, wants to keep interpersonal contacts to a minimum. Each personal visit by a Westerner reminds its citizens once again that life could be different from what it is, that at the very least they would like to have the right to travel across the border.

Third, the forms of less personal interaction that exist have effects that no government can control completely. Writers from the two sides of the wall, for example, meet from time to time, discover that they have deep-seated mutual interests, and go home to write articles and novels reflecting this perspective. Fragmentary evidence strongly suggests that the two-thirds of the GDR population able to receive Western television in their homes are avid viewers, especially of news programs. Consultations among Protestant leaders in East and West paved the way for the decision made by many East German pastors to support a peace movement aimed at disarmament in their own part of the world. Readers of contemporary literature, television viewers, churchgoers, and many others are not insensitive to the message being sent out: "We Germans," it is saying, "have significant interests in common that go beyond our current commitment to mutually antagonistic military blocs. We belong together!"

Finally, it is possible, albeit not very likely, that major political breakthroughs will reunite the city and reverse the trend of declining community. This possibility of reversibility raises an interesting question: What would happen if Berlin were to be reunified today, or next week? Would not the old patterns of interaction, and with them the expectations, demands, and identifications associated with political community, simply reemerge? In other words, have three decades and more of separation *really* made East and West Berliners different from each other?

In seeking to answer this question, it is tempting to think in terms of historical examples. The Poles did not give up their sense of nationality despite a century and a quarter of division under alien rule; and similar nationality struggles were recurrent in the Balkans. Such examples, however, which would lead us to expect a sense of German nationality and Berlin community to persist for many decades to come, may be misleading. The classic cases of reunited nationalities occurred at times and in places in which there was a relatively low degree of organized complexity. Polish peasants in what were then the German, Russian, and Austro-Hungarian empires were fairly similar, more tied to the land and their peasant communities than to elaborate sets of imperial social communications systems. It is by no means clear that the Poland that reemerged in 1918 was the result of spontaneous pressure from the masses, as opposed to an unusual set of international circumstances, effective organization by a small number of leaders, and the willingness of the masses to cast votes in plebiscites. How likely is it that a new international crisis would make the rest of the world accept a reunified Germany and/or Berlin? Moreover, although another element of the Polish case, namely a unifying thrust by determined leaders, may eventually exist in the German situation, what they will face is not a mass of peasants untied to any large-scale and complex system of government and communication, but rather populations with strong sets of interdependencies which are mutually exclusive.

The latter is a more likely scenario for a Berlin reunified at some future time. If the city is politically amalgamated on the basis of new international agreements, it will be fairly easy to rebuild a unified municipal government; and with time, it will be possible to construct the links to tie together divided water and electricity grids, streets and subway lines, and the like. Still more difficult to reconstruct will be the sentimental ties of community. Reunification in the year, say, 2000 will come more than a half century after the city's political division and almost forty years after the appearance of the wall. By then there will be very few Berliners alive who will have a vivid memory of what it was like before 1945, and fewer still who will have any active contacts on the other side of the city. Changing residential preferences, traffic, and other patterns by which people organize their daily lives will by then have produced two cities in a physical sense. East Berliners will be tied intimately to the social, economic, political, and other systems in the German Democratic Republic; West Berliners to quite different systems in the Federal Republic. Rebuilding a common set of expectations, demands, and identifications among Berliners will doubtless be a slow process, quite possibly slower than that which had forced them apart in the first place. Even then, as the history of efforts to merge American towns and cities into larger units suggests, unforeseen issues may arise to hinder reunification.

What seems far less likely in the present circumstances is that a new nationalistic movement firmly grounded at the grassroots level will emerge to force the German governments or those of the victorious Allies of World War II to reunify the country (or, still less likely, Berlin alone). The precondition for such a movement would be the kind of social communications networks which the GDR's government still seems determined to prevent. Free mobility within Berlin and Germany will probably remain an impossible dream until there are no more economic incentives for citizens of one Germany to flee to the other, until pacts have been reached for returning to their country of origin those who have left for political reasons (a possibility that most West German leaders would firmly reject now), and, more generally, until neither country poses a threat to the other. It is unlikely that, in the absence of free mobility, an effective social communications network will emerge in the two Germanies.

The prospects, at least for the foreseeable future, are for the division of Berlin to continue. As each year passes, the underlying basis of political community in Berlin as a whole erodes a bit more. East Berliners become more closely tied to a network of systems that tries as much as possible to ignore the existence of West Berlin, while West Berliners form stronger links to a network of systems in which nongovernmental processes in East Berlin are of little moment. In the place of community, estrangement is growing.

Notes

[1] Peter Paul Nahm, ed., *Dokumente deutscher Kriegsschäden*, vol. IV/2: *Berlin— Kriegs- und Nachkriegsschicksal der Reichshauptstadt* (Bonn: Bundesministerium für Vertriebene, Flüchtlinge und Kriegsgeschädigte, 1967), pp. 5–6, 74–77.

[2] Ibid., pp. 82–83; and Statistisches Landesamt Berlin, *Berlin in Zahlen 1951* (Berlin [West]: Kulturbuch-Verlag, 1951), p. 15.

[3] The enemies of Hitler's Third Reich had never really reached a final agreement on reparations. At Yalta the Big Three had agreed in principle on the demand for reparations, and specific sums, such as Stalin's proposal of $20 billion, had been bandied about; postwar agreements even specified how transfers were to be made. But, in the final analysis, behavior regarding reparations was decentralized, with each occupying power pursuing somewhat different policies in its own zone. See Bruce Kuklick, *American Policy and the Division of Germany: The Clash with Russia over Reparations* (Ithaca, N.Y.: Cornell University Press, 1972).

[4] Nahm, *Dokumente*, vol. IV/2: *Berlin*, pp. 79–83.

[5] See W. Phillips Davison, *The Berlin Blockade: A Study in Cold War Politics* (Princeton, N.J.: Princeton University Press, 1958); and Gerhard Keiderling and Percy Stulz, *Berlin 1945–1968: Zur Geschichte der Hauptstadt der DDR und der selbständigen politischen Einheit West Berlin* (Berlin [East]: Dietz Verlag, 1970).

[6] See my "Political Division and Municipal Services in Postwar Berlin," in *Public Policy 17*, eds. John D. Montgomery and Albert O. Hirschmann (Cambridge, Mass.: Harvard University Press, 1968).

[7] See my "Infrastructural Changes in Berlin," *Annals of the Association of American Geographers 63* (1) (March 1973): 58–70.

[8] See my "The SPD of East Berlin, 1945–1961" (with Ronald A. Francisco), *Comparative Politics 5* (1) (October 1972): 1–28.

[9] Estimated data for 1946 are from Albrecht Kaden, *Einheit oder Freiheit: Die Wiedergründung der SPD 1945–1946* (Hanover: Verlag J.A.W. Dietz Nachf., 1964), p. 320n; data for 1950 and 1961 are from: Sozialdemokratische Partei Deutschlands, Landesverband Berlin, *Jahresbericht*, volumes for 1951 and 1962 (mimeographed).

[10] See his letter to Bishop Hans Lilje, *Obrigkeit: Eine Frage an den 60jährigen Landesbischof* (Berlin [West]: n.p., 1959).

[11] In 1967, at the time Bishop Bengsch was named cardinal, there were 505,000 Catholics in the Berlin bishopric: 256,000 in West Berlin, 110,000 in East Berlin, and 139,000 in the GDR. Data from "Pabst Paul ernannte 27 neue Kardinäle," *Der Tagesspiegel* (Berlin [West]), May 30, 1967, p. 2.

[12] See my "Political Disintegration in Postwar Berlin," in *From National Development to Global Community: Essays in Honor of Karl W. Deutsch*, eds. Richard L. Merritt and Bruce M. Russett (London: Allen and Unwin, 1981). The indicators surveyed (and summarized in the composite index) are: Eastern visitors to West Berlin's municipal theaters, exhibition center, radio tower, and summer garden, 1950–1961; letters and packages sent between West Berlin and the East, 1952–1960; membership in the SPD-East, 1950–1961; and sales of the daily newspaper *Telegraf* to East Berlin subscribers, 1951–1960.

[13] Data in this and the following paragraphs are from my "Interpersonal Transactions across the Wall," in *Living with the Wall: West Berlin, 1961–1985*, eds. Richard L. Merritt and Anna J. Merritt (Durham, N.C.: Duke University Press, 1985), pp. 166–183.

[14] Data from "Bericht über die Durchführung des Viermächte-Abkommens und der ergänzenden Vereinbarungen zwischen dem 3. Juni 1972 und dem 31. Mai 1973," Abgeordnetenhaus von Berlin, 6. Wahlperiode, Drucksache 6/1013, August 1, 1973, p. 7; and subsequent reports.

CHAPTER 3

Berlin Between East and West

Dietrich Stobbe

Europe is in fact a divided continent, and this state of division is most sorely evident in Germany, specifically in Berlin. If you were in Germany today, in 1988, and asked the man on the street, "Why does this situation exist?", you would probably get the answer, "Because of the East–West conflict and because of the Communists." Yet, that response would be only partially correct. The exacerbated East–West tension has certainly deepened the division of Europe, of my country, and of the city of Berlin, but—as history knows—the division lines in Europe were already chosen and drawn by the anti-Hitler coalition during and after World War II. Whoever discusses the division of Berlin must start by discussing Yalta as a direct consequence of World War II, a war which Germany began and lost. The results of that war are most obvious in Berlin. Thus, this city is the place in Germany to think about what Germans have done; it is the place to think about our history and about its consequences for our future. Berlin, once the capital of the German Reich, now exists between East and West.

One should remember that Germany was the last European nation to establish a federal democracy, late in the last century, long after France, England, Spain, and even Austria. The German Reich lasted seventy years, which in retrospect seems a very short time. Berlin was its capital for those seventy years, but for centuries it had served as the capital of the Prussian state. Since World War II, we have had 43 undecided years for Berlin. These 43 years amount to more than half of the time for which the German Reich existed. Now, everyone in Berlin will be confronted with the crucial question: Are Berliners, are Germans, and are the members of the Western Alliance ready and able to see and to understand what our political reality is about? Or do they, do we Berliners and Germans refuse to recognize that a divided country is the consequence of our own history?

One often prefers the simpler idea that the Communists have done what in historical reality we have done to ourselves. We Berliners and Germans must answer the question of whether we accept our situation and what options exist: Morally, can we accept the division? Are we ready to live with the wall? Or do we try to compromise and acknowledge the reality of the postwar power structure in Europe as the necessary starting point for fresh ideas and peaceful change on a continent which is so seemingly unchangeable in its political power structure?

In Berlin, one sees that there is no single easy answer. When the wall was built in 1961, the Germans had to think about the nature of the power structure with which they were confronted. One must remember that our American Allies, together with the French and the British, guaranteed our freedom in the western part of the city, but for the first time in the postwar period, they had to confess that they were unable, in spite of their postwar rights in all four sectors of Berlin, to exercise control or effect change in the eastern part of the city. The Communist regime of East Germany, backed by the Soviet Union, built the wall exactly on the line which marked the border of its sphere of political influence within the city since the end of the war. As the wall was built, American tanks and Russian tanks stayed two inches on either side of that line, and both were unable to move three inches forward to a military confrontation. We have to consider the political meaning of this crucial episode. With that experience, the Germans learned that the United States and the Soviet Union were prepared to maintain and live with the political division lines which were set by the end of World War II.

This had been evident when the German workers fought in East Berlin in 1953, and was reaffirmed by the events in Hungary in 1956, by the several Polish attempts to free themselves of Communist leadership, by the so-called Prague-spring in Czechoslovakia, and by the crackdown on Solidarity. In other words, Yalta, at least in the eyes of those who took part in the process of settling the divided postwar Europe, has created and perhaps historically validated the division of Europe into two conflicting political systems. And after a period of time, when strong hopes for the reunification of Germany and, of course, of the city of Berlin dominated our political thinking, we Germans were left alone to find a way to adjust to the reality of the division.

What we had to learn was that peace is indeed more important than reaching national goals like reunification or—dare I say it—even more vital and pressing than freedom for an Eastern European country. Because with the nuclear war that we would most likely experience in Central Europe, in the event of a military conflict, there simply would be no nations left to enjoy their freedom. So we have had to speak from the position in which these political consequences place us. If it is true that the decisive prerequisite for maintaining peace is an approximate military balance between the superpowers at the lowest possible level, then the other side of the coin is that this military equilibrium, this rough parity, is fixed in the existing power structure of Europe well into the future. This learning experience, together with the Cuban missile crisis and the continuing atmosphere of confrontation between East and West, has most heavily influenced our political decisions in the Federal Republic of Germany.

In Berlin and throughout the west, the result of the discussions in the years following the construction of the wall was a new strategy for the entire Western Alliance. The Harmel Report of 1967 became the political guideline of NATO and was regarded as having been drafted following a common assessment of the power structure in Europe, in Germany, and in Berlin. The Harmel Report was based on the conviction that even countries and alliances with sharply opposing ideologies and different sociopolitical systems share the urgent, overriding concern for peace in a nuclear world.

Thus, the commitment of NATO members to a strong defensive capability was seen as inextricably coupled with détente, that is, with political measures aimed at reducing tension and confrontation between East and West that could spur any actual military conflict. The Harmel Report at once constituted a NATO consensus and paved the way for a policy which was later called German *Ostpolitik*. Ostpolitik was never an isolated German policy; it was made possible precisely because it was integrated, embedded in a political framework shared by the entire Western Alliance and particularly the United States. After eight years in the government of Berlin, I am well aware that between the federal government in Bonn and an Eastern state not a single treaty has been reached which was not approved by the American administration before the German government concluded it.

On the one hand, the NATO decision to pair defense and détente signalled a crucial post–World War II consensus that in a nuclear world, political stability is every bit as essential to security as one's military arsenal. But for the Europeans, on the other hand, détente has also been thought of as a means of restoring vital links between countries which share centuries of history, culture, and traditions. These benefits of détente are maybe less readily apparent to Americans, but in Europe, the rewards of Ostpolitik have shown themselves in economic cooperation, in scientific dialogue, in cultural exchange, and certainly—I can say as a Berliner—in the personal lives of Germans who once again can establish contact with family and friends living in the eastern part of the country.

Western European opinion is extremely sensitive to the state of détente. When détente deteriorated in the 1970s Western Europeans became very skeptical and anxious about the immense nuclear stockpile on the European continent. With strong hopes for an agreement on intermediate range nuclear weapons and the promise of future strategic arms negotiations between the superpowers, Europeans are optimistic. If our own defense efforts are to be accepted and supported by the public, they must be accompanied by parallel political efforts, so that NATO defense strategy is seen as enhancing security rather than jeopardizing it. For any security policy to be credible, it must have the support and belief of the public behind it. Negotiations, arms control, dialogue, and treaties are the fabric of politics. We are now past the period in which politics were ignored and more weapons were deployed, and have moved into a second phase of détente. It is important to note that the German insistence on the preservation of détente is not incompatible with a strong commitment in NATO. Instead, this very conviction stems from the important NATO tradition of the Harmel Report.

Officially, Harmel remains the guideline for NATO, but in the political reality of today, it has been fully dissolved. The relationship between the United States and the Soviet Union is the decisive factor for the security of Berlin. We now operate the city under an agreement which was signed by the four victorious powers, the main powers of which are, of course, the United States and the Soviet Union. Détente has done much to improve the quality of life for Berliners. The postwar Berlin agreement can continue to work sufficiently only as long as negotiations continue between East and West. Berlin would suffer if the negotiations and talks between the superpowers were to fail. We, in Berlin and in Germany, can and should welcome the current mood for negotiations and agreement, and hope that Berlin, too,

TV discussion on September 2, 1981, on the occasion of the tenth anniversary of the signing of the Quadripartite Agreement at the television center, SFB (Radio Free Berlin), Masurenallee, Charlottenburg, with the ambassadors who negotiated and signed the agreement on September 3, 1971. From left to right: Sir Roger Jackling (Great Britain), Jean Sauvagnargues (France), Fritz Pleitgen (ARD correspondent in East Berlin), Pjotr A. Abrassimow (ambassador of the U.S.S.R. in East Berlin), and Kenneth Rush (U.S.A.).—September 2, 1981. Reproduced with permission of the Landesbildstelle Berlin.

will benefit. Therefore, I want to stress: no one can expect that arms control negotiations can be concluded positively in a climate of foreign policy which is deliberately designed as hostile to cooperative East–West relations.

The word *unilateralism* is antithetical to the concept of alliance. We cannot afford unilateral attempts at leadership within NATO, because of the danger that vital interests of the multiple partners of the alliance would thus be excluded. For Germany, and especially for Berlin, but certainly for the health and unity of the whole North Atlantic Alliance, it is essential that Western Europe and America work to develop a common assessment about the nature of the East–West conflict. And I am sure that the Berlin experience will be again at the heart of the matter.

I am convinced that there is no alternative to the Harmel Report's framework of defense plus détente, which is based on the confidence in our own system. We must seek cooperation with the East bloc on issues of common interest like arms control, but at the same time continue to engage in healthy, peaceful competition. The strength of our own system will speak for itself. We are not made weaker by the process of détente; instead, increased communication and exchange with the East cannot help but transmit a clear message about the desirability of freedom of movement and expression, which NATO members share as a democratic political basis. In the interest of Berlin, I hope to see the perception of détente as a "weak" policy corrected. The policy of détente is rooted in the conviction that our system is solid enough to compete, negotiate, and achieve compromise with the Soviet Union, without itself being jeopardized.

Berlin Through the Eyes of a Longtime Member of the German Parliament (Bundestag)

Walter Picard

The *Bundestag* can be compared with the House of Representatives in the United States, although it has more power. In 1965, the year I entered the German Parliament, Berlin was the crucial point of German domestic politics, of the relations between the Federal Republic of Germany (FRG) and the Soviet Union, and of the Western Alliance. The German population, especially the politicians, and above all the members of the Federal Parliament, were used to facing one Berlin crisis after another. The question was only how one would overcome those crises and how much the West would give in.

No doubt, from the very beginning of the division in 1945, the West never took the strong, even stubborn position the Soviet Union did. Germany had risked World War II and had lost it; one of the inevitable consequences was the partition of Germany and of its former capital, Berlin. The basis for the situation and for the development of Berlin after the war was the agreement of 1944/45 between the three victorious powers, Great Britain, the United States, and the Soviet Union, which was finally approved by the heads of state in January 1945 in Yalta. In this agreement, we find the unmistakable statement that Berlin is not a part of the zone of occupation of the Soviet Union by which it is surrounded. Admittedly, in this agreement no guarantee was laid down for free access between Berlin and the Western occupation zones.

A common administrative government of Germany and Berlin could only be carried out as long as the former war Allies had at least a minimum common understanding of the future development of Germany and Berlin. I don't think it is necessary to remind you of all the events which prove that this common understanding had already begun to break down before the war had ended. In 1948/49, when the first serious Berlin crisis occurred, the Western powers realized that cooperation or understanding was no longer possible with their former ally, the Soviet Union.

Since West Berlin was not and is not part of the Federal Republic of Germany like Bavaria, Hesse or the other states of the FRG, the German Parliament always felt responsible; but it was actually limited by Allied reservations to discuss, to pass resolutions, to present petitions to our Allies. The goal of all our efforts in the Parliament has primarily been and

Allied Forces Day, May 21, 1983: Parade in the Street of the 17th of June (between Tiergarten Station, of the city railway, and Großer Stern (Big Star)). First row from left: Division General Jean-Pierre Liron (French municipal commander), Major General James G. Boatner (American municipal commander), Major General Joseph David Frederik Mostyn (British municipal commander); behind them: Klaus Franke (Deputy President of the chamber of deputies of Berlin).—May 21, 1983. Reproduced with permission of the Landesbildstelle Berlin.

still is to take care that Berlin remains, in the view of our Western Allies, the key point where the quality of East–West relations is proved.

Of course, from the beginning of the four-power administration of Berlin in the summer of 1945, there were links between the city and West Germany. But these links, which the Soviet Union had agreed to, were never defined. And it was just a game that the Soviet Union played in testing how far these links could be reduced and weakened or even removed, while the Soviet Union strengthened her influence in the eastern part of the city and later increased the dependence of the German Democratic Republic (GDR) on the Soviet Union.

After the Federal Republic of Germany and the German Democratic Republic had been established in 1949, the partition of Germany and of Berlin was completed. But Berlin was still an open city to some extent, and it was not too difficult and dangerous to leave the GDR via East Berlin, going from there to West Berlin and finally to the Federal Republic. About 3 million

Election of the President of the Federal Republic of Germany (Bundespräsident) on March 5, 1969 in the Ostpreußenhalle at the Funkturm (radio tower), Exhibition Park, Masurenallee, Charlottenburg. In the middle: Dr. Gustav W. Heinemann, elected president.—March 5, 1969. Reproduced with permission of the Landesbildstelle Berlin.

people left the state, which calls itself the State of Workers and Farmers (Arbeiter- und Bauernstaat). This situation ended with the construction of the Berlin Wall in August of 1961.

A few weeks before this date, Khrushchev's Berlin ultimatum of November 1958 had ended, and the Soviet Union had agreed to the presence of the Western Allies in West Berlin. Consequently, they then began to enforce their criticism of the presence of institutions of the FRG; they tried to close the streets and waterways when the Federal Parliament had a session in Berlin or when the president of the FRG was elected in Berlin in 1969.

It was then that President Nixon, visiting Berlin, declared the situation of the city completely inadequate and called on the other three powers to clarify it. The Federal German, the French, and the British governments supported President Nixon's initiative, and Foreign Minister Gromyko responded in July 1969, declaring his readiness for four-power negotiations. These began in March 1970 and led to the Quadripartite Agreement of September 1971, which became effective on June 3, 1972.

As far as the German Parliament was concerned, it followed the negotiations with interest and sympathy. Government and Parliament were always well informed by the Western Allies. When the agreement became effective, there was relief in Germany and in Berlin, and the population approved and welcomed the result on the whole. Yet, it was no secret that there was skepticism about the new role the old capital now had to play. The agreement confirmed the rights and responsibilities of the four powers, following the resolutions and agreements of the time during and after the war, and the present status of Berlin can only be changed by a new agreement of the four powers.

Whereas prior to this agreement the city was a case of public interest—not only in Germany—and a graduated scale of the East–West relations, now the danger arose that Berlin would lose the public interest and be deprived of political efforts. For a while it seemed that the city entered the leeside of politics in Germany. But this situation was not overlooked either by the city government and council or by the Bundestag. There are a lot of federal institutions located in the city in order to show and to strengthen the ties between the FRG and Berlin and to prove the commitments the Bundestag has undertaken. On the basis of existing and guaranteed ties, the FRG supports the city heavily. In all the years I served on the budget committee, I never experienced a dispute concerning financial aid to Berlin. If there was argument, it was only if the financial aid could be used more efficiently in a different way.

From 1951 until 1982, the federal budget was charged by an amount of DM 147 billion. The budget for 1983 made a financial contribution of DM 13 billion to Berlin, more than 5 percent of the total budget. And this huge amount was spent when we had an unemployment rate over 10 percent and a deficit in the federal budget of DM 40 billion or 16 percent of the total.

We do this unanimously because we want the city of Berlin not only to exist but also to be the most fascinating, interesting city, where cultural life is more attractive than anywhere else in Germany. And we want to keep Berlin as the place where modern industry, innovation, and science are of outstanding importance. The Bundestag has done and will do what is possible in order to regain the former position of Berlin as the capital of Germany, even if Germany and also Berlin will remain divided for a long time. The city is indeed the most vital and exciting German city. It still has a special international flair which is still improving. So it makes sense for international business to be represented there. The goal of our strong financial support is mainly to make Berlin an interesting, attractive, international meeting point, and a visit to it a must.

For the German Parliament, and I think also for the German population, including the GDR, Berlin is of a political importance which can't really be

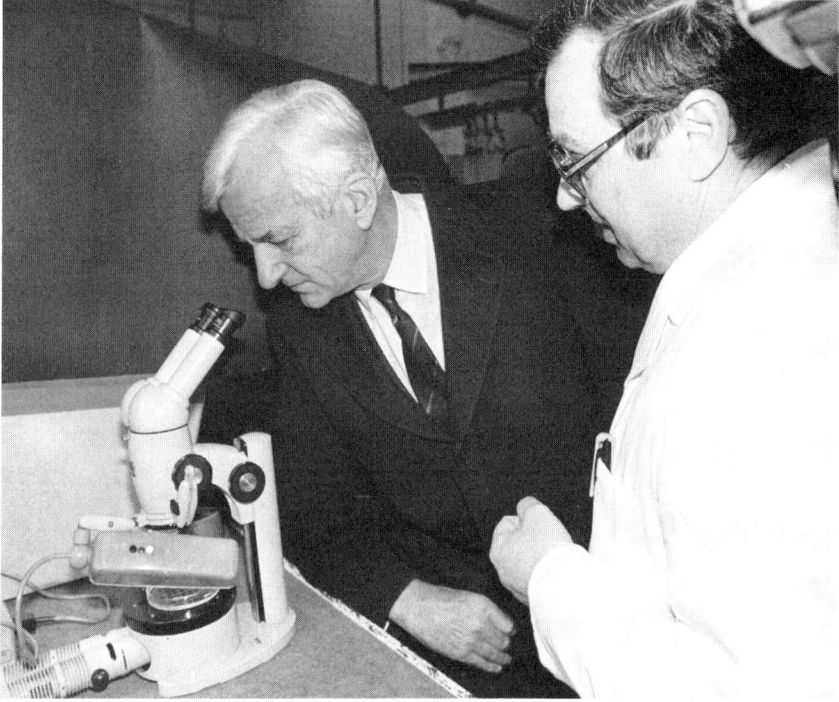

Visit of the President of the Federal Republic of Germany (Bundespräsident) Dr. Richard von Weizsäcker on March 3, 1986 at the Federal Health Office (Bundesgesundheitsamt) at Thielallee 88–92, Zehlendorf/Dahlem.—March 7, 1986. Reproduced with permission of the Landesbildstelle Berlin.

overestimated. It is the outpost of the free world, the showcase of the West, and one shouldn't undervalue the psychological and finally the political influence of the city on the people in our Communist neighbour states.

To a German member of Parliament like myself, who has been on the budget committee for 14 years, the heavy financial support of the former capital is also considered to be a contribution to defending the free world, a clear demonstration that we shall never give in, and that it doesn't make sense for the Soviet Union to increase its military and political pressure. On the contrary, the firm and strong but flexible position of the government and parliament in Berlin and in Bonn is a means to reduce the tensions and to finally come to some kind of solution of the heavy and somewhat dangerous problems oppressing the people in East and West. The question may be asked why Berlin can't stand on its own as other big cities do. The answer is clear enough: Although Berlin is still the most industrialized city in Germany, it suffers a great disadvantage. It is isolated and completely surrounded by the GDR, and there is no exchange of people and goods as was natural before the war. Therefore, the life of the people there and the

Signing of the final protocol of the Quadripartite Agreement of September 3, 1971, on June 3, 1972 in the building of the Allied Command (Alliierter Kontrollrat), Elßholz-straße 5, Schöneberg, after arrangements were made with regard to the measures provided in Section II of the Quadripartite Agreement. At the table the four secretaries of state signing the final protocol by which the Agreement became effective on June 3, 1972. From the right: William Rogers (U.S.), A. Gromyko (U.S.S.R.), Douglas Home (Great Britain), and Maurice Schumann (France). Second row, left: the French embassador Jean Sauvagnargues; left behind Gromyko: the former soviet embassador A. Abrassimow.—June 3, 1972. Reproduced with permission of the Landesbildstelle Berlin.

existence of the city itself is to a large extent an artificial one compared with other German cities like Hamburg or Munich.

The Quadripartite Agreement of 1971 has brought with it a certain stability in the development of the city. But the appearance of this stability may be deceptive and we shouldn't fall into such an illusion. As the ambassador of the Soviet Union to East Berlin declared in 1981, the Soviet Union is now as ever of the opinion that West Berlin is a foreign body and a capitalist enclave in the territory of the German Democratic Republic. Certainly this is in contradiction to the agreement, and we have to face the fact that Berlin is in a situation of insecurity and danger as long as Europe and Berlin itself are parted and an aggressive and inhuman ideology is in power on the other side of the wall and the iron curtain.

Therefore, the former capital of Germany will be a case of high political interest and concern in the German Parliament as long as the present situation lasts.

SECTION II
Development of a Culture

Social Consciousness and Social Causes: Impulses for Social Reform at the Turn of the Century in Berlin

Louis Lowy

At the turn of the century, Berlin had a population of close to two million people. Since 1880 it had grown by almost three quarters of a million. When, in 1871, Berlin became the capital of a united Germany under Wilhelm I as its emperor and Otto von Bismarck as its "Iron Chancellor," Berlin was still 65 percent rural. But by 1900 it had become urbanized. Von Bülow had become chancellor and Wilhelm II emperor by the end of the nineteenth century, when the processes of urbanization and industrialization had come together and when the consequences of these processes had already left their marks on the city and its inhabitants.[1]*

Social Conditions

The industrial revolution produced its inevitable crisis conditions in the social sector here as elsewhere on the European continent, and no less so in the United States.

The "factory system" became a dominant force in the lives of the city's people—unemployment had left many breadwinners without work and income, notably from 1899 to 1910. Child labor and female labor (10–20 percent of the work force) produced disruption in family structures and value orientations. Heightened class consciousness emerged among the population. The labor movement became a significant social and political force; labor strife culminated in numerous strikes with attendant hardships for workers and their families; at the same time, under the leadership of Wilhelm Liebknecht and August Bebel, Marxist ideology underpinned the labor movement. In contrast, Hasenclever, Blos, and Bernstein were instrumental in shaping a liberal reform movement—anti-Marxist in orientation—to enlist support of the people against these poor social conditions and to bring about their amelioration.[2]

The attempt of these social reformers was guided by a philosophy of change from below via grass-roots movements, not unlike the reformers in

---

*See Notes section at the end of this chapter.

other parts of the world at this period in history. Urban conditions for workers in Berlin were characterized by poor housing, terrible, ramshackle flats (slums), poor water supply and canalization, unhygienic garbage disposal, etc. At the same time, a building boom flourished for the well-to-do, and a great deal of construction effort went into erecting institutions, such as orphanages, old-age homes, and hospitals, for the poor, sick, and deserted.[3]

The time was ripe and the stage was set for "social response and action," to use modern terminology. Two major streams of activity emerged: (1) social legislation and (2) private philanthropic efforts.

Social Legislation

In order to take the steam out of the burgeoning social democratic movement, the emperor issued a "Kaiserliche Botschaft," an imperial decree without parliamentary participation, that spelled out a series of social measures.

Insurance of workers against accidents in the workplace, but also for people who could no longer earn a living because of old age or disability, establishing a *Rechtsanspruch* (legal claim), for the first time in history, which, in modern language, we would call the first "entitlement programs."[4] Originally limited to construction and factory workers, the law was extended to white-collar employees in 1911; two-thirds of the cost was borne by employers and one-third by employees. The cost-sharing principle became another milestone in social policy developments on the Continent and in many countries of the world, although at a much later date. The foundations were laid for the design of a welfare state. (In the United States the Social Security Act was passed in 1935.) Eventually, social legislation was expanded to honor claims by unemployed workers to obtain cash benefits, to establish an eight-hour work day, and to abolish child labor.[5]

This was a period of intense political and social ferment. Inequality of income distribution became more apparent and new social classes appeared; there was a greater levelling toward the "middle," despite continued rigidly held positions of privilege by the upper classes and the aristocracy, who were overrepresented in the civil service, the professions, the army, the diplomatic services, and at the universities. Nevertheless, the lower classes made themselves heard through political parties (the Social Democrats, the Communists, the Zentrum), the labor unions, and through social movements in general. Despite the passage of enlightened social legislation, dire poverty was not appreciably reduced among the working and nonworking people. Beggars abounded in the streets, and special police detachments (Armenpolizei) roamed the streets of Berlin to go after the unemployed, the beggars, and the thieves.

Sperlingsgasse, corner Friedrichsgracht (Mitte, East Berlin).—May 1909. Reproduced with permission of the Landesbildstelle Berlin (above).

Hallesches Tor (Gate) with high level railway station (Kreuzberg).—1906. Reproduced with permission of the Landesbildstelle Berlin (below).

Heinrich Mann in his *Der Untertan* (*The Patrioteer*) (1921) presents a vignette describing a typical scene:

> A wet and cold day in February 1892. People 'Unter den Linden' are waiting for something to happen. Police on horseback appears. There—'The Unemployed!' In small squads, walking slowly in formation, they move towards the imperial castle, stop there and stand silently with pale faces, hands in their pockets of well-worn overcoats. . . . They stand there only to show that they exist. The police drives them on to the nearest corner. There they stop again, keep standing and staring at the wall in front of them. This same scene is repeated during the next few days. They become more dogged in their determination. Traffic stops. 'Give us bread and work,' they yell.[6]

In response to such events, and in order to avoid civic disruptions (as well as not to provide ammunition to the "political left"), a system of "care for the poor" (Armenpflege) under public and private auspices was instituted. In present-day parlance, we would refer to this as "public welfare."

Public Welfare at the Turn of the Century

Those who could not support themselves were stigmatized; in fact, they lost civic and church rights, and compulsory work (Arbeitspflicht) was introduced to reduce or eliminate vagrancy. The maxim sounded: "It is the duty of society to care for the poor, but not the right of the poor to claim assistance."

The "Elberfelder System," founded in 1855,[7] adopted the principle that a city has the obligation to take care of its poor; and in order to make this administratively possible, a city was divided into several districts, each headed by a "volunteer chief" (welfare worker) to visit the poor and provide direct relief to them. It was Stadtrat (city councilor) Münsterberg who enunciated the principles of "individualization and decentralization, with services offered directly by volunteers out in the field (Aussendienst)." The "Innendienst" (bureaucratic offices) would later make relief decisions bureaucratically and hence, impersonally.[8] This system remained the basis of public welfare well into the new century. In the United States, "indoor and outdoor relief" and "friendly visiting," as carried out by the State Boards of Charities, the Charity Organization of New York, and other private agencies, and the prevailing philosophy "not alms but a friend" can be looked at as parallel developments.[9] Berlin's poor benefited from the adaptation of the "Elberfelder System" that was established to meet the needs of its poverty striken.

Private Philanthropy

In addition to public relief programs for the poor, religious organizations of all denominations, private individuals, self-help groups, and political parties shared in philanthropic endeavors. Two major principles underpinned these efforts: "voluntaryism and freedom." Increasing concern for the homeless, mentally ill, children and youth who left school early, victims of alcoholism, and others led to the establishment of vacation programs (Ferienkolonien), public nutrition sites (Volksküchen), orphanages, and old-age homes. It became readily apparent that the public and private sectors needed linkages; and the founding of the "Deutscher Verein für Armenpflege and Wohltätigkeit" (today the Deutscher Verein für öffentliche und private Fürsorge [German Organization for Public and Private Welfare] in Frankfurt) became an institutional milestone in the history of German social welfare.[10]

Several outstanding personalities assumed leadership during this period. Only some of them can be mentioned briefly:

Franz Hitze influenced social policy decisively when he became a mover in founding the Catholic Workers' Unions and acted as consultant to other trade unions as well. He was also one of the leading initiators—together with Lorenz Werthmann—of the German Caritas Organization, still one of the top private social welfare organizations in Germany today and part of the world Caritas movement.[11]

Jeanette Schwerin set up the "German Society for Ethical Culture" as a mediator between the well-to-do and the poor and as a group designed to advise the poor how to cope. This was in the tradition of the prevailing philosophy that counseling the poor would lead to the amelioration of their plight, a philosophy prevalent in England, France, and the United States at that time, and still to be found among many segments of the world population today. This "Society" printed an inventory of all social service agencies existing in Berlin in 1893, *A Social Guide through Berlin*, published by Carl Heymann.[12] Dr. Münsterberg, director of the Poor Relief Administration in Berlin in 1897, expanded this guide and created what we would refer to today as a "central information office" of social services programs.[13] Many German cities, such as Köln, Lübeck, Worms, Freiburg, Bochum, Duisburg, Dresden, and many more made a great deal of use of Münsterberg's "invention."

The Women's Movement

One of the benefits of industrialization was increased leisure for many middle- and notably upper-class women. Philanthropy had always been an important form of activity for well-to-do women, but now, no longer satisfied with doing good works on a voluntary basis, they sought the training which would transform them into social workers. Social work became, with teaching, an acceptable occupation for women of the middle and upper classes. An "honor-roll" of such German women at the turn of the century in Germany would include: Dr. Alice Salomon and Helene Peiper in Berlin; Maria Zettler in München; Marie Schmitz in Aachen; and Helene Weber and Christine Teusch in Cologne.

The emancipation and suffragette movement coincided with other historical trends and led to the emergence of social work as a vocation and, subsequently, to its professionalization. These developments could also be traced in the New World—notably in New England (Boston) and New York.[14] Private philanthropy, the women's movement, and social reform, in Berlin as well as in New York and Boston, became intertwined. The vision by individuals, notably—though not exclusively—by "upper-middle-class women," to do something about the social miseries by spearheading a cause and devoting their energies, skill, and time to make things happen was a significant feature in coping with the changing social conditions in Berlin (and other cities) at the turn of the century. The spirit of "noblesse oblige" became retranslated and adapted to the conditions of the late nineteenth century. It led to a powerful awakening of social consciousness which gave rise to social reforms that have left their indelible mark in history. While specific social policies, programs, measures, and organizational structures have changed considerably to keep pace with the convulsive changes during the twentieth century, the legacy has endured and has been the foundation of social policies in hundreds of countries and thousands of cities ever since.

The Emergence of Social Work

At a general assembly of the Deutscher Verein (German Association) in 1907, Albert Levy demanded that people who engage in social welfare activities, under public or private auspices, should not only be motivated by a "good heart," but should also receive systematic training in carrying out helping activities.[15] Levy asked that a social vocation be created. His call was heard, and subsequently the first schools of social work in Germany were founded. Given the circumstances at that time, these first schools were "Frauenschulen" (schools for women). The relationship between volunteers and trained social workers immediately became an issue that has continued to remain one ever since.

To be sure, several courses and workshops for philanthropic workers had existed prior to Levy's call. In fact, it was Dr. Alice Salomon in Berlin and Helene Weber in Cologne—among several others—who offered such courses and training institutes. But only at the turn of the century was it generally recognized that *helping* required specialized knowledge and skills, and that the *calling* of doing good and of bringing about reforms and administering social programs had been transformed into a *vocation*, and eventually into a *profession*.

Alice Salomon was a native Berliner. She was active in the labor movement, in the German and in international women's organizations, and she became instrumental in setting up the first school of social work in Berlin in 1908. She was founder, and subsequently head of the school from 1908 to 1925, and later became the first president of the International Association of Schools of Social Work. She wrote seminal books on social work and social work education and also translated, in 1926, Mary Richmond's *Social Dignonsis* into German. She died in 1948 in New York after her forced emigration to the United States because of Nazi persecution.[16]

On January 30, 1985, a memorial plaque honoring Alice Salomon as founder of the Berlin school was affixed to the present day Fachhochschule für Sozialarbeit und Sozialpädagogik (Undergraduate School for Social Work)[17] in Berlin.

Not until 1920 was social work education in Germany officially sanctioned, first by Prussia and later on by other states in the Weimar Republic. The efforts of the early pioneers had borne fruit. Although the darkness of

Memorial tablet in honour of Dr. Alice Salomon (1872–1948), foundress of the first social school for women (Schöneberg, Goltzstraße 43).—June 1985. Reproduced with permission of the Landesbildstelle Berlin.

the Nazi period and World War II had cast its pall over social welfare, the seeds of social work and social work education in Berlin and the rest of Germany have sprouted again and have led to exciting new developments and significant progress in these fields.

The confluence of industrialization and urbanization and its consequences for the life of the city of Berlin and its people, the first emergence of a "women's movement," the pioneering efforts to arouse social consciousness not only in the church, and among political labor leaders and upper-middle-class women, but also among workers, philanthropists, social reformers, and in the "general public," have created enormous impulses in social welfare policy and social work: (a) entitlements by law to insure against normal risk conditions, (b) social reforms to improve the lot of the poor, the destitute, the handicapped, the aged, abandoned children, and others, (c) linkage of private and public sectors and utilization of volunteers as friendly visitors, (d) creation of social work and training for "scientific philanthropy," and (e) recognition of the indispensability of leadership in advancing human betterment and of the fact that achievements in politics, economics, the arts, and the sciences need to be balanced with achievements in effecting a healthier social environment and social justice.

After the tragic events following the turn of the century, namely the outbreak of World War I, the progressive stance of the Weimar Republic was short-lived, and the nightmare of the Nazi regime appeared to have wiped out the social achievements of Berlin and the Kaiserreich around 1900. But that was not to be!

The social impulses of the period around the turn of the century are of lasting historical, philosophical, and practical significance as they reach into our own decade. Berlin's contributions in the social sector in those days were as significant in its "development of a culture" as were its contributions as an intellectual, artistic, musical, and political center.

Notes

[1] Lange, Annemarie, *Berlin: Zur Zeit Bebels und Bismarcks: Zwischen Reichsgründung und Jahrhundertwende* (Berlin: Dietz Verlag, 1976).

[2] Ibid.

[3] Putzstück, Walter and Hermann Glaser, *Ein Deutsches Bilderbuch: 1870–1918: Die Gesellschaft einer Epoche in alten Photographien* (München: C.H. Beck Verlag, 1982).

[4] Orthbandt, Eberhard, "Der Deutsche Verein in der Geschichte der deutschen Fürsorge," in *Nachrichtendienst des Deutschen Vereins für Öffentliche und Private Fürsorge* (Frankfurt/Main: Vol. 60, May 1980, No. 5, pp. 151–176).

[5] Ibid., p. 156.

[6] Lange, *op. cit.*, p. 728.

[7] Friedlander, Walter and R.Z. Apte, *Introduction to Social Welfare*, 4th ed., (Englewood Cliffs, N.J.: Prentice-Hall, 1974), pp. 11–12.

[8] Orthbandt, *op. cit.*, p. 157.

[9] Axinn, June and H. Levin, *Social Welfare: A History of the American Response to Need*, 2nd ed. (New York: Longman, 1982). Chapters 2, 3, and 4.

[10] Orthbandt, *op. cit.*, p. 156–157.

[11] Schmidle, Paul "Deutscher Caritas Verband," in *Fachlexikon der Sozialen Arbeit* (Frankfurt: Deutscher Verein, 1980), pp. 182–183.

[12] Carl Heymanns Verlag, Berlin, 1893.

[13] *75 Jahre Soziale Arbeit in Deutschland* (Berlin: Deutsches Zentral-Institut für Soziale Fragen), p. 4.

[14] Axinn and Levin, *op. cit.*

[15] Orthbandt, *op. cit.*, p. 159.

[16] Salomon, Alice, *20 Jahre Soziale Hilfsarbeit* (Karlsruhe, 1913).
Salomon, Alice, *Die Ausbildung zum sozialen Beruf* (Berlin, 1927).
Salomon, Alice, "Die Idee einer Hochschule für Frauen," in *Die Erziehung*, 1926, pp. 125.

[17] Direct Communication and invitation to the event from Prof. Dr. H.J. Brauns, Fachhochschule für Sozialarbeit, Berlin, 30 December, 1984.

CHAPTER 6

Jewish Life in Berlin Until the Hitler Period

Leon A. Feldman

Early Beginnings

Berlin traces its beginning back to the year 1237. The first evidence of the presence of Jews was in a local ordinance, dated October 28, 1295, by which wool merchants were forbidden to supply Jews with woolen yarn. Subsequent tax records mention Jews in 1317 and 1363, respectively. Jews lived in what was called a Jewish quarter (Grosser Judenhof), and there was a Jews' Street. Apparently, however, some wealthier Jews lived outside of these areas. Only in 1543, permission was granted for a Jewish cemetery; until then Jews buried their dead in nearby Spandau.

During the time of the Black Death (1347–52), Jewish quarters were burnt, and some of the inhabitants were killed or expelled. Later, Jews once again were permitted to settle in Berlin. This pattern of persecution and sufferance repeated itself so consistently that modern historians would look for the correlated pattern of poor harvests and epidemics to account for outbursts of hatred. Thus in 1446, the Berlin Jews, as well as those of Brandenburg, were expelled, but allowed to return a year later. A few wealthier men were admitted in 1509, while in the following year, the Jews found themselves accused of desecrating the Host. One hundred and eleven Jews were arrested and tried; of these, 51 were sentenced to death, with 38 of them being burnt at the stake on July 10, 1510. All remaining Jews were expelled, and it took until 1539 for their innocence to be established. By 1543—despite the opposition of the townsfolk—Jews were permitted to settle in Berlin again. In 1571 they were expelled once more, this time "forever."

During the next one hundred years, only occasionally did Jews make an appearance in Berlin, and it took until about 1663 that permission to stay permanently was granted to the "Court-Jew" Israel Aron, supplier to the army and the court of the Great Elector. As the result of the expulsion of Jews from Vienna in 1670, some fifty Jews were admitted into Berlin for a period of twenty years on May 21, 1671. They were made to pay huge sums for "protection" and were not allowed to build a synagogue. However, this permission to enter the city, and a subsequent privilege granted to a number of Jews on September 10, constitutes the beginning of a new Jewish community in Berlin. Despite the vocal objections of local inhabitants, the author-

Section, DDK 88/8.—Photograph by Hans-Joachim Bartsch, Berlin. Reproduced with permission of the Berlin Museum, Berlin.

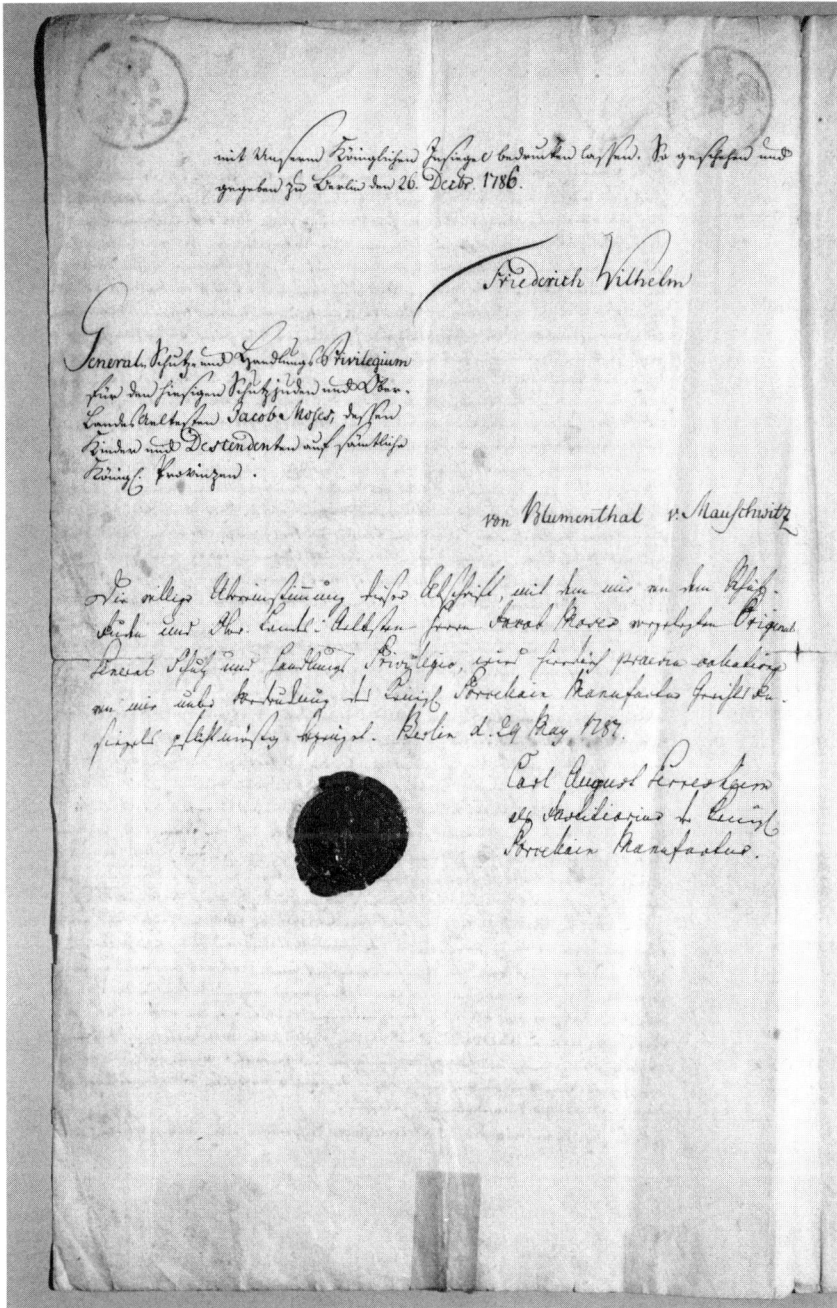

Letter of protection for Jacob Moses, issued by Friedrich Wilhelm II, son of Friedrich II (the Great), king of Prussia from 1786 to 1797.—Berlin Museum, Berlin, Jewish

ities granted "letters of protection" to a considerable number of males. The first census of Jews in Berlin (1700) records seventy families with "residence permits," 47 families without such "protection," and a few itinerant peddlers and beggars: a total of 1000 people.

The male Jews were mostly engaged in commerce, a handful of them in the lending and changing of money. All this while, it was nearly impossible to find employment elsewhere: artisans and craftsmen were tolerated only as long as they were not in competition with any of the guilds. It was the guilds who were most hotly opposed to the admission of Jews. They resorted to accusing Jews of dealing in stolen goods and wanted to restrict Jewish merchants to clandestine dealing in second-hand and pawned goods. Officialdom, however, being interested in raising additional tax money from the Jews, met the demands of the guilds only partially and meanwhile raised the "protection" money and all special fees imposed on the Jews for privileges. The taxed privileges included ritual slaughter, the sale of meat, marriage dues, circumcision of their sons, burial of their dead, and permission to admit additional Jews to their community. At the same time, the authorities limited the number of shops Jews were allowed to keep.

Despite all these handicaps and impediments, Jewish mercantile activities expanded until Jews were ordered to close down every store opened since 1610. Only those members of the community who could raise the sum of 5,000 Thaler could avoid the latest ordinance which made dealing in anything but second-hand goods or pawnbroking illegal.

By 1701 Frederick I (the first "king in Prussia") began a campaign of systematic exploitation of the Jews. He doubled the tax for "protection," ordered levies to maintain an infantry regiment, imposed a special tax on the birth of a child, required exorbitant payments for many other activities, and imposed heavy fines for contravention of these new ordinances. His successor, Frederick William I, the Soldier-King (1713–40), limited the number of "tolerated" Jews to the heads of 120 households, but against special payment allowed that—in addition to the eldest—second and third children could also set up households. A decree of 1730 reduced the number of such households to one hundred; the two eldest sons of a family, however, were allowed to stay and set up houses against the payment of 1,000 Thaler for the eldest and of 2,000 Thaler for the second son. This king also limited economic activity: Jews were prohibited from owning land, in keeping with a ruling imposed in 1697, unless special permission was obtained—again at a price. Property could only be bequeathed to direct descendants, not to wives or any other blood relative. By January 1737, Jews could no longer acquire housing by purchase—a move probably designed to restrict the Jewish population where the number of Jewish families had risen to 234. A new decree set a limit of 120 families (953 people), plus an additional 48 families of "communal officers" (234 people). Five hundred and eighty-four Jews were asked to leave, 387 obeyed. Yet, by 1743, the Jewish population in Berlin amounted to 337 families (or 1945 people).

When Frederick II (the Great) succeeded to the throne in 1740, he denied residence permits to second and third children and restricted the number of "protected" Jews to 150. On the other hand, his revised *General-Privilegium* of 1750 (in force until 1812) granted residence rights to 200 "ordinary" and to 63 "extraordinary" families. The eldest child of an "ordinary" family inherited this right, while the right of residence in the case of an "extraordinary" Jew expired at the death of the holder. Moses Mendelssohn, for all his fame, was unable to secure "ordinary" rights for his children; i.e., at his death in 1786, only an appeal by his widow to the successor of Frederick II saved the family from banishment.

Towards Full Citizenship

For a number of diverse reasons, it was during the reign of Frederick II that the lot of Jews in Prussia improved. Partly this change came about through the influx of other "foreigners": emigrés from French religious persecution, bringing both new crafts, like silk manufacture, and breadth of horizon in the guise of French-speaking scientists and intellectuals whom the young king had attracted to Berlin. Another change in the economic situation arose through the successive Silesian Wars conducted by the king against Saxony, Russia, and Austria. Whereas in particular the Seven Years' War (1756–63) brought trade with other towns to a standstill and created much chaos and unemployment, it gave new urgency to the king's demands for money and supplies. As suppliers to the army and as purveyors to the mint, some Berlin Jews became wealthy, and some were even granted similar rights as those enjoyed by Christian bankers. In 1763, the Jews in Berlin were given permission to go beyond the previous limit of forty houses and acquire up to seventy. The king lost no time to draw on this new wealth: he ordered the Jews to supply a specified amount of silver annually, below the prevailing market price. In 1764 he levied huge sums for "protection" and, as a condition for further privileges, imposed the demand and unusual irritant that each new household accept a blind choice of porcelain from the royal manufacture to the value of 300–500 Thaler, with the strict injunction to sell this far-from-perfect china out of town.

However, the Berlin of the 1760s also saw the burgeoning of new learning, brought about initially by a variety of coincidental intellectual factors in the men and ideas then clustered around Moses Mendelssohn. Interest in learning and emphasis on education as such was not new, it had been in evidence among the Berlin Jews decades earlier at a time when they were not allowed to run a printing press themselves. They could only supply printers and proofreaders for the court preacher Jablonski, who wanted to set up *The Book of Psalms* (1697) and the complete *Bible* (1699) in Hebrew.

The story of Hebrew texts printed in Berlin is extensively documented thanks to Moritz Steinschneider's research in the late nineteenth century. He listed the Jewish printers and the journeymen as well as the texts for which each printer was responsible—and their number is great. Equally great is the number of printers involved, since journeymen were not "protected" and had to leave town every two years or so. Since Frederick I refused permission for a *Talmud* to be printed in Berlin, only the second edition of the Frankfurt-on-the-Oder *Talmud* (1715–22) was issued as the "Berlin Talmud" during the reign of Frederick William I between 1734 and 1739. By 1738, a calendar (Luach) was issued on a yearly basis; altogether there were

Copperplate etching by J.G. Müller, 1785, according to the painting by J.C. Frisch.—
Text: Moses Mendels Sohn—to the king Friedrich Wilhelm II most humbly dedicated
by the Jüdische Freyschule (Jewish Free School) at Berlin, 1787.—Berlin Museum,
Berlin. Photograph: Hans Joachim Bartsch, Berlin, 1988. Reproduced with permission
of the Berlin Museum, Berlin.

so many important rabbinic and other Hebrew texts published in Berlin in the period of 1708 to 1762, that it is an important indication to the demand it had to supply in times where Jews felt increasingly safe from physical oppression so that they could have time to ponder over the educational needs of their offspring.

Under the influence of Moses Mendelssohn, several educational reforms were introduced into the Jewish community of Berlin. In 1778, a "Jewish Free School" was established in conjunction with a printing press. A primer in German, designed and in part written by Mendelssohn and his friend David Friedländer (1750–1834), documents to this day their rational ideas of teaching Jewish children the elements of reading, different alphabets, and numerals in print and script, as well as basic moral tenets. This *Lesebuch für jüdische Kinder* (Berlin: Voss 1779) was held in such high regard that it served as a model for non-Jewish children in German schools.

One of the aims of Mendelssohn, and subsequently that of his circle, was to spread knowledge and awareness of that other, non-Jewish world of culture at their doorstep. Mendelssohn's strenuous endeavour to obtain a fair hearing and ultimately citizen rights, for his coreligionists, demanded of them that they could speak, read, and write German but also that their religious heritage was preserved and transmitted. Thus, towards the latter part of the eighteenth century, Berlin became the center for the printing of Haskalah (enlightenment) books and articles in German, side by side with biblical texts translated into German by Mendelssohn but printed in Hebrew script. Concurrently, three other thrusts happened: (1) a deliberate move to keep alive knowledge of Hebrew as a written and read language by the founding of a society to promote the Hebrew language; it published *The Gatherer* (Ha-me'assef) for several decades, beginning in 1788; (2) by Mendelssohn's work towards creating a legal basis for "civic amelioration" of the lot of Jews in Germany by translating the ritual laws, by helping to formulate an oath acceptable to Jews in German legal proceedings, by working with and influencing leading Prussian jurists like C.W. von Dohm (*Über die bürgerliche Verbesserung der Juden*, 1782) and E.F. Klein (*Judeneid*, 1783); (3) no less important was Mendelssohn's decisive influence on his German intellectual peers, from whom he won in 1763, in close competition with Kant, the competition of the Berlin Royal Academy on a subject proving verities in metaphysics, to his final years. As the only man not in public service, he was one of the 22–24 members who constituted the first of Berlin's three prestigious "Wednesday Societies." Parts of the deliberations on economic, sociological, juridical, and ethic concerns of the day of these top Prussian civil servants—and Mendelssohn—are on record in the issues of Berlin's most intellectual periodical, *Berlinische Monatsschrift*. It was here that Mendelssohn's "What do we mean by 'Enlightenment'?" first appeared in print (1784). Thus, in the last quarter of the eighteenth century, the interaction between Jew and Christian began on an intellectually reciprocal level among men of integrity and concern for the moral and civic welfare of others, irrespective of creed. Towards the end of the eighteenth century, it became possible to meet on a social level, and the salons of Henriette Herz, Rachel Varnhagen, and Mendelssohn's daughter Dorothea Schlegel became the meeting place for both Christians and Jews who came eagerly in order to enjoy high-spirited conversation and to exchange opinions on an intellectual level then not easily found elsewhere in Berlin. It was in this climate that conversions to Christianity began to occur gradually.

Berlin Jewry in the Nineteenth Century

Toleration of the Jews as citizens was by no means a won cause in the Prussia of 1800. The years 1803/04 witnessed an extended, written controversy over the Jewish question, thus enabling the government to take no action. Neither the French Revolution of 1789, the relative tolerance shown by emperor Joseph to Jews in Vienna, nor the Declaration of Independence in North America had helped the Jews as far as definite citizen status was concerned. It took the defeat of Prussia by Napoleon and the resultant influence of French insistence on liberty and equality to bring about the Prussian act of 1809 and the edict of 1812, which finally removed all restrictions on rights of residence, impositions of special taxes, etc. As citizens, Jews were now subject to state as well as to religious jurisdiction. They were required to adopt family names and make accessible their records of births, marriages, and deaths.

Internally, so to speak, the Jews had been governed by statutes approved by Prussia on December 7, 1700. This provided the election of *parnassim* (communal leaders), who were in office for three years. These men were empowered to impose fines for infractions—of which one-third went to the Jewish community chest, the rest to the state. The parnassim had the right to excommunicate members, requiring the consent of the local rabbi and the state. New statutes issued in 1722 and 1723 brought about changes in community administration. The chief parnass was now elected by royal appointment but under the direction of a Jewish community board. This board co-opted a number of *tovim* (lay members) and there was provision for the replacement of members. In 1792 a special three-member committee was set up to handle the community's fiscal matters. After 1812 and the Edict of Emancipation, the organizational structure of the Jewish community faced a void: old regulations had been abolished; new ones had not been formulated. It took until 1837 before new statutes were passed, and until 1854 before Berlin Jews elected a new administration to be in charge of community affairs. It was not and until August 1860 before a new constitution was ratified.

Even more serious were the difficulties that beset the Jewish community in the nineteenth century over the issue of liturgical reform, i.e., a further break with tradition in a community that had had a synagogue since 1714 and a number of very distinguished rabbis. The last of these before 1800, Hirshel Levin, known for his opposition to *Haskalah* (enlightenment), was the only one who had threatened to start a controversy. The reform program initiated by David Friedländer and other supporters was temporarily halted by a state decree of December 9, 1823. It provided that "all divine worship was to take place in the local synagogue and according to accepted custom without any change in language, ritual, prayer or liturgy." Fortunately, such conservatism did not affect scholarship or learning. The year 1819 saw the founding of the Society for the Culture and Science of Judaism (Verein für

Kultur und Wissenschaft des Judentums) by Leopold Zunz, assisted by the historian I. M. Jost and others. The Jewish Free School, founded in 1778, closed in 1825 for lack of funds and was replaced around 1826 by a new school for boys under the supervision of the Jewish community, with Zunz as principal until 1830. In 1835, the community organized a school for girls. In addition to these community schools, there were also some private educational institutions. One, founded in 1807, advocated a liberal Jewish ideology under the direction of Jost (1816 and 1835), while a conservative teachers' seminary opened in 1835. Zunz founded another seminary which functioned between 1840 and 1850, to be replaced by yet another one in 1859.

The Frankfurt-on-the-Oder press had moved to Berlin in 1830 and began to supply the schools with many needed books. In 1834, David Friedländer who had founded his own printing press and publishing firm in 1830, engaged as proofreader the eminent scholar David Cassel. Among the outstanding titles issued in 1862 was the *Code* (Mishneh Torah) by Maimonides, but of particular interest at that time was the work of Michael Sachs, a rabbi not opposed to moderate reforms, who became known for his pioneer work as translator of mediaeval Hebrew poetry and for his rendering into lyrical German of the *Siddur* and *Machzor* (daily prayers and for Feasts and Holy Days). In 1844 this scholarly and temperate man became a third preacher in the Berlin Jewish community.

By this time, a second Association for Jewish Culture had come into being (1840), a reform society had been founded (1845), and a reform congregation soon thereafter, which originally wanted to become autonomous from the community but did not achieve its aim. The high point of its radical reforms occurred during the rabbinic tenure of Samuel Holdheim (1847–60). The next violent confrontation that rocked the Jewish community occurred when many of its members opted for the introduction of an organ into the New Synagogue. Proposed changes in liturgy and the appointment of Abraham Geiger as rabbi provoked the 1869 founding of an orthodox separatist group: the Synagogue Congregation Adass Jisroel, which was formally incorporated in 1885.

One of the conditions for Geiger's appointment as rabbi had been the establishment of an institution of higher learning, later known as Hochschule für die Wissenschaft des Judentums (1872). About the same time (1873) the orthodox group founded a seminary for its students called Rabbiner Seminar für das orthodoxe Judentum. A conservative school, the Jewish Theological Seminary, concentrated on historical Judaism, was functioning in Breslau since 1851. All three institutions for the education of scholars and religious functionaries were still in existence by November 1938, and countless learned rabbis and Jewish academics owe their training and knowledge to them.

Emancipation: Its Demands and Consequences

After 1812, the political history of the Berlin Jews became increasingly enmeshed with that of the Jews of Prussia, of Germany, and with that of the world around them. In Germany itself, Jews began to consider themselves Jews *and* Germans: in the revolution of 1848 Jews were involved not only as

Students in the library of the Rabbi-Seminary (Rabbiner-Seminar) of the Jewish congregation Adass Jisroel, founded in 1869, dissolved around 1942, and re-established in 1986; Artilleriestraße 31, now Tucholskystraße 40, ward Mitte, East Berlin.—About 1935. Reproduced from "Adass Jisroel, die jüdische Gemeinde in Berlin (1869–1942)," West Berlin 1986, p. 63, with permission of the editor Dr. Mario Offenberg, Berlin.

fighters on the barricades and as members of the civic guard but also as orators and journalists. However, notwithstanding the edict of 1812, which granted Jews Prussian citizenship (and all rights pertaining thereto), they continued to suffer from a number of restrictions and handicaps, so that in fact full legal civic equality was not achieved until July 1860. By that time, Berlin represented a stronghold of liberalism and tolerance.

It was in this spirit of freedom and equality that the Jewish community of Berlin in February 1878 petitioned Otto von Bismarck, then chancellor of Germany, to raise the question of equal rights for Rumanian Jews at the Congress of Berlin. At Bismarck's instructions, this was done. The German delegation was to insist that provisions for equal rights for members of all creeds in all the Balkan countries become part of the peace treaty. France, Italy, Austria, and Hungary, at Bismarck's behest, were to discuss the problem before the congress met. When it did, the German delegation based its appeal on a memorandum drawn up by a special committee of renowned Berlin Jews, including the banker Gerson von Bleichröder and the writer Berthold Auerbach.

When the Jewish problem finally came up for discussion in July 1878, the independence of Bulgaria, Serbia, and Rumania was made contingent on affording equal rights to all ethnic groups and religions. This principle was also binding, according to separate resolutions, on Turkey, Greece, and Montenegro. While all countries, except Rumania, complied, Serbia and Bulgaria even included the provision of equal rights for minorities in their constitution. The only opposition at the congress came from the Russian representative. He claimed that the Jews of Serbia, Rumania, and Russia could not be compared with the Jews of Berlin, Paris, London, and Vienna.

It was indicative of the influence of the Berlin Jews in the late 1870s that Bismarck and the congress listened to them and acted on their recommendation. In Berlin itself, Jews increasingly began to make their way into the political and social life of the city. For instance, about one-fifth of the newspapers came to be owned by Jews, or had Jews as editors. Including the *Berliner Tageblatt* and *Vossische Zeitung*, i.e., newspapers widely read at home and abroad, though not by any means voicing government opinion. They also began to play a prominent part in literature, arts, music, and the theater, as well as in other cultural activities. Their distinction in the arts and sciences and in public life aroused a loud reaction in the more conservative circles. Before long, Berlin turned into a center of anti-Semitism that found its supporters among political parties and organizations, and even by such an influential figure as a preacher at court. Odious tirades of a racial, economic, and cultural anti-Semitism blossomed forth, primarily in the 1870s and 1880s. Among its outstanding proponents were the historian Heinrich von Treitschke, the orientalist Paul de Lagarde, and the germanist Adolf Bartels.

This wave of anti-Semitism should not have come as a surprise. From the year 1295 onward, there had been repeated outbreaks of hatred and upsurges of persecution, hostility borne of ignorance and intolerance. Yet the Jewish population in Berlin continued to grow steadily and at an astounding rate since 1812. In that year, the figure stood at 3,000; it reached 12,000 by 1852, 108,000 by 1890, and 175,000 in 1925. However, to evaluate this rise in numbers, it needs to be compared to the total number of Berliners during the same time span: in 1840, Jews comprised about 2 percent of the entire population; the figure stood at 5 percent in 1852 and at 4.29 percent in 1925. (During the period 1811–1828, 1.4 percent of all German Jews lived in Berlin; in 1871 the corresponding figure was 7 percent, and in 1925 it was 30 percent.)

In view of the fact that intermarriage with Christians, apostasy from Judaism, conversion to Christianity, and the decline in the Jewish birthrate had made inroads on the number of Berlin Jews, the rise in the total Jewish population in Berlin has to be accounted for in terms of immigration. Between 1722 and 1795, many Jews arrived from Lithuania and from partitioned Poland, from the province of Posen, and from the so-called Pale of Settlements. These Jews from Eastern Europe were joined by an influx of their coreligionists from Galicia, Poland, and Russia after the First World War. The earlier settlers as well as the newcomers became an important component in the life of the Berlin Jewish community. For the most part, they were very poor but highly motivated to acquire learning and to defend social values. However, mostly they spoke only Yiddish and were determined to maintain a "Jewish way of life," religiously, culturally, and socially.

But was there a one and only "Jewish way of life"? Within the religious and cultural life in the Jewish community in Berlin, orthodoxy and other Jewish ideologies had been in conflict throughout the major part of the nineteenth century. The orthodox Jews accepted only a Judaism that was "Torah-true," i.e., a Judaism as set forth in rabbinic law and lore which was codified by Josef Karo's *Shulchan Arukh* (*The Arranged Table*) (sixteenth century), bringing together the commentaries and teachings known as *Halachah*. Orthodox Jews felt it incumbent upon them to emphasize their stand as guardians of the Torah and its commandments in order to maintain these values in the face of the threat emanating from the desire for reform, *Haskalah*, and the trend towards the secularization of Judaism that had begun to permeate Jewish society in western and central Europe in the first half of the nineteenth century.

Orthodoxy looked upon attempts to adjust Judaism to the "spirit of the time" as utterly incompatible with the entire thrust of normative Judaism. Orthodoxy until today insists that the revealed word of God, rather than the values of any given age, are the ultimate standard for all Jews. Therefore many orthodox believers foresaw the perils about to beset Jewry when civic rights broke down the walls of the ghetto; they feared that exposure to the lure of the modern world might ultimately result in total assimilation. A first alarm was sounded when Moses Mendelssohn translated the *Pentateuch* into German. Numerous conversions to Christianity added to this fear, as did the efforts of the reform movement to transform the character of Judaism in order to facilitate total integration of Jews into modern society. Not only orthodox but also liberal and tradition-minded Jews worried deeply about the future of Judaism. While the liberal and conservative as well as many orthodox Jews remained within the organized Jewish community (Gemeinde), in Berlin and in other cities of Germany, separatist communal and synagogal organs were founded. Fortunately in Berlin, as well as in other parts of Germany, the orthodox and liberal Jews were not rent by irremediable controversy, so that when the need arose in the 1930s, there was cooperation for dealing with all aspects of the tragedy that befell.

Before that time, for example, between 1880 and 1930, Berlin was enriched by eight additional synagogues; in all, in the Berlin community functioned seven orthodox and nine liberal and reform synagogues. In addition, there were many prayer halls and private synagogues; and all groups that were supported by the Jewish community had their own rabbi. Most of the synagogues were destroyed in November 1938.

In the nineteenth century, when Berlin grew into an important commercial and industrial center, Jews played an increasingly important part not only in economic enterprises but also in the intellectual realm. Well known and respected were the banks of Bleichröder, Mendelssohn & Co., the department stores such as Wertheim and Tietz, or men like the engineer Emil Rathenau, founder of the AEG (General Electric Company), and his son Walter Rathenau (assassinated in 1922). Altogether, the list of those outstanding Jews, including those from Eastern Europe, who made their home in Berlin: physicians, scientists, philosophers, artists, writers, jurists, politicians and engineers, reads like a "Who's Who" of the period from 1760 to 1933.

Berlin, the capital of Germany, also became headquarters for a number of national Jewish organizations. (E.g., Deutsch-israelitischer Gemeinde-bund,* founded in 1869; Verband deutscher Juden,† established in 1904; Order of the B'nai B'rith, 1893; Central Verein deutscher Staatsbürger mosaischen Glaubens,‡ 1893; Hilfsverein der deutschen Juden,§ 1901.) Each of these organizations published their own widely circulating journals. The Berlin *Gemeindeblatt*, for instance, reached a weekly circulation of over 60,000 copies.

In 1925, the census of Jews in Berlin had stood at 160,000. By 1935, the number was approximately 175,000. Apart from those who succeeded in fleeing, only very few Berlin Jews survived Hitler's "final solution."

The Cause of Zionism

"Zionism"—a term coined only in 1893 by Nathan Birnbaum—at first met with a lukewarm reception in Berlin, although at a later period, Germany in general, and Berlin in particular, were centers of fervent Zionist support and activities. Opposition to the Zionist endeavors came from the orthodox extremist and from the liberal camps. The Berlin liberal rabbi, Siegmund Maybaum (d. 1919), was among the leaders of the "Protest Rabbiner" and the Central Union of German Citizens of Mosaic Persuasion—known as the Central Verein, (abbreviated C. V.)—launched a concentrated campaign against the movement founded by Theodor Herzl at the turn of the twentieth century. The C. V., founded as a defense organization against the second great wave of anti-Semitism which spread throughout Germany in the nineteenth century, denied every inclination toward Jewish nationalism, i.e., the idea for a Jewish homeland of its own, Hebrew as a national language, a common history and culture—all of which, they believed, to be unrealizable. The organization emphasized that its followers are members of German ethnicity (Volkszugehörigkeit) and are deeply rooted in German culture. Therefore, they concentrated their political involvement in counter-acting anti-Semitism and, from an intellectual point of view, in explaining Judaism and in studying collective prejudices and their damaging effects upon all areas of public life.

The opposing position was taken by the Zionist Organization of Germany (Zionistische Vereinigung für Deutschland), a relatively small group, but with a very active membership, which came to full bloom after the First World War, and then played a very important role in the life of the Jewish community. The Zionists were not homogeneous, and represented within its ranks a variety of ideologies and strategies. The groups included on the right the religious Zionists (called Mizrachi), and on the left the various labor and socialist tendencies. The most prominent faction was the "Cul-

---

*Union of German Israelite Communities.
†Association of German Jews.
‡Central Union of German Citizens of Mosaic Persuasion.
§Federation of German-Jewish Philanthropies.

tural Zionists," who were influenced by the interpretation of Judaism and theory of spiritual Zionism (Geistiges Zentrum-*Merkaz ruchani*) in Palestine as promulgated by Ahad ha-Am. His philosophy of cultural Zionism, which did not emphasize complete reliance on diplomacy to achieve a homeland in the Holy Land, but stressed that the purpose of Palestine was not to resolve the economic and political plight of the Jews, nor alleviate the problem of anti-Semitism for those Jews continuing to live in the Diaspora. In his view, the building of a spiritual center in Palestine would radiate to the Diaspora new teaching and new hope, which would revivify Jewish life there. However, all factions, irrespective of their ideological perceptions had one thing in common: the upbuilding of the Jewish homeland in Palestine, and the denial of or counteracting assimilation.

CHAPTER 7

Cabaret and the Dilemma of Satire in the Early Weimar Republic

Peter Jelavich

The purpose of this chapter is to suggest that the contradictions of Weimar society left two options open to "artistes engagés" or intellectuals of left-liberal persuasion. On the one hand, they could employ a type of social satire that castigated all points of the Weimar political spectrum, and hence developed cynical overtones; or, on the other hand, they could devise an agitational art that espoused radical and revolutionary change, but which held little hope for realization, given Weimar Germany's sociopolitical makeup. Both of these options were artistically productive, but politically sterile; and it is precisely this combination of cultural effervescence and social frustration that one associates with the Weimar Republic. Moreover, interwar Berlin also tends to evoke images of cabaret. Consequently, this essay will focus on the first performance of Weimar Germany's first artistic cabaret, and it will contend that many of the dilemmas that produced the "negativistic" current of Weimar culture were already visible in the program of Max Reinhardt's *Schall und Rauch* ("Sound and Smoke") on December 8, 1919.

The tone of early Weimar cabaret was set by the tragic historical events that framed the birth of the Republic. War, half-hearted revolution, and whole-hearted counterrevolution determined the political spirit of the early Weimar period. World War I, which claimed 9 million lives over the course of four years, took a heavy toll in Germany: nearly two million Germans were killed, and over 4 million more were wounded—in short, one out of every eleven Germans was a casualty of the fighting. By October 1918, it was also clear to the German political elites that the war effort was failing, and they were thus faced with a pressing question: The war having been lost, what could be saved? It was not simply a matter of salvaging German territory, but, more importantly, of rescuing a social, political, and economic way of life. The pillars of Wilhelmine society—the military, the agrarian elites, the industrial leaders, the bureaucracies, the church—wanted to ensure that their domestic power would remain undiminished. This would not, apparently, be an easy task, because before the outbreak of war, the nominally Marxist Social Democrats already had received over a third of the votes cast in national Reichstag elections. Although these social-ists approved war credits in August 1914, the prolongation of the slaughter eventually embittered ever larger sectors of the population against the po-

The German Parliament (Reichstag), built 1884–94, after the plan by Paul Wallot;
Platz der Republik, ward Tiergarten.—About 1930. Reproduced with permission of
the Landesbildstelle Berlin.

litical and economic elites that benefitted from and sustained the war effort.
By October 1918, the German government—which, by that time, meant pre-
eminently the German General Staff—knew that a military collapse at
the front would coincide with a collapse of traditional political structures
at home as well.

In a surprisingly short time, the German generals were able to reach an
accommodation with their old enemies, the Social Democrats, and to forge
an unholy alliance that gave Weimar satirists so much material for their art.
The generals realized that if they persuaded the Kaiser to abdicate, and if
they handed power over to a civilian regime, they would solve two problems. On the one hand, they might be able to gain better peace terms from
the allies, who claimed to be fighting a war "against the Kaiser and for
democracy"; on the other hand, they could place the onus for calling an
armistice and signing a peace treaty on civilian (and preferably socialist)
politicians. The mutiny of sailors at Kiel at the end of October 1918 and the
spread of strikes, mutinies, and demonstrations to other cities in the first
week of November hastened this scenario, which culminated in the abdica-
tion of the Kaiser, the proclamation of the Republic, and the appointment of
Friedrich Ebert, the chairman of the Social Democratic Party (SPD), as
Reich chancellor on November 9, 1918.

On the following evening, Ebert formed a secret bond that exceeded the best hopes of the generals and, some have argued, also sealed the fate of Weimar democracy. A bureaucrat to the core, Ebert epitomized the cautious, revisionist, and (in practice) antirevolutionary spirit of German Social Democracy, which strove for a gradual democratization of German politics and a slow but steady growth of the trade-union movement.[1]* Unfortunately for Ebert, many of the Germans who had taken to the streets in the first weeks of November were more inspired by the works of Karl Marx, to which the Social Democrats paid token homage, and were inflamed by the example of Russia, where a year ago to the week a revolutionary communist party had succeeded in acquiring and maintaining power. On the Russian model, workers' and soldiers' councils (or *soviets*) sprang up throughout Germany, and they demanded a thoroughgoing democratization of politics and socialization of major industries. Similar demands were voiced by the two radical spin-offs from the left wing of social democracy, namely the Independent Social Democrats (USPD) and the Spartacists around Karl Liebknecht and Rosa Luxemburg. Ebert, who had hoped that a constitutional monarchy with a strong parliament would follow the end of war, was initially shocked by the proclamation of a republic, and he was even more horrified by the extreme demands of the councils and the leftist parties. On the one hand, he believed that too rapid a social change would lead to chaos and civil war, as the case of Russia seemed to prove. On the other hand, he feared that, unlike Russia, a civil war in Germany would terminate with a victory of counterrevolution and, perhaps, an abrogation of the few social gains that the Social Democrats had painstakingly acquired over the course of half a century. Thus on the evening following his appointment as Reich chancellor, Ebert held a secret telephone conversation with Wilhelm Groener, a member of the German General Staff. Groener agreed to support the Republic if Ebert promised to use the army to maintain social order against the leftist demands of the council movement, the USPD, and the Spartacists. This offer was happily accepted by Ebert. Five days later, an equally momentous pact was concluded between the great industrialist, Hugo Stinnes, and Carl Legien, the head of the organized trade unions that espoused the "reformist" spirit of social democracy. Stinnes agreed to recognize union officials as the representatives of labor and as equal bargaining partners to capitalists, and he granted an eight-hour workday; Legien, for his part, promised to leave the principle of private property untouched, and to resist calls for socialization of industry from the rank and file.

These alliances, though not irrational from a pragmatic standpoint, were fraught with hypocrisy and contradictions from the standpoint of ideals.[2] Ebert, albeit head of the SPD, had taken power only reluctantly, under pressure from the masses in the streets. As the historian Ernst Troelsch noted, the Social Democratic leaders "adopted the revolution to appease the masses; it was a revolution that the socialist leaders had not made and that, from their perspective, was an abortion, but which they pretended to accept

*See Notes section at the end of this chapter.

as their own long-sought child.''[3] To keep that child in line, the Wilhelmine military, though for so long the enemy of republicanism and social reform, was called in as guardian. Together, the army and the socialist leaders fought against the parties that struggled in practice for the very ideals that the Social Democrats espoused in theory: radical democratization, socialization of industry, and anti-militarism. It was a fight that took on increasingly brutal forms. On December 6, troops under orders from Gustav Noske, the Social Democrat who would soon be appointed minister of defense, fired for the first time on workers demonstrating in Berlin. In early January, a small uprising of Spartacists in the Prussian capital was suppressed, leaving a hundred insurgents dead and their radical leaders, Luxemburg and Liebknecht, murdered while in custody. The quelling of even larger disturbances in Berlin in March cost the lives of 1200 people. While the Social-Democratic government employed reactionary troops of the regular army and the Freikorps against leftist demonstrators, the old order reasserted itself in other areas as well. Most notably, the civil service and the judiciary continued to be manned by prewar bureaucrats and judges, still thoroughly imbued with monarchist and anti-republican values.

We all are familiar with Carl von Ossietzsky's assertion that Weimar was not only a "republic without republicans," but even more a case of republicans lacking a republic. Since the essence of satire is to highlight the discrepancies between ideals and reality, the unholy alliances that held this state together proved a rich harvest for German writers and artists. Much of that harvest was reaped in the cabaret movement. Berlin's first major postwar cabaret was Max Reinhardt's *Schall und Rauch*, which opened its doors on December 8, 1919, over a year after the proclamation of the Republic. Two weeks earlier, Reinhardt had inaugurated his Grosses Schauspielhaus—a former circus hall that seated 3500 spectators—with a performance of Aeschylos' Oresteian trilogy. Soon thereafter, Reinhardt decided that he would open a cabaret to complement and even parody the goings-on of his "serious" theater. Consequently, when *Schall und Rauch* opened in the basement of the Grosses Schauspielhaus, its major number was a politically satirical puppet-play entitled *Einfach klassisch! Eine Orestie mit glücklichem Ausgang* (Simply Classical! An Oresteia with a Happy Ending).

This movement from "serious" theater to cabaret was, in fact, an inversion of the path that Reinhardt had taken before the war. He had been manager of one of the first cabarets of the Wilhelmine era, also named *Schall und Rauch*, which had opened in January 1901. Up to then, Reinhardt had been an actor in modern, mainly naturalist, plays. His excursion into cabaret was caused by his dissatisfaction with naturalist theater, which attempted to create a nearly exact illusion of reality. Naturalism was, for Reinhardt, much too "untheatrical"—it denied the enormous visual and gestural possibilities of the stage. Such true "theatricality" could be found, however, in vaudeville, which combined skits, songs, dance, and other performing arts. Reinhardt's first cabaret attempted to fuse the popular theatricality of vaudeville with the thematic concerns of the educated liberal elite, such as parody of high politics and high culture. Although the first *Schall und Rauch* was successful as a cabaret, Reinhardt decided to return to conventional theater, but with a difference. From 1902 on, his former cabaret troupe, now a theater company, performed classical and modern drama with a much greater degree of vitality and "theatricality" than any other stage in Germany. The plays of Shakespeare, Goethe, Schiller, and others, which had acquired almost museal status and were treated as spoken texts, were enlivened by pantomime, song, dance, imaginative stagings, and other "vaudevillian" devices. This revitalization of elite texts through the infusion of popular theatricality was extremely successful, and it culminated in the first major theater-in-the-round productions of the twentieth century. In 1910 and 1911, respectively, Reinhardt staged *Oedipos* and the *Oresteia* in the (rented) Schumann circus hall in Berlin. Eight years later, Reinhardt purchased that circus hall and revived his production of the *Oresteia*, and he also resurrected the cabaret which, in 1901, had been the starting-point of his theatrical reform.[4]

The main purpose of the new, postwar *Schall und Rauch* was entertainment, not satirical agitation; but given the ostensible absurdity of politics in the early Weimar era, political themes were used as springboards for amusement. *Schall und Rauch* opened on rather traditional (half-racy, half-sentimental) cabaretic notes: there were Pierrot-songs, "Dirnenlieder," and the like. Things picked up, however, with the screening of a cartoon film entitled *A Day in the Life of the Reichspräsident*—a sendup of Ebert, which began as a takeoff on the notorious photograph of Ebert and Noske in swimsuits at the Wannsee, which had graced a recent cover of the *Berliner Illustrierte Zeitung*.[5] Next, Paul Graetz, who would soon become one of the most famous cabaret performers of interwar Berlin, sang some songs with texts by Kurt Tucholsky, including one that described with cynical approval the proliferation of profiteering during the war and postwar months. The song concluded with a few slices against Noske—indeed, by December 1919 it had become *de rigueur* among satirists to attack the Social Democratic minister of defense who repeatedly called in troops to suppress workers' demonstrations.[6]

The high point of the evening came with the puppet play, *Einfach klassisch!*, a topical updating of the *Oresteia*. Agamemnon appears as a king who is one-quarter Greek and three-quarters Prussian: the classical designs on his helmet and on the trimming of his clothing are visually outweighed by his Prussian officer's greatcoat, monocle, and duelling scars.[7] In the first of the three acts, Agamemnon is deposed by Aegisthus, who proclaims a republic with himself as president. Aegisthus is presented as a civilian "Literat und Berufsethiker" (man of letters and professional moralist)[8]—a cross between Friedrich Ebert and Kurt Eisner, the idealistic USPD writer who had been the first prime minister of the Bavarian Republic from November 1918 until his assassination the following February. The same fate awaits Aegisthus, who is killed in the second act by Orestes, an "officer of an Attic Freikorps"[9] who wants to "alte Ordnung schaffen"[10] (establish the old order). In the third and last act, "Woodrow Appollon"—who is described in the cast listing as "perpetually in Yankee-dress, living only in higher spheres"[11]—briefly threatens to restore democracy, but the American's good nature and political ineffectiveness allow Orestes to reassert himself. At the end of the play, Orestes leads a Freikorps unit to the Baltic lands, where the allies had allowed German troops to remain under arms in order to combat the Bol-

shevik threat from Soviet Russia. Secondary figures in the work include a
trio of socialist, liberal, and conservative newspaper editors (described as the
modern equivalent of the Greek chorus[12]), and a singularly tasteless "Elek-
tra of the Salvation Army" who collects money for "starving anti-Semites."

The most basic impression of this puppet play is the fact that all of the
major actors in German history in 1918 and 1919—the Kaiser, the General
Staff, the Freikorps, Ebert, Eisner, Wilson, anti-Semites, and others—are
reduced to a common level of ludicrousness. This trivialization of all sectors
of the political spectrum is made most explicitly in a monologue that Aegisthus, alias Ebert/Eisner, delivers while practicing out with a punching ball:

> It's easy to laugh at me, ladies and gents!
> But do *you* have any more competence?
> Do you think that ruling is such a delight?

(He begins to punch the ball.)

> Attacks from the left, attacks from the right,
> The morning papers help bloody the fight,
> The satirists make fun of your plight,
> With outright spite, they incite and indict.
> The whole thing's lost every trace of romance,
> The hero's pose, the stately stance.
> There's no more crown and no more throne,
> In short: It's just not worth a bone.
> Werfel or Rolland might be your name,
> But brains won't win you points in this game.
> If you try to hang out with intellectual men,
> The dadaists stage a putsch right then. . . .
> In the end you say with a hang-dog face:
> There's just no good in the human race.[13]

The reference to dadaists is very apropos, inasmuch as dada embodied the
quintessential deflation of German politics. Indeed, it should not come as a
surprise that *Einfach klassisch!* was itself a dadaist performance of sorts: the
text was written by Walter Mehring, the puppets were designed by George
Grosz and executed by John Heartfield, and the music was composed by
Friedrich Hollaender. All four of these men have become firmly identified
with "Weimar culture": Grosz as a bitter caricaturist of Weimar politics and
society, Heartfield as a pioneer in leftist political photomontage, Mehring as
the most prolific writer of cabaret texts, and Hollaender as the equally prolific composer of cabaret and vaudeville music (including the songs in *The
Blue Angel*). Of these four, Mehring, Grosz, and Heartfield had been intimately associated with the Berlin Dada movement since the closing months
of World War I. Dada had been inaugurated as a protest against the madness
of a seemingly "civilized" world that had embarked upon the most horrify-
ing slaughter of modern times, where millions of lives were sacrificed for
causes that seemed ever more trivial and absurd as the months and years
wore on. This sense of the insanity and absurdity of politics was prolonged
past the end of hostilities owing to events in Germany, where, as noted
above, a putatively socialist regime conspired with the prewar military elites
to suppress workers demanding genuine socialist reforms. Consequently,

the poems and songs of Mehring, the acerbic drawings of Grosz, and the aggressive photomontages of Heartfield lashed out at both the Social Democrats like Ebert and Noske, and at the reconstituted institutions of the Wilhelmine past—the army, the judiciary, the church.

Such assaults took increasingly provocative forms, such as processions in which the dadaists donned death's-head masks and strung absurdly large cardboard iron crosses around their necks, or the Dada exhibition of 1920, where the public was greeted by a huge dummy of a pig decked out in Prussian uniform. The ultimate travesty of politics came with the antics of Johannes Baader, who facetiously declared himself "Oberdada" and ruler of the world, and who disrupted a session of the constituent assembly at Weimar by tossing around a leaflet with proclamations to that effect. There was bitter irony, however, in the fact that Baader disturbed the assembly during the vote that passed article 118 of the Weimar constitution, which abolished censorship.[14] In short, Baader ridiculed the parliamentary process at the very moment that it gave artistic movements, of which Dada was a part, a greater degree of legal security (at least on paper) than they had enjoyed in the past, and certainly more than they were to possess in the not-too-distant future.

While the dadaists denigrated political activity along a spectrum ranging from social-democratic reformism to the reactionary right, they reserved their approbation for a single movement: the Spartacist (and later Communist) left. Indeed, John Heartfield, his brother Wieland Herzfelde, the radical young director Erwin Piscator, and perhaps George Grosz joined the German Communist Party during its founding congress on December 31, 1918.[15] Subsequently, many of the works of these writers, artists, and directors depicted the misery, exploitation, and suppression of the working classes. Significantly, though, in the early years of the Weimar Republic, Grosz, Heartfield, and Herzfelde rarely depicted the positive aspects of the working-class struggle: they did not glorify the achievements of the workers' movement, nor did they praise the promised communist land of the future. The Berlin Communist newspaper *Die Rote Fahne* lamented Grosz's inability to "juxtapose to his caustic criticism of the bourgeois mug (Fratze) the positive element of today's society, namely the struggle and the heroism of the proletariat,—a fault, incidentally, which is shared not only by George Grosz, but by the manifestations of German revolutionary artists in general. . . ."[16]

The Communists' hostility toward the wholly negative, unconstructive criticism of Grosz, Heartfield & Co. forced the latter to opt either for or against "serious" political commitment. Heartfield, Herzfelde, and later others (like Brecht) chose to toe the party line throughout the 1920s, and they devoted their efforts to political photomontage and journalism in Communist and working-class newspapers. In contrast, Grosz weakened his ties to the Communists after 1925; his progressive disillusionment with the extreme Left had commenced with his disheartening trip to the Soviet Union in 1922. By the end of the decade, Grosz tended to add the political left to his panoply of caricatures, which now spanned the whole political spectrum of Weimar Germany.[17]

This type of satirical nihilism came to dominate much of the "respectable" cabaret culture of the Weimar era; one finds it repeatedly in the songs, poems, and skits of Walter Mehring, Kurt Tucholsky, and Erich Kästner. These masters of satire had no trouble finding material for their barbs in the troubled society and polity of the Weimar Republic, but their efforts did little more than evoke laughter from their middle-class audience[18] and might have contributed to an underestimation or trivialization of political concerns. The political satire of the era had more to do with satire than with politics, and it became a sub-genre of the cabaretic amusement industry. In 1931, when political commitment was called for more than ever, Walter Benjamin lambasted this tendency in an article entitled "Leftist Melancholia." Benjamin accused Mehring, Tucholsky, and Kästner of "underestimating the enemy," and he said of them: "Their political significance exhausts itself in transforming whatever revolutionary reflexes exist in the bourgeoisie into articles of diversion and amusement that are easily consumed. . . . In short, their leftist radicalism is exactly that stance which does not correspond to any political action. It doesn't stand to the left of this or that movement, but rather to the left of possibility pure and simple. At the outset it seeks nothing more than to enjoy itself in negativistic peace. The transformation of the political struggle from a compulsion for commitment to an object of amusement, from a means of production to an article of consumption—that is the ultimate 'hit' of this literature."[19]

Benjamin's impatience with political cynicism is understandable, even though his own political stance was itself not incontrovertible. To be sure, the political coatrack of the Weimar Republic had few hooks upon which writers and artists could happily hang their garments. If one grants that writers and artists of quality tend to be somewhat more idealistic and somewhat more disturbed by contradictions than other people, then it is understandable that they felt estranged by the Weimar Republic. Nevertheless, some historians (with the benefit of hindsight) have deplored the fact that the writers who, like Thomas Mann, grit their teeth and said "yes" to the Republic were few in number—and even Mann's audience must have noted that his espousal of republicanism was somewhat less than wholehearted.[20]

Perhaps, though, one demands too much of the arts by asking them to be political media; politics—especially the brutal politics of Weimar—is carried out in other spheres. Tucholsky himself noted that "social poetry is no social revolution[21]"; and in 1944 Grosz wrote retrospectively: "In former days when I engaged in political and social satire, I often felt its limitations. In portraying and satirizing the events of the passing scene, the artist is like a fiddler scraping on too small a violin."[22] Indeed, one could argue that it was people like Heartfield, Herzfelde, Piscator, and Brecht, whose works spoke for the German Communist Party, that were deluding themselves into thinking that art could effect social change. That was certainly the opinion of Max Reinhardt, who regarded theater and the arts in general as an escape from "the misery of daily existence."[23] He contended that politics offered no hope of salvation or even improvement, because human nature could not be bettered. The populist anti-Semitism that he had encountered as a youth in Vienna as well as the popular war hysteria of 1914 led Reinhardt to tell a friend in 1917: "For me, the most appalling realization is the fact that it does not make a bit of difference whether autocracy or democracy prevails. After all, tyranny does not come from above, it is merely the result of a deeply rooted need of the masses that cannot be eradicated."[24] George Grosz likewise came to share this profound political pessimism. In 1933 he told Herzfelde, his former artistic/political comrade-in-arms: "For the masses, the stupidest, the most foolish, the most tasteless is good enough; that was, is, and remains my motto. If I had thought or experienced otherwise... I would have remained in [the working-class district where I grew up]..., in the midst of the dungheap of the 'little workers' and the 'little people'...."[25] Once one reaches such conclusions about the populace, then one also concludes that the masses want only bread and circuses; and it was a circus—both figuratively and literally—that Reinhardt offered to his public both upstairs and downstairs in the renovated Zirkus Schumann, and that was served up in subsequent Weimar-era cabarets.

Finally, it should come as no surprise to note that such artistic cynicism about politics and the populace was matched by a cynicism about art itself. Reinhardt himself contributed to that attitude. Not only did he despiritualize and (according to many critics) debase the *Oresteia* in the Grosses Schauspielhaus by mounting a circuslike production that emphasized dynamic motion, visual splendor, and technological gags at the expense of the dramatic content; he even went so far as to permit his own "high-cultural" endeavors to be satirized in the programs of his "low-cultural" cabaret, starting with *Einfach klassisch!*. Reinhardt could allow the dadaists to write and mount this production not only because they shared his political pessimism, but also because they radically questioned the utility of art. Already during the war, the dadaists had begun to debunk all of classical and much of modern art; they sought to underscore the contradiction of the German nation, which paid nominal homage to Goethe and Schiller and at the same time conducted the most gruelling of modern wars. As Grosz noted: "Dada was not an ideological movement, but an organic product which arose as a reaction to the cloud-wandering tendencies of the so-called sacred art which found meaning in cubes and gothic, while the field commanders painted in blood."[26] Grosz started to refer to art derogatorily as "Kunscht," and he eventually summed up this view in the motto: "Kunst ist Scheisse" (art is shit). But that attitude did not prevent Grosz from persisting in being an artist of sorts himself.

In conclusion, it may be said that Grosz, Mehring, Heartfield, and the other participants in the first performance of the Weimar Republic's first major cabaret were caught up in a serious dilemma. Although they aspired to be engaged artists, they radically questioned the positive value of both political engagement and art. These mixed feelings were inadvertently brought to the fore when, during the performance of *Einfach klassisch!*, Grosz and his fellow-dadaist Huelsenbeck, who were sitting inconspicuously in the first row, jumped up and shouted loudly to protest their own program. Of course, it was intended to be part of the "fun"—but it also may have symbolized their ambivalence toward their own artistic endeavors. More significant, though, is the fact that their disruption ended with a rather misplaced joke. Even though most of the audience shouted back at Grosz and Huelsenbeck, unaware of their true identities, no one moved to evict them. This led Huelsenbeck to conclude the ruckus with the quip: "What kind of order is this here? Where are the policemen who are to kick us out?"[27] Already in 1919, that line would have evoked little laughter from workers and leftists, and all too soon, it would no longer seem so funny to artists or the liberal middle classes either. The ability to joke about politics and the arts in general, and even about police repression in particular, was very much in the style of Weimar cabaret; but with historical hindsight, one might question whether such cynicism really merited the laughter that it provoked.

Notes

[1] For a critical assessment of Ebert, see Richard N. Hunt, "Friedrich Ebert and the German Revolution of 1918," in Leonard Krieger and Fritz Stern, eds., *The Responsibility of Power: Historical Essays in Honor of Hajo Holborn* (Garden City: 1969), pp. 340–61.

[2] Excerpts from the works of major discussants in the very heated debate over Germany's "November revolution" are presented in Richard N. Hunt, ed., *The Creation of the Weimar Republic: Stillborn Democracy?* (Lexington: 1969).

[3] Ernst Troelsch, *Spektator-Briefe. Aufsätze über die deutsche Revolution und die Weltpolitik 1918/22* (Tübingen: 1924), p. 15.

[4] A fine introduction to Reinhardt's career is Heinrich Braulich, *Max Reinhardt: Theater zwischen Traum und Wirklichkeit* (Berlin: 1969); see esp. pp. 33–169.

[5] The cover is reproduced in Lisa Appignanesi, *The Cabaret* (New York: 1976), p. 109.

[6] For accounts of the revived *Schall und Rauch*, which include brief descriptions of the opening night, see: ibid., pp. 132–38; Heinz Greul, *Bretter, die die Zeit bedeuten. Die Kulturgeschichte des Kabaretts* (Munich: 1971), pp. 190–94; Wolfgang Carlé, *Das hat Berlin schon mal gesehn. Eine Historie des Friedrichstadt-Palastes* (Berlin: 1975), pp. 74–80; Rainer Otto and Walter Rösler, *Kabarettgeschichte. Abriss des deutschsprachigen Kabaretts* (Berlin: 1977), pp. 78–81; and Walter Rösler, *Das Chanson im deutschen Kabarett, 1901–1933* (Berlin: 1980), pp. 155–59.

[7] George Grosz's ink and watercolor sketch for the figure of Agamemnon is reproduced in George Grosz, *Theatrical Drawings and Watercolors*, catalogue, Busch-Reisinger Museum (Cambridge: 1973), fig. 46.

[8] Walter Mehring, *Einfach klassisch! Eine Orestie mit glücklichem Ausgang* (Berlin: 1919), p. 5.

[9] Ibid., p. 6.

[10] Ibid., p. 21.

[11] Ibid., p. 6.

[12] Ibid., p. 8.

[13] Ibid., pp. 19–20.

[14] See the *Berliner Tageblatt*, no. 324, 17 July 1919. The article 117 mentioned in the debates became article 118 of the final document. Both sides of the leaflet are reproduced in Johannes Baader, *Oberdada. Schriften, Manifeste, Flugblätter, Billets, Werke und Taten* (Lahn-Giessen 1977), pp. 48–49.

[15] See Beth Irwin Lewis, *George Grosz: Art and Politics in the Weimar Republic* (Madison: 1971), p. 67.

[16] *Die Rote Fahne*, 14 June 1925.

[17] The political dimensions of the career of George Grosz, as well as his growing disillusionment with the Communist party, are discussed in Lewis, *George Grosz*; and Uwe M. Schneede, *George Grosz. Der Künstler in seiner Gesellschaft* (Köln: 1977).

[18] The middle-class nature of the audience of *Schall und Rauch* was guaranteed by the high cost of the entrance fee; this point is underscored in "Schall und Rauch," in the *Neue Züricher Zeitung*, no. 1979, December 17, 1919. Wieland Herzfelde likewise described dadaism in retrospect as "an internal affair of the bourgeoisie" ("eine Bourgeoisie-interne Angelegenheit"); see Herzfelde, "George Grosz, John Heartfield, Erwin Piscator, Dada und die Folgen, oder Die Macht der Freundschaft," in *Sinn und Form* **23** (1971): 1245.

[19] Walter Benjamin, "Linke Melancholie" (1931), in *Gesammelte Schriften* (Frankfurt am Main: 1972), Vol. 3: 280–81.

[20] Gordon Craig in particular has criticized Weimar-era literati for having failed to give more positive support to the Republic; see his "Engagement and Neutrality in Weimar Germany," in the *Journal of Contemporary History* **2**, no. 2 (1967), 49–63. In contrast, the Weimar intellectuals have been defended by Carl Schorske, among others; see his "Weimar and the Intellectuals," in *The New York Review of Books*, May 7, and May 21, 1970.

[21] Cited in Appignanesi, *Cabaret*, p. 101.

[22] See Herbert Bittner, ed., *George Grosz* (New York: 1960), p. 32.

[23] Cited in Braulich, *Reinhardt*, p. 66.

[24] Cited ibid., p. 74.

[25] Cited in Lewis, *Grosz*, p. 21.

[26] Cited ibid., p. 53.

[27] Cited in Appignanesi, *Cabaret*, p. 133.

CHAPTER 8

Literary and Cinematic Representations of the Great Depression in Germany

Maria Tatar

Satire has long figured as the privileged medium of social criticism. It is hardly surprising to find that the German literary figure of this century who infused fresh life into novels depicting contemporary social circumstances found himself forever moving from the solid ground of the real to the heady atmosphere of the surreal. Heinrich Mann himself was hard pressed to explain just why he could not resist the temptation to supplant sober realism with irreverent satire.[1]* In his case, it was surely not for want of a vivid sense of social realities that he resorted again and again to a rhetoric of exaggeration, distortion, and disfiguration. Yet Heinrich Mann does not stand as an isolated instance of the writer who aims for realism, but ends by creating what Thomas Mann, in an intemperate moment, called *Groteskkunst* (grotesque art).[2] Writers moved by a profound sense of discontent coupled with a passion for reform have throughout the ages found in satire the appropriate literary vehicle for what they perceive to be their social mission.

The art of satire has always flourished in democratic societies, and Weimar Germany was no exception to the rule. *Neue Sachlichkeit* may have been the official label affixed to the artistic achievements of the Weimar Republic, but the works that emerged under the banner of that "New Sobriety" were neither objective nor sober nor matter-of-fact. The much-heralded rage for realism during the 1920s was in fact probably more rage than realism. From the pages of the *Weltbühne*, Kurt Tucholsky railed at the military, the middle classes, and the judicial system; Erich Kästner attacked the sacred cows of the bourgeoisie in his impudent lyrics; Toller, Hasenclever, and Zuckmayer brought satire to the stage in their comedies; and in the visual arts, Otto Dix and George Grosz drew less than flattering portraits of the "ruling class." The secret to their success, according to Kurt Tucholsky, was hatred, the deep-seated hatred of the underdog for the over-privileged. "We were angry. Very angry!" Otto Dix recalled in later years. Rage at the powerful combined with outrage at social injustices fueled the creative efforts of left-wing writers and artists in the 1920s and infused the art of their prose and portraiture with a rare degree of satirical intensity. To call the

---

*See Notes section at the end of this chapter.

works of these particular figures objective, sober, realistic, and free of sentiment is to display a misplaced reverence for the term *Neue Sachlichkeit* and
to foster a profound misunderstanding of the origins and aims of the works
ordinarily associated with it.[3]

If the Expressionist poets and artists of the pre-Weimar era had been
guided by moral idealism and utopian zeal, those who survived into the
twenties soon joined the ranks of what Döblin called "the disenchanted and
the disillusioned" to form a new movement. To be sure, there were those
who prided themselves on their "objectivity" and "sobriety"—Ernst Jünger
and Gottfried Benn are notable examples—but the vast majority (particularly
those on the left end of the political spectrum) recognized that their opposi-
tional politics colored their creative efforts. As Hermann Kesten bluntly put
it, the new breed of artists and writers, by way of contrast to the "pathos-
mongers" of the Expressionist movement, were "ironists, embittered critics
of the prevailing order, satirists, and Voltaireans." Cultural pessimists to the
core, they saw themselves duty-bound to expose the weaknesses, vices, and
injustices of their age and to point the finger of blame at those responsible
for them. They may have looked to their own time and place for their subject matter, but again and again they filtered that reality through the distort-
ing lens of satire.[4]

The epigraph that Heinrich Mann had contemplated for the most renowned of his satirical portraits of Wilhelminian Germany—"This nation is
hopeless"—guided the literary efforts of countless Weimar intellectuals.
Their scathing assaults on capitalism, imperialism, militarism, and a host of
other evils were paired with vitriolic outbursts against social democracy and
middle-class mores. With few exceptions, the serious poets, novelists,
essayists, and artists remained at best a part of the loyal opposition, at worst
the harshest critics of the struggling Weimar government. Small wonder,
then, that they have been charged, in retrospective assessments of their
stance, with unwittingly engineering the collapse of the Republic. Where
they might have offered support—even in the form of constructive
criticism—they mocked and jeered.[5] As Gordon Craig has observed, the
cynical jibes and satirical thrusts of Tucholsky and his like may not have
destroyed the Republic, but they were destined "to hearten the forces of the
right which were bent on the destruction of the Weimar Republic."[6]

Even in their own day, the ironists, critics, and satirists of the literary and
artistic establishment were treated to a litany of charges ranging from hyper-
bole and excessive pessimism to treason and sabotage. "What happened to
the positive side?" Kästner's readers demanded again and again of the author
in letters and interviews. And Kurt Tucholsky, in an indignant essay published in the *Weltbühne*, felt obliged to defend himself and his colleagues
against the accusation of incessant negativism. While Kästner and Tucholsky
pleaded guilty to the charges of their critics, they were hardly prepared to set
aside their pens for the peace pipe. In a country where the bourgeoisie was
profoundly antidemocratic, where military men wore the badge of arrogance
on their uniforms, where bureaucrats valued their position above their function, where politicians conspired with big business to raise profits, Tucholsky found it impossible to take the sting out of his words. "The satirist," he
reminded his readers, "is an offended idealist. He wants the world to be

good; it is bad; and he does battle with the bad." And Kästner echoed these words when he preached in a "sermon" to his readers: "Satirists are idealists." Like Grosz, who felt duty-bound to become a "German Hogarth," Tucholsky and Kästner were drawn to satire for its deep moral impulse.[7]

Weimar's offended idealists had hoped to press for social reforms by magnifying the evils of the day and thereby conveying a sense of urgency and emergency. Yet many unexpectedly found themselves cast in the role of prophets, for in the final years of the Weimar Republic the gap between literary satire and real life began to narrow. Satire often came perilously close to the truth; at times it even seemed to pale in comparison with social realities. To be sure, the first signs that life might rival art in its power to strain credibility came in the early years of the Republic with the inflation of 1923. But at no time did art fall more dramatically short of the mark in describing Germany's economic conditions than in the novels and films set in the time of the Great Depression. When Leonhard Frank, for instance, began writing *Von drei Millionen Drei* (Three out of Three Million), a dreary fairy story of modern times, he hardly dreamed that its title would become an anachronism by the date of its publication in 1932.[8] By then the ranks of the unemployed had swelled to six million.

The economic crisis of the late twenties and early thirties captured the imagination of writers from a broad spectrum of political persuasions.[9] Yet since the vast majority of novels concerned with that crisis were inspired by a sense of compassion for the unemployed, the political allegiances of their authors generally belonged to parties that drew support from the working classes. Compassion alone, however, rarely produced compelling writing. Those novels that described in lurid detail the misery of unemployed workers—Albert Klaus's *Die Hungernden* (The Starving) is a cardinal example of the genre—misfired largely because case studies of welfare clients and recipients of unemployment benefits made for tedious prose.[10]

Pathos was nevertheless an essential ingredient in any account of the Great Depression. And, odd as it may seem, the very writers and artists who had specialized in the art of satire made a point of becoming expert "pathos-mongers" as well. Identification with the downtrodden and passionate sympathy for their plight had been exhibited nowhere more graphically than in the visual art of the twenties. Otto Nagel's urban homeless, Otto Dix's street beggars, and George Grosz's war cripples document the strong social conscience of a postwar generation. For his colleagues, Max Beckmann had formulated a stirring postwar agenda that proved of continuing relevance:

> We will have to take part in the miserable conditions that are to come. . . . At this very moment we have to get as close as we can to man. . . . Moving from a superficial imitation of reality, from a weakly archaic art that has deteriorated into empty ornamentation, and from a falsely sentimental form of inflated mysticism, we hope now to arrive at a transcendental objectivity that issues from a profound love of nature and man.[11]

In practice this meant shifting attention from the "face of the ruling class" to the equally unattractive (but less ferocious) faces of social misfits and outcasts. Panhandlers, streetwalkers, criminals, and invalids: those down on their luck along with the down-and-out found their way onto the canvases of artists who later became renowned for their "Sachlichkeit."[12] But if anger was not conducive to "sober" visual representation, compassion and empathy also did not make for objective portraiture. The harsh and brutal facts of everyday life may have inspired many an artist, but they rarely appeared as such on canvases and in notebooks. Grotesque exaggeration and grim pathos became instead the twin emblems of socially engaged art of the twenties.

In fiction, the unchecked expression of compassion for the underprivileged had a way of deteriorating into virtually unreadable melodrama. The most successful—both in commercial and in literary terms—of the works that chronicled the fate of the unemployed seasoned the pathos of their plots with a healthy dose of social satire. Compassion may have been lavished on the protagonists of their tales, but the society in which these economic outcasts moved served as the target of fierce satire. The decent, upstanding man without a job is contrasted again and again with the deceit and iniquity of employers, of trade unions, of the government, and of urban society in general. Hence, pathos and satire came to serve as the twin motors driving the plots of these novels. The three most memorable depictions of little men caught in economic distress all take as their setting Berlin in the late twenties and early thirties. Hans Fallada's *Kleiner Mann—was nun?* (*Little Man, What Now?*), the film *Kuhle Wampe*, for which Bertolt Brecht and Ernst Ottwalt wrote the screenplay, and Erich Kästner's *Fabian* share a tendency to set individual decency and integrity against urban greed and corruption. Yet each of these works also offers a different perspective on the social origins and consequences of the Great Depression and a different solution to the plight of its victims. In order to understand the extent to which the tension between pathos and satire might turn instructive rather than sensationalistic or destructive, it will be useful to examine these three representative tales of hard times.

Of all the writers who sought to capture the mood of defeat and despair that engulfed millions of Germans during the Great Depression, none was to be more commercially successful than Hans Fallada. Fallada himself was no stranger to the anxieties that beset the "little man" in times of inflation and unemployment. "Those were the days," he recalled in one of his volumes of memoirs. "Those were the hours of deepest affliction! . . . We had nothing—only sleepless nights! . . . The terror of those days is still so much with me today that I pay every bill on the very day it arrives."[13] Yet like the Fallada of fairy tales (from whom the aspiring author Rudolf Ditzen presumably took his pen name), Hans Fallada figured not only as a hapless victim but also as a somber observer of events. "Fallada watched everything as it happened and took it all in."[14]

The novel that catapulted Fallada to literary fame and (at least temporarily) to financial security formulated in its title the question on the lips of the six million unemployed in its year of publication: "Little man, what now?" But Fallada's novel concerns itself not so much with the problem of mass unemployment as with the plight of the lower middle class (*Kleinbürger*) in times of economic crisis. More poignantly than any other author writing in the troubled times of the Weimar era, Fallada records the futile struggle of the *Kleinbürger* to maintain both his personal and economic integrity during

Corner of Friedrichstrasse and Georgenstrasse; in front of city railway station Fried-richstrasse, Mitte district, East Berlin.—1930. Reproduced with permission of the Landesbildstelle Berlin.

the Great Depression. Johannes Pinneberg, the "little man" of Fallada's title, may rise from the rank of clerk and factotum in the dung trade of the provinces to salesman for men's furnishings in a Berlin haberdashery, but ultimately he too finds himself on the dole. And for him unemployment signals more than financial disaster: it spells the loss of bourgeois respectability and marks him a social outcast. By the end of the novel, the white-collar worker is not only without work, but more importantly, he is literally stripped of his white collar—the very emblem of his personal dignity.

If Pinneberg is slow to register his descent from the ranks of a public servant to the level of a public nuisance, it is largely because the shift in his fortunes proceeds only gradually, at an almost imperceptible pace. To be sure, hardly a day goes by without some new crisis. But the course of his life is marked less by the sudden, violent upheavals that organize our retrospective understanding of historical epochs than by the endless series of minor catastrophes that shape and determine the lives of ordinary people.[15]

Fallada gives us history from the bottom up: Black Friday, government decrees, and unemployment statistics recede into the background to make way for accidentally charred dinners, bleak visits to the obstetrician, and heated debates over household purchases. The forty-eight chapter titles that arrest the flow of the novel graphically draw attention to the personal crises that punctuate the lives of the Pinnebergs. Take the following title: "The marriage begins in proper fashion with a wedding trip, but—do we need a stewpot?"[16] This chapter, like many others, begins on an upbeat note but gradually builds to a domestic crisis that, however banal it may seem, illustrates the way in which economic insecurity threatens to subvert marital happiness. Johannes and Lämmchen live in a state of perpetual anxiety, for their austere household budget does not allow for a single accident or unplanned acquisition, be it a child or a stewpot.

If the tight budget that regulates every move in the domestic sphere leads to fear of the unexpected, the stringent quota system at the workplace generates a real sense of terror. On the advice of Herr Spannfuss, an efficiency expert schooled in the methods of Taylorization, Pinneberg's employer introduces a quota system designed both to increase sales and to reduce the payroll. Pinneberg, once the "born salesman," turns into a near parody of Uriah Heep as he struggles to meet his monthly quota. A ruthless competition for clients sets in, leading Pinneberg's colleagues to live daily by the phrase: "Every man for himself!" (p. 138). By fostering a climate of fear and uncertainty, Spannfuss succeeds in pitting the members of the salesforce against each other and driving them into utter isolation. And it is precisely this sense of isolation and lack of solidarity that troubles Pinneberg: "We stand alone. And the others, who are just like us, also stand alone. . . . If we were only workers! They call each other comrade and help each other. . . ." (p. 205).[17]

Fear of unemployment figures both as cause and symptom of Pinneberg's isolation. Unlike his able-bodied colleague Heilbutt, who, as his name implies, swims effortlessly through the troubled economic seas of the time, Pinneberg perpetually struggles to remain afloat.[18] Without his wife Lämmchen, who provides him with the proverbial haven in a heartless world, he would surely have gone under along with countless numbers of his fictional counterparts in novels and films of the early thirties. Pinneberg's marriage serves as "a small, cozy island" in the midst of "the wild, wide world with all its uproar and hostility" (p. 112). There may be no hope for solidarity in the public sphere, but the private sphere holds out the possibility of "being together" ("das Beisammenseinkönnen").

For Pinneberg, as for Fallada, marriage figures as the sole source of relief in troubled economic times. It is the one institution that remains pure and untarnished to stand as a shining example of integrity in adversity.[19] At a time when people are, to quote Lämmchen, "horrible" (p. 147) and when, in Pinneberg's words, they are trained to become "beasts of prey" (p. 132), the little man and his wife succeed in preserving their human qualities and, above all, their integrity (Anständigkeit) by retreating to their blessed isle which offers moments of splendid isolation. In the final analysis, the intimacy of marriage offers the only authentic and lasting consolation. Although Pinneberg's interior monologues ("On the smacker! Right on the smacker, you dog!") and his various private declarations ("Next time I'll be sure to vote for the Communists!") suggest that his political consciousness rises as his fortunes fall, he never finds in the public arena the kind of solidarity that is his in the private sphere.

Much has been written about the sentimental scene that closes Fallada's novel.[20] As the Pinnebergs embrace, they are translated to a higher sphere and, for a moment at least, they transcend their careworn existence. Memory takes them back to the scene of their first rendezvous and repairs the injuries of time. To the minds of most critics, the question formulated in the title of Fallada's novel nevertheless remains unanswered. The author himself, however, declared: "Lämmchen is my answer. I can't think of a better one." At the same time, he conceded that love might not be the proper answer for everyone: "There are only private answers: for each person a different one."[21]

If love was to provide the answer to mass unemployment, there were many who wanted to rephrase Fallada's question. Like Fallada's novel, the film *Kuhle Wampe oder Wem gehört die Welt?* (Kuhle Wampe, or Who Owns the World?) is set in Berlin during the early thirties and poses in its title a question. But there the similarities between novel and film end. It is almost as if Brecht and Ottwalt had heard Fallada's answer to the plight of the little man and, in a gesture of irritation, reformulated his question.[22] If Fallada held that public misery, however extreme, cannot taint private bliss, Brecht and Ottwalt make it abundantly clear that public misery breeds private misery. In *Kuhle Wampe*, the private sphere of the family, rather than serving as a solution, figures as part of the problem.

The first of the three nearly self-contained "dramas" that constitute *Kuhle Wampe* offers perhaps the bleakest cinematic commentary on the Great Depression in Germany. "One Less among the Unemployed" compresses into one brief, eloquent sequence the events leading to the suicide of a young unemployed worker. We catch our first glimpse of Bönicke as he scans the want ads of a local paper. Pocketing the paper, he mounts his bicycle and pedals off with a trail of competitors in his wake. A riveting series of shots alternately shows a cluster of riders and the spinning wheels of their bicycles. The search for work, as Brecht put it, is shown "as work."[23] But beyond that, the visual depiction of this particular job hunt (the subtitle of the sequence reads "The Job Hunt") captures a sense of ruthless competition at breakneck speed even as it comments on the futility of the riders' efforts in the images of the spinning wheels. In this contest, everyone loses.

At home Bönicke finds no consolation for his defeat. What is served up to him along with his evening meal is the sum of folk wisdom distilled in such phrases as: "Hard work goes far" and "Hardworking people get ahead." These time-honored and seemingly timeless adages, intoned by Bönicke's parents, are mocked by crosscutting shots depicting the mad dash of bicycle pedalers who, for all their diligence and perseverance, advance only in space. Bönicke's daily search for work is followed by the daily meal which ends with the daily altercation between father and son. "Every day the same old quarrel"—in these words of the mother (the last spoken words before her son's suicide), it becomes clear that the crushing litany of reproaches at home replicates the oppressive rhythms of the search for work. Although Bönicke does not utter a single word throughout the entire sequence devoted to his pursuit of employment, the motive for his suicide is tellingly conveyed in visual terms by the two shots that frame his leap from the apartment window: the first brings before our eyes a household sampler extolling once again the virtues of hard work, the second repeats the shot of the unemployed cyclists making their way through the city.[24]

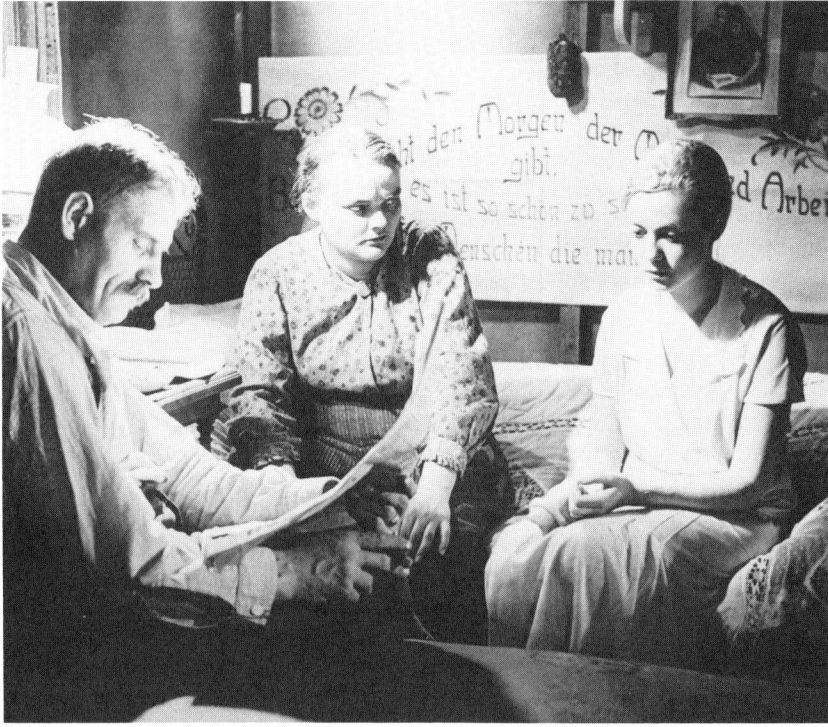

Still from the film Kuhle Wampe, *1932, by Slatan Dudow. Scenario: Bertolt Brecht and Ernst Ottwalt. Music: Hanns Eisler. The saying on the wall reads: "Don't lament the morning that gives trouble and labor; it is so nice to care for people you love."— Actors (from left to right): Max Sablotzky (Vater Bönicke), Lily Schönborn (Mutter Bönicke), Hertha Thiele (Tochter Anni). Reproduced with permission of Stiftung Deutsche Kinemathek, Berlin, and of Christian Fessel, Berlin.*

As Brecht observed, the most astute critic of this opening sequence proved to be the film's censor. Bönicke's suicide, according to this government official, was not depicted as the fate of this or that morbid individual, but rather as a "typical event." "We were stunned," Brecht reported. "We had the unpleasant feeling that we had been caught." The censor had not only discovered but also articulated exactly what the film's producers had intended to convey. Bönicke's act is not motivated by personal frailties or foibles, but instead has its roots in the general economic conditions prevailing in Germany during the last years of the Weimar Republic.[25]

Despite the inexorable logic of the events leading from the search for work to the suicidal leap, there is a way out for Bönicke. But it is left to his sister to find the road leading from isolation and despair to solidarity and hope. Anni and her parents succeed in keeping a roof over their heads during troubled times by moving from the city to the country and from a tenement to a tent, but they do not by any means escape the stifling conditions of petty bourgeois culture. The shots of the colony at Kuhle Wampe reveal that the urban refugees are by no means pioneers working collectively to build a utopian community in nature: rather, these squatters have simply transplanted themselves, along with their bourgeois values and aspirations, to the shores of the Müggelsee. As the Bönickes carry furniture and kitchen utensils into their tent to the rhythms of German military marches broadcast from a radio, the camera records images of men reading papers, smoking cigars, and playing chess. Here, as in the celebrated sequence contrasting Herr Bönicke's absorption in a tabloid account of Mata Hari's physical charms with Frau Bönicke's anxiously intense calculation of living expenses, the ease with which the settlers at Kuhle Wampe slip into their old habits to evade the issues at hand becomes evident.[26]

It is above all in the scene depicting the engagement party of Anni and her fiancé that the bourgeois values of the settlers at Kuhle Wampe are held up to ridicule. From the start, it becomes clear that the guests have assembled for one reason alone. The same law that, for Pinneberg, prevailed in the sphere of work rules at the makeshift table of the Bönickes: "Every man for himself." Whether attacking a pound cake or laying siege to a platter of meat, the guests show no mercy. The celebration turns into a drunken orgy with bride and bridegroom as sober and sobered witnesses to the revels.

Anni's disillusionment with her fiancé Fritz, her departure from Kuhle Wampe, and her return to Berlin mark the beginning of a conversion experience that takes place off-camera before the third part of the film. If the first two segments of Kuhle Wampe chronicle the failure of the conventional family unit to serve as a vehicle of support and solidarity, the last segment documents the stunning success of the workers' sports movement in drawing together young people and lifting their spirits through the sense of a common mission. From the dreary tenements of Berlin and the cheerless tents of Kuhle Wampe, the camera moves to scenes of open-air athletic events and theatrical productions. For these workers, sports events are not merely a form of relaxation and recreation, but rather an activity designed to foster solidarity and to fortify themselves for the struggles ahead. "Learn to win" is the slogan that guides them in their athletic contests. For the masses of workers who experience defeat and demoralization on a daily basis, these events are intended to represent the one opportunity for triumph. "Forward" (Vorwärts), the first word of their song of solidarity, stands in stark contrast to the image of the endlessly spinning wheels seen in the athletic competition of the film's first segment.

It is in this milieu that Anni and Fritz are reunited, presumably to rebuild their relationship on a sounder basis. If the future is not entirely rosy for the couple, the two are nonetheless braced for what lies ahead by a new sense of strength in class solidarity. The coda to the film makes it clear that Anni and Fritz have parted company with their dispirited elders to join the ranks of an idealistic, younger generation that shares its resources, engages in collective activities, and promotes a sense of hope through solidarity.[27] The message delivered by Kuhle Wampe rings as loudly and clearly as the words of Gerda that end the film: the solidarity of radical, revolutionary youth figures as the one hope for salvation.

While Fallada and Brecht both point the way to victory over economic adversity through solidarity, Erich Kästner ends his novel Fabian with the defeat of the isolated individual. Fallada's isle of domestic solidarity and Brecht's vanguard of revolutionary youth represent visionary ideals that are tested and discredited in the course of Fabian's trials in Berlin. The counterpart to the visionary ideals that are proclaimed in the final passages of Fallada's novel and in the final frames of *Kuhle Wampe* is an apocalyptic dream of spiritual decadence and physical carnage that occupies the dead center of Kästner's novel. In a belated preface to the novel, Kästner stressed that he had aimed above all to sound a warning signal to his readers. His panoramic survey of life in Berlin during the early thirties was no mere mirror of reality; instead it deliberately disfigured and distorted the social realities of the times. Mordant satire figured as Kästner's weapon in the struggle to stir the conscience and consciousness of his contemporaries. "If that can't help," he declared, "then nothing can do any good."[28]

Kästner's Berlin is a city that breeds vice and corruption: "Crime resides in the east, deceit in the center, misery in the north, debauchery in the west, and decadence lives in every quarter."[29] The city's feverish state of hyperactivity in the erotic sphere is symptomatic of an advanced state of paralysis in the moral sphere. For Kästner, the ultimate source of that moral paralysis can be traced to the spiritual depression attending periods of economic depression. The sluggishness of the economy does much to create a climate of apathy and moral stagnation—what one character aptly describes as spiritual apathy ("die Trägheit des Herzens," p. 31). Yet there are those who refuse to succumb to the prevailing disease of the times, which is not to say that they are at ease with their times. Jakob Fabian, the hero of Kästner's novel, remains immune to, if not untouched by, the afflictions of his age.

Fabian is less a model of moral activism than of moral stoicism. He is forever standing on the sidelines, both a spectator and—given the moral climate of the times—often a voyeur. "I am watching and waiting," Fabian states. "I am waiting for the triumph of decency" (p. 81). Even when Fabian joins the ranks of the unemployed and drifts from one quarter of the city to the other, he is driven more pointedly by his curiosity than by the desire to find employment. Yet this curiosity has its limits. While Fabian eagerly accepts every invitation to explore various lurid scenes of urban dissipation, he generally draws the line at participation.[30] As one character grumbles, for Fabian the world is little more than a "window display" (p. 120). It is surely no coincidence that the unusual name of Kästner's protagonist is paronymous with that of Fabius Maximus, the Roman general who never risked direct confrontation with the enemy.[31]

Salvation in the private sphere and solidarity in the public arena are both discarded as possibilities in the course of Fabian's odyssey. To be sure, Fabian briefly entertains hopes of establishing a middle-class version of Pinneberg's domestic idyll, but these hopes are dashed by the loss of his job. He also never seriously contemplates the possibility of emerging from his isolation by seeking political alliances, in large part because he has never set much store by systems that promise to regenerate society. "What good is a divine system when men remain swine?" (p. 66), Fabian asks his friend Labude, a political activist. Fabian's skeptical attitude toward politics is confirmed by the encounter he witnesses between a Communist and a National Socialist. These two representative "politicians" seem genuinely

George Grosz: "At Five o'clock in the morning," 1921—Berlinische Galerie Berlin. Reproduced with permission of Berlinische Galerie, Berlin, and of Wolfgang Petrick, Berlin.

serious about lowering the numbers of the unemployed, but they do so by shooting at each other.

If Fabian fails to find a vision to guide him, he is nonetheless a man tormented by visions—visions decidedly apocalyptic in tenor. In the chapter devoted to Fabian's nightmares, Kästner proved himself the literary equal of such contemporary artists as George Grosz and Otto Dix.[32] Fabian's dream landscape offers no visionary alternative to the prevailing social conditions; instead, it intensifies and deepens the mood of utter hopelessness pervading the novel. Even in his dreams, Fabian remains the passive observer, a silent witness to an inflated version of the depravity in his age. The first of the two central dream images takes shape beneath a glass floor on which Fabian kneels to get a full view of the heady activity below him: "Fat, naked women with worry wrinkles across their bodies sat at tables and drank tea. They wore torn stockings and had straw hats around their necks. Necklaces and earrings sparkled. One of the old ladies had put a gold ring through her nose. Fat men sat at other tables, half naked, hairy as gorillas, with top hats, some in lavender briefs, all with fat cigars between their thick lips." (p. 119). The orgy of random sexual couplings that follows stands in stark contrast to the tender embrace of the Pinnebergs at the end of Fallada's novel: lust and passion supplant love and marriage in Fabian's vision of society.

Fabian flees this scene to enter a new arena of human action. The next spectacle to which he bears witness figures as a pageant of human greed. Lined up on an endless staircase stand people from all walks of life, each diligently rifling the pockets of the person on the next step. Towering above them all, Labude proclaims the dawn of a new age and announces that decency must prevail at last. Shots ring out, and this second segment of Fabian's dream ends in an orgy of violence and bloodshed. Labude's vain attempt to usher in a new era of peace and solidarity proves futile in light of the reigning spirit of antagonism.[33] Just as Fabian's great expectations for domestic solidarity ended in lost illusions, so Labude's dreams of political solidarity turn into a nightmare of human carnage.

The story of Fabian deliberately ends on a bleak note, for Kästner's intention was to so move his reader that he would leap up after reading the novel, pound his fist on the table, and shout: "Things must be different." "Times are dark. I won't give you a whitewash," the author declared in a celebrated response to readers mystified by the unrelieved pessimism of his poetry. Kästner believed it his duty to stretch the truth, to magnify the follies and vices of his age, in order to carry out his mission in the area of what he called "adult education." Like his literary antecedents in the school of satire, he offers both a passionate indictment of the evils in his day and a silent appeal to virtue and reason. Kästner himself confessed that he wrote with the express hope that his satirical barbs would shame men into becoming "just a tiny bit better."[34]

That Kästner's novel bore an urgent moral message did not escape the attention of his contemporary readers. In the very year that witnessed the publication of Kleiner Mann—was nun?, Hans Fallada applauded the wisdom that emerged from the pages of Fabian: "Be decent. Don't get taken in! Stay decent."[35] Fallada, like Kästner himself, conveniently forgets that Fabian's moral posture is never a very comfortable one. As the exponent of decency, Fabian survives only as long as he remains a passive observer standing on the fringes of society. Once he swings into action—and he does so only on the final page of the novel—he perishes. Kästner seems in fact to be at pains to emphasize that Fabian lives in a world where decency is incompatible with survival. That moralists will continue to perish until the world is made safe for decency remains the abiding lesson of the novel.[36]

According to Heinrich Mann, German literature finally went public in the era of the Weimar Republic.[37] Writers no longer felt obliged to confine themselves to "private matters"; instead they treated topical subjects of immediate general concern. The postinflation phase of the Republic witnessed the flowering of genres designed specifically to accommodate the representation of contemporary social realities. This was the era in which the *Tatsachenroman*, the *Zeitstück*, and *Gebrauchslyrik* gained widespread currency.[38] Modes of representation that appropriated the stuff of everyday life for literature and the arts (reportage, montage, photomontage, and documentary art) stood in the vanguard. It goes without saying that writers and artists drawn to those particular genres and modes of representation aimed to convey the facts of everyday life, the hard realities of the here-and-now. Yet whether focusing on the consequences of the Great War, of the inflationary period, or of the Great Depression, few succeeded in registering and recording those facts in a matter-of-fact manner. Invariably political stances shaped the subject matter; personal perspectives colored the manner of presentation even when no explicit stands were taken. The "new sobriety" never really implied objectivity; rather it signalled the moment of awakening to social realities after the visionary excesses of the Expressionist movement. Political conditions in the 1920s and 1930s were such that they rarely lent themselves to unbiased objective reporting: Weimar's troubled domestic panorama with its array of competing solutions for the same problems hardly made for nonpartisan accounts.[39]

In the short life span of the Weimar Republic, few issues commanded greater attention than the economic crisis of 1929–1933; it is to the credit of writers in that regime that they seized the opportunity to give shape to so paramount a matter in both novels and films. The protagonists of their works enlist our sympathy in much the same way that the careworn faces and hollow eyes staring at us from the canvases of Otto Nagel and Käthe Kollwitz move us to empathize with the unemployed. Novels and films set squarely in the time of the Great Depression as a rule feature underdogs, blameless victims of economic pressures who stand as models of long-suffering, patience, steady purpose, and stoic decency. They may become victims, but they also engage in a heroic struggle to retain their personal integrity and to stay "decent." Few writers could describe the symptoms of social malaise during the Great Depression without slipping into pathos, even the most brittle prose had a certain sentimental edge when it took the unemployed as its subject matter.

As a foil to the pathos of the little man's plight stand the institutional sins of capitalism, government, and politics along with the human evils of avarice, gluttony, and greed. These become the targets of critical assaults and satirical thrusts. The Expressionist faith in the inherent goodness of man gave way in the twenties to an intensely cynical view of human nature—so much so that it is tempting to translate "Neue Sachlichkeit" as the "New Cynicism." The phrase "Man is a beast" took on the character of a slogan; writers and artists alike set about demonstrating the truth of that proposition by holding a mirror up to the "mugs" of their contemporaries.[40] In Fallada's *Kleiner Mann—was nun?*, rapaciousness is singled out as the bane of society; it is an attribute that afflicts employers and efficiency experts right along with widows renting out flats, and Pinneberg's own mother. *Kuhle Wampe* offers

an indictment of government policies and civil procedures, yet it also casti-
gates the smug complacency of petty-bourgeois manners. And Kästner's
Fabian may deplore politics and messianic socialism, but he is even more
appalled by the lust and greed of the urban populace. The failures of the
economic and political mechanisms of the Weimar government are made
eminently clear in each of these accounts, but the citizens of the regime are
also not spared.

Pathos and satire may be the paired motors that drive the plots of these
novels and films, but one of those two motors is also generally more powerful than the other. Fallada's *Kleiner Mann—was nun?*, for instance, focuses
largely on Pinneberg's struggle to maintain his integrity in the face of economic adversity. As a result, his story is suffused with a kind of lyrical pathos
that culminates in a sentimental idyll marking the triumph of decency. In
Kästner's *Fabian*, by contrast, the fortunes of the protagonist are given less
weight than the events he witnesses. Like Isherwood's famous camera with
its shutter open, Fabian passively registers and records the colorfully sordid
world of Berlin in the early thirties. The satirical portrait of that world gives
the story of Fabian a cynical tenor that ends with the defeat of decency. In
the final analysis, both Pinneberg and Fabian remain aloof from politics and
the public arena to take refuge in the privacy of sentimentality and cynicism.

Kuhle Wampe takes us from the islands of private bliss and the seas of
private despair into the public realm of party politics. Yet it too draws on a
tension between pathos and satire—a tension that is never resolved in favor
of pathos and sentiment (as in *Kleiner Mann—was nun?*) or in favor of satire
and cynicism (as in *Fabian*). Pathos permeates the introductory sequence.
No matter how matter-of-factly Bönicke's suicide may be executed (the
film's censor noted that Bönicke prepares for his final leap with the aplomb
of a man peeling cucumbers), it remains profoundly moving. The next
scenes, most notably the move to Kuhle Wampe and the engagement party
celebrated there, take advantage of satire to censure petty-bourgeois manners. The mood shifts once again to pathos with shots of the athletic contests
sponsored by the workers' sports movement. The visual impact of that
pageantry may be more exhilarating than it is touching, but the words
intoned to the music accompanying the young athletes' efforts cast a dark
pathos over the otherwise buoyant atmosphere of the scene. These workers,
we learn, buy their equipment with the "pennies of want" and secure their
subway fare by going hungry. From the tenements of Berlin, they stream to
the sports arena to escape the "crushing struggle for existence" and to mar-
shal their forces for the battle ahead. Finally, the coda to the film, by setting
the fatuous sophistry of the bourgeoisie against the shrewd reasoning of the
working classes in an animated discussion of the international economic
crisis, fuses satire with pathos. This last contrast between a chorus of
stodgy pedants and the voices of robust idealists leaves us with a clear vision
of both the problem (apathy) and the solution (action) to the economic
ills of the day.

Each of the three works considered in this context has been heralded as a
prime example of the sober, restrained style of "Neue Sachlichkeit." While
all three of their authors share a concern with contemporary social conditions and spare no effort in exposing the factual origins and consequences of

the economic distress besetting their protagonists, not one of them can be said to strive for objectivity or moderation in describing the status quo. Whether the accounts of these writers are colored by soul-stirring sentiment, irreverent cynicism, or an admixture of the two, they all draw on satire and pathos to mark the boundary between oppressors and victims, between problems and solutions. To expect ideological objectivity and nonpartisan factual reporting from accounts of contemporary social and economic conditions is perhaps unrealistic, if not unreasonable. The writer who undertakes the task of giving literary shape to the plight of six million unemployed workers is far less likely to engage in sober realism than in social criticism.[41] If his social mission compels him to suffuse realism with pathos, his critical stance leads him to dip his pen in satire. *Neue Sachlichkeit* was situated somewhere between the poles of pathos and satire, but few writers of the era ever succeeded in resisting the impulse to move to the right or the left of that stable center.

Notes

[1] As Heinrich Mann noted in response to his publisher's comments on the burlesque elements of *Im Schlaraffenland*: "Reality as I observe it produces a great deal of caricature and eccentricity. Should I get rid of that? I don't know. Maybe it is exactly what is capable of further development?" See *Heinrich Mann 1871–1950: Werk und Leben in Dokumenten und Bildern*, ed. Sigrid Anger (Berlin: Aufbau, 1971), p. 84. On the blend of realism and satire in Heinrich Mann's works, see especially Ulrich Weisstein, "Heinrich Mann. Besichtigung eines Zeitalters," in *Zeitkritische Romane des 20. Jahrhunderts: Die Gesellschaft in der Kritik der deutschen Literatur*, ed. Hans Wagener (Stuttgart: Reclam, 1975), pp. 9–36.

[2] See Thomas Mann's tirade against the "expressionist-satirical social novel" (a thinly disguised reference to the writings of his brother) in *Betrachtungen eines Unpolitischen* (Frankfurt a. M.: Fischer, 1956), pp. 557–58.

[3] Tucholsky's observations appear in the essay "Fratzen von Grosz," in his *Gesammelte Werke*, ed. Mary Gerold-Tucholsky and Fritz J. Raddatz (Reinbek bei Hamburg: Rowohlt, 1960), III, p. 42. Dix made his remarks about the anger of his generation in a conversation with Maria Wetzel. See Fritz Löffler, *Otto Dix: Leben und Werk* (Dresden: VEB Verlag der Kunst, 1977), p. 34. Wieland Schmied's now classic and often cited definition of *Neue Sachlichkeit* as an artistic movement characterized by fidelity to the representation of objects, sobriety and sharpness of vision, a tendency to focus on the everyday objects of life, etc., has done much to perpetuate the mistaken notion that *Neue Sachlichkeit* is a fundamentally realistic form of art. See his *Neue Sachlichkeit und Magischer Realismus in Deutschland, 1918–1933* (Hannover: Schmidt-Küster, 1969).

[4] Alfred Döblin's statement can be found in his *Schicksalsreise: Bericht und Bekenntnis* (Frankfurt a. M.: Josef Knecht, 1949), p. 165. Döblin refers specifically to those disenchanted by party politics, but his phrase holds true for those who had lost their illusions about Expressionist ideals. Jünger's words on the importance of "Sachlichkeit" appear in his preface to *In Stahlgewittern*. Benn's comment on the sense of "Nüchternheit" he had developed owing to his scientific training appears in the essay "Lebensweg eines Intellektualisten," in *Gesammelte Werke*, ed. Dieter Wellershof (Wiesbaden: Limes, 1961), IV, p. 28. Hermann Kesten drew his telling contrast in "Brutstätte allen Unheils: Alfred Döblins erster Exil-Roman," rev. of *Pardon wird nicht gegeben* by Alfred Döblin, *Die Zeit*, Sept. 15, 1961, p. 17.

[5] On the cynicism of left-wing intellectuals, see especially Golo Mann, "The Intellectuals," *Encounter*, 4, No. 6 (1955), pp. 42–49, and *Deutsche Geschichte des neunzehnten und zwanzigsten Jahrhunderts* (Frankfurt a. M.: Fischer, 1958), pp. 700–18.

[6] Gordon Craig, "Engagement and Neutrality in Weimar Germany," *Journal of Contemporary History* 2 (1967), pp. 49–63. For a spirited yet balanced defense of these writers, see Istvan Déak, *Weimar's Left-Wing Intellectuals: A Political History of the "Weltbühne" and Its Circle* (Berkeley: Univ. of California Press, 1968), pp. 222–28. On criticism from the right, see Kurt Sontheimer, *Antidemokratisches Denken in der Weimarer Republik: Die politischen Ideen des deutschen Nationalismus zwischen 1918 und 1933* (Munich: Nymphenburg, 1962).

[7] For Tucholsky's defense, see "Wir Negativen," in his *Gesammelte Werke*, I, pp. 372–77. His remarks on satire appear in the essay "Was darf die Satire?" (*Gesammelte Werke*, I, pp. 362–64). For Kästner's "Eine kleine Sonntagspredigt," see his *Gesammelte Schriften* (Köln: Kiepenheuer & Witsch, 1959), V, pp. 117–20. Harry Graf Kessler reports Grosz's declaration in his *Tagebücher, 1918–1937*, ed. Wolfgang Pfeiffer-Belli (Frankfurt a. M.: Insel, 1961), p. 119.

[8] Leonhard Frank, *Von drei Millionen Drei* (Berlin: Fischer, 1932). For a brief discussion of the novel in the context of Frank's literary œuvre, see Klaus Weissenberger, "Leonhard Frank. Zwischen sozialem Aktivismus und persönlicher Identitätssuche," in *Zeitkritische Romane*, pp. 54–75.

[9] Jürgen C. Thöming makes this point in his astute analysis of *Arbeitslosenromane*. See "Soziale Romane in der Endphase der Republik," in *Die deutsche Literatur in der Weimarer Republik*, ed. Wolfgang Rothe (Stuttgart: Reclam, 1974), pp. 212–36.

[10] Albert Klaus, *Die Hungernden: Ein Arbeitslosenroman* (Berlin: Der Bücherkreis, 1932).

[11] Max Beckmann, "Schöpferische Konfession," in *Tribüne der Kunst und Zeit*, ed. Kasimir Edschmid (Berlin: Erich Reiss, 1920), pp. 63–64, 66.

[12] The dark side of "Neue Sachlichkeit" is perfectly captured in a letter by Heinrich Zille to Otto Nagel. Zille finds in Nagel's somber paintings of beggars, prostitutes, and invalids the quintessence of modern art. See Wieland Schmied, *Neue Sachlichkeit und Magischer Realismus*, p. 250.

[13] Hans Fallada, *Heute bei uns zu Hause* (Stuttgart: Rowohlt, 1943), p. 32.

[14] "Die Gänsemagd," in *Kinder- und Hausmärchen gesammelt durch die Brüder Grimm* (Stuttgart: Reclam, 1978), p. 164. Jürgen C. Thöming also finds in this phrase from "Die Gänsemagd" the principal inspiration for adopting the pen name "Fallada" ("Hans Fallada. Seismograph gesellschaftlicher Krisen," in *Zeitkritische Romane*, pp. 97–123).

[15] According to Jürgen Manthey, Fallada had read with keen interest and profit Siegfried Krakauer's study *Die Angestellten* (*Hans Fallada in Selbstzeugnissen und Bilddokumenten* [Reinbek bei Hamburg: Rowohlt, 1963], p. 88). Fallada was no doubt struck by the following passage in that work: "We should unburden ourselves of the illusion that it is chiefly great events that shape man. The small catastrophes that are the stuff of daily life influence him more deeply and permanently. Man's fate is primarily dependent on a series of such miniature events." (*Die Angestellten aus dem neuesten Deutschland* [Frankfurt a. M.: Frankfurter Societätsdruckerei, 1930], p. 74).

[16] Hans Fallada, *Kleiner Mann—was nun?* (Hamburg: Rowohlt, 1950), p. 22. Further page references to passages from the novel will be to this edition. The translations, here and elsewhere, are my own.

[17] On the twin themes of fear and isolation, see Helmut Lethen, *Neue Sachlichkeit 1924–1932: Studien zur Literatur des "Weissen Sozialismus"* (Stuttgart: J.B. Metzler, 1970), pp. 156–67. Andrew Weeks also discusses Pinneberg's growing sense of alienation from his co-workers (*The Paradox of the Employee: Variants of a Social*

Theme in Modern Literature, Germanic Studies in America, no. 35 [Bern: Peter Lang, 1980], pp. 115–24).

[18] On the significance of Heilbutt's name and the names of other characters in Fallada's œuvre, see Theodor Lemmer, "Hans Fallada: Eine Monographie," Diss., Freiburg in der Schweiz, 1961, pp. 58–68.

[19] On the institution of marriage and the paramount role of women in Fallada's works, see H.J. Schueler, *Hans Fallada: Humanist and Social Critic* (The Hague: Mouton, 1970), pp. 39–63, and A.V. Subiotto, "*Kleiner Mann—was nun?* and *Love on the Dole*: Two Novels of the Depression," in *Weimar Germany: Writers and Politics*, ed. A.F. Bance (Edinburgh: Scottish Academic Press, 1982), pp. 77–90.

[20] In the preface to his dramatization of Fallada's novel, Tankred Dorst observed: "The sentimentality . . . stems from the fact that both Lämmchen and Pinneberg look for the solution to their problems in the very smallest unit, with each other." See *Hans Fallada/Tankred Dorst: Kleiner Mann—was nun?* (Frankfurt a. M.: Suhrkamp, 1972), p. 5.

[21] The two statements are cited by Jürgen Kuczynski ("Hans Fallada: 'Kleiner Mann—was nun?'—oder: Macht und Idylle," in his *Gestalten und Werke: Soziologische Studien zur deutschen Literatur* [Berlin: Aufbau, 1969], pp. 350–58).

[22] Though Brecht and Ottwalt are generally credited with writing the screenplay, Hermann Herlinghaus notes that Slatan Dudow, the Bulgarian director of *Kuhle Wampe*, withdrew his name as their collaborator for political reasons. See "Slatan Dudow—Sein Frühwerk," *Filmwissenschaftliche Mitteilungen* 3 (1962), 703–70.

[23] Bertolt Brecht, "Der Film 'Kuhle Wampe,'" in *Bertolt Brecht: Kuhle Wampe. Protokoll des Films und Materialien*, eds. Wolfgang Gersch and Werner Hecht (Frankfurt a. M.: Suhrkamp, 1969), p. 92.

[24] That Bönicke's suicide was also motivated by the elimination of unemployment compensation for workers under the age of twenty-one did not escape the attention of the censors. Explicit references to Bönicke's knowledge of the recently enacted emergency decrees eliminating his benefits were subsequently cut from the film. For the comments of the censors on this episode, see *Bertolt Brecht: Kuhle Wampe*, pp. 104, 115, 124–5.

[25] For Brecht's comments on the censor, see his "Kleiner Beitrag zum Thema Realismus," *Bertolt Brecht: Kuhle Wampe*, pp. 93–96.

[26] For an astute analysis of the Mata-Hari sequence, see Reinhold Happel, "'Kuhle Wampe oder Wem gehört die Welt?' Eine exemplarische Analyse," in *Film und Realität in der Weimarer Republik*, ed. Helmut Korte (Munich: Hanser, 1980), pp. 198–200.

[27] A number of commentators have criticized the stark contrast drawn between the generations. See especially Siegfried Krakauer, *From Caligari to Hitler: A Psychological History of the German Film* (Princeton, N. J.: Princeton Univ. Press, 1947) and Rack/Gremm, "Kuhle Wampe," *Film* 4, No. 1 (1966), pp. 45–46. Wolfgang Gersch, however, sees in the film a celebration of the revolutionary proletariat ("Exposition und Modell: Sozialistisches Menschenbild im deutschen proletarisch-revolutionären Film vor 1933," in *Sozialistisches Menschenbild und Filmkunst: Beiträge zu Kino und Fernsehen* [Berlin: Henschel, 1970], pp. 271–91).

[28] Erich Kästner, *Gesammelte Schriften*, II, p. 10.

[29] Erich Kästner, *Gesammelte Schriften*, II, p. 81. Subsequent page references to passages from the novel will be to this edition.

[30] As Rudolf Arnheim puts it, "Fabian does not participate, he stands behind the camera." ("Moralische Prosa," *Die Weltbühne* 27 [1931], pp. 787–90). "This hero," writes Volker Klotz, "is not a hero, not even an antihero, he is a tester and observer (*eine Sonde*)." See "Forcierte Prosa. Stilbeobachtungen an Bildern und Romanen der Neuen Sachlichkeit," in *Dialog: Literatur und Literaturwissenschaft im Zeichen*

deutsch-französischer Begegnung. Festgabe für Joseph Kunz, ed. Rainer Schönhaar (Berlin: Erich Schmidt, 1973), pp. 244–71.

[31] John Winkelman makes a connection between Fabian's name and both the Roman general and the English socialist society. See *Social Criticism in the Early Works of Erich Kästner*, Univ. of Missouri Studies, no. 4 (Columbia, Missouri: Curators of the Univ. of Missouri, 1953), p. 28.

[32] Dirk Walther draws this pertinent analogy between Fabian's dream and the work of Grosz and Dix. See *Zeitkritik und Idyllensehnsucht: Erich Kästners Frühwerk (1928–1933) als Beispiel linksbürgerlicher Literatur in der Weimarer Republik* (Heidelberg: Carl Winter, 1977), p. 254. For an analysis of Fabian's dream, see Kurt Beutler, *Erich Kästner: Eine literaturpädagogische Untersuchung*, Marburger Pädagogische Studien, no. 1 (Weinheim: Julius Beltz, 1967), pp. 124–127.

[33] Egon Schwarz neatly distills the message of Fabian's twin visions: "The principle 'Everyone against everyone' in the economic realm corresponds in a perfectly logical reversal to the sexual slogan 'Everyone with everyone.'" See "Erich Kästner. Fabians Schneckengang im Kreis," in *Zeitkritische Romane*, pp. 124–45.

[34] Kästner's remarks on the message of *Fabian* are cited by Rudolf Arnheim ("Moralische Prosa," p. 790). The response to his readers comes from the poem "Und wo bleibt das Positive, Herr Kästner?" (*Gesammelte Schriften*, I, pp. 214–15). And Kästner's desire to strengthen the moral fiber of his contemporaries is expressed in "Eine kleine Sonntagspredigt: Vom Sinn und Wesen der Satire" (*Gesammelte Werke*, V, pp. 117–20). On Kästner as "Schulmeister," see Kurt J. Fickert, "Moral Ambiguity in the Weimar Republic: Kästner's *Fabian* Revisited," *Germanic Notes* 14 (1983), 51–54.

[35] Hans Fallada, "Auskunft über den Mann Kästner," *Die Literatur* 34 (1932), pp. 367–71. Hans Meyer finds the same message in the novel. See his "Beim Wiederlesen des 'Fabian' von Erich Kästner," in Stephan Hermlin and Hans Mayer, *Ansichten über einige Bücher und Schriftsteller* (Berlin: Volk und Welt, n.d.), pp. 93–96.

[36] Helmut Lethen makes this point (*Neue Sachlichkeit*, p. 145).

[37] Heinrich Mann, "Die geistige Lage," *Gesammelte Werke* (Berlin: Aufbau, 1960), IV, pp. 334–62.

[38] Lothar Köhn makes this point. See his "Überwindung des Historismus: Zu Problemen einer Geschichte der deutschen Literatur zwischen 1918 und 1933," *DVJS* 49 (1975), p. 133. And Klaus Petersen also emphasizes the predominance of topical genres in his "'Neue Sachlichkeit': Stilbegriff, Epochenbezeichnung oder Gruppenphänomen?" *DVJS* 56 (1982), 469.

[39] Horst Denkler notes that only those authors who strove for social change identified themselves with *Neue Sachlichkeit*. See his "Die Literaturtheorie der zwanziger Jahre: Zum Selbstverständnis des literarischen Nachexpressionismus in Deutschland—Ein Vortrag," *Monatshefte* 59 (1967), p. 312, and "Sache und Stil: Die Theorie der 'Neuen Sachlichkeit' und ihre Auswirkungen auf Kunst und Dichtung," *Wirkendes Wort* 18 (1968), p. 173.

[40] It was George Grosz who made the declaration: "The verist holds a mirror up to the mug (*Fratze*) of his contemporaries." Nearly every major painter of the 1920s asserted man's beastly nature. For Grosz's statement, see *Die Kunstismen*, eds. El Lissitzky and Hans Arp (Erlenbach-Zürich: E. Rentsch, 1925), p. 11.

[41] On this point, see Helmut Gruber, "The German Writer as Social Critic, 1927 to 1933," *Studi Germanici* 7 (1967), p. 259.

CHAPTER 9

Berlin Culture in Exile, 1933–1945

Thomas S. Hansen

For Ilse Fang

On May 10th, 1933, National Socialists in Berlin staged their first ceremonial book-burning in front of the university. In this auto-da-fé, thousands of books were incinerated whose ashes represented the growing deadly threat Hitler's regime posed to German life and learning. Heinrich Heine, a refugee of the previous century, had prophesied all too precisely the result of such tactics, writing in 1820 of book-burning: "That was merely a prelude; where books are burned, they end up burning people."[1]* In those flames of fifty years ago, over one half of the 134 titles destroyed were by native Berliners—a disproportionately high number which suggests that something about Berlin writers made them especially obnoxious to National Socialism. In search of such characteristics, this essay proposes to examine the fates of several representative Berliners who sought exile when their works were banned and their lives threatened following Hitler's seizure of power. They are all intellectuals who had already left a mark on Berlin's culture before 1933 when, by necessity, they traded their endangered but familiar existence in Germany's capital for the traumas of life as refugees. The subject matter suggests a division of the material into the following sections: Berlin's importance as a prelude to culture in exile; the situations of several Berliners who fled the city in 1933; the tendency of the exiles to perpetuate or abandon traditions established in Berlin before 1933; and, finally, an examination of the image of Berlin in exile literature.

In the exodus of anti-Nazis, Marxists, and prominent Jews that began in 1933 with the official Nazification policy of *Gleichschaltung* and continued through 1941, we can count over two thousand writers alone, not to mention the thousands of other refugee intellectuals and artists. Of the Berliners among them, we must ask what, if anything, reflects an enduring debt to the culture of the city they abandoned. Can one define some Berlin temperament that survived the uprooting and transplantation of exile? The answer, in a few cases, is certainly "yes." Kurt Tucholsky, whose satirical humor embodies the Berliner essence of the 1920s, captured certain qualities of the city when he suggested for his own epitaph a proverbial characterization: "He had a warm heart and a big mouth." For the Berliner Paul Erich Marcus (who wrote under the pseudonym of PEM), these characteristics were the

---
*See "Notes" section at the end of this chapter.

Professor Dr. Walter Jens (President of the P.E.N.-Centre of the Federal Republic of Germany) opening the series of events on the Day of the Book (Tag des Buches) in the Academie of Arts (Hanseatenweg 10, Tiergarten).—May 8, 1983. Reproduced with permission of the Landesbildstelle Berlin.

foundation of the abrasive yet appealing temperament of Berliners per se. These were the qualities that got them through the defeat of World War I and the shattered hopes of the inflation. PEM wrote in exile of Berliners, such as Tucholsky, during the twenties:

> Gradually they had learned to think only of today and, at best, about tomorrow, and behind this there lurked a sense of "after us the deluge.". . . People somehow got by . . . , cursed, made coarse jokes, and suffered in silence with pursed lips. The "Gemütlichkeit" which had been baptized with the water of the Spree was concealed behind brassy insolence.[2]

Like all the world's great metropolises Berlin has a mystique all its own, which forms those who come *to* the city as well as those who have *left* it. It is salutary to recall in this context of twentieth-century exile and banishment that Berlin has also exerted a magnetism attracting foreign talent. Historically, the most important such immigration was the influx of Huguenots who fled persecution in Roman Catholic France in the seventeenth century to find asylum in Berlin at the invitation of the Elector Friedrich Wilhelm of Brandenburg. The French colony prospered to such a degree that by 1685 one-third of the total population of 15,000 consisted of French refugees.

"The Great Elector receives refugees in his States," 1782. From the Berlin Museum, Berlin. Photograph: Hans-Joachim Bartsch, Berlin. Reproduced with permission of the Berlin Museum, Berlin.

Festive days at Kreuzberg 1979; cultural program of the Office of the Arts Kreuzberg in cooperation with the Bethanien House of Artists (Künstlerhaus Bethanien), in the background.—August 28, 1979. Reproduced with permission of the Landesbildstelle Berlin.

Writers of great stature, among them Friedrich Baron de la Motte Fouqué and Theodor Fontane, traced their ancestry to this stock. Being a great metropolis, Berlin has had an uncanny way of assimilating the foreign and provincial while transforming them, changing itself subtly in the process. Adoptive Berliners from Mecklenburg, Pomerania, or Paris have all enriched the city with their own contribution to *Berlinertum*. Currently, the city is home to a new subculture of displaced citizens. The Turkish presence in Berlin has unmistakably solidified into a second generation of bilingual, bicultural "native Berliners" who have begun to produce their own literature reflecting the Turkish experience in West Germany. The verses of Aras Ören (b. 1939) are but one example of this growing body of works that document the protean quality of *Berlinertum*.

The literary climate that evolved in Berlin during the nineteenth century—after Fontane's unsentimental urban novels had shaken German letters out of its provincialism—had by the 1880s become a laboratory for avant-garde experimentation. In the Deutsches Theater, the drama of Naturalism, which had proved distasteful to the conservative Viennese public, found its stage in Berlin. Here was the center where, as the theater critic

Julius Bab recorded in exile, the foreigners Ibsen, Tolstoi, and Zola converged to produce a German literature of class conflict and social conscience.

Berlin's role in the nation's literary life did not go unchallenged, however, and by 1900 the cultural power assembled in the nation's capital caused backlash among the provincials. An Alsatian, Fritz Lienhard, stirred up such sentiments with the slogan "Away from Berlin!" He demanded a decentralization of intellectual life and an ethical foundation of culture untainted by the "decadence" of the big city and its internationally flavored literary "-isms." Lienhard's antiurban outburst adumbrates the "Blood and Soil" aesthetic that fueled the book-burnings of 1933 and featured Berlin writers so prominently. The cosmopolitan milieu of the city was alien to the ethic of *Heimatdichtung* (anti-urban, rural literature) and primitive racial ideals.

The first thirty years of the twentieth century saw no diminution of the city's cultural ascendancy. The great flowering of Expressionist art and literature is as unthinkable without this urban matrix as is the Berlin Dada movement. The following artists, writers, journalists, or publishers—all either Berliners or active in Berlin before 1933 and exiles thereafter—belonged to these circles: George Grosz, Walter Mehring, John Heartfield, Richard Huelsenbeck, Johannes R. Becher, Carl Einstein, Wieland Herzfelde, Ernst Toller, Alfred Wolfenstein, Rudolf Leonhard, Paul Zech, Else Lasker-Schüler, Kurt Hiller, and Albert Ehrenstein. Jakob van Hoddis was taken from an insane asylum in 1942 to die in an unidentified concentration camp. The philosopher-writer Salomon Friedländer (pseud. Mynona), whose "grotesques" *Secrets of Berlin* appeared in 1929, emigrated at the age of 62, only to die in poverty and neglect in Paris in 1946. Walter Hasenclever, Kurt Tucholsky, and Walter Benjamin had already taken up part-time residence in France before the seizure of power; all were to commit suicide in exile. Ernst Erich Noth, whose autobiographical Berlin novel *Die Mietskaserne* (1931) described urban poverty and proletarian life, fled to France where he made the rarely successful transition to writing in an adopted language. Siegfried Kracauer's reports from Berlin in the pages of the *Frankfurter Zeitung* were philosophical vignettes on the lives of the common man that read like Döblin's literary texts recast for the feuilleton. Kracauer emigrated to Paris, then to the United States, where (writing in English) he set the theoretical foundation for modern film criticism. Of course, the greatest evocation of the city for its own sake in German literature was Alfred Döblin's *Berlin Alexanderplatz* (1929). In that novel the images that incessantly assault all of Franz Biberkopf's sensory organs force the reader to experience the overwhelming, disjointed chaos of Berlin. Berlin Alexanderplatz represented to the Nazis the epitome of the so-called asphalt literature fostered by Berlin.

Most intellectuals in Berlin (as in the rest of Germany) were taken by surprise by the events of January 1933. A few biographical anecdotes suffice to demonstrate the point. Lion Feuchtwanger, who in 1930 had clearly depicted the success of fascism in his novel *Erfolg*, was later to shake his head in dismay at his own purchase of a house on the outskirts of Berlin in 1932. Similarly, Brecht had purchased a country house in Bavaria in the same year with the royalties from *The Threepenny Opera*, although he was not permitted to enjoy the rural life for long. In 1933 he wrote laconically: "After seven weeks of real wealth, we left the property; soon we fled across the border."[3] Furthermore, not all intellectuals immediately perceived the necessity of escape. The actor Fritz Kortner was indecisive about forsaking Berlin. He had moved to Ascona in 1932, only to return to Berlin in a few months. On January 31, 1933, he conveniently left Germany to tour Scandinavia with a troupe from the Deutsches Theater and was not to visit the city again until 1947.[4] For many not threatened with arrest, the dangers appeared temporary. It took considerable prodding from the French ambassador, for example, to persuade Heinrich Mann to leave Berlin. After the burning of the Reichstag, Döblin reluctantly packed one small suitcase and left for Switzerland, thinking to himself, "It was just an outing in order to let the storm blow over."[5] Gustav Regler dwells in his autobiography upon packing up his library, thereby exploring the metaphor of burying a dying culture. In search of comfort, Regler walked down Unter den Linden reading Tucholsky, only to find the satirical figure of Herr Wendriner objectified as never before. He lamented the change wrought by the Nazis: "Berlin is now dying before our eyes, incorruptible Berlin, the Berlin of Heinrich Zille and Käthe Kollwitz, of Klemperer, Bruno Walter . . . the names come like a torrent— Berlin!"[6] George Grosz recounted how he was warned in a dream to flee the city and accept a teaching position in the United States. The theater critic Alfred Kerr, whose radio broadcasts in 1929 had predicted a Nazi victory, packed his rucksack despite a high fever in order to slip over the Czech border disguised as a hiker.

In the autobiographies of the generation born between 1880 and 1910, the trauma of actual departure becomes a topos. The account of Kurt Hiller, the Expressionist publisher and pacifist who in 1934 was released from a concentration camp, is symptomatic of the imagery of this separation:

> On the 28th of September 1934 I left Berlin. The journey from Friedenau to the Anhalt Station—in the complete awareness of the fact that I, dyed-in-the-wool Berliner, would never again see the city of my home, or Germany—was no small matter. I seemed to myself to be a gray shell devoid of life. I was also without tears. For the moment without hope. I lacked completely that which is called *vis vitalis*. Dejection would be the wrong word for it. Debilitated creature, spiritual half-corpse, mechanically trying to save its existence. My condition left just enough strength to buy a ticket to Dresden and get on the right train."[7]

An interesting footnote to the problem of psychological separation can be found in Martin Gumpert, physician and friend of Thomas Mann, who did not leave the city until 1936, yet recorded an unconscious existential preparation for his exile. In the early 1930s, Gumpert packed his bags and slipped off to a small hotel around the corner from his office. Then, walking the pavement, he experienced his native Berlin with the alienation of a stranger. In his autobiography he recalled, "Never had a city seemed more joyous, more magical than this home which surrendered itself to me only when I had rejected it."[8] The eye of the Berliner in this experiment in alienation registers the presence of an imaginative aura which reveals itself only to the "estranged" observer. When the experience is not self-induced, however, but the result of banishment, the joyous déjà vu vanishes and the imaginative quality is internalized. The exile, who experiences the city of home just as vividly, does so with an overwhelming sense of dependence and vulnerability.

The refugee existence, brutal as it was, by no means spelled the end of Berlin humor in exile. The musician-composer Friedrich Hollaender, who had become famous in the 1920s for popular cabaret songs as "Von Kopf bis Fuß," [From head to toe] mused in his memoires about packing for an escape. He mocked the emigrés' initial delusions about the duration of Hitler's power:

> What do you take along on an escape? There is no escape guide book on the market. . . . What does an escape suitcase look like—the only one that you're allowed carry with you? . . . Of course, this may not be anything more than an overnight case, a weekend valise; after all, the most spirited high-jinks don't last longer than from Saturday to Monday. Just a bachelor party till the morning birds sing. The toothbrush is always the first thing that goes in. It removes the bitter taste and the nicotine yellow of the previous day. Warm underwear, because it's always cold away from home. On the other hand, the electric shaver already seems to belong to the pattern of days past. The untended stubble is already your first disguise. Because when you hear the knock—the terrible knock on the door—it is good if you aren't the same person you were the day before.[9]

Friedrich Hollaender's metaphorical luggage prompts the question: just what aspects of *Berlinertum* could indeed be exported? What qualities of this city's personality survived the sea change of exile? To begin with, the visual artists and the musicians had, by virtue of their media, an easier time continuing their pre-1933 activities and acclimating professionally to their adopted homelands than did those whose skills were based in the German language. The photographer Lotte Jacobi has said that merely by aiming her camera at a subject, could she continue the art she had practiced so successfully in Berlin.[10] A similar case might be made for the architect Walter Gropius, a founder of the Bauhaus who was at Harvard University after 1937. Through his buildings as well as his role as educator he had enormous impact upon the aesthetics of North American design. In the field of music, which Bruno Walter in his autobiography termed the "universal language," there was little difficulty for the accomplished German artists to communicate.[11] Walter, who conducted in Vienna from 1933 to 1938, eventually settled in the exile community in Beverly Hills. Friedrich Hollaender, of the same emigré community, represents a remarkable success story in his transference of a Berlin style of popular music to Hollywood. In his twenty-three years in California, he scored around 175 films and wrote many successful songs for big stars such as Bing Crosby and Marlene Dietrich. With true Berlin swagger, Hollaender calculated that by composing for the movies, the length of his musical output dwarfed Wagner's œuvre. Kurt Weill, popularly remembered as Brecht's musical collaborator on such works as the *The Threepenny Opera* (1928), *The Rise and Fall of the City of Mahagonny* (1927–29), *Happy End* (1929), also made a success in American show business. Weill sensed what was needed to succeed in America and, being adaptable, began to distance himself from his former role of young modernist composer who had been judged against Paul Hindemith. After 1940 Weill considered his most important competitor Richard Rodgers, a composer who could not represent a more extreme pendulum swing of values. Weill wrote the music for *Lady in the Dark*, *Knickerbocker Holiday*, and *Lost in the Stars*, achieving great success but losing his earlier intellectual following who never forgave him his popularity. Through Hollaender and Weill, the culture of Berlin was indeed exported—and quickly assimilated by American show business. Very few of the emigrés, however, although they dreamed of the financial rewards possible in the American entertainment industry, were able to shift their styles with equal success to popular culture. Their attempts to gain from this potentially lucrative market represented compromises with earlier styles and aesthetic standards that were doomed to fail.

When we examine the case of the visual arts in exile, we also find Berliners gradually being absorbed by their new adopted homeland. George Grosz, the vicious satirist of Berlin's bourgeoisie, found relaxed happiness in New York City. His mood in exile stood in such stark contrast to his earlier Berlin style that the works he produced after 1933 are a far cry from the grotesque caricatures of *Ecce Homo* or *The Face of the Ruling Class*. In exile Grosz turned to nature, and his painting developed an idealistic, even heroic strain. In his autobiography he recalls intentionally casting off his "earlier German personality like an old worn-out suit."[12] In the relative comfort of America, the abrasion of Berlin's dirt, which had been the source of his earlier artistic vision, was absent. Unfortunately for his art, that abrasion proved to have been an irreplaceable inspiration, and Grosz never attained that unique mordant style that had helped to define Berlin during the Weimar Republic.

Berlin's cinema had such a pervasive influence in exile (chiefly in Hollywood) that documenting it would have to be far more exhaustive than a brief overview permits.[13] Suffice it to say, that it was through Hollywood that German exile culture probably made its most indelible mark on the United States. Berlin's UFA studios had, of course, been exerting influence outside Germany before the seizure of power; therefore, the subject is not neatly contained within the period of 1933 to 1945.

Although Berliners scored true artistic and professional successes in the American film industry, the attempts of the most formidable theatrical producers fared far worse. Three towering figures of the vibrant theater life of Berlin in the 1920s—Max Reinhardt, Erwin Piscator, and Leopold Jessner—never achieved the success in exile that they deserved. Because their careers were so intimately a product of Berlin's interwar life, they are good examples of the difficulties that plagued the "export" of cultural material.[14] The failures of exile theater embodied in these three directors showed that mere translation, without appropriate cultural transformation, could not continue a tradition. Too strict an allegiance to the past, combined with language barriers, financial problems, theater politics, and the standards of a strange entertainment industry that did not view theater as a moral force, hampered Berlin's theater professionals in America. Only the German-speaking stages of Switzerland afforded the exile theater the possibility of true continuity as well as innovation. The Zürich Schauspielhaus became the new home to many theater people and dramatists from Berlin. Exile plays of Brecht,

Georg Kaiser, Ferdinand Bruckner, Friedrich Wolf—all dramatists whose works had stirred Berlin audiences during the Weimar Republic—premiered in Zürich. This ensemble was a direct link to the Brecht-Ensemble in postwar Berlin where standards and techniques established in exile provided the norms for subsequent interpretations of Brecht's dramas.[15]

Unlike visual artists, architects, musicians, or film directors, writers in exile were hampered, not helped, by their very technical accomplishments. The more wedded they were to the subtleties of their native language, the less likely they were to find success in a new tongue. Most of them never developed the ability to adapt to new readers and new markets. In the literature written outside Germany after 1933, Berlin's *genius loci* is no longer the vital, compelling presence in German literature that it had been. Although it is a multifaceted body of writing, exile literature remains to a great extent topical, born of historical conflict, and very much a mirror of refugee existence. In poetry, frequently the most private of genres, homesickness and existential isolation often dominate. Vienna (or Prague), however, most consistently become the object of this nostalgia. Berlin, for some reason, seldom evokes the same sense of tragic loss. Perhaps the brutality of political events in Berlin caused such deep emotional pain to the exiles that poetic nostalgia was impossible. Perhaps the Berlin personality itself—in which Tucholsky had praised humor tempered with hard-nosed tenacity—helped prevent sentimentality under the circumstances. When Brecht evokes Berlin in his poetry, for example, he stresses political crimes and human suffering, inflating these to mythical proportions when he equates the city with Sodom and Gomorrha. Yet Brecht never rejected Germany or its capital. His description of Berlin as "Unbewohnbar/Und doch unverlaßbar" [unlivable, yet unleavable],[16] captures the tension of the exile's double bind.

Walter Mehring was a novelist, dramatist, poet, cofounder of the Berlin Dada movement, and quintessential Berliner. His verses remain the touchstone for *Berlinertum* in exile. The first strophe of the "Ode an Berlin," written in exile in his own Berlin dialect, betrays an inability to despair utterly that High German could not have conveyed in this situation:

> Manchmal berliner ick aus'm Traume—
> Und soo' ne Träne kullert mir auf't Schemisett.
> Ick höre ummassu:
> "Nu sind wa frei im deutschen Raume!"
> Ne, Emil; nich, det ick Dir flaume,
> Aber Emil, angter nanu (entre nous):
> Jloobst'n det? Jloobst'n det?[17]

Mehring's odyssey was to carry him through French internment camps to Spain, via Martinique, to Hollywood, then New York and, avoiding his native Berlin, eventually to Switzerland after the war, where he died in 1981.[18]

Tracing the image of Berlin in exile literature underscores a perennial human phenomenon: At a moment of separation, the object of loss claims us, etching itself indelibly on the mind. Retreat binds the exile to the land he has lost, which in retrospect is transformed by the act of remembrance that simultaneously negates, conserves, and idealizes. Berlin lives in various

Synagogue at Fasanenstrasse 79–80, Charlottenburg. Photograph taken on April 16, 1941. Heavy damage during the "Crystal Night" (Kristallnacht) on November 9, 1938. (The photograph might also reflect damages caused by the first aerial attacks of the R.A.F. in March and April 1941.) Over and over again eyewitnesses confirmed that this synagogue suffered brutally during the Crystal Night. Reproduced with permission of the Landesbildstelle Berlin.

guises: the colorful anecdotes of autobiography, the politicized visions of Georg Kaiser's or Brecht's antifascist dramas, the socialist-realist prose fiction of Jan Petersen and Bernard von Brentano, and the lamentations of Mascha Kaléko's poetry. Klaus Mann's *Mephisto* (1936), set in the intrigues of Berlin's theater world under the Third Reich, traces from beyond Germany's borders the channels of power and influence in the capital. *Berlinertum* and the city's essence per se are unimportant for Mann, however, whose youthful theatrical attempts had met with hostility in the city.

No writer produced a successor to *Berlin Alexanderplatz* in exile, least of all Döblin himself. Nonetheless, the city remained at the center of his literary imagination. The novel *Pardon wird nicht gegeben* [No pardon granted] (1935) is obviously set in Berlin although the city is never mentioned by name. In this autobiographical work, Döblin explores the complicated dynamics of his own family while depicting the failed revolution of 1918/19 (again, unspecified in the fiction). The four novels of the cycle *November 1918* (begun in 1937) pursue this historical theme, incorporating events Döblin had witnessed in Berlin. The novels, while evoking the capital after

World War I, attempt to trace the genesis of fascism in Germany. As the saga evolves, however, Döblin interweaves a story of the protagonist's conversion—an autobiographical element that parallels his own embracing of Catholicism in exile.

Whereas Döblin's exile works did not preserve the aura of *Berlin Alexanderplatz*, the city did not relax its grip on him. In 1940 Döblin wrote a letter from St. Germain. While recounting his activities in France, he makes a slip of the pen, writing: "Approximately twice a week we go to Berlin."[19] Noticing the error with humor, he corrects the wrong word to "Paris." Mere force of habit? Perhaps: yet, after seven years in exile, an internalization of place that best corroborates Brecht's dictum of the city as: "unlivable, yet unleavable."

A final example from prose fiction serves to capture the true literary preservation of *Berlinertum*. The young Kurt Lehmann, who was born near the Schlesischer Bahnhof [Silesian Station], did not become a writer until he fled his native city at age 26. His first novel born of the refugee experience, "Ein Mensch fällt aus Deutschland" [A man drops out of Germany] (1936) was published under the pseudonym of Konrad Merz. The work virtually breathes the temperament of Berlin. "I didn't lose my heart in Heidelberg, but rather in Berlin-Moabit," says the youthful protagonist Winter.[20] This diary-cum-epistolary novel of the self-styled "Spreesprößling" [Spree offspring] is an account of undercover existence in Holland where Merz found asylum from 1934 to 1945. The style delights one with unexpected word play and grotesque humor. The sentences move with a powerful tempo and have an edge honed on Tucholsky's style. In one passage Winter exults in receiving the most desirable of commodities:

> In the evening there was a package from Ilse waiting for me at the post office. A heart made of cake. In the middle of the street I bit into its center. I took a bite. What's that? Paper? I kept biting. What the heck? My passport! Ilse baked the passport into the heart. I'm here again. I exist officially. "Nationality: 'Prussian." Is that true? "Build: unfortunately extant." "Profession: foreigner." "Eye color: prohibited." "Face: disagreeable." "Identifying characteristics: incredibly hungry." "Place of residence: on earth, *poste restante*."[21]

Ein Mensch fällt aus Deutschland is unique, being both a record of exile as well as a novel in which *Berlinertum* lives, absorbed into the spirit of the hero who claims: "I am the Berlin that has dropped out of Berlin."[22]

Those exiles who were drawn back to Berlin after 1945 had to confront their fragmentary memories with the rubble of reality. PEM compared his return with a visit to Pompeii: "The city squares and houses looked like the ruins of a perished world. Or was it as though I had come to visit my own grave."[23] The imagery of death that pervades this rediscovery of the city echoes the same fear the exiles had uttered upon fleeing. The culture that many had tried to preserve abroad—though it had not utterly vanished at home—seemed extinguished at last.[24] This feeling of the end of a sensibility is recorded by Günter Kunert, born in 1929, who described his experience as a teenager scrambling over the debris, exploring the ruins of Berlin. It dawned upon Kunert in later years what quality of the city his generation had been deprived of. In that "lost time" before 1933 that was familiar to him only from books and stories, the city had seemed a place of harmless pleasures where Hitler was a caricature and Kästner's Emil and his detectives roamed the labyrinthine streets. It is a vision reminiscent of Walter Benjamin's great exile work *Berliner Kindheit um 1900* [Berlin childhood around 1900], which had similarly played upon memory and desire to reconstruct a fictionalized personality of an earlier era. *This* city of memory was not to be reborn from its own ashes. With the eradication of all traces of E.T.A. Hoffmann's haunts, of Raabe's Sperlinggasse, of the underworld around the Alexanderplatz, the disappearance was—in Kunert's word—"magical."[25] An external world that had been internalized through the literary imagination was removed.

Yet, Kunert's requiem is premature. It obscures the fact that contemporary writers continue as never before to exploit the imaginative promise of this city tinctured with legend. Although the terrain has changed, the urge to map it has not. One need only to think of the vibrant literary scene in the city and of the writers whose works have helped create a new urban literature in East and West: Uwe Johnson, Ulrich Plenzdorf, Ingeborg Drewitz, Günter Kunert, Peter Schneider, Barbara König, to name but a few.[26]

To close these ruminations, the final word must go to an exile. Ernst Bloch, a philosopher with a literary gift, perceived Berlin in 1932 on the brink of decisive change. Although his sentiment—with all its imaginative as well as geopolitical prescience—is by now half a century old, it remains a timeless reaffirmation of Berlin's vitality: "Other cities are often mere ghosts of a better past . . . Berlin is possibly—what other choice is there—the ghost of a better future."[27]

Notes

[1] "Das war ein Vorspiel nur, dort wo man Bücher verbrennt,/Verbrennt man am Ende auch Menschen." Heinrich Heine, *Werke in dreizehn Teilen* (Leipzig, Vienna, Stuttgart, n.d.), Teil 5, p. 16. *Note*: All translations from the German are by T.S. Hansen.

[2] "Langsam hatten sie gelernt, nur an das Heute und bestenfalls an's Morgen zu denken, und 'Nach uns die Sintflut' lauerte irgendwo dahinter. . . . Man fand sich irgendwie . . . ab, schimpfte, machte dreckige Witze und litt mit zusammengekniffenen Lippen still vor sich hin. Die mit Spreewasser getaufte Gemütlichkeit verbarg sich hinter Kaltschnäuzigkeit." PEM [Paul Erich Marcus], *Heimweh nach dem Kurfürstendamm* (Berlin: Lothar Blanvalet, 1952), p. 177.

[3] "Nach sieben Wochen echten Reichtums verließen wir das Besitztum, bald/ Flohen wir über die Grenze." "Zeit meines Reichtums." In: *Gesammelte Werke in 20 Bänden* (Frankfurt/Main: Suhrkamp, 1967), vol. VIII, p. 419.

[4] Fritz Kortner, *Aller Tage Abend* (Munich: Kindler, 1959), p. 419ff.

[5] "Es war ja nur ein Ausflug; man läßt den Sturm vorübergehen." Quoted in Hans-Albert Walter, *Deutsche Exilliteratur 1933–1950*, vol. I (Darmstadt: Luchterhand, 1973), p. 218.

[6] "Nun stirbt Berlin vor unseren Augen, das unbestechliche Berlin, das Berlin von Heinrich Zille und Käthe Kollwitz, von Klemperer, Bruno Walter . . . die Namen überstürzen sich—Berlin!" Gustav Regler, *Das Ohr des Malchus. Eine Lebensgeschichte* (Frankfurt: Suhrkamp, 1975), p. 196.

[7] "Am 28. September 1934 verließ ich Berlin. Die Fahrt von Friedenau zum Anhal-

ter Bahnhof, in vollem Bewußtsein, daß ich Urberliner meine Heimatstadt, ja Deutschland niemals wiedersehen werde, war keine Kleinigkeit. Ich kam mir vor wie ein graues Gehäuse ohne Leben. Auch ohne Tränen war ich. Zunächst auch ohne Hoffnung. Das, was *vis vitalis* heißt, fehlte mir völlig. Niedergeschlagenheit wäre ein falscher Ausdruck. Entkräftete Kreatur, seelische Halbleiche, die mechanisch ihre Art Existenz retten will. Der Kräftezustand reichte gerade noch aus, die Fahrkarte nach Dresden einzulösen und den richtigen Zug zu besteigen." Kurt Hiller, *Leben gegen die Zeit* (Reinbek: Rowohlt, 1969), p. 297.

[8] "Niemals erschien mir eine Stadt heiterer, zauberischer als diese Heimat, die sich mir erst hingab, wenn ich sie verstieß." Martin Gumpert, *Hölle im Paradies. Selbstdarstellung eines Arztes* (Stockholm: Bermann-Fischer, 1939), p. 230.

[9] "Was nimmt man auf eine Flucht mit? Es gibt keinen Fluchtführer im Handel zu kaufen. . . . Wie sieht die Fluchtreisetasche aus? Die eine, die man mitnehmen kann. . . . Freilich—dies ist vielleicht nur ein 'overnight-case', ein Wochenendkoffer, denn der beste Spuk währt nur von irgendeinem Sonnabend bis zu irgendeinem Montag. Ein Polterabend nur, bis die Morgenvögel schreien. Die Zahnbürste ist immer das erste, was hinein muß. Sie beseitigt den bitteren Geschmack und das Nikotingelb des vergangenen Tages. Das warme Unterzeug, denn es ist immer kalt außer Hause. Der Rasierapparat hingegen scheint schon dem verflossenen Gleichlauf der Tage anzugehören. Die unbedienten Bartstoppeln sind bereits die erste Verkleidung. Denn, wenn es klopft—das schreckliche Klopfen an der Tür—, ist es gut, wenn man nicht der gleiche ist vom Tag zuvor." Friedrich Hollaender, *Vom Kopf bis Fuß. Mein Leben in Text und Musik* (Munich: Kindler, 1965), p. 274–275.

[10] Conversation with the author (March 1983).

[11] Bruno Walter. *Theme and Variation.* Trans. by James Galston (New York: Alfred Knopf, 1946), p. 245.

[12] George Grosz, *A Little Yes, A Big No* (New York: The Dial Press, 1946), p. 30.

[13] See the several essays on the topic in *Deutsche Exilliteratur seit 1933.* Vol. I, *Kalifornien.* Eds. John M. Spalek and Joseph Strelka (Bern and Munich: Francke, 1976).

[14] On Piscator in exile, see John Willet, *The Theater of Erwin Piscator* (New York: Holmes & Meier, 1979); Edward Harris, "Max Reinhardt." In: *Deutsche Exilliteratur nach 1933, op. cit.,* pp. 789–800. See also John Baxter, *The Hollywood Exiles* (New York: Taplinger Publishing Co., 1976), pp. 186–194; Marta Mierendorff, "Leopold Jessner." In: *Deutsche Exilliteratur seit 1933, op. cit.,* pp. 738–747.

[15] See Werner Mittenzwei, *Exil in der Schweiz* (Leipzig: Reclam, 1978) chapter 3, "Das Zürcher Schauspielhaus . . .", p. 350ff.

[16] Bertolt Brecht, *Gesammelte Werke, op. cit.,* vol. IX, p. 533.

[17] "Sometimes I utter Berlin dialect in my dreams—/And such a tear rolls onto my shirtfront./I keep hearing/'We are now free in German territory!'/Naw, Emil, not that I'd pull your leg,/But Emil, just between us (entre nous):/D'ya believe it? D'ya believe it?" Walter Mehring, *Staatenlos im Nirgendwo. Die Gedichte, Lieder und Chansons, 1933–1974* (Düsseldorf: Claassen, 1981), p. 11.

[18] For more on Mehring in exile, see Thomas S. Hansen, "Walter Mehrings antifaschistische Romane; ein Beitrag zur politischen Prosa im Exil." *Jahrbuch für Internationale Germanistik,* Reihe A, Bd. 5: *Deutsche Exilliteratur—Literatur im Dritten Reich,* 1980, pp. 132–140.

[19] "Etwa 2 x wöchentlich fahren wir nach Berlin." Alfred Döblin, *Ausgewählte Werke in Einzelbänden.* Ed. by W. Muschg, Briefe (Olten and Freiburg: Walter, 1970), p. 240.

[20] "Habe . . . mein Herz nicht in Heidelberg verloren, sondern in Berlin-Moabit," Konrad Merz. *Ein Mensch fällt aus Deutschland.* Nachwort von Ingeborg Drewitz (Hamburg: Konkret Literatur, 1978), p. 92.

[21] "Abends erwartete mich dann ein Paket von Ilse auf der Post. Ein Herz aus

Kuchen. Mitten auf der Straße biß ich mittenhinein. Ich biß. Was ist das! Papier? Ich biß weiter. Was soll das? Mein Paß! Ilse hat den Paß in das Herz gebacken. Ich bin wieder vorhanden. Wieder abgestempelt, "Staatsangehörigkeit: 'Preußen'". Ist das wahr? "Gestalt: leider vorhanden". "Beruf: Ausländer". "Farbe der Augen: verboten". "Gesicht: unangenehm". "Besondere Kennzeichen: Hat mächtigen Hunger". "Wohnort: auf der Erde, postlagernd". *Op. cit.*, p. 56–57.

[22] "Ich bin das aus Berlin gefallene Berlin." *Op. cit.*, p. 32.

[23] "Wie die Reste einer untergangenen Welt sahen die Plätze und Häuser aus. Oder war es, als käme ich, mein eigenes Grab zu besuchen." *Heimweh nach dem Kurfürstendamm, op. cit.*, p. 12.

[24] Paul Gurk, Martin Kessel, Oskar Loerke, Hans Fallada, none of whom emigrated, all wrote "Berlin" novels between 1933 and 1945. See also the operetta by Walter Kollo from the period, "Berlin, wie es weint und lacht." An important document of the city's enduring vitality in the immediate postwar years is the *Berliner Almanach 1947*, eds. Walter G. Oschilewski and Lothar Blanvalet (Berlin: Lothar Blanvalet Verlag, 1946).

[25] Günter Kunert, "Diesseits des Erinnerns." In: *Berlin, ach Berlin*, ed. Hans Richter (Berlin: Severin und Siedler, 1981), pp. 20–29.

[26] See the anthology *Berlin* [sic]. *Contemporary Writing East and West Berlin* (Santa Barbara, California: Bandanna Books, 1983) for a wide selection of younger writers.

[27] "Oft sind andere Städte bloße Gespenster besserer Vergangenheit; . . . Berlin ist möglicherweise—es bleibt keine Wahl—das Gespenst einer besseren Zukunft." Ernst Bloch, "Berlin aus der Landschaft gesehen." In: *Verfremdungen II. Geographica* (Frankfurt: Suhrkamp, 1965), p. 37.

CHAPTER 10

The Grandchildren of Grosz and Kirchner: Realism and Violence in Postwar Berlin Art

Eckhart Gillen

Exhibitions of recent paintings from West as well as East Germany have met with head-shaking and astonishment in both Western and Eastern Europe. When the exhibition *Ugly Realism* was shown at the ICA (Institute of Contemporary Arts, London) in 1978, English art critics backed away from the aggressive attacks of the Berlin painters and pointed out how basically different the English art tradition was. As one reviewer put it, "Never deprived of the democratic outlets of criticism and constitutional control, the English nation and her artists could afford the dangerous luxury of being apolitical. Things are quite different for Germany. . . . The politically committed artist seems to be a figure of the Weimar Republic but can, in fact, be traced back at least to the lampooning in Luther's time. . . . British art, to this day, is landscape-oriented, with all that implies space, slowness, calm; even our townscapes are apt to be versions of landscape."[1]* John Willett, in his study of the culture of the Weimar Republic, *The New Sobriety* (London, 1978), writes: "Such intensification of conflict, the emphasizing of differences rather than reconciliation, is, for better or worse, a very German way of looking at things."

In Moscow, too, Soviet art critics reacted with skepticism to the first presentation, in 1975, of new painting from the German Democratic Republic (GDR). The tendency of GDR artists to show everything "very obviously, very directly, very unmercifully" is traced back to the fact that from the beginning it has been "unfortunate and tragic" for German art that "the best artists were often forced into opposition against their own nation." The so-called *conflict paintings* of the 1970s in East Germany quite provocatively left behind the official optimism of that boringly homogeneous Socialist Realism, which since 1945 has been the only style sanctioned in the countries of Eastern Europe. Many artists in East Berlin and East Germany, like their counterparts in West Berlin, have begun to hark back to the traditions of German Expressionism and Verism, to the reluctant acceptance of the functionaries.

Translated from German by John Gabriel, Berlin.
*See Notes section at the end of this chapter.

Yet already in 1924, when the first comprehensive German art exhibition was shown in Moscow and Leningrad—with works by Grosz, Dix, Pechstein, Felixmüller, Schlichter, and others—these styles horrified the Soviet critics, one of whom wrote: "These pictures really give you the creeps. Possibly because in these Expressionist caricatures, in these grotesquely distorted naked bodies... in all of this carefully and Teutonically labored description of the most gruesome details, one detects an undercurrent of a certain sadistic joy."[2] Mr. Fedorov-Davydov went on to say that these artists unconsciously revelled "in all of this horridness" and derived what he called "a sick pleasure from depictions of erotic pathology."[2] This criticism from the Left did not prevent the Nazis from denouncing the Verists of the 1920s as "cultural Bolsheviks."

Looking back to what in Germany is sometimes called "Hour Zero," the defeat of the *Third Reich*, which to many of those who experienced it was something like a natural catastrophe, I shall attempt to show that West Berlin, the walled-in remainder of the capital of the *Reich*, has had to bear the consequences of the Second World War in prosperous West Germany's stead. As a showcase of Western capitalism, one might expect it to be a glossy demonstration of affluence, but it is surprisingly gloomy and without the veneer of wealth of other West German cities. An English visitor to the exhibition *Berlin: A Critical View* remarked spontaneously, "Ultimately, it was West Germany who won the war—Berlin was the only loser."

Berlin is an ugly town in need of care. Buildings have fallen into disrepair, the grey plaster crumbles off nineteenth-century facades riddled with bullet holes. Ruins, bombsites, and large areas of wasteland are common features, especially near the wall. The old neoclassical embassies near the Tiergarten slowly rot in a wilderness of weeds, rubble, and tin cans, their former occupants having moved to Bonn. Not far away, the Reichstag now stands empty—a mausoleum to a nation that no longer exists. The wall even encroaches on this building, blocking off the back entrance as if to emphasize that the Russians still have a foothold. "This absurd city is no accident. It has history; and it must face up to it," said Heinrich Albertz, a pastor and former mayor of Berlin.

Helmut Middendorf, one of the young "violent painters" from the lofts of Kreuzberg, once remarked, "Berlin is such an incredibly ruined, ugly city... I think Berlin is *the* city where you get the strongest feeling of what a city is." His painting entitled *Bridge*, of 1980, is a manifestation of this experience. In a poem on Middendorf's paintings, Franz Meyer-Siemermann wrote: "Ponderous terrible blocks of flats against a sky mystic and wonderful, ultramarine blue: So we see the morning rise blue in our Kreuzberg living-room window after an all-night drunk: 'Journey to the End of the Night'."[3]

The photographer Michael Ruetz recalled: "When I had moved to Hamburg and to the normalcy of the Federal Republic... I missed the signs of decay which so dominated Berlin and produced the piquant flavour of a past life. I found it extremely difficult to stand the 'normal' atmosphere of this bourgeois city."[4]

What fascinates artists so much about this decrepit city? Do they see Berlin as some archaeological excavation, a gigantic, slightly morbid open-air

Hartmut Bonk, Berlin: Images of Gods in the Loft (Götterbilder auf dem Dachboden). 1986/87. With permission of the artist.

museum that illustrates what Marx, in the introduction to his *Grundrisse*,[5] called "... the divisions and the conditions of production of all those defunct forms of society from whose ruins and elements it is built and whose remains, many not yet superseded, it drags along within it...?" The site of the Reichstag was once one of the many drill grounds located outside the city walls (which have since been replaced by the wall). It was here that Albert Speer, Hitler's general building inspector, had planned to erect his gigantic temple for the future world capital of Germania. Beneath this castle in the air, people now play football on the weekends and roast their sausages. The great railway stations, Potsdamer Bahnhof and Anhalter Bahnhof, were torn down after the war. Berlin has been relegated to a sidetrack, cut off; the sites of the former stations are now huge vacant lots. The ruined facade of Anhalter Bahnhof stands in its wasteland "like the ruins of an aqueduct in the Roman Campagna." Artists like Raffael Rheinsberg search the ground there for traces of a present now become the past. Not far from there, Karl-Horst Hödicke (an afficionado of Kirchner's Berlin street scenes, former student of the abstract expressionist Fred Thieler, and Helmut Middendorf's teacher at the College of Art) painted his *Gobi Desert* of 1978, an image of the wasteland outside his studio window. It is difficult to imagine that this was once Postdamer Platz, the city's most bustling intersection. Today the view is cut off by the back wall of the new National Library;

Hödicke painted it, as Eberhard Roters as the Director of the Berlinische Galerie once wrote, like "the radiant golden yellow cape of some distant island"; and the series of Berlin cityscapes that Hödicke executed from 1976 to 1978 he called "the melancholy of empty monuments".[6] Forbidding as rugged cliffs, modelled in stark contrasts of light and dark, the buildings of Dessauer Strasse with their vacant black gaps of windows look like some long-abandoned ruin. The choice of colors and his approach suggest that Hödicke may well have followed the instructions of "How to Paint Big-City Scenes" that the Expressionist Ludwig Meidner wrote in 1914: "When you paint Berlin, use only white and black, not too much ultramarine and ochre, but plenty of umber."

Meidner's plea to his fellow artists that "it's high time we started painting our home, the big city"[7] marked the beginning of an indigenous tradition of Berlin cityscapes that reaches from Ludwig Kirchner and Max Beckmann to George Grosz and Karl Hubbuch, from Werner Heldt to K.H. Hödicke and, in the 1980s, Rainer Fetting and Helmut Middendorf.

The Expressionists, Verists, and neo-Expressionists have not, however, seen their home city in terms of a home, a comfortable, familiar place; the urbanization process set in motion by industrial development has made it a very unhomely and frightening place indeed. The poet Alfred Wolfenstein once cried out "This is no home / Just give it a try! / No cozy love / All fight and buy! / And buildings flutter whipped / By light, noise, hiss, and scream. / And I homeless, pathless / O streets, drug me, drug me!"[8] Ludwig Meidner's painting *Burning City* of 1913 shows Berlin, metropolis and home of banking empires, industry, and great department stores, as an eternal battlefield whose denizens, helpless, aggressive, disoriented, see their wishes for warmth and human security swallowed up by the great competitive machine. And Meidner described his apocalyptic visions in "How to Paint Big-City Scenes": "Bombardments of hissing window rows, careening balls of light... Human fragments... The buildings beside us seem to topple and crash." In his autobiography *Mein Leben*, written in 1919, Meidner explained his feelings: "A sharp painful need compelled me to tear down everything with straight lines, verticals...to build ruins, buildings rent mournfully asunder...My mind bled with terrible happenings. All I saw were...burned-out cities, apocalypses...For already the monstrous storm that was about to engulf the world had bared its teeth and cast a garish yellow shadow across the days."[9]

Some impending catastrophe also seems to be prophesied by Helmut Middendorf's *Airplane Dream* of 1982, a painting he executed for the recent *Zeitgeist* exhibition in Berlin. The destructive potential of the bomber, a black crucifixlike shadow, merges with the disquieting blue of the night sky. With Middendorf, the Expressionist metaphor of night becomes a screen on which suppressed fears and desires are projected. As the side of human existence opposed to the daylight rationality of the reality principle, night is the realm of the unconscious (Middendorf's *The Bridge* is another good example of this). In this sense Middendorf has made of his image what Wolfgang Max Faust called "a projection point for open significances." He has avoided any restriction of the subject's meaning to, say, fear of war, the threat of atomic war to humanity, and the like.

How little justification there is in the charge that the young "violent" painters are merely camp-followers of the great Berlin Expressionists is shown by another cityscape of Middendorf's, his *Hovering Red*, of 1980. The compositional idea is, admittedly, Expressionist, an allusion to the canvas which Conrad Felixmüller painted in 1925, on the death of his lifelong friend Walter Rheiner, an Expressionist poet. Helplessly clutching at a curtain, a syringe in his hand, Rheiner's body floats in final, painful ecstasy between the illuminated abysses of city streets and night sky. In the hypersensibility of the addict, the Expressionists found a symbolic state, a state of no longer being able to find sustenance in the meaningless artificial paradises of the city, in whose anonymity one tried to hide, to forget. Felixmüller, himself involved in the Expressionist movement, saw the danger of letting oneself drift, which carefree masochism, into the "lowest abandonment" of the individual who feels himself misunderstood by society. His painting *The Death of the Poet Walter Rheiner* marks a turning-point in his style to a more dispassionate and objective realism.

Middendorf's hovering human figure is a far cry from this feverish vision, the pathos with which the Expressionists criticized modern civilization. He builds a symbolic bridge between reality and hallucinatory vision—the spirit of the city, a discharge of anonymous streams of energy from people living in the joyless sea of Kreuzberg flats, raises waves of color and form on its surface like those described by Georg Heym in his poem, "The God of the City": "The red belly of evening glows to Baal / . . . He thrusts his butcher's fist into the night. / He shakes it. A sea of fire races / Down a street. And searing bright / Smoke devours them, until dawn's first traces."[10]

While for Heym the city was dominated by the demon of violence and negation, Middendorf's spirit exudes a strange and unsentimental optimism for he is anything but a prophet of the "no-future" generation's disillusioned activism. His aim is to fascinate and to irritate us without proclaiming any new style, new direction, new manifesto. This attitude on the part of the "violent" painters of the 1980s likewise divides them from their Expressionist forefathers. Their younger counterparts no longer believe that the world can be made to fit into symbols. In their pictures they record intense moments of emotion, capture their reactions to life as if in a photographic flash.

The new movement has no programmatic images. It was different with the artists who experienced the horrors of the First World War, in whom "the conscience of the planet throbbed mightily" and who believed that "what politics has bungled, artists will set right. . . . We believe in the redemption of humanity through art."[11] Meidner exclaimed, "Painters, poets . . . Who is going to fight for the good cause if we don't?"[12]

The Crier, painted by Carl Hofer in 1924, is a symbolic wanderer in the night, who alone raises his voice in the midst of a silent and desiccated world. And in 1926, George Grosz painted his *Self-Portrait as Warner*. The revised socialist realism of the sixties in East Germany again took up the figure of the warner or accuser, if only to put what they called a "concrete political message" into his mouth. Willi Sitte's *Crier II* of 1964, said East German art historian Hermann Raum, expressed a "great artistic liberation" brought about by a "comprehensive identification of the artist with the historic mission of his country. . . . The crier, representing the history-shaping class, increasingly articulated the unity into which Sitte merged with the party that trained him."[13]

After 1945, in the face of a situation in which an entire people had implicated itself in the crimes of the Nazi regime, the accusatory voice in art died down to a general complaint. Modern art had been ruthlessly attacked as decadent by the Nazis and had been replaced partly by a vulgarized naturalism and partly by an academic style notable for its prurience. All this crushed belief, in Germany, gave in to the humanist mission of art. Bernard Schultze, an abstract expressionist artist, recently recalled the "change that Otto Dix went through, that terrible change when he began painting those idyllic landscapes on Lake Constance (e.g., *Fruit Trees in Blossom*, 1948) and almost denied his early work (e.g., *War*, 1929–32, center panel of a tryptich). That style couldn't be developed any further, of course; that was over and done with. Accusations, riddled bodies, destruction—nobody wanted to hear any more about that, right, because they'd been through the real thing, seen it close up. So it was back to the ivory tower, out to explore other fields."[14]

The reality of the bombed-out, ghostly cities had outdone the Surrealists' wildest nightmare imaginings: "Can any more Surrealist de-compositions exist than those photographs of blasted cities?"[15] asked Hans Sedlmayer, who in his book *Verlust der Mitte (Loss of the Center)* mounted in 1948 a polemic against modern art as one expression of the demise of any universally binding Western, Christian view of man and his world. The postwar generation, completely disillusioned and under the spell of Sartre and existentialism, felt, as Hann Trier, another abstract painter, put it, "an incredible skepticism with regard to all such concepts as 'religiousness', 'humanism', 'Western civilization'—values that art was suddenly supposed to communicate."[16] Gottfried Benn summed up the prevailing mood well when he wrote that people expected art to put back in place the center that did not hold: "Art must, people say, *must* restore the center. . . . Art must represent human beings in the image of God. Well, does anything else exist but the image of God? That would be news to me. Art, let it be known, *must* do absolutely nothing!"[17]

For example, Werner Heldt, who spent the 1930s in Berlin, went into what is called "inner emigration." The reality of crime and cruelty that became official government policy after Hitler's democratically legitimated takeover of power on January 30, 1933, was too much for the rational mind to grasp and to cope with. In the face of incomprehensible historical events, Werner Heldt reached at the conclusion that realism in art, insofar as it was based only on nonartistic categories of logic and causality, could not communicate what it meant to live under a rule of tyranny. In order to penetrate the reality of this "collective hallucination," this mass psychosis, Heldt wrote, artists would have to "regress to a primitive mental state in which the primitives, very small children, and dreamers can live without ill. This is the magic world of symbols."

The illustrations in the epoch-making book *Artistry of the Mentally Ill*, published by the Heidelberg psychiatrist Hans Prinzhorn in 1922, and Carl Gustav Jung's researches into the collective unconscious, awoke in Werner Heldt "memories of ancient shapes known from dreams. . . . It was as though... our real and present world was only a kind of thin layer of lava under which that other world incessantly boiled, like fiery liquid magma."[18] Heldt returned to these thoughts of 1935 in a speech he gave at the opening of an exhibition of the *École de Paris*, held in 1947 at the Gerd Rosen Gallery, which the year before had given Heldt his first postwar showing in Berlin. Heldt recalled: "In 1937, when the great breaking of images began with the exhibition of so-called decadent art, Werner Gilles told me that some of his paintings had hung there too, alongside drawings by a mental patient. The caption beneath them read, 'Where's the difference?'" Heldt answered this question with another question: "Where's the resemblance?" and then replied that the similarity lay in "a hallucinatory vision"[19] which brought back to the surface of consciousness archaic images, the archetypes of human history. This vision exploded the bounds of all mechanistic explanations of the universe and rendered the individual's own sensations and feelings accessible to him again.

More convincingly than all the theories advanced by art historians and critics, these insights on the part of many German artists both inside and outside Nazi Germany, go far toward explaining what at first seems a baffling phenomenon: the fact that after 1945, the aggressively critical Verism with which artists reacted to the attrition of the First World War was neither continued by its still-living representatives—among them Grosz, Dix, and Rudolf Schlichter—nor was it taken up by the younger generation of artists.

Let me give an example from a still quite unknown field, that of German art in exile. Heinz Lohmar, German Communist party member since 1931, arrested by the Gestapo in 1933, escaped to Paris where, in 1936, he painted *The Superbeast* under the influence of the Surrealists and Max Ernst. The mimetic elements of this image, such as the steer's skull, an archetype of barbarian, chthonic brutality, the monstrous hand giving the fascist salute, snakes' heads and insects, emerge only in suggestions from an amorphic pictorial structure. In the end, Lohmar's message is reduced to the statement that, as Georges Bataille wrote in "Divine Eros": "violence is mute." And as the Expressionist Otto Pankok noted fatalistically in his diary: "Evil, up to now contained, has been unleashed and the world is sliding towards hell."[20] Words like these reveal the helpless and tragic situation of those German artists in exile who, in Paris in 1935, came together in a Popular Front to defend culture against barbarism.

The canvas entitled *Barbaropa*, painted by Heinz Trökes in 1947, is another such Surrealist-influenced attempt—the artist definitely had Max Ernst and Salvador Dali in mind—to digest the traumatic experience of Nazi terror, as already expressed by the painting's title in which the words "barbarian" and "Europe" are combined. Again the visual metaphor of a petrified bull's head appears, supported by Daliesque poles, in a forbidding desert landscape. French Surrealism, which was not seen in Germany until 1946 in an exhibition at the Berliner Stadtschloß (Berlin City Palace), seemed to German artists in the late 1940s the only style adequate to express "an amorphous and anarchic world." The denizens of this world were described by H.E. Holthusen in 1947 as "survivors of a shipwreck... driftwood of a civilization gone to pieces, living in a fantastic dreamlike city that sprawls out among heaps of debris and mountains of rubble... who have

Werner Heldt, Berlin: "Berlin at Sea" ("Berlin am Meer"), 18.5 × 30 cm, lithography; from the file "Berlin," 1949—Sprengel Museum, Hannover. Reproduced with permission of the Sprengel Museum and of Werner Heldt, Berlin.

witnessed with their own eyes and their own bodies a world-inundating catastrophe."[21]

In a series of ink drawings and oil paintings, Werner Heldt again and again varied the theme *Berlin at the Sea (Berlin am Meer)* a symbolic image which appeared to Heldt with the force of an apparition when he returned to Berlin from an English prisoner-of-war camp. The gutted buildings and piles of rubble evoked in him the vision of an abandoned city that had fallen victim to a second Deluge. The war as a Deluge or Descent into Hell—such titles of postwar German paintings fit in with official political parlance in which Germany's defeat was invariably referred to as "the collapse," calling up visions of some natural catastrophe for which human beings cannot be held responsible. Heldt wrote the following about his *Berlin at the Sea*: "In my paintings I have always depicted the victory of nature over human works. Everywhere under the asphalt of Berlin lies the sand of Brandenburg. And that sand was once the floor of the sea."[22] This image of cycles in which nature reclaims what human hybris has erected, reduces historical events to inevitable strokes of fate. Surrealism indeed seems the best way to express this philosophy, because it "takes things out of their defined [i.e. historical] spaces and out of their recorded times and resituates them between space and time," said Heinz Trökes in a lecture on Surrealism given in 1946 at the Gerd Rosen Gallery in Berlin. Werner Heldt felt a spiritual affinity with Charles Meryon, who in his *Etchings of Paris* depicted the ocean with a whale, a sea-snake, and mythological creatures, rushing into the Quartier Latin around the Saint-Étienne-du-Mont church. With cool topographic precision, Meryon portrayed those parts of the old city which Baron Haussmann had earmarked for demolition, the scenes, as Werner Heldt wrote in a text on Meryon of about 1947, of "terrible vices and crimes."[23]

Heldt, whose last paintings were completely abstract, "passed by like some insignificant piece of flotsam", in the words of Hans Kinkel. The claims of a new art, the *Universal Language of Abstraction*, as a book title of the period had it, were so imperative and were defended so eloquently by such critics as Will Grohmann and Werner Haftmann that even artists basically unconcerned by the style were unable to resist it. Heldt's *Berlin Buildings with Stovepipe* of 1954 just misses being an exercise in modish design. Not a few abstract artists used the "total freedom" to find themselves, which, according to Haftmann, abstraction offered, to adapt their compositions for sale to manufacturers of dressmaking materials and wallpapers. Manfred Bluth, now a member of a group called the *New Splendour*, who paints in the style of Caspar David Friedrich or Boecklin, once confessed: "Yes, I went through all those struggles between objective and non-objective art personally, too. . . and naturally I tried. . . to paint in a more abstract style. . . . [Later] I felt ashamed of myself for sacrificing myself to the Zeitgeist like that."[24] Long after abstraction in art had carried the field at *documenta I* in 1955, such pundits as Grohmann and Haftmann started a virtual religious war over the new art, set off by a remark made by Carl Hofer, who had in 1945 been named Dean of the influential Berlin Hochschule für bildende Künste (College of Art). Abstract art had reached a dead end, Hofer had said; and it was not until ten years later that the Berlin air had cleared sufficiently for Hofer's work to be exhibited again.

Many artists agreed with Hann Trier: "What we were surrounded by were ruined, impoverished cities. Now was that reality? No, it wasn't a new reality, it was the result of old and bad politics. . . . We wanted to do something new, not paint bombscapes!"[25] Poverty and ruins did not fit at all well into the picture of a country embarking on an optimistic new era. A welcome way out was to open those doors to the unconscious, employ that "psychic automatism" which the Surrealists had proclaimed in their first manifesto back in 1924. By letting the brushhand go and by ignoring the dictates of the conscious mind, the gestural painters exclaimed, "Look, we're alive—we've made it through!" After the French Surrealists had fled to the United States in 1941 and 1942, the movement came back to Europe rechristened in various ways—abstract expressionism, action painting, art informel, abstraction lyrique, tachisme, or simply "un art autre." Berlin saw the new American painting for the first time in 1951, in an exhibition that included works by Pollock, Motherwell, and Rothko among others.

Werner Haftmann wrote that "Total freedom was possible because the social order had been smashed anyhow." Destruction of traditional form as an aesthetic sign of social liberty was predicated on the work of art being absolutely open, ambiguous and hence not claimable by any political tendency.

The autonomous work of art took up a position vis-à-vis society and created new realities: "Realities," as Haftmann wrote, "of a harmonious character, pure, internally consistent fabrics of form and color."

Wieland Schmied has summed up the development of abstract art into an ideology during the 1950s. "In parallel to political and economic developments and with the change of mood from 'We escaped by the skin of our teeth that time' to 'Now we're somebody again'," he writes. "Not the look of abstract art changed but the sensations associated with it, from an expression of the most profound self-doubt to a pose of proud self-assurance. The ideology of abstraction was marked by a naive belief in progress and had the advantage of being convenient. It made it easy to come out in favor of the modern and at the same time get over the past. With abstraction, artists could speak the international language of form and simultaneously, in the simplest way, repudiate Nazi art."[26]

In 1962 the so-called fully abstract informal art of the fifties could still be exhibited under the title *The Present to 1962* at the Haus am Waldsee in Berlin, mounted to provide a "feast for the eye." Ten years later many of the same paintings hung in the same rooms under the title *Subject: Informal. On the Structure of Another Era*. Here the canvases were subjected to ideological criticism and shown against a background of historical documents that raised the question of whether artists' claims to autonomy, to being absolutely independent of society or politics had not been grist to the mill of an apolitical, affluent society. When reunification was shelved in favor of economic and military integration in the Western Alliance, this met with little resistance as long as annual growth rates continued to double. Not much more was asked of Germans whose anti-Communism had survived the Hitler regime in a latent form than "to vote every four years for the CDU [Christian Democratic Union party] and otherwise keep their nose out of politics," as Countess Dönhoff wrote about the Adenauer era in *Die Zeit*.[26a]

Obviously between the unquestioning identification with abstract art in 1962 and the critical look back at it in 1973 the conservative restoration of the 50s has been questioned in the meantime; and the "boring fifties" were superseded by the "roaring sixties." During the fifties West Berlin had figured as a "bulwark of freedom" and an "island in the communist sea," holding fast to the illusion of soon becoming the capital of a reunified Germany. The continually increasing numbers of refugees from what was officially known as the Soviet Zone made its collapse seem imminent in 1960 and 1961, and when the wall went up on August 13, 1961, the shock was deep. Almost two decades were to pass before West Berlin artists dared to take the wall as a subject for their work. Hödicke's canvas *The Beauty and the Beast* (1979) and Rainer Fetting's *Van Gogh at the Wall* (1978) and *Setting Sun over East Berlin* (1979) are statements by a generation that had learned to live with, or at least to see sarcastically, this monument of German history, an attitude well expressed in one of the popular songs of Lilli Berlin, a New Wave singer:

> "Come on over to East Berlin—insane
> They don't let everybody in—insane
> 25 marks admission fee
> Heavy sounds and a lot to see
> The people have the power here—they're nervous
> Not a thing for them to fear—but the Secret Service
> Take a look through Brandenburg Gate—insane
> Too bad it's sealed off with a grate
> It's okay, we'll take the train
> Looking forward to East Berlin
> Nice people who're really in—insane
> It's all over with West Berlin."[27]

In an aggressively anti-Communist climate which for intellectual justification had to rely on the doctrine of totalitarianism, the popular version of
which was "Reds are as bad as Nazis," the well-adjusted students of the
fifties soon began to develop a critical consciousness that in 1967/68 led to a
confrontation with the establishment and a student revolt in Berlin. This
growing political awareness in artistic and intellectual circles fell into the
same period as a revolution in the visual arts: the confrontation of German
abstract painters with Pop Art from England and the United States and with
New Realism from France. Comparisons of paintings by Fred Thieler, a
tachiste (*Composition D-20-56* of 1956) and by his award-winning student
Peter Sorge serve to realize the scope of the change this brought about; or by
Professor Hann Trier (*The Fall*, 1961) and his student Hans-Jürgen Diehl
(*Nesting Place*, 1976). In the tense situation caused by the building of the
wall, this return to figuration fell on particularly fruitful ground.

Two years after the celebration of purely retinal art at the Haus am Waldsee, the first exhibition of *New Realists and Pop Art* in Germany took place
at West Berlin's Akademie der Künste (Academy of Art). With the works of
such artists as Arroyo, Blake and Dine, Johns, Lichtenstein, Oldenburg,
Paolozzi, Pistoletto, Rauschenberg and Rivers, Rosenquist, Warhol, Wessel-
mann, Hamilton and Hockney, Arman and Guttuso, a bridge seemed to
have been built to all those apparently forgotten artistic approaches of the
twenties which took a skeptical view of the realities of the day. Soon, in
1964, a group of German artists (Baehr, Diehl, Petrick, Sorge, Lüpertz, and
Hödicke), all of them graduates of the Berlin Hochschule für bildende Künste (College of Art), formed a self-help gallery in Kreuzberg, called *Grossgörschen 35* after the address of the premises. They rediscovered the big-city
iconography of the twenties, used set-pieces from reality in the shape of
news photographs and comics, and revived collage and montage techniques
(Wolfgang Petrick, *Paradise*, 1965; *In the Garden*, 1972–73). They understood realism in its broadest sense, as an operative method for analyzing a
sick society, a method by which the viewer, alienated by the abstract and
incomprehensible processes of consumer society, might better recognize his
own situation. This "critical realism" of the Berlin brand was meant as a
shock therapy, consciousness-expanding and, hopefully, in the end bringing
about an improvement in the patient's condition (Wolfgang Petrick, *Bird's
Eye*, 1972; *Housewife*, 1969). Wolf Vostell symbolized the ossification of
interpersonal relations by casting human bodies in concrete; and in his happening *Disasters of War* (after Goya) staged at the Berlin-Grunewald station
whose ramp over which Berlin Jews were led to their deaths at Auschwitz is
still visible.

The year 1964 also saw René Block open his gallery in Berlin, a gallery
that was to become the second important focus of the city's artistic activity
during the sixties. René Block called the work of his artists, among them
K.P. Brehmer, Hödicke and Vostell, with an ironic twist on the Socialist
Realism to the east "Capitalist Realism", following a happening of Konrad
Lueg and Gerhard Richter on October 11, 1963, in a Düsseldorf furni-
ture store: Lueg and Richter declared, as a demonstration for "Capitalist
Realism", the entire inventory of the store, as it stood, to be a work of art.[28]

Both the Grossgörschen group and the Capitalist Realists around the

Wolfgang Petrick, Berlin: "State of Affairs" ("Zustände"), 1976, 130 × 110 cm, lead and colored pencils—Berlinische Galerie Berlin. Reproduced with permission of the Berlinische Galerie, Berlin, and of Wolfgang Petrick, Berlin.

Gallery R. Block took Berlin Dada as their jumping-off point. Vostell wrote in retrospect: "My first critical paintings for Berlin in 1964 . . . were the beginning of my new, realistic, and socially critical school arising from Berlin, shaped by Berlin's history, pretested by Dada."[29] In both groups, at least throughout the sixties, political commitment on the part of artists was again in high favor. According to Jürgen Waller, another Berlin realist, "the artist's privilege of expressing himself . . . [involves] the moral duty to relieve society of some of its responsibility."

This moral rigorism of the mid-sixties, encouraged by an extremely emotional debate on an extension of the time limit for the prosecution of war crimes, led many German intellectuals to take up a problem that had been long suppressed or dealt with only superficially, namely that of making peace with the past. In 1967, Alexander and Margarete Mitscherlich analyzed the reasons behind the avoidance of this problem in their much-acclaimed book, *Die Unfähigkeit zu trauern* (*The Inability to Mourn*). They found: "From a backward, aggressive nation under National Socialism we turned, phenotypically speaking, into an apolitical, conservative nation. This is relatively easy to explain in terms of our lack of curiosity about or psychological interest in the motives that made us become the followers of a leader who led us into the greatest material and moral catastrophe in our history. . . . We invested all of our energy . . . in repairing what was destroyed, building up and modernizing our industrial potential, all the way down to the appliances in our kitchens."[30]

It was this period that saw the first hesitant attempts on the part of Berlin artists to address this subject. In 1967, for example, twenty-five years after the SS massacre in the Czechoslovakian village of Lidice, René Block organized an exhibition entitled *Hommage à Lidice* in which twenty-two German artists of the generation born between 1930 and 1938 took part, among them, from Berlin, K.P. Brehmer, K.H. Hödicke, Bernd Koberling, and Stephan Wewerka.

In East Germany, by contrast, anti-Fascist program painting—large, historical canvases—had long been a part of the official policy, for, of course, the leftovers of Nazism, those "Bonn militarists out for revenge," were all in Western Germany. Willi Sitte in particular devoted himself as early as the fifties and sixties to such subjects as *Lidice, Massacre*, and *Memento Stalingrad*. For his depiction of the *National Committee for a Free Germany*, in which officers of the Wehrmacht behind Soviet lines attempted to convince the German army to surrender, Sitte chose the pathos-ridden formula of a triptych with predella. With his painting *The Survivors* of 1963 we are asked to associate "a direct appeal to responsible political behavior." It goes without saying that the forms in this work possess "no autonomy of any kind," since, as East German art historian Hermann Raum concludes, "what counts is their substantive content."[31]

In contrast to Willi Sitte's emotion-laden approach to aesthetics, Brehmer works with such everyday, seemingly innocent elements as postwar overprints of Nazi stamps—Hitler's portrait defaced overnight by the words "Germany's Corrupter"—as if that could eradicate the past.

In the early seventies, another West Berlin painter of the Critical Realist persuasion, Ulrich Baehr, took up the subject of what might be called the

Ulrich Baehr, Berlin: "Deutsche Torsi im Olympia Stadion", 1971; photograph: Riki Kalbe, Berlin. Reproduced with permission of Mr. Ulrich Baehr and Mrs. Riki Kalbe, Berlin.

body language of power. He has solidified these gestures in a number of sculptures such as his *German Torsi*; and in his painting entitled *Five Persons Sitting in front of a Paradise*, done in 1975–76, Baehr excerpts the Allied leaders at the Yalta conference.

When the bombardment of North Vietnam began in 1965, the first organized student actions started on the campus of West Berlin's Free University. On March 26, 1966, Wolf Vostell demanded, in a satirical happening-manifesto in New York: "Instead of dropping bombs on North Vietnam, the U.S. planes ought to bombard the population with fried chicken, chewing gum, Coca Cola, popcorn, cream pies, brassieres, Kleenex, plastic flowers, postcards of The Wall, goldfish, crocheted doilies, freedom bells, lipsticks. . . ."[32] The accompanying illustration was Vostell's silkscreen print of 1968, *B 52*, with actual lipsticks dropping out of the aircraft's bomb doors. In 1973 Peter Sorge drew his embittered *Mr. America*.

When the student Benno Ohnesorg was shot by a policeman during a demonstration against the Shah of Iran's visit to Berlin on June 6, 1967, the hitherto nonviolent student protest movement began to escalate. A concerted campaign on the part of the Springer Press, which controls over 70 percent of the Berlin news market, stamped the students as criminal elements, and the Berlin Senate, university administration and police tended to agree. In the House of Representatives, the Socialist German Students Organization (SDS), which had already been expelled from the Social Democratic party in 1961, was publicly compared to the Nazis. The fact that during the seventies a terrorist group took its name from the ominous date of the Ohnesorg shooting—"The 2nd of June Group"—led many commentators to denounce the entire student movement as preparing the way and providing sympathizers for the terrorist acts of later years.

Although the Berlin Realist painters did sympathize with the victims of a climate of latent violence and fear, many of them produced works characterized by an ironic distance to the events of the protest years. Johannes Grützke, for example, reversed cause and effect in his painting *Benno Ohnesorg Gets his Gun* of 1968: flanked by a guard of faceless zombies, victim becomes culprit. Rudi Dutschke, the student leader who in April 1968 was shot down on the street, is made to look ridiculous by Grützke, whose *Anonymous Triumph* of 1969 shows him in a theatrical pose. Grützke's *Demonstration* of 1968, finally, gives us a worm's eye view of what looks like a very bad music-hall turn, and his *S. Freud, K. Marx, H. Marcuse, and Julius Grützke*, painted the following year, unites the idols of the student movement with the artist's son. Evidently fearing objections, Grützke explains: "Because I paint only from my own mirror image, I disarm all those who accuse me of laughing at others in my work. It is always me—and I do not see the world as better or worse than myself."[33]

His view "that pictures have no effect, that art has never brought anything about" is shared even by painters who, like Arwed Gorella, worked actively for political change during the student movement. Gorella, one of the founders of the New Society for Visual Art in 1969, reflected in his canvas *Lenin, January 1924*, those doubts about the heroic status of revolutionaries that arose during the phase of general resignation after the failure of the student revolt. He pictures Lenin, half paralyzed by a series of strokes, weighted down by cogitation, seated in a wheelchair. (The canvas was removed from an exhibition of West Berlin artists in Moscow.) Behind him, a grimy track leads from the shining halls of theory to the depressing reality of an industrially underdeveloped Soviet Union. And from a poster that graced the walls of many a student's room back then, Karl Marx looks doubtfully down on the man who put his ideas into practice.

In 1972, with a change of members, the Critical Realists formed the Aspect group and once again attempted, in 1977, the year of the European Council exhibition *Tendencies of the Twenties*, to legitimate their "veristic" methods by making direct reference to Otto Dix's triptych on big-city life of 1927/28. Their *Principle of Realism*—the title of a travelling exhibition from 1972 to 1974—was gradually hollowed out during the reform-happy years of the Socialist–Liberal coalition in Bonn until all that remained as a routine "ugly realism." While Otto Dix could still say in the early twenties that he had the feeling that "a side of reality existed that had not yet been portrayed —the ugly side," the shock effect of Klaus Vogelgesang's drawings, executed with old-masterly precision if not obsession, is simply no longer shocking. One critic of Vogelgesang has written: "His draftsmanly virtuosity conserves him as if in a deep-freezer which retains the natural color of peas

without convincing us that they are in any way fresh from the field."
"Where in Grosz's drawings it is obvious that his anger has left no room for
contemplation, Vogelgesang gleefully ruminates his shock effects." Another
reviewer comments that, "True, these Germans as Hermann Albert paints
them... probably actually do look like that. But that's just the problem.
What is meat to a caricaturist or a journalist is poison to an artist." They
no longer portray the castoffs of society, prostitutes or soldiers, like Grosz
did; they depict the man on the street, that "Mr. Everybody whom they
themselves possibly harbor. Their repetition of motifs often inspired by
photographs of sexual or political brutality has brought forth a brand of
program-painting that tends to hysterically confirm rather than deplore
what they attack."[34]

A Critical Realism that had become tired and academic soon provoked the
students of these realists, some of whom had in the meantime become pro-
fessors, to open their own self-help galleries and rent studio space together.
Students of Wolfgang Petrick, himself a founding member in 1964 of the
Grossgörschen 35 group, established a studio in a factory loft on Kulmer
Strasse; students of another charter member of Grossgörschen 35, Karl
Horst Hödicke, organized their own exhibitions in the Gallery on Moritz-
platz. Among them were Helmut Middendorf, Rainer Fetting, Salomé, and
Bernd Zimmer, who were soon to become known far beyond Berlin's borders as a result of the show *Violent Painting* held at Haus am Waldsee in
1980. Although it is true that these artists oppose the in the meantime repeti-
tive rhetoric of their teachers, they conduct this operation, unlike the Critical Realists in the early sixties, without the aid of a theoretical program and
without making any particular moral or political claims for their paintings.
They have again taken up, seemingly effortlessly, the urban themes that were
a tradition in Berlin at the latest beginning with Meidner and Kirchner.

The experience of the Critical Realists of the city, however, has little in
common with Expressionist sufferings of the lonely individual surrounded
by a decaying and vice-ridden metropolis. They move like *Big-City Natives*
(H. Middendorf, 1980–1981) through an *Electric Night* (1981) of disco-
theques, bars, cafés, squares, and streets like human fish in a gigantic aquar-
ium. "Human bodies jerk like lightning through the apocalyptic discorock
night. Rock 'n' roll on the dance floor of the 'Jungle'. A canvas inferno in
ultramarine blue, black, and red—downtown, in the center of nightly neon
ecstasy."[35] This description by Franz Meyer-Siermann applies well to
City of the Red Nights II (1982).

The experiences that Middendorf's paintings convey come across without
help from the critics. They are accepted and understood spontaneously, in
the same places that gave rise to them, in *SO 36* (1980), for instance. For such
rock-music halls in Kreuzberg, the artists created huge canvases and even
appeared on stage there: "Basically we're all rock stars who didn't make it.
Middendorf used to appear with his guitar, Zimmer plays a good bass
guitar," and Salomé sings and plays with the band 'Geile Tiere'. For the first
time, an avant-garde has emerged which apparently feels no gap between the
lonely misunderstood artist and the philistine mass of the kind that Paul
Klee complained of when he wrote, "No people supports us." They express
the feelings of a cool generation: "Take it easy, live your life, but live it

loosely. Don't try to change the world, try to change your attitude towards it. Prefer escape to confrontation and arrange to give your desertion the ironic look of conformity."[36] In this changeover from alienation to disinterest, Pascal Bruckner and Alain Finkielkraut, writing in their *Little Handbook of Everyday Survival*, see a "Renaissance of romanticism" springing from a widespread disgust with normalcy. Escaping from the mundane strictures of the rat race, they rediscover for themselves the city of night as an adventurous and mysterious realm: "Nighttime with its colorful fauna of sleepless wanderers, prostitutes, gigolos, alcoholics, gays, guitar players, funny saints—in the great capitals these night hours carry a scent of secrecy, a whiff of the forests and the vagabond life. You swim in darkness, through a motionless and voluptuous air that caresses you, invites you to stay awhile, bathe in it and forget about going home. . . . You pass by desirable mirages, prowling around for no reason, with no goal. . . . The serious busy capital breaks. . . into completely unrelated pieces,"[37] say Bruckner and Finkielkraut. And the revolution is nothing but "a fallen dream."[38] Why worry about progress, development, plans for the future? "Don't think of tomorrow, I'm living now," says Salomé. "From now on, all that exists is adventure, projects without meaning, a love of chance, a pure desire for intensity,"[39] and a visible rendering of feelings, wishes, dreams, and desires uncensored by the mind. "And let me tell all you cold grey mice to your face, leave me alone, because I've got nothing to do with your thing," sings Lilli Berlin.[40]

Notes

[1] Georg von Gehren, "London/Berlin 2, A Critical Look," in: *Art + Artists*, January 1979, p. 36.

[2] A. Federov-Davydov, *Press and Revolution*, November–December 1924, pp. 116–123.

[3] Quoted from: *Gefühl und Härte. Neue Kunst aus Berlin* (cat.), ed. by Ursula Prinz and Wolfgang Jean Stock, Art Society Munic, Munic 1982, p. 71.

[4] Quoted from: *Berlin—A Critical View. Ugly Realism 20s–70s* (cat.), ed. by Sarah Kent and Eckhart Gillen, Institute of Contemporary Arts and the Berliner Festspiele GmbH, London-Berlin 1978, p. 254.

[5] Karl Marx, *Grundrisse der Kritik der politischen Ökonomie*, 1857/58, reprint of the Moscow edition 1939/1941, Francfort/Vienna.

[6] E. Roters, in: K.H. Hödicke, *Bilder 1962–1980* (cat.), Haus am Waldsee, Berlin 1981, pp. 7, 12.

[7] Quoted from: *Kunst und Künstler* (art magazine), Berlin 1914.

[8] Quoted from: *Menschheitsdämmerung*, ed. by Kurt Pinthus, Berlin 1920.

[9] Manuscript.

[10] Quoted from: *Menschheitsdämmerung*, ed. by Kurt Pinthus, Berlin 1920, p. 7.

[11] Manifesto of the "Vereinigung für neue Kunst und Literatur," Magdeburg 1919, quoted from: Helga Kliemann, *Die Novembergruppe*, Berlin 1969, p. 59.

[12] Quoted from: *An alle Künstler!* Berlin 1919.

[13] Quoted from: *Catalog Willi Sitte*, Kunsthalle Rostock, Rostock 1971, p. 9.

[14] Quoted from: *Grauzonen-Farbwelten* (cat.), Neue Gesellschaft für bildende Kunst Berlin, Berlin 1983, p. 292.

[15] Hans Sedlmayer, *Die Revolution der modernen Kunst*, Hamburg 1955.

[16] Quoted from: *Grauzonen-Farbwelten* (cat.), Berlin 1983, p. 287.

[17] At above, p. 241.

[18] Werner Heldt, "Einige Beobachtungen über die Masse," quoted from: Wieland Schmied, *Werner Heldt*, Köln 1976, p. 77.

[19] At above, p. 90.

[20] Quoted from: *Widerstand statt Anpassung* (cat.), Berlin–Karlsruhe 1980, p. 67.

[21] H.E. Holthusen, *Der unbehauste Mensch*, Munic 1964, p. 128.

[22] Quoted from: Wieland Schmied, *Werner Heldt*, Köln 1976, p. 66.

[23] At above, p. 95.

[24] Quoted from: *Grauzonen-Farbwelten* (cat.), Berlin 1983, pp. 315–316.

[25] At above, p. 319.

[26] Quoted from: *Kulturpolitisches Wörterbuch Bundesrepublik Deutschland/DDR im Vergleich*, ed. by W.R. Langenbucher, R. Rytlewski and B. Weyergraf, Stuttgart 1983, p. 101.

[26a] Quoted from: Thema: *Informel. Zur Struktur einer 'anderen' Zeit* (cat.), Städtisches Museum Leverkusen. Schloß Morsbroich, 1973/ Haus am Waldsee Berlin 1973, p. 16.

[27] Osterberlin-Wahnsinn, quoted from: *Lilli Berlin*, Süss und erbarmungslos, produced by Micky Wolf in June, 1982, music: Manfred Optiz/Harald Grosskopf, text: J. Barz; distributed by the Ariola Group of Companies.

[28] René Block, *Grafik des Kapitalistischen Realismus*, Berlin 1971, pp. 31–35.

[29] Quoted from: *Wolf Vostell—Retrospektive 1958–1974* (cat.), Neuer Berliner Kunstverein/Nationalgalerie Berlin, Berlin 1974, p. 13.

[30] Alexander and Margarete Mitscherlich, *Die Unfähigkeit zu trauern*, München 1967, pp. 18–19.

[31] Quoted from: *Catalog Willi Sitte*, Kunsthalle Rostock, Rostock 1971, pp. 39/40.

[32] Quoted from: René Block, *Grafik des Kapitalistischen Realismus*, Berlin 1971, p. 21.

[33] Quoted from: Thomas Schroeder, "Der Maler Johannes Grützke," *ZEIT—Magazin* No. 38, 1974, p. 26.

[34] Karl Heinz Bohrer, "Die Deutschen, ihr Selbsthaß und sein Abbild," quoted from: *Frankfurter Allgemeine Zeitung*, 6.12.1978, No. 271, p. 25.

[35] Franz Meyer-Siermann, quoted from: *Gefühl und Härte* (cat.), Munic 1982, p. 71.

[36] Pascal Bruckner/Alain Finkielkraut, *Das Abenteuer um die Ecke. Kleines Handbuch der Alltagsüberlebenskunst*, Munic 1981, p. 182.

[37] At above, pp. 230–231.

[38] At above, p. 254.

[39] At above, p. 265.

[40] Verpiss Dich! Quoted from: *Lilli Berlin*, at above, no. 27.

CHAPTER 11

Literary and Cultural Life in West Berlin

Ingeborg Drewitz

Look at the map of Berlin. Follow the border between East Berlin and West Berlin. Better still, walk along the border. You will find that West Berlin forms a large semicircle around the city center of Mitte, as can be seen on any map of Berlin since the mid-nineteenth century. Up until 1945 Mitte was also *the* cultural center of Berlin. West Berlin has been cut off from this center since 1945; its isolation was not, however, complete until the building of the Berlin wall in 1961, and for some years after the Second World War the outstanding places of cultural interest in the city center Berlin–Mitte remained places of all Berliners. The most important ones were the Friedrich-Wilhelm-University, today Humboldt University, founded in 1810, the museums, the former Prussian State Theaters, most of which were destroyed during the Second World War, e.g., the German State Opera (Deutsche Staatsoper). From 1945 to 1955 it was in the Admiralspalast on Friedrichstraße, but it was rebuilt and reopened in 1955 at its old location Unter den Linden. The German Theater (Deutsches Theater) on Schumannstraße, founded in 1883, survived the war. From 1949 to 1954, it housed the Berliner Ensemble of Bertolt Brecht and Helene Weigel which, since 1954, has found its place in the theater on Schiffbauerdamm. The Comic Opera (Komische Oper) on Behrenstraße, a house for opera, musicals, and ballet, reopened in 1947, the Metropol-Theater, a stage for operettas and musicals, in 1945 at the Colosseum; Schönhauser Allee. In 1955, it moved to the Admiralspalast when the German State Opera returned to its old location Unter den Linden, and it has been there since.

For some years after 1945, numerous smaller popular theaters were also outstanding places of cultural interest, "Theater was, up until 1948, the year of the currency reform, of unimaginable importance in Berlin" wrote Friedrich Luft in 1972 in his foreword to *25 Jahre Theater in Berlin, Premieren 1945–1970*.[1]* And, of course, of continuing importance were, and still are, the former Prussian State Library (Preußische Staatsbibliothek) Unter den Linden, now State Library Berlin-East, and the University Library (Universitätsbibliothek). The list is not exhaustive. Many of these institutions had been reduced to rubble by 1945.

---

* See Notes section at the end of this chapter.

In West Berlin the Technical School, founded in 1799, known since 1879 as the Technical College (Technische Hochschule) and since 1946 as the Technical University, and the Dahlem Museums were comparatively unscathed and could be used partially. The Municipal Opera / Deutsche Oper Berlin (Städtische Oper / Deutsche Oper Berlin) and the Schiller Theater had to be rebuilt. Despite the handicaps, cultural work in all districts began to flourish again as early as in the summer of 1945. Cultural departments were set up to support artists at the local level. As one of their most important tasks in the early years, they issued certificates of employment that entitled artists to receive food rations. Few cultural department directors tried to encourage activities on a more wide-ranging level. Notable exceptions here were Dr. Skutsch in the house am Waldsee in Zehlendorf, who promoted music and literature and put on performances of Georg Kaiser's plays, and, later, Dr. Kämpfer in Wilmersdorf, who started a chamber opera. The Palace-Park Theater (Schloßparktheater) in Steglitz put on its first performances in the summer of 1945, in the former stables of the old Prussian diehard Wrangel; Jürgen Fehling directed in a Zehlendorf cinema; the Young Artists' Group, a youth organization of the Democratic Renewal Alliance (Kulturbund zur demokratischen Erneuerung) formed under Russian occupation shortly after the fall of Berlin, held workshop discussions for young writers, painters, sculptors, stage-set designers, and musicians. It also organized concerts in the Titania-Palast-Cinema in Friedenau. One of the most celebrated guest performers was Yehudi Menuhin. The Hebbel Theater in the street with changing names (Königgrätzer Strasse before 1933, Saarlandstrasse from 1933 to 1945, Stresemannstrasse after 1945) became for the years from 1945 to 1951 the most important theater in the Western sectors of Berlin. Jean Paul Sartre came here for the performance of *The Flies*, Thornton Wilder came, and Wolfgang Borchert's *Outside the Door* had its Berlin premiere there where postwar youth met, wrapped in coats and blankets in the winter. But they also went to the Deutsches Theater in the Russian Sector to see Brecht's *Mother Courage*, and to some of those 200 theater groups of various sizes who performed in cellars, barracks, private rooms, gymnasiums, and church halls. Bookshops displayed their selection mainly from the second-hand section, and new publications soon began to appear. The Aufbau Verlag in the Russian Sector started publishing in the first year after the war. Many dates and facts prove that the Berlin of the terrible postwar years was a very lively city in terms of culture. The first radio broadcasts (for example) came in May of 1945; the studios in the Masurenallee were occupied by Russian troops, but soon the Norddeutscher Rundfunk Berlin (North German Radio Berlin) was set up in a house on Heidelberger Platz in Schmargendorf. RIAS (Radio in the American Sector) was founded in 1945 and broadcast from near the Winterfeldplatz. The first newspapers appeared in September. At first the cinemas showed mainly Russian films, but after the Western allies had taken over their occupation zones of Berlin in the summer of 1945, the films shown were mainly those of the occupying nations.

Looking back over this period, I think that the most important cultural event was the first and only Congress of Writers which was held in 1947 in West and in East Berlin, and emigrants as well as authors from all provinces of the former German Reich were invited. The meetings in West Berlin took

The first German Writer's Congress, October 4–8, 1947. Kammerspiele des Deutschen Theaters, ward Mitte, East Berlin. President of honor Ricarda Huch. Photograph: Abraham Pisarek. Reproduced with permission of Dr. Ruth Gross, Berlin.

place in the "Prälat" in Schöneberg, a beer and dance hall with a garden which had often been the venue of mass festivities for Nazis of lower rank. It had survived the war more or less unscathed and, with its large rooms, was well suited for conferences.[2]

Why was this congress the most important event, at a time when exciting developments were happening in the theater, at a time when German youth was moved and heartened by the offers of reconciliation? I think it is because this congress for the first time underlined the power conflict between socialism and capitalism, between the United States and the Soviet Union, in the cultural sphere. Ricarda Huch, the honorary president of the congress, made a memorable speech in which she talked of the crucial task the Germans were facing: to expiate their historical guilt. (Ricarda Huch had resigned her membership in the Prussian Academy of Arts in 1933, following the expulsion of Heinrich Mann and Käthe Kollwitz and, later, of the Jewish members of the academy.) She called upon the delegates to honor the memory of those who had fought against the Nazi regime and who had been executed. It was her last speech. She left Jena in the Russian zone of occupation to move to the West, where she died only three weeks later.

As a result of the currency reform in 1948, many postwar activities collapsed for economic reasons. However, the bomb sites were slowly cleared and new buildings rose up; but the isolation of West Berlin became increasingly evident and an inescapable fact. From 1952 the borders between West Berlin and the surrounding countryside, the Mark Brandenburg, were closed for twenty years. Air, rail, and road corridors were set up, an interzonal passport was introduced for journeys between West Berlin and the Federal Republic of Germany (FRG), and customs regulations hampered a resurgence of Berlin's industry. The city lost its preeminent position as headquarters for the main publishing companies and, despite the Berliner Philharmonie (Berlin Philharmonic), the excellence of its theaters, and the impressive cultural achievements of the reconstruction era, it lost its place as *the* German cultural center. To stop the slide the Berlin Festival was started in 1951 in West Berlin; this half-city was to retain its shop-window function as a center of culture and it succeeded. West Berlin continues to attract visitors from both German states as well as from the whole world. It has regained some of the aura and magnetism of the "golden twenties;" West Berlin remains one of the most interesting centers of German theater, and its

Bauhaus Archives, Klingelhoferstrasse 13–14, Tiergarten; design: Walter Gropius; laying of the cornerstone, May 1976, formal opening, January 12, 1979.—August, 1981. Reproduced with permission of the Landesbildstelle Berlin.

State Library, Potsdamer Strasse 33, Tiergarten (Stiftung Preussischer Kulturbesitz/ Prussian Cultural Heritage Foundation); architect: Hans Scharoun. In the fore- ground: Potsdamer Brücke (bridge) und Landwehrkanal (channel).—August, 1979. Reproduced with permission of the Landesbildstelle Berlin.

position as a musical center has been stabilized. Thanks to the International Building Exhibition held there in the mid-fifties, it has also reclaimed its place as an architecturally significant city, even though the competition was daunting. The city renewal (Stadterneuerung) of Berlin–Kreuzberg and the International Building Exhibition (Internationale Bauausstellung) in 1987 are other examples of West Berlin's regained architectural significance.

In East Berlin, the quality of theater was also remarkable, especially at the Komische Oper and the Schiffbauerdamm Theater and, of course, because Bertolt Brecht, having returned from the United States, lived and worked in East Berlin where he and Helene Weigel started the Berliner Ensemble in 1949. The museums in East Berlin were well looked after and the former Prussian State Library (Preußische Staatsbibliothek) was open to the public. Its stock of holdings, however, was reduced. Since 1940, during the Second World War, the holdings of the Prussian State Library Unter den Linden had progressively been evacuated in order to preserve them in castles, cloisters, mines, etc., situated throughout Germany. There existed, by the end of the war, about thirty salvage locations, the bulk of the books and a huge part of the precious special collections being located in the western occupied zones of the former German Reich. Holdings of the former Prussian State Library which had been evacuated to the eastern occupied zone of Germany were returned to their old location Unter den Linden and became the basis of the now German State Library Berlin East (Deutsche Staatsbibliothek Berlin-

Ost). Holdings which had found asylum in western regions of Germany were brought together in Marburg during the fifties and in the early sixties were forwarded to several locations in West Berlin where they were kept until the new State Library, Foundation of Prussian Cultural Heritage (Staatsbibliothek, Stiftung Preußischer Kulturbesitz) on Potsdamer Straße, built by Hans Scharoun from 1967 to 1978, was ready to accommodate them. Prior to the end of 1978, access to these holdings of the former Prussian State Library was difficult, but since the 1st of November, 1946, books, already replaced on the shelves of the University Library of Marburg, could be hired out. And in West Berlin, on the 17th of September, 1954, the Amerika-Gedenkbibliothek / Berliner Zentralbibliothek (America Memorial Library / Berlin Central Library) was founded as a public library. It increased its stock over the years and has now become one of the most-used libraries in West Germany.

Free University of Berlin, Auditorium Maximum; Altensteinstrasse 40, Dahlem district. November 4, 1954. Reproduced with permission of the Landesbildstelle Berlin.

In 1949, the Freie Universität Berlin (Free University Berlin) was founded in Dahlem, West Berlin. Cofounders were professors and students: students who for political reasons were not accepted at the Humboldt University in the Soviet Sector of Berlin, and professors who did not agree with political prerequisites for university studies, teaching, and research. Honoring the mutual decision to work at a free university, its students were granted codetermination in administrative and academic decisions. This was a new structure which did not please the traditional universities in West Germany though it had come about without discussions as a matter-of-factness grown out of the attitude of the founders of this university, professors and students, united by their desire for academic freedom. Soon, the Free University had outgrown its original campus and achieved a solid academic reputation, despite the misgivings from traditional universities in West Germany. It was not without a certain touch of irony of history that, from 1967 to 1969, the Free University produced, along with Frankfurt and Heidelberg, many of the leaders of the student revolution, first and foremost Rudi Dutschke.

Other important cultural events during the fifties and sixties include the extension of the Dahlem museums, the restoration of Schloß Charlottenburg, the reconstitution of the Prussian Academy of Arts (Preußische Akademie der Künste) as the Academy of Arts, the building of its new house on Hanseatenweg by Werner Düttmann, the building of the Neue Nationalgalerie (New National Gallery) by Mies van der Rohe, the building of the Berliner Philharmonie and the Neue Staatsbibliothek, Stiftung Preußischer Kulturbesitz (New State Library, Foundation Prussian Cultural Heritage) by Hans Scharoun, the building or rebuilding of schools, sports facilities, churches, and the start of the Berlin Film Festival, the foundation of the Deutsche Film- und Fernsehakademie Berlin (German Film and Television Academy Berlin) as well as the foundation of the Hochschule der Künste (University of Arts) for pictorial art, music, and theater. . . and more. The destruction during the war had been so immense, and the rivalry with East Berlin tailed off after the building of the Berlin wall.

Although I emphasized the Writers' Congress of 1947, I have said very little about literature and writers in the city. West Berlin was no longer a real or innovative literary center. As mentioned before, the major publishing houses moved away in the fifties. Furthermore, a glance at the theater programs of this time shows very few premieres of plays by contemporary German authors. There was too much German literature of the twenties to catch up with, and publishers of plays were besieging their editors with translations from British, American English, and from French. The works of the English "angry young men" attacking the staleness of petit-bourgeois postcolonial society were also at the height of their popularity at that time. Plays not dealing with bombings or genocide had an irresistible appeal. From the mid-fifties on, the trend was increasingly away from the examination of war, prison, and post-war experience, and from the reflection on what kind of state the Federal Republic of Germany should be. Well, throughout the country existed small groups of writers but only one of them became important and widely known, and even this one did not create a new German literary movement. One met, one discussed finished works, works in the state of being finished or in progress, and tried to further one another, but one did not even think of arriving at a common and binding new literary manifesto. In Berlin, the writers who had formed the Group of 12[3] began to go their own different ways from 1952 onwards as their works were published. Gottfried Benn, who had been enthusiastic about Jens Rehn's first novel *Nichts in Sicht* (Nothing in Sight), died in 1956. A few weeks later Bertolt Brecht, who had promoted a number of young Berlin authors, including Horst Bienek and Arnim Juhre, died in East Berlin. Bienek was now in prison in Workuta. Brecht and Paul Dessau had been forced to make changes in the opera *Lukullus*. East Berlin and the German Democratic Republic (GDR) no longer had a literary center either, even though literature held a place of pride in the state's cultural policy. In the Federal Republic, a number of writers with both political consciousness and literary ambition contributed to the magazine *Der Ruf* (*The Call*) and established in 1947, after their magazine had been banned by the American occupying authorities, annual meetings which under the label Group 47 soon emerged as *the* literary center of West Germany. By 1953/54, it had become a kind of literary stock exchange; publishers and radio editors regularly attended the conferences. The first conference outside West Germany was held in 1954, in Cap Circeo, south of Rome. At that time, the examination of recent German history seemed to have been concluded. In 1955, 1962, and 1965 the Group 47 met in West Berlin where Wolfdietrich Schnurre, one of its founders, lived. Some Berliners were invited to the conferences of the Group 47 but the group developed no particular bonds to Berlin.

The particular reality of life in West Berlin, with its hundreds and thousands of refugees coming in daily by Stadtbahn (street car) and underground, its subsidized affluence despite steady but slow emigration to West Germany: this reality was as little reflected in contemporary literature as was the problem of German fascism. Reality, quite clearly—so the argument ran—was the "material of experience in movement" and as such could not be interpreted. Of course, Berlin and Berlin authors were on the alert. Robert Wolfgang Schnell, Günter Bruno Fuchs, and sculptor Günter Anlauf founded the gallery Die Zinke in Kreuzberg, the first step towards the discovery of Kreuzberg as a bohemian district. Günter Grass, who had written *Die Blechtrommel* (*The Tin Drum*) in Paris, returned to Berlin in 1960. His success in Group 47 was the drumbeat which heralded an era of renewed literary interest in recent German history. Uwe Johnson moved to West Berlin before the wall was built. His first novel, *Mutmaßungen über Jakob* (*Suppositions about Jacob*), dealt with life in the GDR at the time of the Hungarian uprising in 1956 and was a major success. The Berlin branch of the German Authors' Association held a congress on nonfiction books, which started to make an impact on the postwar book market.

After the building of the wall, a deliberate policy of promoting young authors was introduced, by giving them grants to live in Berlin. However, this undertaking was—and still is—too inadequately financed to produce any significant impulses. A major impulse did, however, come from the Ford Foundation, which awarded substantial grants to authors wishing to live in Berlin for a year. Ingeborg Bachmann was one of the beneficiaries, as was Witold Gombrowicz, who coined the phrase "the glittering thing West Berlin," an apt description of the Berlin of the early and mid-sixties. Walter Höllerer, professor at the Technical University, organized well-attended readings by authors in the largest lecture hall and in 1963, he founded the "Literary Colloquium," which also serves as a meeting place, a workshop, a small publishing company, and a film production center. Writers from the GDR as well as from the Federal Republic read from their works at the Siegmundshof students' residence hall of the Technical University. After the building of the wall, this was a sensation.[4] From 1965 on, the Association of

German Writers also began to make important contributions to the city's literary activities. It invited Nelly Sachs and Mascha Kaléko back to her home town and sponsored the first exhibition on the literature of emigration, written by the authors of the New York Aufbau Verlag. It drew attention to the literature by and on workers in the sixties as well as to Turkish literature—there were large numbers of Turkish guest workers in the city by now. It stressed the importance of the literature of resistance in Latin America and of revolutionary writing in Greece and Portugal. More and more literary pubs and cafés opened up, even in the years of the student revolution with its slogan "literature is dead." Klaus Wagenbach founded his publishing house in Berlin, and the Rotbuch Verlag consolidated its position after a split. The Oberbaum Verlag and the Elefanten Presse were founded as the alternative publishing scene became increasingly important throughout West Germany. The Schaubühne on Hallesches Ufer, still the most renowned of West Berlin's Theaters, now on Lehniner Platz, performed the works of a number of young playwrights. The literature and work circles started literary workshops; galleries included readings in their programs; and the Neue Gesellschaft für Literatur (New Society for Literature) developed its programs from 1974 onwards. The Authors' Bookshop (Autorenbuchhandlung) was founded, the second of its kind in West Germany, the shareholders being several hundred authors, whose works are permanently available there. Then there was the opening of a new cultural center in Carmer Strasse. This center houses the Young Booksellers' Club run by Klaus Peter Herbach. Political bookshops abound in this area, and around the corner are the headquarters of the DAAD (German Academic Exchange Service), which awards grants to artists so that they can spend a year in Berlin. Berlin is a lively city: about 800 authors live there; most of them, however, merely vegetate because the radio and TV stations do not have enough programs to accommodate so many writers, the newspaper scene is extremely limited for such a large city, and the theater managers and publishers do not go into the writers' cafés looking for authors. Nonetheless, new initiatives are starting up constantly, such as theater groups and street theaters, if the weather permits. The Bethanian Arts Center (Künstlerhaus Bethanien) at Mariannenplatz in Kreuzberg, for example, was formerly a hospital and was saved from demolition by a local citizens' action group. It is now a cultural center with studios, a fine refectory, and exhibition rooms. It is also a meeting place for the Turkish population of Kreuzberg. Here, Turkish artists seeking political asylum can work and exhibit their art.

West Berlin: a city to live in. A city with a strangely and dangerously hectic atmosphere, where everyone is preoccupied with himself and scarcely notices the others, a fact which particularly strikes writers expelled from the GDR who are now living in West Berlin. Authors who have sought political asylum in the city are equally aware of its atmosphere. Well-known authors have left the city or leave it for long periods. They are rarely seen in the pubs these days. Berlin is a city to work in if you try to read and explore the reasons for this particular atmosphere instead of feeling hustled by the city's hectic race. Sensitiveness towards political developments is one of the preconditions of artistic work in Berlin; without it, it is impossible to grasp the city's reality.

Some years ago I argued that West Berlin is the fifth center of German literature in Europe—the others being West Germany, East Germany, Austria, and Switzerland. And I would like to repeat this claim and to stress that Berlin literature—as all city literature—has primarily been literature by outsiders who have come to live in the city. Berlin literature cannot be limited in meaning to literature written in the Berlin sociolect. There is no Berlin school comparable to, for example, the Viennese school. Anyone who has read the Berlin-based magazine *Litfaß*, edited by emigré Assen Assenov, will be fully aware of this. Berlin is a city that remains in an absurd political situation, a city in constant danger of losing the balance of this absurdity. Life in this city compels authors to heighten the precision of their feeling, their perception, and their hearing; no Berlin author can escape this rule. Here we find the brilliant expression of rage in the work of Yaak Karsunke; melancholic cynicism in Botho Strauss; injured love turning into laughter in the work of Günter Bruno Fuchs; pleasure in disgust in the recent prose of Christoph Meckel; half laughter and half indictment in the work of Peter Schneider; laughter, which sticks in the throat, at petit-bourgeois inhibitions (Robert Wolfgang Schnell); self-analysis in the precise and impersonal style of Wolfdietrich Schnurre; leaflet-style texts and analytical plays for young people by Volker Ludwig and Eckart Hachfeld. All these works are just as much Berlin literature as the pounding rhythms I try to give my prose, and which Uwe Johnson used so successfully in his "Stadtbahn" (city railway) text.

The influence of Romance literatures in Berlin has always been slight. Today this influence makes its presence felt in the work of the Chilean emigrant Antonio Skarmeta and in the works of Argentinian writers who have escaped persecution. The main impact has been in the political text, in films, and in the discovery of the literature of resistance. The influence of twentieth-century North American literature in the new Latin American texts in unmistakable.

Berlin is also a place where diverse influences can converge and cooperate. The most notable example of this is expressed in the films which director Peter Lilienthal and scriptwriter Antonio Skarmeta have produced. In recent years, we have also seen the discovery of modern Turkish literature, this, too, being a literature of resistance, in which European and Turkish traditions meet. In translation, this literature also has its recognized place in the Berlin cultural scene.

Look at the map of Berlin. Follow the border between East and West Berlin. Better still, walk along the border. Then you will realize by your own experience that to live, write, paint, draw, sculpt, or compose in this city is to be confronted daily with the reality of absurdity.

Notes

Dr. Ingeborg Drewitz, writer, coshaper, and coorganizer of democratic literary and cultural life in West Germany, died in 1986. The last proofs of this chapter were read by the editor and by Dr. Dietger Pforte, Director of the Section Literature, Library- and Archive-System at the Senate for Cultural Affairs, Berlin.

[1] Registration of the theater premières in Berlin during the first twenty five years after the Second World War, edited by order of the Senate of Berlin, 1972, p. 12.

[2] The information by Ingeborg Drewitz, a very reliable personality as well as a highly careful writer, can't be doubted. However, all files of the Prälat in Schöneberg prior to 1953 having been discarded, and up to now no proof could be found that meetings of that congress also took place in the Prälat. Photographs show that the Deutsches Theater on Schumannstraße was at least its prominent "stage." Testimonies about events in the Prälat in Schöneberg would be highly appreciated.

[3] From the beginning of the fifties up to approximately 1956, some writers and one musician met for literary workshops at least twice if not four times a month in the homes of members. Hence, twelve was set as the upper limit for the number of participants in a meeting. The Group of 12 never made its public appearance. As Bernhard Drewitz remembers, it started after the Working Group of Young Artists, founded in 1947, had split. "Motor" of the Group of 12 was Joachim Cadenbach. Besides him, Arnim Juhre and Ingeborg Drewitz kept the group alive for some years. Some others joined the meetings quite regularly, among them Johannes Hendrich, Jens Rehn, Alice Frommholz, and Maria König, the life companion of J. Cadenbach. They were the core of the Group of 12.

[4] These readings took place from 1964 until 1966. The organizers were Burkhard Mauer, who later became a dramatic producer, and a student named Wege. The readers came from both half-cities and from the GDR as well as from the FRG. From the GDR came, e.g., Paul Wiens, Johannes Bobrowski, Volker Braun, Sarah and Rainer Kirsch, Jens Gerlach, Karl Mickel, Günther Deike, and Heinz Czechowski; from West Berlin, e.g., Friedrich Christian Delius, Marianne Eichholz, Günter Grass, Christoph Meckel, and Volker von Törne. The most spectacular event was probably a discussion on February 5, 1965, in the Academy of Arts, directed by Uwe Johnson and with the participation of Paul Wiens and Günter Grass.

Personal Experiences in a World Capital

CHAPTER 12

Berlin's Portrait in Prose

Walter Höllerer

Berlin became a modern metropolis at the end of the nineteenth century, and it was then that—with Theodor Fontane—Berlin prose achieved the quality of world literature, and young writers found an honest critic and promoter. The Literary Colloquium Berlin (Literarisches Colloquium Berlin), founded in 1963, works in an old house of that time on Lake Wannsee, and inscribed on this house, in big letters, is the year it was built: 1885. It was once the home of an industrialist. Then, Berlin was hailed in the following way by the poet Julius Hart:

Die Fenster auf!	Open the windows!
Dort drüben liegt Berlin!	Berlin is over there!
Dampf wallt empor und Qualm!	Steam is rising, smoke!

An enthusiastic poem! Smoke was welcome at that time as a positive symbol of industrial activity. Open the windows! Steam is rising, smoke!

In 1889, naturalistic stories called "Papa Hamlet" appeared by an author by the name of Bjarne P. Holmsen; Scandinavian authors were successful in early naturalism. Hidden behind the Norwegian pen name, however, were the two German writers Arno Holz and Johannes Schlaf, and the Berlin of backyards and cold water flats made its appearance in German prose.

With Holz began the many attempts to use action snapshots of Berlin from which universal models for modern literature could be built. Out of elements from Berlin, a whole universe was constructed, quite uniquely, for example, by authors such as Scheerbart, Carl Einstein, Alfred Döblin, Paul Gurk, Erich Kästner, to Gabriele Tergit, Uwe Johnson, and Christa Wolf—to name but a few.

Holz lived for a time in a garret in Berlin-Wedding, a working-class residential district of the city. In his giant epic *Phantasus* (1898), a combination of verse and rhythmic prose, he brings together glimpses of his Wedding surroundings, his own biography, and the universe. He sees the streets of Berlin in the morning in living color; he writes, for example, of a bakery boy on the back of a hearse:

On the end of a funeral car, next to a basket of rolls
piggy back
a bakery boy
happy and content
and
whistling
his legs dangling, the wagon trotting,
the fog swallows him up.

I will return to this snapshot of a morning in the streets of Wedding.

Behind such beginnings of naturalism stands the figure of the great Berlin novelist Theodor Fontane, the author of *Jenny Treibel*, who lent a younger generation of writers his good will, his sympathy, and his criticism. His scenes of salons, of the bourgeoisie and the aristocracy, his rides and walks through the Grunewald and on the Kreuzberg capture the literary portrait of Berlin.

At the beginning of the twentieth century, Berlin became more and more bustling, even hectic. Just before the outbreak of the First World War in

Alexanderplatz with the Berolina (monument), from the Königstrasse; Mitte district, East Berlin.—1898. Reproduced with permission of the Landesbildstelle Berlin.

1914, the city was inundated with the apocalyptic visions of the early Expressionists. "The End of the World" runs the title of a poem by Jakob van Hoddis which reflects the atmosphere: "The hat flies off the burgher's pointed head." We are reminded of pictures like those of George Grosz. The glowing god of the city, the burning god of money and war, Baal, sits among the factories, as Georg Heym saw it. The din of war was heard in advance by the poets. From a century ago, the cry of Bertha von Suttner's *Down with Weapons!*, still rang in one's ears whilst visions of horror and ultimate destruction pushed into the foreground. Owing to Kurt Pinthus, these facts are known worldwide as far as poetry is concerned. The Berlin Expressionist prose is still rather unfamiliar; it is compelling but enigmatic, spilling over with metaphors, and imbued with Berlin black humor.

An example is Jakob van Hoddis's "Doctor Hacker's End," in a city seen as a battlefield of feelings, thoughts, intrigue. Dr. Hacker's end is the end of a man who tries, in this city of Berlin, to reflect on reality and facts, e.g.; who, in the city of Berlin, has visions; who, in the city of Berlin, dreams of great halls made of black rock; who dreams of a stairway for giants, and who stumbles down these stairs for giants. Hacker argues with a pale, high-strung young man. He bangs his head against the wall. He shouts: "A different world, a new world!" By the end of the story, it reads: "He put on his coat and rushed out of the house. The streets were empty. A milkwagon rattled by. The chairs stretched their legs out of the café windows. A little white dog ran across the street and ate him up."

Alfred Lichtenstein belonged to the group of young Berlin Expressionists. He was the creator of the coffee house "Café Klößchen" (Café Meatball), and the inventor of the poet Kuno Kohn. "Lame Day came limping in. Smashed the rest of the night with an iron crutch. The half-extinguished Café Klößchen lay there in the soundless morning, a shining piece of glass. In the background sat the last customer. Kuno Kohn had sunk his bobbing head down into his own hunchback. His whole body cried out without a sound."

The Café Meatball of Lichtenstein's story was Berlin's most famous literary café, the "Roman Café." It was there that writers of the magazine *Sturm* and the publisher Herwarth Walden met; it was there that the first Dada-voices were heard, the first impulses of Surrealism felt. Carl Einstein. The Charon-People, and the Cosmologists.

Many of the young writers were to die in the First World War: Alfred Lichtenstein, August Stramm, Ernst Stadler, Georg Trakl, and others. The Dadaists created a counterculture to the structures of Western civilization—regulated and then destroyed by military means. At the end of the First World War, people thought that military slogans had finally been exhausted.

The Twenties. Let's take the year 1923, the year of the great inflation in Germany. The value of the mark on September 30, 1923, $1 = 50 million marks; on October 22, 1923, $1 = 40 billion marks. On November 15, 1923, the new currency was introduced, the so-called Rentenmark ("Pension mark"). Everybody's savings were lost.

In 1923 Kurt Schwitters writes his story "Auguste Bolte," which takes place in Berlin. It is a story which parodies computer logic and computer structure, in connection with modern city structure. Remember: the com-

Roman Café (Charlottenburg); left: Budapetser Strasse, right: Tauentzienstrasse from the Auguste Viktoria Platz.—About 1935. Reproduced with permission of the Landesbildstelle Berlin.

puter, as a technical instrument, wasn't even invented at this time! But computer thinking was imaginable, especially in a city like Berlin. Auguste Bolte finds herself in a situation in which she can make decisions only in the most absolute way, yes for yes, no for no; no subtle distinctions in between. In this manner, she races through the city, wanting and trying to keep in touch with people, groups of people, while in the meantime these groups are subdividing into smaller groups. During this hectic activity, running here and there, she must gradually jettison her possessions, rid herself of encumbrances, literally down to her clothing, and so she gets poorer and poorer. She does all of this not with the intention of living as such, but to attain the academic goal of becoming a "Dr. leb.," a Doctor vitae, a doctor of life. It's to no avail that there's a typical Berlin advice-giver in the story, the Berliner ne'er-do-well standing on the street corner and calling over to the preoccupied and over-wrought Auguste: "Nonsense, Auguste, better get married!" And what is the last stop of this "computer run" through the city of Berlin? At the end of the story, Auguste is standing on military training grounds, the outcome of a yes-yes-no-no computerized curriculum vitae. As a post scriptum, Schwitters parodistically notes: "The hammer hovers above. The catastrophe approaches."

To me, the history of the story is of special interest. It was written in 1922, the year of my birth. In 1923, it was published. In 1963, we revived the completely forgotten story and published it in my magazine *Akzente*. And in 1983, the year of Mr. Computer in the U.S.A., I could recommend it to everyone.

In 1929, the great Berlin tableau of Alfred Döblin, *Berlin Alexanderplatz*, appeared: a universal novel, with Berlin's role comparable to that of predecessors like Dublin in *Ulysses* and Manhattan in Dos Passos's *Manhattan Transfer*. A city novel with Berlin's rhythm and Berlin articulation, Berlin slang, Berlin body language, the sign language of the city districts and social classes; with the Berlin system of transportation and its social structures. With the psychic problems of Franz Bieberkopf in the late twenties: the political struggles that ruled the streets and seized the minds of people, in the middle of Berlin, in Wedding, in Moabit. But this novel is not just a Berlin novel; it is also a novel by the author of *Mountains, Seas, and Giants*, a mythological novel. The present serves as an example for mythical reality. Statistics—like that of the slaughterhouse, for example—go together with pagan and Greek and Hebrew mythologies.

In 1931, shortly before the Third Reich, a novel of a female Jewish journalist from Berlin reached the bookstores: Gabriele Tergit's *Käsebier Conquers the Kurfürstendamm*. The novel is not known well enough. It wasn't until 1977, when it was brought out in a new edition, that it was really discovered. During the Third Reich it was taken out of circulation. The novel shows the speculating Berlin of the Kurfürstendamm, the journalistic milieu, the rituals of art, of the entertainment industry and its promoters; it depicts the ruin of a limited but well-meaning popular actor: big money uses him for a while for big business. In part, the book can be read as a Berlin *roman à clef*, if you like; the authoress worked for the *Berliner Tageblatt* and based her characters on real people.

By assembling a number of Berlin pictures and images, Gabriele Tergit caught the beginning of the Hitler era in Berlin. A few chapters were published in the magazine of the Literary Colloquium Berlin (LCB) *Sprache im technischen Zeitalter* (Language in the Technical Era), vol. 80, October 1981, and in the LCB book *Autoren im Haus* (Authors in the House) in 1982.

The mood in Berlin, the sudden change of opinion in newspaper editorials, in the courts, in intellectual circles, the indecisiveness in Berlin Jewish families, the false hopes, the destructive optimism in Berlin at the beginning of the thirties—it's all there for you to read about firsthand.

For example, to quote from Tergit on the last public protest of intellectuals in Berlin on February 20, 1933, in the Krolloper (Kroll Opera House): "The beautiful room was almost empty. Instead of a thousand people there were about fifty who'd appeared. Underneath the lectern sat a police officer. He stared into an opened file folder. Tönnies (one of the assembled intellectuals and friends of G. Tergit in the Berlin of the Weimar Republic) spoke about academic freedom. Olden (another) spoke about freedom of the press. Wolfgang Heine, fraternity student, social democrat, minister of justice after 1918, spoke about freedom of assembly. The police officer let Tönnies and Olden speak. As Heine read a sentence from 1904 or 1905, the police officer said, 'The meeting is declared closed.' And that was that."

Roman Café (Charlottenburg); left: Budapetser Strasse.—1946. Reproduced with permission of the Landesbildstelle Berlin.

Gabriele Tergit was over thirty at the time. I was eleven in 1933. The eleven-year-old got some news by way of Berlin. On May 10, 1933, in the public action called "Against the un-German Spirit," the books of undesirable writers were burned in Berlin. I was told that my favorite author was among them—Erich Kästner. My favorite book then was *The 35th of May*.

The city of Berlin was for me, largely on account of Kästner, a city of literature. There was Kästner's fictional Uncle Ringelhuth in Berlin, and besides, I had a real uncle in Berlin, too, and he had books as well. I visited him in 1936. We had to read then in school, as a requirement of the Nazi regime, a selection from Ernst Jünger's *War as an Inner Experience*. The book maintained that the basic order of life was that of the army, of military order, no matter what area of life one is talking about. Jünger's images and his thesis were offensive to me. I was walking with my uncle through the streets of Berlin Tempelhof, the area he lived in, and I asked him what kind of writer Jünger was. My careful uncle said. "They say he's a good stylist." "What's a good stylist?" "Someone who knows how to express himself well." "Well, is this Jünger a good writer then?" "You'll have to find that out for yourself," my uncle replied. He was a clever didact, just like Kästner's Onkel Ringelhuth in *The 35th of May*. That remark started me down the long literary and critical road.

Truth and reality in Berlin in the forties was destruction. A number of prose works gave a picture of the destruction and portraits of the destroyed city: for example, Margaret Boveri's *Days of Survival, Berlin 1945*. In her many scenes and dialogues, without hate and artifice, she rendered the service of abolishing the stereotypes of the enemy. Stereotypes existed, and continue to exist, chiefly in opposition to the Russians, but also to the Americans. Margaret Boveri tore down the stereotype through observation and through narration of direct confrontation in Berlin. Here is a sample of her experience of the city she knew, in altered circumstances: "May 8, 1945. I rode my bike into the city for the first time, for the first time too in a dress, instead of the filthy dirty pants I'd been wearing for weeks. The nearer I came to the zoo, the more desolate it got. The Gedächtniskirche seen from Kantstraße looks really strange. The spires were meant originally to be pointed, but from the impact of the many bombs, the central one is all rounded off and the smaller ones flattened." The writer Wolfgang Koeppen experienced something similar in finding the Roman Café, that focal point of Expressionist literature, totally demolished.

In and around Berlin in the thirties and forties, many writers met their death: in prisons, in transit, in death cells, on the gallows, in concentration camps, in air raids, and through suicide: Gertrude Kolmar, Jakob van Hoddis, Carl von Ossietzky, Jochen Klepper, Albrecht Haushofer, Felix Hartlaub, and others.

Berlin after 1945: at first it was one Berlin, then Berlin with four zones, then finally Berlin in two halves, separated by a wall into an eastern half and a western half. The most typical Berlin Berliner among writers after 1945 was Günter Bruno Fuchs. "Berlin Berliner" means: born in Berlin. Again and again, in verse and in prose, he practiced the principle of permeability between the two city halves, in his written and actual journeys and city wanderings. An example to many, he practiced to be a kind of naive "good soldier Schweik" writer, dealing with politics. Fuchs portrayed in his prose work the East–West statute that keeps Big Brothers in one's own home. He imagined it this way: next to a West Berliner stands an American. Next to an East Berliner stands a Russian. At least that's the way it is in the mind of the Berliners. The result is this Fuchs story:

> On the street corner stands a snowman. Next to the snowman stands a man. Next to the man stands a second snowman. Next to the second snowman stands a second man. The two snowmen are listening to the conversation of the two men. The two men don't notice and go on talking as usual.

The story is a description of the climate in Berlin as well as advice on how to behave for citizens living in a mutual political disaster.

Similar "good soldier Schweik" stories, written by a young unknown author by the name of Arthur Knoff, have been published by the Literary Colloquium in the fifth volume of the LCB editions. They are simply called *Stories*. On closer look, the author isn't so unknown: it is the well-known writer Günter Grass whose only short stories are published there. The photo on the cover of the book doesn't show Günter Grass but Anna Grass instead, albeit sporting a moustache. The story "Slow Waltz" in this volume portrays Günter Grass's Berlin as a place of agent activities. Of course, the poetic images of Fuchs and Knoff don't tell everything about the divided city. In her Berlin stories, Ingeborg Drewitz portrays that fate: division which causes alienation among Berliners from different parts of the city.

In two descriptions of the city, the serious difficulties of communication

Meeting in the garden of the Literary Colloquium Berlin (Am Sandwerder 5, Wann-see district) on the occasion of the event called "Summer Nights Dream".—1985. Photograph: Renate von Mangoldt. Reproduced by permission of the Literary Collo-quium Berlin and Mrs. Renate von Mangoldt, Berlin.

are explored, one written in the East and one in the West. The one in the East is by Christa Wolf, with the title *The Divided Sky*; the other, *Two Views*, written in the West, is by Uwe Johnson. In another book by Christa Wolf, called *Cassandra*, she writes not just about the difficulties of com-munication but especially about the dangers of war in our time. She shows very penetratingly the hopes which are connected with the peace movement in both parts of Berlin. It is a peace movement that comes from the people themselves and is not manipulated by official political forces from the out-side.

Let me come back to my opening image from Arno Holz: you remember, the bakery boy whistling on the back of the hearse, on a Berlin morning, in Berlin-Wedding, the fog enveloping him.

I was in Wedding a few years ago looking for a spot from where I could look down over the whole area. I found an artificial hill, a big old bunker from the Second World War. They wanted to blast it out of existence after the war, but it was so well constructed that they couldn't get rid of it. It was left there and the top was planted over. In a couple of spots, you could look down into the empty dark belly of this concrete hill. It was early in the morning when I was there. From down below came the city sounds of Wedding. And up there on the top you suddenly heard other remarkable sounds:

BUNKERBERG BERLIN-WEDDING

The hill, made of concrete, slopes
down into bomb nights.
Out of the concrete
on top the steel mesh
sings
excitedly, loudly
with all-out effort and quicksilvery,
a tiny bird.

Is this the Berlin situation? Or is it the situation of all men? "The sound makes the music," goes the old German saying. Or: "It's all in the way you say it." The sound and the fury. How far will today's sounds take us? The sound of speech brings people together. The sound of speech draws them apart. To me, this observation concerns not merely our modest field of literature.

CHAPTER 13

The Portrait of Berlin in Lyric Poetry

A. Leslie Willson

Founded around 1230, rather late by European standards, Berlin became a mighty metropolis by the end of the nineteenth century, after decades of increasing distinction as a center of commerce, government, industry, art, and culture. Poets enjoyed the central location of the city and its exposure to music, art, and publishing. But poetic inspiration—finding private love, abstract longing, and encounters with nature more attractive and popular— was not inclined to commemorate the city itself. Berlin was no different from a dozen other cities when it came to poetic portrayal, and a mountain fastness or the unearthly beauty of a desolate heath were more likely to be memorialized in verse than the streets and monuments, and the bustle of a city. Drama, even on a small and intriguing scale, is an essential part of a poem—and cities were not yet dramatic; certainly not to the extent that Berlin became dramatic as time went on.

Poems in which Berlin figures—as a city, as the populace of a city, as a historical monument—cannot be characterized as chronicles. Poetic treatments of Berlin in one or another of its aspects rather resemble photographs, snapshots, anecdotes, or snatches of conversation. Description may take place, but it is severely limited by the very form of the poetic vehicle. Nevertheless, the city does emerge, as do its residents and the historical events that define it.

There are today more poets per square kilometer in Berlin than in any other city in East and West Germany. My research produced over forty, most of them contemporary, who have treated the city in poetic form. Not all are residents of Berlin; some have moved away from either East or West Berlin, either voluntarily or by force, and some have taken up residence there, drawn by the vitality of the city that has persisted despite ravages of war and political upheavals. Berlin is a paradox—not one but two cities; a unique place—West Berlin is an island surrounded by an essentially hostile host; Berlin is an exasperation to its residents, both East and West; Berlin is a symbol of past glory, a scene of present frustration, an unyielding presence in the minds and souls of Germans East and West. Berlin is magnetic.

One of the earliest modern treatments of the city is by a visitor from Switzerland, Gottfried Keller, who in the poem "Berliner Pfingsten" (Whit-

Unter den Linden (formerly via triumphalis of Berlin), Mitte district, East Berlin; at right: opera house; in the background: palace.—1901. Reproduced with permission of the Landesbildstelle Berlin.

sun tide) wrote an early and mild version of a twentieth-century slogan: "Make love, not war." Sometime in mid-century, when Keller (born in 1819) was still a young man, he described a street scene with the exuberant exultation of youth.[1]*

In the early years of the twentieth century, Frank Wedekind wrote a poem dealing with the pending political travail that lay in wait for the monarchy. In an amusing but nonetheless earnest way, it warns not to impute certain zoological characteristics onto the person of the king. The poem is entitled "Der Zoologe von Berlin" (The Zoologist of Berlin). It relates the story of an incautious zoologist whom a policeman arrests after an ostensible defamation of the king, who has evidently been given an animal epithet. The poem alludes to anarchists and state informers, but despite the plight of the luckless zoologist, who gets a year in jail because of his inappropriate remark concerning the monarch, the poem hints at the fascination Berliners still have for animals, particularly those on display in the zoo. The zoo becomes a bit of Berlin that is more than simply cages, that is also broad expanses of

---

*See Notes section at the end of this chapter.

The Tiergarten (Zoological Gardens), Tiergarten; southwestern section, Landwehr-kanal.—May, 1981. Reproduced with permission of the Landesbildstelle Berlin.

lawn and tree-shaded promenades.[2] Probably in the early years of the century, Arno Holz echoed the sentiments of Gottfried Keller in a poem with the title "Brücke zum Zoo," (Bridge to the Zoo)[3] whose center of action is located near a bridge that leads to the zoo.

The zoo is a great attraction in this most urban of cities, and from it poets lead their readers to its surroundings and beyond—to streets, houses, squares, waterways, and, above all, to people interacting with the city. The desirable location of a street receives the attention of Aldona Gustas in a poem from the seventies entitled "Jebensstraße" (Jeben Street)[4]. The preference of a place to live in proximity to the zoo, as well as the scarcity of housing in Berlin in the seventies, is expressed in the following poem by the late Günter Bruno Fuchs:

TO THE HOUSING BUREAU, TIERGARTEN[5]

We would like
on behalf of my family

> to apply for the
> apartment at 40 Huttenstraße,
> one-and-a-half rooms
> with kitchen and
> without a bath.
> Moabit
> is well located for us. I work
> here in a small café. My wife
> hasn't far to go when our
> two boys, both a year
> apart, want to go swimming
> in the canal right at the end
> of Huttenstraße
> in the summer.
>
> (Up to now
> we've never had water nearby.)
>
> I have
> looked at the apartment. Find it
> good. My papers are coming to you
> from the Housing Bureau
> in Kreuzberg, because there's no
> vacancy there right now.

The traffic in human desire that centered in the early part of the century in the vicinity of the Alexanderplatz is mentioned in the poem "Meine Groß-mutter, z.B." (My Grandmother, e.g.) by East German poet Kurt Bartsch, one of several in which he memorializes his sturdy and indefatigable grandmother.[6]

In the early years of the twentieth century, on the eve of war and surrounded by the unrest of exploited workers, the city became the subject of laments, protests, and warnings of the Expressionist poets. Though most did not mention the city by name, the specter of the ravenous heathen god Baal became for them a symbol of the destructive forces at work in the great city. But even then the city was loved, despite its oppressive masses.

In those years Johannes R. Becher, in the poem "Berlin! Berlin!," called the city a "cement rose," magically illuminated by lanterns.[7] Georg Heym wrote three poems in which Berlin plays a role, not only in their titles. The first, "Berlin I," is full of the noise and storm of traffic, but toward evening the city dwellers are lulled by a dreamy twilight.[8] Ernst Blaß, in the poem "Kreuzberg 1," catches the enormity of the city and the mixed anxieties of its residents, the fury and fire of disaster, the ambivalent attitude of its citizenry.[9] In the poem "Blauer Abend in Berlin" (Blue Evening in Berlin), Oskar Loerke describes the oceanlike, strandlike character of the heaving city, which tosses its human flotsam and jetsam like a great sea.[10] Kurt Bartsch used a tale told by his mother to capture the restless mood of the city and the impending political changes in the poem:

SHOTS SCREAMS STILLNESS

While my father's fighting with the police,
My mother's making soup for the commune
Three bowls apiece, she says, fighting makes you hungry.
What is it? asks Thälmann. Gulash soup, says my mother.
She got the money for the meat from her sister
Whose name is Mary, who has TB, and who's a streetwalker.
Afterwards they all sit companionably together
At Hoppe's, on Fischerstraße, the gramophone is playing
The *Internationale*, it's May, the door
To the restaurant is open, outside two men
Wearing brown shirts pass by. Bunch of shits,
Says my mother. Yes, says Otto, while
My father orders beer for everybody and again
Puts on the *Internationale* PEOPLES HARK
The sirens shots shouts stillness

(*Kaderakte*, 13)

Then came the disaster that reduced the city by a million residents, turned
it into rubble, and split it into opposite halves. Shortly after the war, in 1948
at Easter, Robert Wolfgang Schnell expressed unquenchable hope at a historically reminiscent moment in a poem entitled "Easter 1948 at the Grave
of Kleist."[11] The might and the glory of Berlin past is conjured up in an
elegiac poem by Günter Eich from the years immediately following the war.
It is called "Berlin, Hafenplatz" (Harborplace).[12] But the tenacity of hope
and the immediacy of a vital present against the background of a devastating
past is found in Walter Höllerer's poem:

BUNKERBERG BERLIN-WEDDING[13]

The hill, made of concrete, slopes
down into bomb nights.
Out of the concrete
on top of the steel mesh
sings
excitedly, loudly
with all-out effort and quicksilvery,
a
tiny bird

Günter Grass, in his long poem "The Great Rubble Woman Speaks,"[14] im-
mortalized the woman who sat amidst the rubble pounding the mortar from
bricks so that the city could make use of them in its insistent rebuilding.

> The city the city
> strewn all about lies Berlin,
> with firewalls it leans against winds
> that come out of the east south west, out of the north
> all intent on freeing the city.

The city survived, came alive with amazing agility, and exotic sights walked the streets again, like a memorable glimpse once noted by Elisabeth Langgässer in her poem "Berlin, Negress on Friedrichstraße."[15] The city asserted itself amidst the broken, exposed firewalls, erstwhile keepers of advertising slogans and now a symbol of the city's broken body. Those firewalls are acknowledged by Grass in the poem "Firewalls." The last line of the poem is a presage of the distress and unrest that enveloped the young people of Berlin in the sixties, caught, as they were then, by currents of the enduring cold war and the heated outrage over Vietnam:

FIREWALLS

> I greet Berlin by thrice
> butting my forehead
> on one of the firewalls.
>
> Impeccably sawed out
> it casts a shadow there
> where your property once stood.
>
> A soap ad and its blue survived
> on one of the walls to the north;
> now it's snowing, which proves nothing.
>
> The wall advances toward me
> blackly without firewall inscriptions,
> it looks over my shoulder.
>
> Until a single snowball sticks.
> A boy threw it because something
> deep inside him was all wrong.

(Grass, 76)

Then came a visible and audible sign of the sentiments that wrought a divided city. In 1961, in a few days of hectic travail, a wall was erected through the center of Berlin, physically separating the two hearts that beat in that one body. Volker Braun epitomizes the viewpoint that loyally adheres to the policies of the Germany east of the wall in his poem "The Wall,"[16] which reads in part:

1

Between the unusual cities that have
The same name, amidst all the concrete
Wrought iron, wire, smoke, the shots
Of motors: in this unusual land's
Marvelous monument stands out from all that
A construction, noticeable among the marvels,
In this astonishing land
Foreign soil...

...Terrible
A border of stone, it
Prevents what knows
No border: war. And it contains
In a peaceful land, for it must be strong
Not weak, those who run off to the wolves
The lambs...

2

Who behind newspapers
Bark at the concrete, singed
By radio signals, bolt from the dust
Of building sites or at the barbed wire
Harp among their buddies and
Scrape tunnels under the churches: the
Blind chickens will find themselves
Caught in gunsights.

. . .

No wall separates us

That's crap made of concrete, get
Rid of it, with blowtorches
Cut it to bits, with crowbars
Level it to the ground: when they no longer
Head off at the risk of their hides,
Maul the wall down. When those who
Want to change borders are powerless
Break down the border. The last tank
Will crush it and vice versa.
So that it's gone.

But leave it for now.

But another citizen of East Berlin, Kurt Bartsch, has a different view of the
wall, a personal and private view that involves his now-dead grandmother.
The poem is entitled

HADES

My grandmother, much beaten old woman
(Her husband, a miner, died of drink)
Lies buried at the wall between East and West.
When I go to her in the summer/winter
Into the realm of the dead (ivy barbed wire
Grows from the graves, Warning! BORDER AREA)
I have to have a permit, which I show
On demand to Cerberus,
Guardian of Hades, disguised as a People's Policeman.

(*Kaderakte*, 54)

Wall at the border to East Berlin, Zimmerstrasse (Kreuzberg district).—November, 1983. Reproduced with permission of the Landesbildstelle Berlin.

W. Alexander Bauer, in the poem "The Wall," paints a sober and sad portrait of the wall.[17] That portrait takes on lighter tones in a poem characteristic of the resilient Berliner, exemplified by Karl Oppermann in "Berliner Chic."[18] Yaak Karsunke, in his poem "berliner mauer," (Berlin

Wall) describes how the children of West Berlin adapt to an intrusive, visibly
separating object such as a wall.[19]

The existence of the Berlin wall made the separation of the two cities,
painfully felt by residents of both, even more definitive. Kurt Bartsch comments on the now restricted access and egress in his poem

STILL LIFE WITH CLEANING WOMAN

Grass grows between the dead rails
Here the commuting train once traveled
From West to East East to West
THE DOORS ARE CLOSING STAND BACK
The rails are rusting, the bridges
Cross over dead streets, the streets
Blocked by walls, concrete, so
I won't run off, says Trudie. Oh,
Such extravagance for one who can
Do nothing but wipe off steps, scrub floors
She smiles, so we've got
To stay here, don't you think?

(*Kaderakte*, 57)

One of the most-used crossings into East Berlin is the Friedrichstraße Rail
Station, where residents of West Berlin and strangers with passports can
enter East Berlin for a few hours (until midnight) without a visa or other
special documents. In an anecdotal poem entitled "Bahnhof (Station)
Friedrichstraße,"[20] Dieter Schlesak describes the feelings of such a visitor
from the West after an evening of theater in the East, the visitor (and his East
German hosts) being ever mindful of the midnight deadline that hangs over
wandering apparitions. Karl Oppermann, in a short poem, wryly points to
the potential strength built into human beings, lodged in the brain alone:

NATIONAL SECURITY

Naked we crossed the border
the customs official warned us:
Import of weapons
is prohibited.

(*Mauer*)

Bertolt Brecht watched for a few years over the most prominent theater and
theatrical troupe in the world of German theater before the wall was built.
Kurt Bartsch records a vision of Brecht in the following poem:

CHAUSSEESTRASSE 125[21]

Brecht sits as always, you know,
In the rocking chair and snow
Falls on the graves below
Brecht rocks to and fro
And sucks on his cigar
That never cooled by far
Smoke climbs black from the roof peak
The winter has already gone weak
His cap hangs on its nail
Sleet falls as does hail
Soon there'll be lettuce (until
You'll have had your fill)
Brecht rocks on as then
He's happy once again
Then it's eight at night
No one turns on a light
When I look over there
The rocking chair is bare.

But unlike his compatriot Brecht, who remained in good standing with the East German authorities until his death, Wolf Biermann found himself forbidden to perform in public for many years prior to his expatriation in 1976. The predicament of Biermann awakened the sympathy of fellow poets in the West, as in the poem by Johannes Schenk,[22] dedicated to Biermann in 1969:

I'LL BRING YOU A FRIEDRICHSSTADT PALACE

When we cross the border on Sundays
in my left pants pocket I'll stick
with the penny
with the whiskey bottle
or in my jacket a Friedrichsstadt palace
with 7000 people for you
we'll set it up at your place
Your mother will make Chinese tea
and the people from my pants pocket
will take seats in your hurdy-gurdy
one or two on the ukele
and your friend in the belly of the guitar
when you sing
We're already looking forward to it Natasha
and I and the other 7000
I hope when we cross the border
my pocket won't bulge much
Open the door for us now

Reiner Kunze, himself an expatriate of East Berlin, describes his experience listening to a Biermann song, recorded by the sharp-witted, dulcet-voiced cabaret singer in the seclusion of his East Berlin apartment:

WOLF BIERMANN SINGS[23]

In my room the tram screeches along
it screeches from Biermann's record so,
who when he recorded the song
had no studio.

He sings of Barlach's great despair,
we all feel that scar,
since we all know the ban that's there
and listen to the streetcar.

Poets sympathize with poets; many poets like and admire other poets, and poets in East and West Berlin write about their fellow poets. Volker Braun has recorded a lyrical reminiscence of a visit by Hans Magnus Enzensberger. He also felt a kinship to West Berlin poet Christoph Meckel, noted in his poem "An Meckel."[24] Elke Erb, too, mentions her husband, compatriot East Berliner Adolf Endler, in the poem

POETS DWELL IN THE CENTURIES[25]

Poets dwell in the centuries,
this one in that, that one in this, one overlaps,
One right in the middle like another who also dwells in the middle.
Well and good. Endler stretches from '30 to '90 in his.
Otherwise, poets also dwell in apartments like this one,
Which Endler owns, for example, small quarters, sixth floor,
Without bath, backside, outside toilet, but sunny.
When the poet Endler sticks his head out of the window,
he's looking to see whether the trash cans are empty.

In the sixties and early seventies, West Berlin became a battleground. In its streets and parks an aroused youth, troubled and yearning for peace, caught up in a worldwide turmoil of doubt and questing, argued and demonstrated and came into conflict with established authority. Wolf Biermann wrote a song about the assassination attempt on radical critic Rudi Dutschke.[26] The temper of the times was caught by the late Nicolas Born in 1968 in his poem "Berliner Para-Phrasen."[27] At about the same time, Yaak Karsunke outlined one aspect of the mood of Berlin in the following poem:

TAXI TO THE VIETNAM CONGRESS

Berlin, 17.2.1968

to the Technical University? Will we
even get there?
the street people are meeting there!

a man driving a taxi gives information
when nobody's asked him, sees red
when he sees a red traffic light, gives off gas
when he steps on the gas, says such a thing
& once there was no such thing
once there was still order
at least order & today
well, you say so yourself

he drives behind the past
steps on the gas when he sees red
answers when no one has asked
hands back change, takes the tip
steps on the gas & drives on
with a worndown profile

a man
in a taxi

(*Karsunke*, 18)

The East German denial of Wolf Biermann's reentry led to a succession of departures from East to West, some forced by pressure and others willingly undertaken. In 1977 Jürgen Fuchs left East Berlin. No departure from home is easy, and the poets like other expatriates did not easily fit into new surroundings. Fuchs mentions the difficulty of acclimatization in a poem entitled simply "25.9.78":[28]

25.9.78

You need maybe five years, then you'll be
like this here, he says and makes a
gesture. I came in '71
in a car trunk. For some
it goes quicker, for others slower,
he says and shrugs his shoulders.

And a year later, in another short poem, he still thinks of the other Berlin:

NEVER
is the street empty in front of my house
Cars always drive past
In four lanes

Where to
And why
I don't know

I know only
That two years ago
My street was another street
And my house another house

Günter Kunert's removal from East Berlin in the summer of 1979 left
behind much bitterness. Kunert has a keen eye and sense of form. In several
poems he encompassed the East Berlin scene, as in "Berliner Nachmittag"
(Afternoon).[29] He intones a somber view of existence, as in "Berliner Toten-
tanz" (Dance of Death).[30] And a poem like his "Anzeige Berlinerisch"
(Advertisement) [*Fortgang*, 42] presages a worldwide wasteland. His own
creeping and increasing discontent, and his realization that he is not alone in
feeling so, manifests itself in the poem "Mitbürger" (Fellow Citizen).[31] But
it is a scene like the one he describes in the poem "Belagerungszustand"
(State of Siege) that impelled him to take the step he had resisted and that
finally drove him away from the East and into a small village in the West,
away from the sights and smells and pressures of Berlin:

STATE OF SIEGE[32]

No matter where to leaving whatever
always
sure of the reason: Because Sunday
and in front of my house three cars
hour after hour
in the back seat Marx Engels Lenin Stalin
ad usum Delphini

They come directly from the headquarters
of Utopia in Berlin-Lichtenberg
smoke and read newspapers and
expect the counter-leap
of my poor and timorous words
freshly hatched migratory birds
pathfinders
to a place where a conversation about trees
is not muffled by silence
to a place where nobody
shuts off speech

And after moving his wife, six cats, and a treasured collection of Biedermeier toys to Itzehoe, Kunert bade a melancholy farewell to the city he loved in lines he entitled simply "Berlin."

BERLIN

There's nothing more
to describe. Instead
concrete scoffs at all remembering
and boxes up inhabitants forever.
Gone the inscrutable labyrinths
wretched rooms gloomy stores
and the Sansouci of deafening taverns
every evening
the gleaming gravity of toiletry shops
full of color and brushes made
by real blind people and old women
framed by windows
were guarantees for endurance and permanence.
Patiently and silently
time corroded in factory courtyards:
a lively song of death
and in the darkness
of a soon-forgotten driveway entrance
lurked bliss without name:

Now everything is named and measured
recorded and torn down
and nothing left there
to describe.

(*Abtötungsverfahren*, 43)

But Berlin endures. Even with the overabundance of elderly people, noted by Rainer Malkowski in his somewhat sarcastic poem "Altenpark in Berlin" (Park of the Elderlies in Berlin),[33] the birth of new Berliners is celebrated, as by the transplanted Viennese poet Gerald Bisinger in "Jetzt als Sohn Johann August" (Now as Son Johann August),[34] which is about his son born in Berlin in 1977. In another poem, in which he muses about for whom he might be writing, Bisinger strikes a personal tone seen more and more by Berlin poets: it is the Berlin of everyday existence, a personal, enjoyable, comfortable, fussy, loving existence. A poet such as Gerald K. Zschorsch can condemn both the parts of the city and their functionaries and establishment leaders, as he does in the poem "Friede doch den Hütten, Krieg den Palästen" (Peace to the Huts, War against the Palaces)."[35] Or Frank-Wolf Matthies, also formerly at home in the East, can celebrate the city of Berlin with its Western visage as he sees it now and which he expresses in his poem of liberation and hope:

NO LONGER OF WINTER[36]

& even like that the city is
as lovely & as tender as my
lover: saturday and
sunday at the midday
of darkness or
monday in Berlin's
zone 45. yes
even like that & all shrewdness
baffles me. knocks me over
or like what's left
of twenty cigarettes
what's left of soot
& pain. like honeyed kisses

or like rike
when she hums a song

   . . .

yes, the city is like her
I muse & stand at the window
with the tea glass (franz
joseph practices standing up
with mother mathilde)
or she is like the city
(but the comparison is lame)
although: the city is lovely

& like rike
when she hums a song

& proud, man, it is proud
(which is good)—the dialect
crosses the yard: laughs & waves
up—who can do anything
to me? what do I care
about microphones, brain specialists
& dreams written down. yes indeed
sir, I salute the
diplomat cemetery & I
salute the wall & make
a song for françois villon
& the strength is there again
to push the cause ahead (ours: yours
& mine—the others'),
to show impatience
: she does that & the city does
(in my heart the beginning
of two february eyes)

> & like rike
> when she hums a song

Berlin is still the goal of eager visitors from beyond the city's limits. The island-city visited by West Germans has its charms. A typical visit results in sending postcards to friends back home, an occupation witnessed in many a Berlin bar, as described by F. C. Delius in his poem "Zeig mal dein Visum" (Show Me Your Visa).[37] The mood of the city is quite different than it was ten or fifteen years ago. Delius, in the poem "Ruhige Minute in Steglitz" (Silent Moment in Steglitz), catches the present repose mixed with hope for the future (Delius, 73). But it takes the observant eye and ear of a visitor like famous Munich poet Wolf Wondratschek to sum up the vitality of Berlin, the resilience of its citizenry, and the enduring wit and tenacity of Berliners in the poem

KEMPINSKI[38]

> The taxi driver takes the following standpoint:
> "they shoulda torn down Berlin and rebuilt it
> in the West, on Luneburg Heath or wherever;
> all we do here is what the Russians want
> —and it sometimes works and sometimes never."
>
> The old restroom lady laughs,
> when I mention an election booth.
> She would like to have a go at it,
> "but ya can't do that when you got nary a tooth!"
>
> The hotel maid is in love
> and politics is not for her.
> Berlin? "She's an old lady
> who dreams no more of a lover."
>
> The night porter makes it short.
> What's the choice, after all?
> The East is Communistic
> and the West is sentimental.

There it is: Berlin, in the fancy of poets, but not an imaginary Berlin, not an abandoned Berlin, rather a city that has lived through upheavals almost beyond description, a proud city that will continue to change and struggle and be. The image presented here barely touch the statements of poets who try again and again to come to terms with the marvel that is Berlin. Much more has been said and written; much more will be said and written. Poets move on; but poems and Berlin remain.

Notes

Poems translated by A. Leslie Willson, with one exception: "Bunkerberg Berlin-Wedding," which was translated by the author Walter Höllerer. The original German texts are given in the Appendix.

[1] In *Mein Gedicht ist die Welt I. Deutsche Gedichte aus zwei Jahrhunderten*, ed. Hans Bender (Frankfurt am Main: Büchergilde Gutenberg, 1982), p. 311.

[2] Bender, *Mein Gedicht*, pp. 339–340.

[3] Bender, *Mein Gedicht*, pp. 355–356.

[4] In *Berliner Malerpoeten*, ed. Aldona Gustas (Berlin: Nicolaische Verlagsbuchhandlung, 1974), p. 35.

[5] Günter Bruno Fuchs, *Die Ankunft des großen Unordentlichen in einer ordentlichen Zeit* (Berlin: Wagenbach, n.d.), p. 68.

[6] Kurt Bartsch, *Kaderakte* (Reinbek bei Hamburg: Rowohlt, 1979), p. 14. Further reference in the text under *Kaderakte* and page number.

[7] In *Mein Gedicht ist die Welt II. Deutsche Gedichte aus zwei Jahrhunderten*, ed. Wolfgang Weyrauch (Frankfurt am Main: Büchergilde Gutenberg, 1982), p. 49.

[8] Georg Heym, *Gedichte*, ed. Christoph Meckel (Frankfurt am Main: Fischer, 1968), p. 55.

[9] Weyrauch, p. 116.

[10] In *Das große deutsche Gedichtbuch*, ed. Karl Otto Conrady (Kronberg/Taunus: Atheneum, 1977), p. 765.

[11] Gustas, p. 100.

[12] Weyrauch, p. 257.

[13] Walter Höllerer, *Gedichte 1942–1982* (Frankfurt am Main: Suhrkamp, 1982), p. 199. English translation of poem by Höllerer.

[14] Günter Grass, *Gesammelte Gedichte* (Darmstadt: Luchterhand, 1971), p. 153. Further reference in the text under Grass and page number.

[15] Weyrauch, pp. 242–243.

[16] In *In diesem Lande leben wir*, ed. Hans Bender (Munich: Hanser, 1978), pp. 96–98.

[17] W. Alexander Bauer, *Straßen der Unrast. Gedichte* (Munich: Delp, 1971), p. 1.

[18] Karl Oppermann, *An die Mauer geschrieben* (n.p., n.d.), unnumbered page. Further reference in the text under *Mauer*.

[19] Yaak Karsunke, *Reden & Ausreden* (Berlin: Wagenbach, 1969), p. 35. Further reference in the text under Karsunke and page number.

[20] Dieter Schlesak, *Weiße Gegend—Fühlt die Gewalt in diesem Traum* (Reinbek bei Hamburg: Rowohlt, 1981), p. 95.

[21] Conrady, p. 1077.

[22] Johannes Schenk, *Die Genossin Utopie* (Berlin: Wagenbach, 1973), p. 13.

[23] Conrady, p. 1062.

[24] Volker Braun, *Gedichte* (Leipzig: Reclam, 1979), p. 134.

[25] Elke Erb, Keiner schreit: Nicht! (Berlin: Wagenbach, 1976), p. 20.

[26] In *Vaterland, Muttersprache. Deutsche Schriftsteller und ihr Staat von 1945 bis heute*, ed. Klaus Wagenbach, Winfried Stephan, and Michael Krüger (Wagenbach: Berlin, 1979), pp. 265–266.

[27] Wagenbach et al., p. 264.

[28] Jürgen Fuchs, *Tagesnotizen* (Reinbek bei Hamburg: Rowohlt, 1979), p. 51. Further reference in the text under page number.

[29] Günter Kunert, *Warnung vor Spiegeln* (Munich: Hanser, 1970), p. 59.

[30] Günter Kunert, *Im weiteren Fortgang* (Munich: Hanser, 1974), p. 41. Further reference in the text under *Fortgang* and page number.

[31] Günter Kunert, *Unterwegs nach Utopia* (Munich: Hanser, 1977), p. 90.

[32] Günter Kunert, *Abtötungsverfahren* (Munich: Hanser, 1980), p. 50. Further reference in the text under *Abtötungsverfahren* and page number.

[33] Rainer Malkowski, *Was für ein Morgen* (Frankfurt am Main: Suhrkamp, 1975), p. 55.

[34] Gerald Bisinger, *Gedichte: Auf Leben und Tod* (Basel: Nachtmaschine, 1981), pp. 12–13.

[35] Bender, *Lande*, pp. 66–67.

[36] Bender, *Lande*, pp. 68–70.

[37] F.C. Delius, *Kerbholz. Gedichte* (Reinbek bei Hamburg: Rowohlt, 1983), p. 97.

[38] Wolf Wondratschek, *Chuck's Zimmer* (Munich: Heyne, 1981), p. 274.

Appendix

AN DAS WOHNUNGSAMT TIERGARTEN
Günter Bruno Fuchs

Möchten uns
im Namen meiner Familie
bewerben um die
Wohnung Huttenstraße 40,
anderthalbe Stuben
mit Küche und
ohne Bad.
Moabit
is jünstig für uns. Bediene
hier in einer Speisejaststätte. Meine Frau
hats nich weit, wenn unsre
zwee Jungs, beede ein Jahr
aussenander, mal schwimm jehn wolln
im Sommer gleich im Kanal
von der Huttenstraße
am Ende.

(Bis jetzt
Hatten wir keen Wasser in der Nähe.)

Habe mir
die Wohnung besichtigt. Findse
jut. Papiere bekommen Sie rüberjeleitet
vom Wohnungsamt
Kreuzberg, weil da im Augenblick
allet voll is.

SCHÜSSE SCHREIE STILLE
Kurt Bartsch

Während mein Vater sich mit der Polizei prügelt
Kocht meine Mutter Suppe für die Kommune
Drei Teller für jeden, sagt sie, Prügeln macht hungrig.

Was gibt es, fragt Thälmann. Gulaschsuppe, sagt meine Mutter.
Das Geld für Fleisch hat sie von ihrer Schwester
Die Mary heißt, Tbc hat und auf den Strich geht.
Nachher sitzen sie alle gemütlich zusammen
Bei Hoppe, Fischerstraße, das Grammophon spielt
Die *Internationale*, es ist Mai, die Tür
Zur Kneipe offen, draußen gehen
Zwei Mann in Braunhemden vorbei. Scheißhaufen
Sagt meine Mutter. Ja, sagt Otto, während
Mein Vater Bier bestellt für alle und noch mal
Die *Internationale* auflegt VÖLKER HÖRT
Die Sirenen Schüsse Schreie Stille

(Kaderakte, 13)

BUNKERBERG BERLIN-WEDDING
Walter Höllerer

Der Berg, betoniert, fällt ab in
Bomben-Nächte.
Aus dem Beton
auf der Stahlkralle
singt
aufgeregt, laut
mit aller Anstrengung und quecksilbrig
ein
winziger Vogel.

DIE GROSSE TRÜMMERFRAU SPRICHT (EXCERPT)
Günter Grass

Die Stadt die Stadt
Hingestreut liegt Berlin,
lehnt sich mit Brandmauern gegen Winde,
die aus Ost Süd West, aus dem Norden kommen
und die Stadt befreien wollen.

BRANDMAUERN
Günter Grass

Ich grüße Berlin, indem ich
dreimal meine Stirn an eine
der Brandmauern dreimal schlage.

Makellos ausgesägte,
wirft sie den Schatten dorthin,
wo früher dein Grundstück stand.

Persil und sein Blau überlebten
auf einer Mauer nach Norden;
nun schneit es, was gar nichts beweist.

Schwarz ohne Brandmauerinschrift
kommt mir die Mauer entgegen,
blickt sie mir über die Schulter.

Ein einziger Schneeball haftet.
Ein Junge warf ihn, weil etwas
tief in dem Jungen los war.

(*Grass*, 76)

DIE MAUER (EXCERPTS)
Volker Braun

1

Zwischen den seltsamen Städten, die den gleichen
Namen haben, zwischen vielem Beton
Eisen, Draht, Rauch, den Schüssen
Der Motore: in des seltsamen Lands
Wundermal steht aus all dem
Ein Bau, zwischen den Wundern
Auffallend, im erstaunlichen Land
Ausland. . . .

. . . Schrecklich
Hält sie, steinerne Grenze
Auf, was keine Grenze
Kennt: den Krieg. Und sie hält
Im friedlichen Land, denn es muß stark sein
Nicht arm, die abhaun zu den Wölfen
Die Lämmer. . . .

2

Die hinter den Zeitungen
Anbelln den Beton und, besengt
Von den Sendern, sich aus dem Staub machen
Der Baustellen oder am Stacheldraht
Unter Brüdern harfen und
Unter den Kirchen scharrn Tunnel: die
Blinden Hühner finden sich
Vor Kimme und Korn.

. . .

Uns trennt keine Mauer

Das ist Dreck aus Beton, schafft
Das dann weg, mit Schneidbrennern
Reißt das klein, mit Brecheisen
Legts ins Gras: wenn sie nicht mehr
Abhaun mit ihrer Haut zum Markt
Zerhaut den Verhau. Wenn machtlos sind
Die noch Grenzen ändern wollen
Zerbrecht die Grenze. Der letzte Panzer
Zerdrückt sie und sie ihn.
Daß sie weg ist.

Jetzt laßt das da.

HADES
Kurt Bartsch

Meine Großmutter, vielgeprügelte Alte
(Der Mann, ein Bergarbeiter, starb am Schnaps)
Liegt an der Mauer zwischen Ost und West begraben.
Wenn ich im Sommer/Winter zu ihr gehe
Ins Reich der Toten (Efeu Stacheldraht
Wächst aus den Gräbern, Achtung! GRENZGEBIET)
Muß ich ein Schriftstück haben, dieses zeige
Ich auf Verlangen vor Herrn Cerberus
Wächter des Hades, verkleidet als Volkspolizist.

(*Kaderakte*, 54)

STILL-LEBEN MIT PUTZFRAU
Kurt Bartsch

Gras wächst über die toten Gleise
Hier fuhr einst die S-Bahn
Von West nach Ost Ost nach West
DIE TÜREN SCHLIESSEN ZURÜCKBLEIBEN
Die Schienen rosten, die Brücken
Überquern tote Straßen, die Straßen
Mit Mauern verbaut, Beton, damit
Ich nicht stiften gehe, sagt Trude. Ach
Soviel Aufwand für eine, die nichts
Kann als Treppen wischen, Fußböden scheuern
Sie lächelt, da muß man ja
Hierbleiben, finden Sie nicht

(*Kaderakte*, 57)

STAATSSICHERHEIT

Karl Oppermann

Nackt passierten wir die Grenze
der Zöllner warnte:
Einfuhr von Waffen
verboten.

CHAUSSEESTRASSE 125

Kurt Bartsch

Brecht sitzt wie eh und je
Im Schaukelstuhl und Schnee
Fällt auf die Gräber hin
Brecht schaukelt her und hin
Und lutscht an der Zigarr
Die nie erkaltet war
Rauch steigt schwarz aus dem Dach
Der Winter ist schon schwach
Die Mütze hängt am Nagel
Es fallen Stein und Hagel
Bald gibt es Blattsalat
(Bis man genug von hat)
Brecht schaukelt noch ein Stück
Er hat noch einmal Glück
Dann ist es abends acht
Kein Licht ist angemacht
Da seh ich einmal her
Der Schaukelstuhl ist leer.

ICH BRING DIR EINEN FRIEDRICHSTADTPALAST

Johannes Schenk

Wenn wir sonntags über die Grenze gehen
stecke ich in meine linke Hosentasche
neben den Pfennig
neben die Schnapsflasche
oder in die Jacke einen Friedrichstadtpalast
mit 7000 Menschen für dich
den bauen wir auf bei dir
Deine Mutter macht Tee aus China
und die Leute aus meiner Hosentasche
setzen sich in deine Radleier
ein oder zwei auf die Ukulele
und deine Freundin in den Gitarrenbauch
wenn du singst
Wir freuen uns schon drauf Natascha

ich und die andern 7000
Hoffentlich wenn ich am Grenzer vorbeigeh
beult die Tasche nicht so
Mach schon mal die Tür auf für uns

WOLF BIERMANN SINGT
Reiner Kunze

Im zimmer kreischt die straßenbahn
sie kreischt von Biermanns platte,
der, als er die chansons aufnahm,
kein studio hatte.

Er singt von Barlachs großer not,
die faßt uns alle an,
denn jeder kennt doch das verbot
und hört die straßenbahn.

DIE DICHTER WOHNEN IN DEN JAHRHUNDERTEN
Elke Erb

Die Dichter wohnen in den Jahrhunderten,
Dieser in jenem, jener in diesem, einer lappt über,
Der andere mittendrin wie der andere, der auch mittendrin wohnt.
Schön und gut. Endler erstreckt sich von 30 bis 90 in seinem.
Sonst wohnen auch die Dichter in Wohnungen wie dieser,
Die z.B. der Endler besitzt, Quartierchen fünfter Stock,
Badlos, Hinterhaus, Außenklo, aber mit Sonne.
Wenn der Dichter Endler seinen Kopf zum Fenster rausstreckt,
Sieht er nach, ob die Müllkübel leer sind.

TAXI ZUM VIETNAM-KONGRESS
Yaak Karsunke

:berlin, 17.2.1968

zur technischen uni? na komm wir
da überhaupt hin?
da tagt doch der pöbel!

ein mann fährt ein taxi, gibt auskunft
wenn keiner gefragt hat, sieht rot
wenn er rot sieht an ampeln, gibt gas
wenn er gas gibt, sagt sowas
& damals da gab es das nicht
damals da gabs doch noch ordnung

wenigstens ordnung & heute
na sagen Sie selber

er fährt der vergangenheit nach
gibt gas wenn er rot sieht
gibt antwort wenn keiner gefragt hat
gibt kleingeld heraus, nimmt das trinkgeld
gibt gas & fährt weiter
mit abgeriebenem profil

ein mann
in einem taxi

(*Karsunke*, 18)

25.9.78
Jürgen Fuchs

Du brauchst vielleicht fünf Jahre, dann bist du
so, wie das hier, sagt er und macht eine
Handbewegung. Ich bin einundsiebzig
gekommen, im Kofferraum. Bei dem einen
geht es schneller, bei dem anderen langsamer,
sagt er und zuckt mit den Schultern.

NIE
Jürgen Fuchs

NIE
ist die Straße vor meinem Haus leer
Immer fahren Autos
Vierspurig vorbei

Wohin
Und warum,
Weiß ich nicht

Ich weiß nur
Vor zwei Jahren
War meine Straße eine andere Straße
Und mein Haus ein anderes Haus

BELAGERUNGSZUSTAND
Günter Kunert

Wohin auch immer wovon weg
ist immer

der Benennung sicher: Weil Sonntag
und vorm Hause drei Autos
Stunde um Stunde
im Fond Marx Engels Lenin Stalin
ad usum Delphini

Sie kommen direkt aus dem Hauptquartier
der Utopie in Berlin-Lichtenberg
rauchen und lesen Zeitung und
erwarten den Widersatz
meiner armen und zaghaften Worte
frisch geschlüpfte Zugvögel
Wegbereiter
dorthin wo das Gespräch über Bäume
kein Schweigen mehr bindet
dorthin wo keiner einem
die Sprache verschlägt

BERLIN

Günter Kunert

Da ist nichts mehr
zu beschreiben. Stattdessen
verhöhnt Beton alles Eingedenken
und verschachtelt Bewohner für immer.
Fort die unergründlichen Labyrinthe
klägliche Zimmer düstere Läden
und das allabendliche Sansouci
betäubender Kneipen
der glanzvolle Ernst der Seifengeschäfte
voll Buntheit und Bürsten gebunden
von wirklich Blinden und alte Frauen
von Fenstern gerahmt
bürgten für Dauer und Fortbestand.
Geduldig und schweigend
korrodierte in Fabrikshöfen die Zeit:
eine lebendige Weise von Tod
und im Dunkel
einer schon bald vergessenen Toreinfahrt
lauerte das Glück ohne Namen:

Jetzt ist alles benannt und vermessen
abgeheftet und niedergerissen
und nichts mehr da
zum Beschreiben.

(*Abtötungsverfahren*, 43)

NICHT MEHR VOM WINTER
Frank-Wolf Matthies

& auch so ist die stadt
schön & zart wie die
geliebte : samstag wie
sonntag am mittag
der finsternis oder
montag in der berliner
fünf&vierzig. ja
auch so & alle klugheit
verblüfft mich. haut mich um
oder wie der rest
von zwanzig zigaretten
von ruß & schmerz der
rest. wie honigküsse

oder wie rike
wenn sie ein lied summt

. . .

ja, die stadt ist wie sie
denke ich & stehe am fenster
mit dem theeglas (franz
joseph probt mit mutter
mathilde den aufstand)
oder sie ist wie die stadt
(aber der vergleich hinkt)
obwohl: schön ist die stadt

& wie rike
wenn sie ein lied summt

& stolz, mann, stolz ist sie
(was gut ist)—volkmund
geht übern hof: lacht & winkt
hoch—wer kann mir denn
jetzt noch was? was kümmern mich
mikrophone, die hirnspezialisten
& traumprotokolle. jawohl
mein herr, ich grüße den
diplomatenfriedhof & ich
grüße die mauer & mache
ein lied für françois villon
& die kraft ist wieder da
um die sache (unsere: deine
& meine—der anderen)
anzuschieben, die ungeduld zu zeigen
: das macht sie & die stadt

(in meinem herzen der anfang
von zwei februaraugen)

& wie rike
wenn sie ein lied summt

KEMPINSKI

Wolf Wondratschek

Der Taxifahrer vertritt folgenden Standpunkt:
"det Berlin hättn se abreißn solln und im Westen
wieder aufbaun, Lüneburger Heide oder wo;
wir machen hier ja doch nur, wat de Russn wolln
—und det jeht mal so, mal so."

Die alte Toilettenfrau lacht,
als ich die Wahlen erwähne.
Sie möchte auch zubeißen
"aber det jeht nich ohne Zähne!"

Das Zimmermädchen ist verliebt
und Politik ganz piepe.
Berlin? "Det is ne alte Frau,
die träumt nich mehr von Liebe."

Der Nachtportier faßt sich kurz.
Was steht zur Wahl?
Der Osten ist kommunistisch
und der Westen ist sentimental.

CHAPTER 14

A New Yorker's Berlin

Richard Kostelanetz

I must open with a confession of my most profound secret, a secret so dear to me that I hesitate to share it, except that it tells a truth known to everyone who knows me: I am a New Yorker, a native, born and bred, who has lived there his entire life, except for occasional forays "out of town," as I call the rest of the world. I am a confirmed New Yorker, a profound New Yorker. My New York has been visually represented in the classic Saul Steinberg drawing in which the Hudson River is halfway across the visible world and everything west of it recedes into the distant horizon. The truest test of my New Yorkerness is that I don't like to leave New York, and rarely do so in fact, even in the hot summertime. For many years I left only on rare occasions, and then usually to give lectures around the country (customarily getting home as quickly as I could), or sometimes to visit on my own initiative one of only two places: San Juan, Puerto Rico, which everyone knows is really a suburb of New York, and Jerusalem, which can also be experienced as an extension of New York. For years colleagues advised me to go to Europe. Europe, they told me, would do wonders, sheer wonders, for my artistic career; but I don't speak languages other than English, or New Yorkese, and have no inclination to learn. As I was doing wonderfully enough at home, thank these colleagues, I rationalized that I would go to Europe only when, as we say in New York, someone made me an offer I could not refuse!

Perhaps a decade or so ago this friend, Dick Higgins, told me about a certain Berlin DAAD [German Academic Exchange Service] grant. They give you a stipend, he said, and ask nothing of you, not even that you always be in Berlin. Zwowie, I thought to myself, those guys must be what we in New York call Sugar DAADys. Since I had never been to Germany, let alone to Berlin, a city I first of all associate with my main artistic hero Moholy-Nagy, I filled out the two-page application, but wasn't accepted. That didn't hurt, because I was in my gut none too eager to move my butt to Berlin or Paris or Los Angeles or any of those other places where rising hot artists are supposed to camp out. Besides, the rejection letter was written in German, which I cannot read.

Some years later I received an encouraging personal letter, written in English, from a man who was then the director of the DAAD Berliner Künstlerprogramm, Herr Karl Ruhrberg. So I applied again without thinking too much about it. It never occurred to me to do what many other DAAD applicants have done—make an advance visit to Berlin with the aim of befriending and perhaps impressing members of the selection committee. Indeed, unlike most of the other applicants, I could scarcely generate any fantasies of myself ever being in Berlin (or anywhere else outside home). The chief's encouragement notwithstanding, I received in the mail another German letter that told me, according to a German-reading friend, that I did not score this time either, which was more of a relief than a disappointment, because I honestly did not know how or if I was going to get out of New York if I won, while I assumed that DAAD would never give me a stipend for labor in my favorite workplace, my Manhattan studio.

For some reason, I applied again at the end of 1979, even though Herr Ruhrberg had departed to a greener pasture, while his successor was someone who had never encouraged or even written me at all, Prof. Dr. Wieland Schmied. This time I declared in the application itself that I would diddle DAADy no more; this would be the last time I was going to look at those two pages. That ultimatum would cost me nothing, I figured, since the alternative was more time home in New York, which is, of course, the fellowship I want and enjoy most of all—my grant of grants, so to speak. Nonetheless, my threat must have driven the selection committee into paroxysms of solicitousness, because in April 1980 came into my mailbox a special-delivery invitation to spend a year, twelve whole months (!), in West Berlin. This letter was, thankfully, in English; if it had been in German, I might have thrown it out unread.

As you can by now perhaps imagine, this good news caused not unqualified joy but neurotic anxiety, a crisis that no sugary promise of generous amounts of Deutschmarks could assuage: Oh my God, I thought, how was I, a provincial New Yorker, going to leave my home, with my typewriter, my library, my toilet and my bed, to spend more than a week, let alone whole months or even a full year, in some godforsaken place well off Saul Steinberg's map of my world. One good friend, a former Künstlerprogramm recipient, told me how she lasted only a few weeks in Berlin, but she had a problem with Germany per se, while my problem was anywhere, or everywhere, so far *out of town*. Another friend who knows me very well was prepared to bet me—to bet me against me, so to speak—that I wouldn't last more than two weeks in Berlin, and I didn't have enough confidence to invest in myself. In other words, I wasn't so sure that once I got to Berlin I could actually stay there, even if I could in the process take my friend's money, on top of sugar DAADs. When colleagues said they envied my going to Berlin, I instinctively offered them the grant in my stead. "Just show up and tell them that you are Richard Kostelanetz," I would advise, *sotto voce*; "Nobody there knows what I look like."

I nonetheless informed Barbara Richter, my principal contact at DAAD, that I would arrive the following April, but in fact I did not get there until May, 1981, having canceled at my own expense more than one PanAm New York–Berlin superbudget plane reservation. I did not dare sublet my SoHo loft, even though it could fetch me many pretty pennies in rent, because I feared I might at any moment get homesick and want to hurry back into my own familiar lair. In fact, I came back home in late July for a month, but returned to stay in Berlin not until the following spring, as originally scheduled, but only until the end of that next October, as DAAD had fortunately agreed to my proposal to divide my twelve months in half, or into two half-years. Instead, for the winter, I went—you guessed it—back home to New York. I thus returned to Berlin in April, 1982, and stayed for six more months, until the end of September, except for my customary month back home in the middle.

But, please, don't misunderstand my confessions about going home so much. I love Berlin. I love Berlin like I love New York, which it resembles in many ways. Indeed, I love Berlin so much that whenever I'm there I don't like to leave it. Whereas many of my colleagues on the Künstlerprogramm were flying here and there around Europe, while my German friends were always going off to Italy—this habit being, incidentally, the most visible sign of the continuing influence of Johann Wolfgang von Goethe—I did most of my traveling to East Berlin, which you know is comparable to visiting Brooklyn from New York or Cambridge from Boston. You perceive it as a radically different world; yet it is close enough to allow you to get back home at night. Indeed, what distinguishes East Berlin from Brooklyn or Cambridge is that in East Berlin the *Volkspolizei* have parietal rules reminiscent of those we had in my residential American college twenty-five years ago. Like the housemothers who then supervised the girls' dormitories, these *Vopos* want your butt out of their place by midnight. This nightly housecleaning has advantages as well as obvious disadvantages. Let's say you meet an attractive woman in East Berlin and she takes you home. Or an attractive man and he takes you home. And you are enjoying each other, but you really don't want to spend the night with her or him. You can be sure, as sure can be, that she or he won't object when at 11 o'clock you leap up and say, "Gotta get home." You can't always do this in Brooklyn or Cambridge.

Why do I like Berlin? First of all, I am a city boy, and Berlin is a real city, as Boston is a real city, while Providence and San Diego, say, are not. (Nor are those prosperous towns of the *Ruhrgebiet*, no matter how hard they try to pose as cities.) Better yet, Berlin is a civilized city, first of all in the abundance of stylish architecture or buildings that reveal imaginative thinking about design, and then in its pervasive greenery: trees on nearly every street, the little gardens in the fronts and backs of houses, those numerous little parks that dot the city, in addition to the expansive fields and woods of the Tiergarten and the Grunewald. In the past three decades, West Berlin was rebuilt to satisfy two illusions—*that there has been no war and that there is no wall*; and the city's ability to make you forget those two truths is one clear measure of its current civility. Another measure is its creature comforts, which include not only tree-lined streets that are largely safe at night, bars that stay open past midnight, and sidewalks wide enough to accommodate both cafés and crowds, but lakes right *in town* that are suitable for swimming. Where else outside New York can one spend a warm June day at the area's best beach and still get to the country's best opera, the best theater, and the best orchestra at night? Where else can you spend a hot August day at a good beach and then choose among a hundred movies at night? Who needs to go to the country when so much of the country is already in the city?

Kurfürstendamm (ward Charlottenburg), in the direction of Breitscheidplatz; in the background: Kaiser-Wilhelm-Gedächtniskirche (Emporer-Wilhelm-Memorial-Church).—May 1982. Reproduced with permission of the Landesbildstelle Berlin.

Berlin, like New York, has always been a promised land, a magnet for adventurers seeking experiences unavailable at home, a metropolis of opportunity for industrious people from somewhere else, whether Eastern Europe or the Eastern Mediterranean; and even in hard times, this promise of possibility is a spiritual quality you can feel. So it distresses me doubly to hear some Berliners speak of wanting not just to restrict the immigration of Turks but to send them home. Such talk reminds me of the fact that Spain in 1492 brought its subsequent decline upon itself by expelling both the Jews and the Moors, leaving nobody to pay the Spanish taxes—because the Spanish nobles didn't pay taxes—and no laborers to do the dirty work. Berliners should know better than to usher their own demise. (If the Jews are gone, and when the Turks go, who will be next?) Berlin was a promised land for me as well, for reasons I'll mention later. My own principal difficulty in living there, aside from the language problem that I'll also discuss later, reflects my New Yorkness: I was always getting lost, or arriving late at strange addresses, because I could never master the problem of getting efficiently around a city whose streets are not numbered!

Berlin has not the uniformity of rural life but the stark contrasts typical of great cities. In New York one is struck by the discrepancy between rich and poor, especially where the offices and housing of the very rich are in close proximity to the very poor. In Jerusalem, the stark contrast is not between Arab and Jew—a difference more evident in the Galilee—but between the religious and the secular. In Berlin the most striking gap is between West and East. Berlin remains the only place in the world where you can not only peek into the Other World with your own eyes, you can actually go visit it at any time with your own feet, without the forbidding nuisance of needing to obtain a travel visa. In Berlin you can literally take a subway under the Iron Curtain and come out on the other side, right at Freddy's Street, as I call it—*Friedrichstrasse*, they say—in the heart of East Berlin, which doesn't look like a Western city, because it isn't a Western city. Where West Berlin is colorful, with neon signs and people in all sorts of contemporary haircuts and colorful dress, East Berlin's drab anonymity reminds the Western visitor of another world decades past. For an especially vivid sense of the difference, just go on a summer Friday night from the main streets of East Berlin, which become barren after sundown, to the Kurfürstendamm, the main drag of West Berlin, where the weekend party goes well into the night, and you will observe a contrast as great as that between 86th Street and 125th Street in New York, albeit different. Especially if you have read, as I have, some wise guys explaining how West and East are coming to resemble each other, you will be hit with a contrast that to be believed must likewise not only be seen with one's eyes but must be experienced in the body.

This proximity to the Other World is something that West Berliners take for granted, I know; but the more you think about it, the more extraordinary it is that there, as nowhere else, everyone can take the public subway over to the other side, for the regular fare, on a ride no longer than that between Manhattan and Brooklyn, or between Boston and Cambridge. This stark contrast I mentioned before—the stark contrast between West and East—is, we know, largely the creation of a capitalist conspiracy, whereby the West pays millions upon millions to keep West Berlin looking so good, and then yet millions more—*sub rosa, unter der Mauer*, under the Wall, so to speak—to keep East Berlin looking so grim. (This last secret, which I hesitate to share with you, came from a very authoritative source: It was told to me, in typical Berlin fashion, by a nude mermaid, a woman with nothing to hide, so to speak, swimming next to me in the Wannsee.)

Seriously though, Berlin has something else that is very special, something I take to be the ultimate mark of a civilized city: public transportation so abundant, cheap, and comprehensive that you can live there comfortably *without* ever owning an automobile. By that criterion, it is clear, New York is civilized as Los Angeles is not; Boston is civilized as Chicago is not. Never, but never, will I voluntarily live where a car is necessary; and I know from personal experience that you don't really need one in West Berlin, in part because you cannot go very far. In a city of just over two million people, a million rides are taken each day on the subway alone; buses are even more popular. One sign of the popularity of Berlin's public transportation is the abundance of snackstands, places where you can buy wurst and soda or beer for a little more than a dollar. Simply wherever routes of public trans-

portation intersect in Berlin, you will see a sign reading *Imbiss*, or snack; and
though I am scarcely well-traveled, I never saw so many snackstands anywhere else. Since beer in these stands is no more expensive than soda pop, no
wonder we Americans can call people who patronize them excessively *imbe-
ciles*. My problem with cars, if you want to know, is not that I don't know
how to drive—I *do* know how—but that in my gut I regard passenger cars
as essentially unsafe. They break down at inopportune moments, leaving
you stranded. They kill more people in a day around the world than air-
planes kill in a year. They also drown out the sound of bicycles that, at least
in Berlin, are even more likely than cars to crash into you. We are coming to
realize that cars are presently more dangerous to life and limb than dark
streets or even contemporary wars. When you saw a body smashed apart in
1946, you were rightly reminded of the War; if you see a body similarly
broken now, we all know that nine times out of ten a car did it. Since
Berlin is a hothouse for avant-garde social experiments, I'd like to propose
that Berlin take the radical initiative of becoming the first great city of the
world to abolish private cars.

*View from the Grunewaldturm (Grunewald Tower) across the Havel toward Span-
dau (ward), with the new residential settlements at the Heerstraße.—About 1970.
Reproduced with permission of the Landesbildstelle Berlin.*

There are other nonobvious things to be said in favor of Berlin. The first is
that since no one has country homes, you need not turn down invitations for
weekends that are likely to be boring. The second is that Berlin is the only
German city where you don't need to know German, just as New York is
probably the only American city in which people live quite well without

ever really learning English. Berliners, like New Yorkers, are accustomed to the abundant presence of people who scarcely know the official language. Berliners are thus accustomed to speaking slowly, to finding an intermediary who speaks your language, to mime, and to do all the other sensitive things that people do to communicate without words. I speak again from personal experience, because, when it comes to learning foreign languages, I am an utterly hopeless American. I may have a large personal library, but every European who visits me notices instantly a fact that escapes my American colleagues: nearly all the books are in English. DAAD offers its guests free German lessons. Well, I never got them, because Barbara Richter decided that I didn't know enough *rudimentary* German even to begin the DAAD lessons. So I spoke English to everyone in Berlin, regardless of whether or not they claimed to understand it. When I telephoned strangers, for instance, my opening words were not the customary cheery German salutation of " 'Tag. Kostelanetz" ("Good day. Kostelanetz") but an apprehensive "Speak English?" The only people to criticize my incapacity to my face were Berlin intellectuals who wanted to believe that fluency in other languages is the surest sign of superior intelligence, and my apoplectic apartment house superintendent, who was endlessly annoyed that I could not be moved by her suggestions, her criticisms, and her threats. (Thus does strange bedfellows a monolingual make.) My incapacity should not be considered a total loss, however, because I discovered methods of communication, as well as pleasures, that would be unavailable to me in New York. One of my favorite Berliners is my publisher Peter Gente, whose English is just about as good as my German; and we have spent lots of time together, simply enjoying each other's company, while saving our serious conversations for the presence of a translator.

Before I got to Berlin, I was often told that everyone there speaks English, good English, because they learn it in school. This, in my experience, is not quite true. The many folks from elsewhere—mostly *Gastarbeiter*, or guest workers—speak no English at all. As for Teutonic Berliners, it is more accurate to say that they understand English, not only because of having studied it in school for several years, but because of American pop culture; yet, unless these Germans have spent considerable time in an English-speaking country, they are, in my observation, usually reluctant to *speak* English. My first experience of this last truth came at the meat counter of the neighborhood grocery store. The first time I went there, perhaps my first week in Berlin, I heard the familiar sound of American radio, the Armed Forces Network, which plays U.S. rock music every hour for fifty-five minutes followed by a zippy five-minute newscast from New York or Los Angeles. Since everyone behind the meat counter appeared to be listening to this familiar American news program, I said, "Hi. How much is . . . ?" There was a pause during which the clerks suddenly looked at each other anxiously. It became quickly clear that none of them *spoke* English, or perhaps none *wanted to speak* English!

What art did I make as a guest of Berlin? Essentially, I tried to do what I do *not* do at home. Since I tend to spend most days in New York at my typewriter, I did not bring it with me; and when I needed to rent one in Berlin, the German keyboard, with its crossed-up letters and, worse, its misplaced semicolon, so infuriated me that I gave up typing for the duration. (Even at the typewriter, you see, I remained a hopelessly culture-bound New Yorker). My mail from home was not forwarded, because I did not want to spend as much time dealing with it as I do at home. With neither a typewriter nor mail, I figured, my life in Berlin would necessarily be different from that in New York. Fortunately, I was able, soon after I arrived, to work on a radio piece, a *Hörspiel*, as they say, that exploited a particular quality that Berlin shares with New York. Both are international towns in which many languages are spoken. Wanting for years to do a radio piece about the sound of the language of prayer—an ambitious piece that combined my love for Johann Sebastian Bach with my love of *Finnegans Wake*— I recorded sixty ministers in over two dozen languages and then mixed their spoken words on a twenty-four-track audiotape machine. By this process, I made *Invocations*, as it is called—a 62-minute *Hörspiel* (radio play) that was first aired on Sender Freies Berlin and later played on radio stations in Canada, Australia, Holland, and the United States; and it has just appeared in the experimental music series of Folkways Records as my first solo record. Given such linguistic variety, *Invocations* could be made in only a scant few cities of this world: New York, of course, Paris, Jerusalem, Singapore perhaps, and Berlin.

During my first tour of Berlin, I also lectured about American literature, wrote talks for the local radio station, and began another *Hörspiel*, this entirely in German, *Die Evangelien* (the Gospel), that was aired over Westdeutscher Rundfunk in the fall of 1982. My friend Eberhard Blum, who is both a flutist and an incomparably dexterous speaker, asked me for a text he could perform, and the poem I produced, composed of continuously overlapping German words, is indeed something that he and only he can read. The poem itself appeared, in its original German form, in the highly respected Austrian avant-garde journal, *Protokolle*, thereby making me a certified Germany Aspiring Poet (so *aspiring* that I speak no German!), in addition to my earlier American titles. I also began a highly experimental film, *Epiphanies*, that was excerpted for the *Projektionen* series of Sender Freies Berlin television, which asked for a German sound track that, wonder of wonders, I likewise produced with the assistance of German speakers. And that new *Hörspiel* about the Gospels was nominated for the Karl-Sczuka-Prize, which, alas, was won not by me but by another American and DAAD Stipenliat Alison Knowles. It would have been a special pleasure to tell my old friend the theater artist Bob Wilson, who wins West German theater prizes even though his command of German equals mine, that this *amerikanische Gastarbeiter*, whose German vocabulary is insufficient for the grocery store, had likewise won one of those art prizes that Germans, in contrast to Americans, value so highly. One truth that should not go unnoticed is that American cultural institutions are rarely so generous toward European artists who do not speak English.

Until I got to Berlin, I made only short radio pieces—5- to 7-minute works at best, instead of 62-minute extravagances—because we in America have neither the resources for making nor the taste for broadcasting (and paying for) such sophisticated radio. We didn't before I left for Berlin, and we still don't now, and are not likely to do so for many, many years. So, when I returned to Germany in 1983, it is scarcely surprising that my principal mission was the production of another long radio piece—this one composed of sounds peculiar to, you guessed it, New York City. In other words, I produced in Germany a *New York City* I could not do in New York, or anywhere else in America for that matter. Incredible, but true. And need I say that all this high-class radio art would not have happened, had DAAD not made me this gilded offer that not even a *meshugah* New Yorker could refuse. For that alone I kiss each morning my gold-framed, dog-eared photograph of the DAADy capo, Don Wieland Schmied. And on Sundays I dutifully kiss the photographs of all the other Berlin writers on the selection committee—Walter Höllerer, Ingeborg Drewitz, K.P. Herbach. . .

I discovered my last major Berlin project in an extraordinary place that remarkably few Berliners have seen or visited, let alone know about: The great Jewish cemetery in Weissensee, a northeast section of East Berlin. With 115,000 graves, this is, first of all, the largest Jewish cemetery between Warsaw and New York; but aside from its size, it has a cultural coherence that makes it quite unlike any other cemetery, Jewish or otherwise, that you or I have ever visited. This is not a historic Jewish graveyard, with ancient stone, like the ones in Worms or Prague; it is a modern graveyard, founded in 1880,

Cemetery of the Jewish Community, ward Weissensee, East-Berlin, Herbert Baum Straße 12.—November 1966. Reproduced with permission of the Landesbildstelle Berlin.

that stands as an utterly exemplary artifact of visual history. Most of its stones were laid in Berlin's golden years, when Jews, though less than five percent of the city's population, made such a strong impression that Berlin was known throughout Germany as a Jewish city; and these graves from the classic modern period establish within the cemetery itself a contrasting standard for the stones laid after 1935. Thus, the stones of the great Jewish cemetery tell not only of individual lives but of a Berlin lost—a Berlin of style, wealth, confidence, and culture. Indeed, as this graveyard evokes the glorious past more vividly than anything else I ever saw there, there is good reason to consider it the principal surviving relic of the classic Berlin. Because the experience of the cemetery is so special, as well as illustrative of principles of visual history that have long interested me, my initial plan was to make a book mostly of black and white photographs, a small-format paperback with two photographs to a page, for over two hundred pages, because my theme is best evoked through abundant detail. Though this original component of the project has yet to find a publisher, other parts of it have acquired auspicious backers.

Along with my Berlin film colleague, Martin Koerber, and the Literarisches Colloquium, I also received a grant to make *Ein Verlorenes Berlin* (A Lost Berlin), a 20-minute documentary film about the cemetery. Later Inter Nationes gave us sufficient support to prepare five more films, in English, Swedish, French, Spanish and Hebrew, each not with translated subtitles or overdubbing but fresh sound tracks of authentic testimony of ex-Berliners speaking those languages. These films have been shown at international festivals around the world and won festival prizes.

You can understand by now that I like Berlin as a city rich in culture, in activity, in variety, in tolerance, in surprises, and in friends—a city abundant in all the things and qualities that make true urban living more attractive than rural life. *Ich bin Berliner*, which I know is not the same as *ein Berliner*, which is what John F. Kennedy called himself. ("Ein Berliner," everyone should know, is argot for a certain kind of doughnut.) *Ich bin Berliner*, not only because it resembles New York, but it is still, to my senses, a Jewish city, just as New York is a Jewish city and Jerusalem is a Jewish city, but not with only a few Jews, alas—five to seven thousand, instead of 200,000— which is a tragedy about which some things can still be done. Tell your Jewish friends, as I tell mine, that Berlin is *not* West Germany, and indeed it isn't, especially to Berliners, who customarily speak of taking a "trip to West Germany" as though it were a distant country. I tell them about the cemetery and all that it reveals about the traditions of Berlin. I mention the absence of anti-Semitism, which a Jewish friend of mine who grew up in postwar Berlin attributes to the city's geographical isolation. German anti-Semitism, she once explained to me, tends to come into the cities from the surrounding countryside; but Berlin's countryside, she elaborated, is another country, whose peasants are forbidden to come in. My friend Edgar Hilsenrath, whom the German press infallibly identifies as a "Jewish novelist," told me that he came to live in Berlin, after twenty-seven years in New York, because it was the only place in the German-speaking world where he did not feel intimidated by beer-drinking Germans.

And now that Berlin has persuaded me to leave home, not once or twice but seven times—count 'em, seven times; that's a new record for me—why don't I propose redrawing Saul Steinberg's map, placing Berlin just west of New York's Rockaway Point, beyond the southern edge of Brooklyn, very much in need of a connecting subway.

CHAPTER 15
Berlin as a Music Center

Wolfgang Stresemann

Musical life in Berlin developed relatively late. When the city became the capital of the Mark Brandenburg, a very small state located in the middle of Europe, Berlin was involved in many wars. There was neither time nor money for outstanding cultural activities. The Kurfürsten (electors) and, afterwards the kings of Brandenburg-Prussia, who were primarily interested in the extension of their territory, attacked their neighbours and were attacked by them. These conditions did not provide any particular encouragement to develop music as other big cities did, e.g., Vienna, Dresden, and Leipzig.

It was not before the reign of Frederick II, the Great (1740–1786), that music began to play a more important role in Berlin, at least in nearby Potsdam where the Prussian king resided. This great war hero was, on the other hand, a remarkable flutist and a talented composer. In 1747, he summoned Johann Sebastian Bach (1685–1750) to his court and commissioned one of Bach's great works, the *Musical Offerings*. After Bach's death, one of his sons moved to Berlin and tried to establish a Bach tradition at a time when even the name of this great composer had almost been forgotten. Thanks to his teacher Carl Friedrich Zelter (1758–1832), one of Goethe's closest friends, the young genius Felix Mendelssohn-Bartholdy (1809–1847), became involved in these endeavors. He discovered and conducted Bach's *St. Matthews Passion* for the first time in a kind of concert performance with the choir of Zelter's Berlin Singakademie (Berlin Singing Academy). This performance in 1829 was a rousing success; it is considered an important event in music history. From that time on, Bach's fame grew all over the world and so did the renown of Berlin as a center of music. Yet not too much remains to be said about the first half of the nineteenth century. There was an opera, to be sure, which was subsidized by the king of Prussia according to a rather old tradition. But this opera, quite a conservative institution, did not offer much of interest. Strangely enough, there was no orchestra of great artistic level. The court did not consider an orchestra essential, especially since the orchestra of the opera gave a few concerts, although of minor significance.

It was up to a private musician, Benjamin Bilse (1816–1902), to form an orchestra in 1867. Bilse had no sponsors. In order to avoid a deficit, he had to arrange concerts every day, except on Sundays. On Monday, Bilse only performed works by his idol Richard Wagner (1813–1883). On Tuesday, old, so-called classical music was played; Wednesday was reserved for works with the choir; on Thursday, Bilse's musicians played dance music. Each Friday, new compositions were introduced, while on Saturday the program was devoted to light musical entertainment. These concerts were especially popular and became famous as "engagement concerts."

The above facts disclose some insights into the general situation of the orchestra: Bilse was conductor, general manager, and organizer all in one, and he had to put up the necessary money as well as to make sure that he got it back. He deserves great credit for his unswerving enthusiasm and his keen interest in modern music, i.e., the music of his time. So, the Bilsestrasse (Bilse Street) in Berlin rightly reminds us of this musician. Although his orchestra never reached any artistic heights, it paved the way for the birth of the Berlin Philharmonic Orchestra. Richard Wagner conducted the Bilse orchestra twice, and other renowned guest conductors, among them Arthur Nikisch (1855–1922), led Bilse's men in more or less rehearsed concerts. But, of course, this kind of orchestral work could not go on forever. Berlin, by now the capital of a unified Germany, was bound to become a cultural center. Something had to happen.

In 1882, a small provincial orchestra—of only 48 musicians—gave a few concerts in Berlin under the direction of the famous Hans von Bülow (1830–1894). Berlin audiences were amazed by the outstanding level of the performances, yet shocked when they compared Bülow's musicians with those conducted by Bilse. The small orchestra came from Meiningen, the tiny capital of the Thuringian dukedom of Sachsen-Meiningen. What was possible in Meiningen had to be impossible in Berlin? There was a rebellion against Bilse soon after the appearance of Bülow's orchestra. Fifty-two, mostly younger members refused to continue to work under the conditions Bilse had imposed on them. They left the orchestra and formed one of their own. This was the beginning of the Berlin Philharmonic Orchestra in 1882, a very critical beginning indeed. There were no rich people to support the "rebels," and the Prussian king could not be persuaded to provide some money. The young musicians were left to their own devices. They went to a notary and pledged their own money, their own fortunes, for any debts the new orchestra would incur. In that way, they helped themselves and God helped them further on as often occurs when brave people take important matters into their own hands regardless of possible consequences. Each year, the orchestra faced bankruptcy and was finally saved in some miraculous way. Its plight awoke interest and mobilized people, among them a businessman who actually wanted to become a musician: Hermann Wolff. He gave the musicians of the orchestra artistic advice, got them a new hall, the Old Philharmonie, which was destroyed in 1944, and eventually succeeded in finding a top conductor: the very same Hans von Bülow who, five years before, had created such a sensation in Berlin. Hans von Bülow trained the Berlin Philharmonics from 1887–1894 and laid the technical and musical foundation of this orchestra. Serious programs, emphasizing the works of Richard Wagner, Beethoven (1770–1827) and Brahms (1833–1897), were introduced. Bülow, conducting the orchestra for seven years, was the first great musician to put his stamp on the musical life of Berlin.

After Bülow's death in 1894, Hermann Wolff was rather at a loss to find a successor. For two years, guest conductors appeared; one season was given to Richard Strauss (1864–1949), the great composer, once assistant conductor to Bülow in Meiningen. Finally, Wolff learned about Arthur Nikisch, a musician of multiple gifts, half Hungarian, half German, and his enormous stature as a conductor. In 1884, Nikisch conducted in Leipzig the first night of the *Seventh Symphony* by Anton Bruckner (1826–1896); from 1889 to 1893 he was conductor of symphony concerts in Boston, and from 1893 to 1895 opera director in Budapest. From 1895 up to his death in 1922, he conducted the Gewandhauskonzerte (concerts of the orchestra in the house of the cloth-maker's corporation) in Leipzig as well as the subscription concerts of the philharmonic orchestras in Hamburg and also in Berlin, for Nikisch agreed to become Bülow's heir; and with him at the helm a new era began for the Berlin Philharmonic Orchestra. Nikisch indeed had so much charisma that Berlin audiences soon fell in love with him, especially the ladies. He was a kind of magician, a sorcerer who would evoke the most beautiful, enchanting sound from his orchestra. Thus, he fascinated the orchestra as well as his listeners. He also fascinated them by performing new works that he introduced to Berlin. Nikisch conducted Tschaikovsky (1840–1893), Bruckner, Mahler (1860–1911), and other composers which the majority of the listeners did not yet know, because Bülow had not cared to program them. The repertoire of the orchestra grew by leaps and bounds. Within a few years, Nikisch became a conductor recognized worldwide. He took the orchestra to Paris, Petersburg—then the Russian capital—to Vienna, and many other places. For more than a quarter of a century, he worked with the Berlin Philharmonic until his death in January 1922.

Nikisch died completely unexpectedly, and I still recall the terrific shock everybody felt in Berlin. I was about to finish school. We, too, were moved by his relatively early death—at the age of 67—and we shared the feeling of our parents and grandparents that it would be difficult if not impossible to find an adequate successor. Who could replace this unique conductor? At first general despair prevailed. And yet it took only a relatively short time to find the right person. Hermann Wolff had died twenty years before; his widow, Louise Wolff, soon to be called "Queen Louise", took over. Thanks to her remarkable personality and to her complete knowledge of music and musicians, she played a dominating role in Berlin's musical life, especially during the twenties. Now it was up to her to engage, with the consent of the orchestra, a new man. Her choice was Wilhelm Furtwängler, age 36. Furtwängler (1886–1954), already well known in Berlin as the conductor of the concerts given by the Staatskapelle, the orchestra of the State Opera, became the third great conductor of the Berlin Philharmonic. He achieved miracles, led the orchestra to new heights and, after a few years, was, like the late Nikisch, Berlin's most beloved conductor of the time. Before Furtwängler followed Nikisch as chief conductor of the Berlin Philharmonic as well as of the Gewandhausorchester Leipzig, he was opera director in Mannheim from 1915 to 1919, with numerous engagements also in Francfort, Vienna, and Berlin. He was closely connected to the Vienna Philharmonics and took them as well as the Berlin Philharmonics on extended tours throughout Europe and the United States.

In comparison to Nikisch, Furtwängler's approach to music was entirely different. A remarkable idealist for whom every note was almost sacred, he tried to convey the deeper significance of all the great works he scheduled. What was behind the notes seemed to interest him more than the written music. He was not necessarily outstanding in rehearsals, but the moment he stood in front of the orchestra, his power of inspiration was felt by everybody. It seemed that the music carried him away, but he also got additional inspiration from his audiences, which were completely spellbound. Unfortunately, we have only relatively few recordings by Furtwängler. No wonder, since he actually disliked recording sessions. He needed an audience and at first complained bitterly about the necessity of making music with no listeners around.

Furtwängler is now considered *the* representative of the great German musical heritage. However, people forget that he also introduced Strawinsky's (1882–1971) *Le sacre du printemps* to his subscribers, which at its world première in Paris, in 1913, caused one of the greatest theater scandals. He even went on to première the first composition of Schönberg (1874–1951) which was written in the new twelve-tone style, the *Orchestra Variations*, opus 31. At the end, there was almost a revolution among his loyal subscribers, the Philharmonie was turned into a madhouse, nobody seemed to have the slightest sympathy for Schönberg and his new theory. Furtwängler himself admitted he was not quite sure about the work, but as the conductor of the Berlin Philharmonic, he considered it his duty to acquaint Berlin audiences with such a daring piece, even at the risk that it would not be understood. Indeed it was not and it could not be understood, because of a lack of preparation time. Furtwängler had three or at most four rehearsals. Karajan (born 1908), who later tried very hard to familiarize the Berlin Philharmonic with the same piece, needed several years of almost unending rehearsals and several performances until he was satisfied with his rendition. He explained to the orchestra that they must play the *Variations* like the *Eroica*, that it was necessary for them to know every note, every phrase, until the whole work would become part of themselves. Eventually Karajan recorded the Schönberg-Variations by seating the orchestra differently for each of the variations (the whole work is somewhat overorchestrated), and thereby achieved such a beautiful balance that he no longer likes to program Schönberg for a regular concert where, of course, he cannot change the seating of his musicians. It does speak for Furtwängler and his courage that he introduced the *Variations* already as early as 1927.

When the Nazis came to power, Furtwängler continued to play Mendelssohn. He also gave the first performance of three pieces of Hindemith's (1895–1963) opera *Mathis der Maler*. This time the audience gave him tremendous ovations. It was known that Hindemith was considered "persona non grata" by the Nazis. What a splendid opportunity for the Berliners to show their strong dislike for the Nazi regime!

From 1933 on, modern music became most popular in Berlin. The few compositions which were consented to by the Nazis received great and prolonged applause. Of course, the Nazis did not like that; they started a campaign especially against Hindemith. When Furtwängler noticed the rising storm, he wrote an article in which he defended his programming of Hindemith's music, which at that time reflected the composer's return to tonality. Furtwängler attacked "certain groups"—he meant the Nazis—who failed to understand Hindemith's development, and those "certain groups" went into action. Furtwängler had to resign his position as chief conductor of the Berlin Philharmonic Orchestra as well as his position at the State Opera. There was no comment in the Berlin newspapers. People were disgusted, but nobody dared to oppose the powerful Nazis. Furtwängler left the city to devote his time to composing. Guest conductors took over. To get out of the miserable situation, the Nazis chose what always has been the best way out of a musical calamity—to give a Beethoven cycle! Up to this day, Beethoven concerts are always sold out. However, one discovered very soon that Furtwängler was irreplaceable. Therefore, the Nazis called him back, and Furtwängler returned to become the head of the Berlin Philharmonic once again. But he did not go back to the Opera and agreed to conduct only a limited number of subscription concerts in the Philharmonie. Was Furtwängler's decision right or not? One fact is sure: by returning to his old orchestra, he saved his musicians from all those minor Nazi conductors who most certainly would have changed the orchestra's stature as an internationally recognized first-rank ensemble. He helped many orchestra members and their wives who were endangered by the Nazis, and he arranged that the Nazis eventually left the orchestra more or less untouched, with the result that, in 1945, after the defeat of the Third Reich, a new Berlin Philharmonic Orchestra was founded within a few weeks after the capitulation on May 8th.

Once more the orchestra was lucky. They found a young Rumanian musician, Sergiu Celibidache (born 1912), a real genius, a man of explosive temperament who soon dominated the orchestra, although at that time he hardly had any experience as a conductor. He acquainted the musicians and the audience with new works by Shostakovich (1906–1975), Ravel (1875–1937), and Prokofiev (1891–1953) and took the orchestra on tour, until Furtwängler could return and again head the Berlin Philharmonic.

When Furtwängler died in November 1954, there was once more a sense of general despondency. Who could replace the giant? People went as far as to suggest the disbanding of the orchestra. What utter nonsense! Great conductors come and go. There will always be a solution in times of crises, especially if the orchestra is an independent body which enjoys the right of artistic self-administration as in the case of the Berlin Philharmonic: the orchestra members select their permanent conductor and also choose the Intendant (their musical and administrative director). In case of a vacancy in the orchestra, any applicant has to play in front of the entire ensemble. After the audition, a discussion takes place and subsequently a vote. The applicant needs a majority of the orchestra members to get engaged for a year of probation. At the end of this year, another vote is cast, and this time, for the final engagement, a two-third majority is required, as well as the agreement of the permanent conductor who has veto power. The orchestra cannot impose a musician on him he does not like. On the other hand, the permanent conductor cannot force the orchestra to accept a musician he favors if the orchestra is opposed.

After Furtwängler's death, many people expected Sergiu Celibidache to succeed him, and so did "Celi" himself, as one used to call him. He was so sure of his forthcoming engagement that he announced he would dismiss twenty members of the orchestra once he had been appointed. Celibidache, of course, was badly advised to make that kind of statement. No orchestra is pleased to hear such announcements, and the Berlin Philharmonic was no exception. Their members got together and, after some debate, decided that the right man to work with was Herbert von Karajan, who in 1938 had already caused a sensation as guest conductor for the Berlin Philharmonic.

Karajan, born in 1908 in Salzburg, had worked in Ulm and, in 1934, at the age of twenty six, was called to Aachen where he became the youngest German general musical director. In 1938, he conducted a performance of *Tristan and Isolde* at the Berlin State Opera which became a legend as the conductor became "the prodigy Karajan" ("das Wunder Karajan"), as the press put it. Since 1938, Karajan has remained in close relation with Berlin, conducting primarily at the State Opera. After the collapse of the Reich, he left Berlin but returned in 1954 to lead the Berlin Philharmonic through a few programs, each time leaving a great impression on the orchestra, although his interpretations were a far cry from those of the beloved Wilhelm Furtwängler. That there had been tensions between the two conductors was well known. Yet the orchestra thought highly of Karajan and now urged their Intendant to offer him, not Celibidache, the position of permanent conductor. Karajan accepted "mit tausend Freuden" (with a thousand joys). Until today, he has been at the helm for more than 30 years and has almost become his own legend. He has the reputation of being a perfectionist, which is absolutely true. He is also famous for eliciting the most glorious sound from his musicians, and in addition, he is an interpreter with a tremendous sense for the big line and for the structure of any composition. Like his predecessors he has enlarged the repertoire of the orchestra by adding the main works of the *Vienna School*, Mahler's great symphonies, avant-garde music by Henze (born 1926), Nono (born 1924), Penderecki (born 1933), and others. I am not in favor of superlatives, but one has to admit that Karajan and his orchestra present a unity which, at the present time, cannot be found anywhere else. How lucky conductor and orchestra are if they can make music together for more than a quarter of a century as was also the case with Ormandy and the Philadelphia Orchestra!

Everybody knows that Karajan is not an easy man, but on the other hand, he is not as arrogant a person as he sometimes seems to be. He is actually a shy person, who finds it difficult to make friends, and often he does not know how to get along with his own orchestra, his "family," as he likes to call the Berlin Philharmonic, noted for the "eloquence" of some of their members during rehearsals. Yet, in most cases they do what Karajan wants them to do, because they are vitally interested in the music they play. Karajan's authority is never doubted. He is respected by his musicians without exception, and they do love to play under him because he possesses the marvellous gift of relaxing his orchestra without ever losing full control of music and musicians. He told me that it took him almost twenty years to achieve this capability. There are too many conductors who rule over the orchestra like dictators, determined to take care of the slightest detail. Karajan gives his musicians more freedom, he makes it possible for them to bring out the very best they can give. Yet, he never ceases to be their leader.

In addition, one fact must be realized: Karajan and the Berlin Philharmonic would never have reached such phenomenal heights without an adequate hall. Therefore, I would like to describe the Neue Philharmonie, a round hall, built by the renowned architect Hans Scharoun in 1963. At the beginning, it was rightly considered an experiment in line with the typical character of Berliners who like to do things off the beaten path, out of the ordinary, as people who want to experiment. Thus, when architects were asked to compete for the new concert hall, the first prize was awarded to Scharoun's

Concert hall of the Philharmonie Matthäikirchstr. 1, ward Tiergaten; built 1960–63; architect: Hans Scharoun.—October 16, 1963. Reproduced with permission of the Landesbildstelle Berlin.

design, which, indeed, was revolutionary. He dispensed with what most concert halls so far had been maintaining: a distinct separation between those who make music and those who listen, a separation which originated in the Church. Scharoun obviously preferred the theater in the round. He put the orchestra in the middle—although not the mathematical centre— with the audience surrounding it on all sides. This arrangement was new for the listeners, who now faced each other, and it proved a new experience for the conductor, too, because his work could be witnessed by a large part of the audience. Some conductors therefore refused to come to Berlin. Others got used to the hall. Karajan felt very happy to be in the center of the Neue

Philharmonie; as to the audience seated behind the orchestra and watching him keenly, he could not care less—he conducts with his eyes closed.

The hall is now generally recognized as a perfect success. It greatly enhances communication between the audience and the performers; one really does not seem to distinguish where the orchestra begins and the audience ends, and vice versa. It is all one. One feels like a big family, sitting so close to the strings that the slightest mistake can be heard.

When the hall opened, people wondered about the acoustics. I, too, was a little worried about it, especially after our acoustical expert had spoken of a "calculated risk," an experiment. As a matter of fact, we did have some trouble; the strings would not sound right, the wind instruments almost overwhelmed the strings, and the brass had a rather brutal sound. It took a couple of years before the acoustics were sufficiently improved. Now, after some more changes of the podium, I can say with a good conscience: the hall sounds excellent, it is one of the big attractions of Berlin. For visitors who cannot attend a concert, there are special tours during the day to guide them around the Philharmonie. In the meantime, Scharoun's innovation has inspired other architects (examples are the new Gewandhaus in Leipzig and the concert hall in Denver). To summarize: those who want to listen to a first-rate orchestra as well as to a top conductor, performing in a modern hall designed by a true genius—a unique hall which, so to speak, plays its own part during a concert—in Berlin will have an experience which—I state this in all modesty—no other city in the world can offer.

The Berlin Philharmonic orchestra gives more than a hundred concerts every year, plays 30 to 40 concerts on tour, and does many recordings which are quite popular. Many orchestra members devote themselves to chamber music; there are several string quartets, the Bläser Oktett der Berliner Philharmoniker (The Wind Octet of the Berlin Philharmonics) and other ensembles. Since the spring of 1988, they play in the new Chamber Music Hall, also called "The Small Philharmonie," which was opened, although it was not quite finished then, on the 28th of October, 1987, for one week during the celebrations of Berlin's 750th anniversary.

Right now the Berlin Philharmonic receives a subsidy of almost 17 million Marks. Since the income is low due to the low prices for the tickets, subsidies serve as a prerequisite for concerts and facilitate the work of the Intendant. He must not solicit for funds; he is not even permitted to ask for money unless he is in need of special contributions for a particular purpose—for instance in 1982, the celebration of the 100th anniversary of the Berlin Philharmonic.

Besides this leading orchestra, which is indeed one of the greatest cultural assets of Berlin, there is another internationally-known orchestra subsidized partly by Berlin, partly by Bonn, and indirectly by the two radio stations, Station Free Berlin (SFB) and Rias (Radio in the American Sector). Right after the war, Rias founded an orchestra of its own, the Rias orchestra, which today is called the Radio-Symphony-Orchestra Berlin. It is a marvellous orchestra, and still close to my heart, because I was its first Intendant between 1956–1959. This orchestra, too, has been led by outstanding conductors. The first one was the eminent Ferenc Fricsay (1914–1963), often praised as a second Furtwängler. Fricsay, whose recordings are still in demand, died at the age of 48, a terrible loss for the world of music. He was succeeded by Lorin Maazel, the former director of the Vienna Opera, presently chief conductor of the Pittsburgh Symphony. Then, a very young and promising conductor—not even 30 years old—has taken charge: Ricardo Chailly, an Italian, who may become one of the most noted conductors of the world and is already wanted by many orchestras. He soon will follow a call to Amsterdam.

A third orchestra is the Symphony Orchestra of Berlin (SOB). It is a fine group of about 70 musicians, playing excellent music for especially low prices. Responsible for its presently high artistic standard is an American conductor: Theodor Bloomfield, who headed the orchestra for many years. He is a splendid musician and a real educator. Bloomfield wanted to expand the orchestra and asked the Berlin Senate for higher subsidies. When he did not get his way, he resigned, but he still appears as a guest conductor. His place was taken by the young and very gifted Indian, Nathaniel Nazareth, who has been very successful in the Philharmonie as well as in the hall of the *Musikakademie* (Academy of Music) where the symphony orchestra alternately gives concerts. So there are three important orchestras to be heard in

René Kollo (left, Siegfried) and Horst Hiestermann (Mime) in "Siegfried," "The Ring of the Nibelungen, second day" by Richard Wagner; photograph taken at the occasion of the new staging by Friedrich Götz at the Deutsche Oper Berlin Wagnerstr. 10, ward Charlottenburg, on March 21, 1985. Reproduced with permission of the Landesbildstelle Berlin.

Berlin, all of which take part in the Berlin Festival held during the month of September. And, of course, there is the opera, called Deutsche Oper Berlin. Its season, like those of most leading German operas, extends over more than ten months. Performances begin at the end of August and continue until the end of June. Director (or General Manager) Götz Friedrich (born 1930), a well-known stage director, is a guarantee for excellent performances, an interesting program, new productions, and an ensemble of fine singers, among them many Americans. Götz Friedrich's wife, Karen Armstrong, presently heads the list of at least ten prominent Americans of whom all Berlin music lovers are rightly proud. The repertoire includes Berg's (1885–1935) *Lulu*, Janáček's (1854–1928) *Aus einem Totenhaus*, Puccini's (1858–1924) *La Fanciulla del West*, Korngold's (1897–1957) *Die tote Stadt*, the famous operas by Wagner, Verdi (1813–1901), Puccini (1858–1924), Mozart (1756–1791), etc. The orchestra of the opera house (Generalmusikdirektor [chief artistic director]: Jesus Lopez-Cobos) is of first quality, and the same is true for the fantastic ballet which, indeed, deserves a house of its own. To run an opera house with performances every night and to maintain

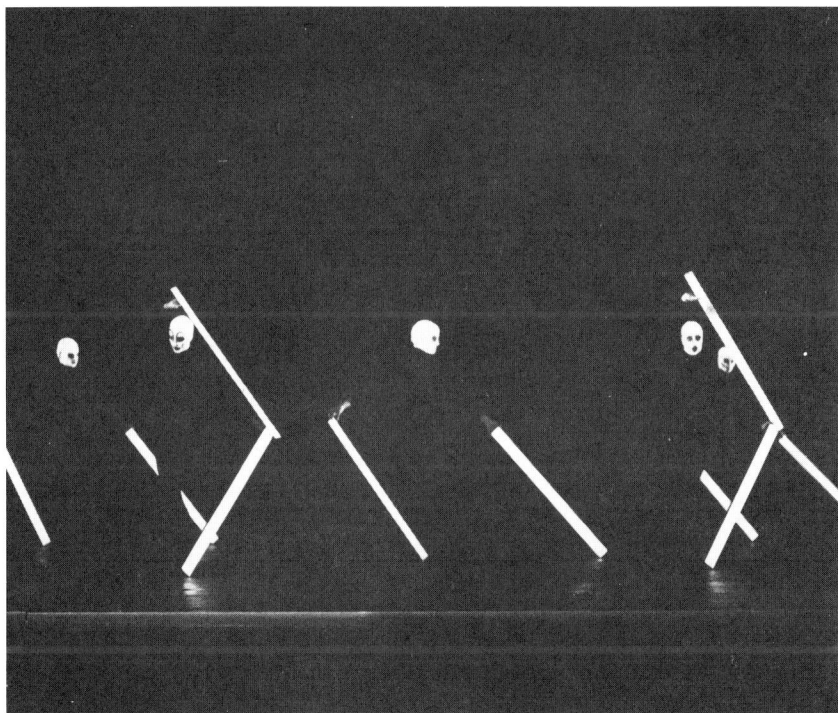

"Lichtknall—eine apokalyptische Odyssee" ("Light-bang—an apocalyptic Odyssey"), Ballet in three sections: harmony—light-bang—reminiscences (Harmonie—Lichtknall—Erinnerungen). Music and idea: Erhard Großkopf; choreography: Lucinde Childs; conductor: Michael Heise.—Deutsche Oper Berlin, ward Charlottenburg. November 13, 1987. Reproduced with permission of the Landesbildstelle Berlin.

a high level, is almost impossible. Yet, Götz Friedrich and his ensemble have turned it into reality. The proof? A sold-out house nearly every night.

A last word may be added about the musical events during the September festival. Its director, Ulrich Eckhardt, is a very imaginative man who always has something new to offer. When the 100th birthday of the Berlin Philharmonic Orchestra was to be celebrated, he proposed a joint program to the orchestra. A "Mahler Festival" was suggested, comprising all symphonies and other orchestral works of the Austrian composer, who had been boycotted by the Nazis. Karajan would do both the 6th symphony and the 9th; guest conductors, partly with their own orchestras, were supposed to take care of the other symphonies and lesser-known compositions. And so it happened. Besides Karajan, the Philadelphia Orchestra gave a moving performance of the 1st symphony; Haitink and his Concertgebouw Orchestra chose no. 3 and no. 7; Abbado and the London Symphony played no. 5; Kubelik, with the Bavarian Radio Orchestra, selected no. 2; the German Philharmonic Youth Orchestra, a quite remarkable group, offered a fine rendition of symphony no. 4; Jesus Lopez-Cobos and his opera orchestra programmed *Das Lied von der Erde*, while the Radio Symphony Orchestra under the baton of Ricardo Chailly presented the unfinished symphony no. 10 in the Cook-version. Besides all of these, Mahler-Lieder and his youthful *Das klagende Lied* could also be heard. The reception of this Mahler-Festival was most gratifying: all concerts were sold out! Berliners and many visitors from out of town attended the performances.

In 1983, the festival honored *György Ligeti* (born 1923), Anton von Webern (1883–1945), and sponsored performances of some very important Russian music written between 1900 and 1930 that had been neglected in Berlin as well as in Russia.

There was a time when Berlin—according to many observers—was the music center of the world. The conductors Furtwängler, Bruno Walter (1876–1962), Erich Kleiber (1890–1956), Leo Blech (1871–1958), and many other great musicians, for instance Fritz Kreisler (1875–1962) and Bronislaw Huberman (1882–1947), lived and performed in Berlin, sometimes at the same time. Schönberg taught there and so did Hindemith. In the old capital of Germany, contemporary music was regularly played. Stravinsky, Bartók (1881–1945), Prokofiev—to mention only a few—appeared as soloists in their own works and created much interest within the—as it was then called—"avant garde." At the same time, Richard Strauss, Hans Pfitzner (1869–1949), and other prominent composers who were born in the middle of the nineteenth century were applauded and appreciated by a large majority of musical audiences. The clash between old and new music produced what we may rightly call the cultural "Golden Twenties." But these are *tempi passati*. They can never be repeated for one single reason: even if one would manage to assemble the greatest artists in Berlin, one would never get the same kind of old Berlin audience that included so many Jewish people, who formed an especially receptive part of the listeners. They are gone forever.

Today, Berlin is still a music center of importance. As a matter of fact, if one would combine a visit to West and East Berlin as well, one could go to three splendid opera houses, attend concerts played by at least five to six

Percy Heath, Modern Jazz Quartet; photograph taken during the Berlin-Jazz-Days 1983 from October 27–30 in the Philharmonie, Matthäikirchstr. 1, ward Tiergarten. Reproduced with permission of the Landesbildstelle Berlin.

orchestras, and enjoy innumerable other musical events on both sides of the wall. During the fifties, Berliners of the western part of the city could easily become acquainted with Russian and Slavic composers, Janáček, Shostakovich, Dvořák (1841–1904), and others, and find at the Comic Opera under the direction of Walter Felsenstein remarkable representations of works by both eastern and western composers, put on the stage in opposition to the "culinary" representation of operas. But after the wall was built, East Berlin is (still) nearly as far away from West Berlin as are Leipzig or Dresden, those two other cities, now parts of the GDR, which have always been competing with Berlin. Now, we seldom visit East Berlin. It is a terrible nuisance to cross the border.

Everybody knows of the crises in Berlin, especially during the sixties. One may still feel a certain tension near the wall when an East Berliner tries to come over and fails. But this should not prevent one from visiting our fair city which offers so much. It is still a place where great music is played by great musicians. Although divided by the wall, but not divided in spirit, Berlin is worth a trip. If you have a chance to see the former German capital, do not hesitate. You may be assured of a warm welcome.

CHAPTER 16
Filmstadt Berlin

Ronald Holloway

Nowhere in the Federal Republic of Germany is the climate for filmmaking as fortuitous as it is in Berlin. Forget production studios and an infrastructure of film professionals. We are speaking in this case about a tradition, an atmosphere, a spontaneous inducement ("itch," if you will) to pick up a camera, sling some sound equipment over the shoulder, and go out and shoot a movie. We are talking about Filmstadt Berlin.

Scene: A young man in military fatigues with a wooden rifle in his hand is crawling on his belly across the Kurfürstendamm. He raises his head every couple of meters to gaze out towards a distant shore like a long-distance swimmer, and now and then he cries out "Deutschland!" The camera pans to *Wessies* (from *Wessiland*: jargon for West German tourists in Berlin) gawking along the sidewalk. Finally, along come the two expected policemen, who stop the traffic to pick up the "war protester" out of the middle of the Kudamm and lug him to the curb—right into the range of focus of Knut Hofmeister, who's been taking all the action in with his trusty Super-8 camera-and-sound unit. "Oh, you're making a movie," obliges one of the irritated but friendly cops. Shortly thereafter, *Deutschland!* (1981) could be seen at the Arsenal-Kino in "The Long Night of Super-8" program scheduled by the International Forum of Young Cinema during the Berlinale.

Cut to Strasse des 17. Juni in Berlin-Tiergarten. A familiar face is playing bag lady; in fact, she's scolding pimps, streetwalkers, and other passers-by who intrude upon her staked-out territory in the city park. It's Erika, the Berlinale's festival photographer, and she's doing her bit in a typical Lothar Lambert movie. Only, this Underground classic is eventually to launch the director and his "family of friends" into the public eye. *Tiergarten* (1979) is quintessential Berlin Underground.

Blend to a bustling *Kneipe* (pub) flowing over with a shooting crew from the German Film and Television Academy Berlin (DFFB). This last-ditch rum-shop is peopled usually by boozers and roués of every sort, but today a couple of "real actors" have stepped into the skid-row roles to accommodate Uwe Schrader in the making of his diploma feature film *Kanakerbraut* (1983). A compassionate statement on Berlin's subculture ("Kanakerbraut" is lingo for befriending a Turk), the DFFB production went on to win a German film prize and further recognition at Cannes in the Week of the Critics section.

Fade to a bridge over the Spree. Signs have been posted the day before, and the traffic over the Alt-Moabit-Brücke was rerouted on this particular evening. Then the arc-lamps go on, and cameraman Franz Rath rides the back of his Arriflex along a rail straight up to the bridge—just as an approaching car grinds to a halt, and a corpse is thrown over the side into the water. *Rosa Luxemburg*'s (1986) last shot is in the can.

Berliners are long accustomed to the city's character as an all-around "movie location." No one is sure how many productions get made here annually. But *TIP-Magazin* does know where you can go to see them screened and discussed at scattered venues across the city. For that matter, I've been phoned time and again by one filmmaker acquaintance or another to meet him in a private home or a factory loft for a premiere of "something new or different." Many a roomy apartment is fully equipped with cutting-tables, coop offices, and make-do studios. J. Hoberman of the *Village Voice*, and a confessed New York admirer of the Berlin Underground, is right when he says: "The thing that's interesting about Lambert is that it looks like he learned editing as he went along!"

That's what I mean when I say that the "climate" in Berlin is particularly inducive to filmmaking of any sort, one might even say "seductive." And it's been that way for all of the current century. Often Paris and Hollywood are named as the places where moviemaking came into its own, while Berlin is historically overlooked for some unforgivable reason. Yet the archives testify (as film restoration now becomes commonplace) that here was one of the authentic cradles of cinematic art.

Numbered among the city's film pioneers were Ottomar Anschütz (1846–1907), who invented the instantaneous shutter; Max Sklandanowsky (1863–1939), whose Bioskop projections in the Wintergarten Theater preceded the Lumière Brothers' show at the Grand Café in Paris by a full month in 1895; and Oskar Messter (1866–1943), whose experiments with the maltese cross for projection and synchronized "sound movies" (1903) were later superseded by the German film industry he helped to found on Friedrichstrasse in the heart of Berlin. One of his featured "Messter-Girls" was Henny Porten, for whom a worthy retrospective was organized by the Stiftung Deutsche Kinemathek Berlin at the 1986 Berlinale. Little doubt, Berlin was a European capital of moviemaking long before Robert Wiene's *Das Kabinett des Dr. Caligari* (*The Cabinet of Dr. Caligari*) appeared in 1919 to impress as the birth of the legitimate "art film."

The "dream factories" began being constructed as early as 1910 in Tem-

---

Photograph on p. 205

Sequence of the film "The Cabinet of Dr. Caligari" by Robert Wiene, 1919. Werner Krauß as Dr. Caligari. Reproduced with permission of "Stiftung Deutsche Kinemathek," Berlin, and Christian Fessel, Berlin.

Turning operations in the glassy studio (Glasatelier) of the Projection AG (limited company/stock corporation)—Union Berlin.—1913. Reproduced with permission of "Stiftung Deutsche Kinemathek," Berlin, and Christian Fessel, Berlin.

pelhof and Neubabelsberg, Woltersdorf, and Johannisthal. The Golden Era of German Expressionism owes much to the great cameramen, set designers, and other film professionals working inside studios for the most part. But there were other forms of filmmaking just as personally satisfying and creatively challenging to be cited alongside the memorable Ufa-productions: Lotte Reiniger's silhouette animation, Walter Ruttmann's experimental *Berlin—Die Sinfonie der Grossstadt (Berlin—Symphony of a Great City)* (1927), Hans Richter's avant-garde abstract films, Robert Siodmak's *Menschen am Sonntag (People on Sunday)* (1929) and Slatan Dudow's *Kuhle Wampe* (1932).

Ulrich Gregor in his essay *"Von der Traumfabrik zur Werkstatt: Film-Metropole Berlin"* (*From the Dream Factory to the Workshop: Film-Metropolis Berlin*) is right when he states that a *"Berlin-Mythos"* ties the traditions of the past together with the movements of the present. The extention of Ruttmann's *Die Sinfonie der Grossstadt* is Alfred Behrens's *Stadtbahnbilder (Cityscapes and the Berlin Stadtbahn)* (1981), both set into stylistic motion by the throb of rail transportation into or around the city. Siodmak's *Menschen am Sonntag* has its fitting sequal years later in Dieter Köster's and Hannelore Conradsen's *Berliner am Sonntag (Wild Clique)* (*Berliners on Sunday*) (1983). And the first graduating classes of the DFFB produced "worker films" in homage to the "proletariat cinema" exemplified by Dudow and Brecht's *Kuhle Wampe*. The parallels are as natural as they are varied.

Berliners feed on their film traditions nearly every day of the year. Besides the internationally distinctive Berlinale-cum-Forum event scheduled annually each February, the "Friends of the German Kinemathek" run programming all year around comparable to that of any cinémathèque in Europe. Gerhard Lamprecht, whose modest-scale Berlin films of the silent period set standards, brought his vast collection of films and cinemabilia to the Stiftung Deutsche Kinemathek and gave unsparingly of his time to DFFB students and "Friends" visiting the Arsenal-Kino, the first of the Off-Kudamm venues for alternative film programming. Today, two decades later, there are more than two dozen of these theatres supplying a hungry film audience with the best all-around movie fare found anywhere in Germany.

Festivals have become a byword in this "cultural Las Vegas"—indeed, all the arts receive a fair share of the attention, with film programming often enough supplying a deftly conceived side-attraction. But pick up a copy of the monthly *Filmszene* anytime, and you will find a "Festival of the Fantastic Film," a *"Kinder-Kino-Initiative,"* a "Week of Low-Budget Films," or an "International Short-Film Festival"—in addition to national film weeks from Taiwan, Ireland, New Zealand, the Basque Country of Spain, and a full-scale mounting of "Classics of the Animation Film."

The town is a haven for specialists. Gero Gandert of the Berlin Kinemathek painstakingly seeks out rare manuscripts and lost film prints for purchase from the estates of German and Austrian emigrants who shared in some significant way in Berlin's illustrious film past. Rolf Giesen, a world authority on special effects, has collaborated with Frank Schlegel on founding their FuturEffects Studio in a factory loft around the corner from the

Third International Film Festivals Berlin, 1953; opening showing in the Gloria Palast (Gloria Palace), Kurfürstendamm (ward Charlottenburg) on June 18, 1953. Reproduced with permission of the Landesbildstelle Berlin.

Bauhaus Museum. Alf Bold champions the cause of avant-garde filmmakers at the Arsenal in Berlin and the Collective for Living Cinema in New York. The filmographies and factual accounts of directorial careers in the hands of Hans Helmut Prinzler and Helga Belach are impeccably accurate each time the retrospective rolls around as an integral part of the Berlinale.

Writers and artists dabble in filmmaking here from time to time. Peter Stein's film version of his own stage production at the Schaubühne of Nicol Williams's *Klassenfeind (Class enemy)* (1983) is an integral work of art in its own right, demonstrating beyond any doubt that film and theatre can be creatively wedded. Writer Alfred Behrens has displayed a unique talent as a visual scenarist in the award-winning *Stadtbahnbilder* and *Walkman Blues* (1985), both poetic statements on the city and its everyday reality. Stage and screen actress Verena Rudolph changed directions in the middle of a successful career to enroll at the DFFB, a decision that appears to be a correct one if the promise of her diploma short, *Lucy* (1984) (about a long-lost aunt living today in Harlem), is any indication. Michael Bartlett, an American musician and member of the Radio Symphony Orchestra in Berlin, felt compelled to invest his earnings in a self-financed low-budget feature, *Konzert für die rechte Hand* (*Concerto for the Right Hand*) (1986), a debut that won him overnight recognition at the Mannheim festival and is all the more striking for the musical structure and rhythm of the narrative.

Foreign filmmakers on a DAAD (German Academic Exchange Service) grant usually prefer to settle in Berlin for their artist-in-residence term. Andrei Tarkovsky and Istvan Szabo were among the more distinguished resident DAAD artists, but the list has also included Yvonne Rainer, Stuart Sherman, and Clemens Klopfenstein. Klopfenstein, the Swiss-German winner of the *Max-Ophüls-Preis* in Saarbrücken for *E Nachtlang Füürland* (*All Night Long*) (1981) in 1982, used his DAAD opportunity in Berlin to make a striking visual short about his impressions of living in Kreuzberg, *Das Schlesische Tor* (*The Silesian Gate*) (1982). Some artists don't even need an invitation to go out and shoot something in Berlin. The Columbia University semiotics professor, Sylvère Lotringer, for example, simply flew into town, hired a video team, and in typical Gotham Underground style put an ad in the local paper to enlist a company of film enthusiasts to collaborate with him on a two-week project titled *Second-Hand Hitler* (1986). Lotringer's books are translated and published by Merve Verlag Berlin—indeed, one of them, *New Yorker Gespräche* (1983), features an interview with filmmaker-performer Stuart Sherman.

It is difficult to say just when Berlin became a vibrant city for a unique film subculture. But let's mark it down arbitrarily with the founding of the Berlin Film Academy twenty years ago in 1966. The advent of the Student Revolt in 1968 pushed classes on theory and history into the background, whereupon a number of students went out into the streets to document life-and-times in the raw. Others honed a neoproletariat film esthetic to a fine art in the movement known as the "worker film"—and German television (particularly Westdeutscher Rundfunk [WDR] Cologne) joined ranks by supporting the movement's leading exponents: Christian Ziewer, Max Willutzky, Marianne Lüdcke, and Ingo Kratisch. The founding of the International Forum of Young Cinema in 1971 as an integral part of the Berlin film festival helped to solidify the movement and paved the way for Berlin filmmakers to make a name for themselves internationally.

About the same time, those who were refused admission to the DFFB—among them Rainer Werner Fassbinder, Werner Schroeter, Rosa von Praunheim—broke out on their own to become respected filmmakers espousing personal statements over sociopolitical themes. Praunheim, followed by Robert Van Ackeren, Frank Ripploh, and others, thus pointed the way towards a fruitful independent Berlin film production. Feminist cinema was to get a share of the action as well: Ulrike Öttinger, for example, walked the lines between both the Underground and the Cine-Feminists.

At the same time, however, the Cine-Feminists grew out of the passion and commitment of the film academy's worker-film movement. Directors like Helke Sander and Marianne Lüdcke were among the first DFFB graduates who sought to combine the two esthetics. Their platform, in turn, was to become the International Forum of Young Cinema at the Berlinale. Thus it was not by accident that the *Frauen und Film* (Women and Film) journal was to have its base of operations in Berlin.

Both DFFB students and Berlin film buffs naturally took a great interest

Studio Drei (Studio Three) of the DFFB Berlin (German Film and Television Academy Berlin), Pommernallee 1, ward Charlottenburg. Shooting operations (Dreharbeiten) for the film "The Purloined Letter" by Stepan Benda, after E.A. Poe, August 1987. Photograph by Christian Fessel. Reproduced with permission of "Stiftung Deutsche Kinemathek," Berlin, and Christian Fessel, Berlin.

in the restoration of low-budget, socially engaged classics produced under the Weimar Republic. The films of Werner Hochbaum, Phil (Piel) Jutzi, and Gerhard Lamprecht were particularly cherished—indeed, Jutzi's *Mutter Krausens Fahrt ins Glück (Mother Krausen's Journey to Heaven)* (1929) and *Berlin Alexanderplatz* (1931) became cult films among the "New Left" post-1968 generation. Heinz Rathsack, whose double function as head of both the DFFB and the Kinemathek, painstakingly put together retrospectives of these forgotten minor masterpieces in cooperation with historians and archivists in the German Democratic Republic (the last was the Peter Pewas retro in 1979).

If nothing else, these low-budget classics demonstrated how to film in the streets, how to obtain a high degree of realism by seeking out actual locations, and how to find ways of releasing the films to appreciative audiences via a self-sufficient distribution and exhibition system. Further, the desire to restore these classics as authentic portaits of Berlin ("pieces of time," as to speak) has led to archival perservation work on films dating from *Die*

Sinfonie der Grossstadt and *Menschen am Sonntag* of the 1920s to *Kuhle Wampe* and *Mutter Krausens Fahrt ins Glück* of the 1930s up to even Roberto Rossellini's *Germania Anno Zero* (*Germany Year Zero*) (1947). The recent retrospective, "*Berlin. Innen und Aussen*," illustrates the historical importance of this undertaking. Just as significant is the inspirational factor involved in the making of Dieter Köster's *Berliner am Sonntag* and Alfred Behrens's *Stadtbahnbilder*, regardless of whether or not the directors' relationship to the Jutzi and Ruttmann forerunners be conscious or not.

Besides the DFFB and the DAAD imput, there was also the Literarisches Colloquium as a think-tank center of creativity in all the arts. Filmmakers like George Moorse and Helma Sanders-Brahms, Horst Kurnitzky, and Marion Schmid, benefited in particular from the supportive liberality of this institution situated in picturesque Wannsee on the shores of Lake Havel. Since this is an establishment for fostering creative artistic talent, its ties to DAAD and the newly founded Film and Media Art section of the Academy of Fine Arts in Tiergarten, the latter under Peter Lilienthal and Eberhard Fechner's administration, are natural and fortuitous in supporting a spontaneity on the Berlin filmmaking scene.

A word should be said about Sender Freies Berlin (SFB) as well. Not only has SFB provided a professional outlet for many DFFB graduates (Wolfgang Tumler, Dieter Köster), but this ARD (First German Television) station also has collaborated with New German Cinema filmmakers (Ulrich Schamoni, Peter Lilienthal) on individual film and television coproductions. Further, Michael Strauven, SFB's film moderator (appearing on the *Kino* program), has consistently offered Berlin filmmakers a platform for discussing their latest projects with the general public. And on the other side of town, across the street from the former UFA-Studios at Tempelhof (today named BUFA), the Berlin production facilities of ZDF (Second German Television) provide a ready contact to locally based producers, such as Regina Ziegler and Joachim von Vietinghoff.

Lately, a new video and television experiment—PK Berlin, the Berlin cable station in Wedding—has activated several independent groups in the city, who share in the Open Channel and Mixed Channel public-service programming. A video cooperative like "medienoperativ" has contributed much to the formation of a video chronicle of cultural and social activities throughout the city.

Berlin filmmakers have their own umbrella organization Berliner Arbeitskreis Film (BAF). Well over 100 active filmmakers are members of this loosely knit group, while a reported 100 more have registered for membership by virtue of having made Super-8 films or 16-mm shorts. BAF has at least served to tie together scattered splinter organizations into a core group when film policies are being discussed or made at the Berlin Senate. It is especially visible during the annual Berlinale in February and the festivities surrounding the German Film Prizes in June.

Many prominent producers and distributors prefer being based in Berlin. Manfred Durniok (*Mephisto*, 1981), Artur Brauner (*Bittere Ernte/Angry Harvest*, 1985), Herbert Baumann (*Einmal Ku'damm und zurück/A Berlin Love Story*, 1985), Horst Wendlandt (*Otto—der Film/Otto—The Film*, 1985), and the aforementioned Regina Ziegler (*Die Reise/The Journey*, 1986) and Joachim von Vietinghoff (*Laputa*, 1986) are genuine Berliners. Wim Wenders (Road Movies) and Chris Sievernich (Delta) have offices here. Two of Germany's major independent distribution companies, Jugendfilm (Jürgen Wohlrabe) and Tobis (Horst Wendlandt, Kilian Rebentrost), work exclusively out of Berlin, while Basis-Film distributes Berlin and Kuratorium productions. The Berlin branch of the renown Geyer-Werke film laboratory on Harzer Strasse in Neukölln maintains direct contact with top German cameramen and is justly famous for contributing to the international reception of such festival entries as Wim Wenders's *Paris, Texas* (1984), Werner Herzog's *Nosferatu* (1978), Maximilian Schell's *Der Fussgänger* (*The Pedestrian*) (1974) and Margarethe von Trotta's *Rosa Luxemburg*. The headquarters of the German Federal Film Board (FFA) is located in Berlin; as the administrative arm of the Ministry of Economics in Bonn, it maintains a supportive link to the German Film Export Union (EXU) in Munich.

For Berlin's 750th anniversary celebrations in 1987 an exhibition on Berlin as a film center was presented in the planned Filmhaus Esplanade. Once restored, this extensively reconstructed former deluxe hotel for nobility (skirting the Berlin Wall in Tiergarten) will house in the future certain key film organizations and institutions (Kinemathek, "Friends of the Kinemathek," BAF), in addition to providing Berlin with a needed archival vault and cinémathèque screening facilities.

As far as the nooks and corners are concerned where all this Berlin filmmaking activity can be found, the general designation is Kreuzberg. Because of its roomy factory lofts and cheap housing, students migrate to Kreuzberg to participate in one of the richest subcultures since the New Yorkers discovered SoHo in Manhattan. Here are not only "film freaks," but also pop bands and alternative theatre groups and artist colonies. Rudolf Thome (*Berlin Chamissoplatz*, 1980) is a Kreuzberger through and through, but so also are Manfred Stelzer (two films on the Georg-Rauch-Haus) and documentarists Johann Feindt and Klaus Volkenborn (*Der Versuch zu leben*/*Trying to Stay Alive* (1983) about an emergency ward in a Kreuzberger hospital). The Künstlerhaus Bethanien offers regular directorial seminars in this converted landmark hospital now serving as a major cultural center.

Still, all things considered, some guiding principles plus a liberal subsidy system have to be underscored as the primary causes of Berlin's flowering status as a film production center. These are found, respectively, in the Berlin Senate and the Berlin Film Fund (*Berlin-Effekt*). The Berlin Senate, particularly the Senator for Cultural Affairs, Dr. Volker Hassemer, has made it a continuing practice to support alternative art forms. As a result, the city is booming with musical groups, alternative theatre, video cooperatives, a Panke-Halle for the plastic and graphic arts, and a stimulating Berlin Underground. One has only to pay a visit to the UFA-Fabrik in Tempelhof—as foreign journalists did during the last German Film Prizes—to catch the spirit of a 70-member commune "occupying" the grounds of the former film laboratory and postproduction facilities of the Ufa-Studios. The UFA-Fabrik runs on its grounds one of Berlin's "Off-Kudamm" venues, in addition to maintaining a youth hostel, a performing circus, an organic bakery, a continuous program of stage presentations, and a barnyard farm for children to visit.

The Berlin Film Fund (BFF)—founded in 1978 under the administration of Dr. Günter Struwe, then managed from 1979 to 1987 by Dr. Hubert Ortkemper and now by Hans Robert Eisenhauer—has become over the years the life-blood of Berlin film production across the board from international projects to modest low-budget films of every type and genre. Once a filmmaker receives BFF aid, he can then combine other subsidy grants (Kuratorium junger deutscher Film, Ministry of the Interior, FFA funding, television coproduction) to get a promising script before the cameras and into postproduction with relative ease. In effect, the Berlin Senate offers a credit loan that has to be paid back only if the production makes a profit at the box office.

One would think that with the risks down to the minimum many would take undue advantage of BFF largesse and liberality. And, of course, some tax-shelter flops are reported to have been produced here. But the very climate in Berlin for winning grudging favor from one of the most knowledgeable and demanding film audiences in Europe prevents at least the genuine Berlin filmmakers from spoiling their chances far into the future. Indeed, the spirit of competition makes for adventure, spontaneity, and outright enthusiasm.

The proof of the pudding is found in the Berlin Film Tour throughout cultural and university centers in North America and in Asia during the 750th anniversary celebrations in 1987 and Berlin's celebration as the "Cultural City of Europe 1988." Two phases of Berlin Film Production, the commercial and the alternative, are presented in the tour. On the first level, festival entries are highlighted to promote Berlin as a more than seductive location for international coproductions. On the second, a selection of low-budget films offer an overview of the very life-style of Berlin with all its enticing and contradictory aspects.

Over the past eight years, the Berlin Film Fund has nursed some 200 films to production and release. The BFFs record at major international film festivals is enviable. In fact, even when funding could not be made available for a local project, the desire itself to "go out and shoot something" in Berlin proved to be an avenue of approach to subsidy funding on the next turn around. Further, due to the recent policy of opening up BFF credit funding to low-budget and (in 1987) television productions, the responsibility was felt to conduct a seminar and ongoing experiment on fostering scriptwriters (instead of leaning too heavily in the direction of writer-director *Autoren*). The seminar was held at the Literarisches Colloquium in the summer of 1986, while a new emphasis on the skills of scriptwriting is currently being introduced at the Berlin Film and Television Academy.

Festival selections in the Berlin Film Tour are remarkable in that many of these have also been the key attractions of the past few German film seasons. Otto Waalkes and Xaver Schwarzenberger's *Otto—der Film* (*Otto—The Film*) (produced by Wendlandt for Tobis release) broke box-office records in 1985 and is the most successful German production since the last war. It was shot on the lot of the CCC-Filmkunst Studios in Spandau. Its sequel, *Otto—der neue Film* (*Otto—The New Film*), released in 1987, has now confirmed Waalkes as a major box-office attraction in Germany.

Margarethe von Trotta's *Rosa Luxemburg*, the official German entry at the 1986 Cannes festival, was the fifth film the prominent woman director has shot in Berlin. Her cameraman, Franz Rath, worked with the Geyer Lab's Hans-Joachim Rabs on giving the film an extra historical polish by muting or fading the colors via a "color-bleaching" process.

Markus Imhoof's *Die Reise* (*The Journey*) (1986), the official German-Swiss entry at Venice in 1986, is the latest (and arguably the best) filmed statement on the social and political background to the 1968 Student Revolt movement and the subsequent phenomenon of the Baader–Meinhof group. Berlin's Regina Ziegler was the German coproducer.

Helma Sanders-Brahms's *Laputa*, selected for the Certain Regard section at the 1986 Cannes festival, takes the viewer on a windmill journey through Berlin on a single day. The very fact that the spoken language is French, that the city is compared to Swift's fictitious island in *Gulliver's Travels* (for West Berlin is truly an island), and that the principals are a French architect and a Polish photographer caught in a hopeless East–West love affair—all these elements reflect the political reality of Berlin in pell-mell fashion.

Peter Timm's *Meier*, (1986), winner of the 1987 Ernst Lubitsch Prize (awarded by Berlin film journalists), zeroes in on the reality of two Berlins separated by a foreboding wall as no other film before it—with the possible exception of Reinhard Hauff's *Der Mann auf der Mauer* (*The Man on the Wall*) (1982) based on Peter Schneider's story with the same title. The protagonist lives and works in East Berlin (where most of the film is set), but he is the beneficiary of two passports (to explain how that happened is what the film is all about) and can waltz his way as a happy "brigadier" of a wall-papering crew between the socialist and capitalist systems—until one night he gets caught at the border pawning off the wrong passport!

Lienhard Wawrzyn spent a good part of a year living in East Berlin while researching the background for *German Dreams* (1985). This fiction-documentary, or documentary-drama, deals with the fate of a mother and her teenaged daughter who have paid a bitter price (a jail term for the mother) to reach the "Golden West"—only to find that dreams are far from reality in trying to adapt to the life-style of West Berlin.

Herbert Ballmann—like Timm and Wawrzyn, a director who knows the ways of the German Democratic Republic firsthand—was inspired by a true incident to make *Einmal Ku'damm und Zurück* (German title translates "Once to Kudamm and Back"). It's the story of a cook in the Swiss embassy *in der Hauptstadt der DDR* (in the capital of the GDR) who accommodates his East Berlin girlfriend by stashing her away in the trunk of his Mercedes to cross back and forth over the border at will with his diplomatic passport. All goes well—until an unforeseen automobile accident spills the beans and causes a political ruffle at the Four-Powers level. For her performance in this film, actress Ursela Monn won an Ernst Lubitsch Prize in 1985.

Besides Uwe Schrader's prizewinning *Kanakerbraut*, there are at least two other films made by Berliners that deal with the "skid row" fate of a city that stays up all night without ever rolling up the sidewalks. One is the Dieter Köster documentary, *Ein rauschendes Leben* (*A Drunken Life*) (1984), in which the bars and *"Kneipen"* provide the backdrop for a study of social drinking from the top to the bottom of the economic scale. The other is

Thorsten Näter's *Zeit der Stille* (*Time of Stillness*) (1986), a black-and-white portrait of two lonely people who suffer through the cold amenities of the Christmas holiday season—until the silence is broken when they come into contact with each other on the phone purely by accident.

Marcel Gisler's *Tagediebe* (*Hangin' Around*) (1983), a prizewinner at Locarno in 1985, takes the pulse of the free-and-easy younger generation in Berlin today. An "open city" in the true sense of the word, this odd status is reflected in the meanderings of three individuals from "outside Berlin" subletting an apartment while the owner is away. All are artists in Kreuzberg without a portfolio to speak of. The insights are offered by a Swiss filmmaker who studied at the DFFB, and they are not too far distant from another tongue-in-cheek low-budget feature by Helmut Berger, Anja Franke, and Dany Levy (the latter another Swiss filmmaker who has settled in Berlin-Kreuzberg) titled *Du Mich Auch* (*The Same to You*) (1986) chosen for the Week of the Critics section at the 1987 Cannes festival. And finally there's the impressionist short, *Das Schlesische Tor*, by DAAD exchange artist Clemens Klopfenstein. This Swiss filmmaker compares Kreuzberg to street scenes experienced in Tokyo and Hong Kong, and its soundtrack complementing the images is a sheer delight.

Some of the best portraits of Berlin involve music at the experiential level. Peter Fratzscher's *Asphaltnacht* (*Asphalt Night*) (1980) started a series off by capturing the attraction of the city for rock groups, jazz musicians, and blues musicians. Another feature of the same phenomenon is found in Alfred Behrens's *Walkman Blues* and specifically on the soundtracks of Martin Theo Krieger's *Zischke* (1986) and Berger, Franke, and Levy's *The Same to You* (a moaning saxophone sets the tempo). Even a DFFB student couldn't resist the urge: Otmar Hitzelberger titled his humorous short film on the goings-on in a hospital ward *Klinikblues* (*Clinic Blues*) (1986). And finally a musician-turned-filmmaker, Michael Bartlett, "composed" an independent low-budget feature film like a city symphony: *Concerto for the Right Hand*.

The best of the original Berlin films usually deal simultaneously with the sunny and the shadowy side of life, whether thematically or stylistically. Diethard Küster's *Va Banque* (1986) features three down-on-their-luck would-be bankrobbers fumbling their way through an armored-car heist, driven to their deed as much out of boredom as of a desire to get rich. The coup succeeds, but a fourth con man makes off with a share of the loot—and everyone in the end gets off scot-free! Berlin filmmakers have compassion for the underdog. Mehrangis Montazami's documentaries—*Männerrecht* (*A Mother's Plight*) (1981) and *Kindertränen* (*A Child's Tears*) for instance—defend the human rights of Turkish foreign workers in dilapidated areas of Kreuzberg and elsewhere in Berlin, even though one supposes that things might be worse for the same families back in Turkey. Also, Jeanine Meerapfel's *Die Kümmeltürkin geht* (*Melek Leaves*) (1984) goes far out of her way to question the justice of deporting Turkish workers after the same have spent years working various unskilled-labor jobs in the city. And Berlin films are, more often than not, committed to a cause even when analyzing the weaknesses of that commitment. Ula Stöckl's *Der Schlaf der Vernunft* (*Reason Asleep*) (1984) leaves little doubt that women's emancipation (viewed by means of Euripides' classic *Medea*) is a thorny path any way you look at it, personally and intellectually.

In this case, one Berlin filmmaker could stand for the whole. Martin Theo Krieger's *Zischke* grew out of the DFFB graduate's work for other Berlin filmmakers as a cameraman—among them for Reinhard Münster on *Dorado* (*One Way*) (1983), a hilarious spoof of the entire history of New German Cinema's stylistic traits. In *Zischke* the eternal circle prevents everyone in the story from attaining his or her aim, often enough that disruption caused by the blind acts of others involved in the same merry-go-round of affairs: an abandoned teenager, a young prostitute without a pad, a Lebanese actress fighting off the advances of a stage director, two illegal Arab exiles seeking asylum in West Berlin with falsified passports, a trio of plain-clothes cops whose numbers include one tainted by corruption. Filmed in black-and-white, the images coupled with the soundtrack offer a rare density in capturing the atmosphere of the city in alienated wintery surroundings. Yet when Zischke (short for Christoph) tries half-heartedly to catch a train at Bahnhof Zoo to run away from the city and join his father in Italy, he somehow manages to miss it. For better or for worse, his destiny is to be found here in Berlin.

CHAPTER 17

Berlin as a Theater Center

Joachim Werner Preuss

Berlin is a theater center—this is a commonly accepted status, but embraced in this notion now is the political fate of the city, which has changed as a result of the Second World War. Until 1944, when "total war" was declared by the Nazi Propaganda Minister Goebbels and theaters were closed, Berlin was not only the *Reichshauptstadt*, the political center, but it was also the capital of German theater. Undeniably.

Theater in Berlin today (we speak here of West Berlin) is now once again in transition. It can be explained only if one also looks at history, and this means, as far as Berlin is concerned, at the environment too.

There was a time when it really meant something to be *the* German theater center! For Germany, this did not come about as naturally and as matter of fact as was the case with other theater centers e.g., Paris, Vienna, and London. Theater history in Berlin began relatively late, if the sparse chronicles, surviving the many wars, are to be believed. According to the very vague reports, interest in theater began in Berlin in the middle of the sixteenth century, more than a hundred years later than elsewhere. This interest, instigated by Joachim II, the Kurfürst (elector) of Brandenburg, consisted of educational exercises in speech and conduct, practised with "poor town youth" in cloisters. The theater resulting from these exercises still remained mostly dialogues for a courtly pastime, and the religious schools of the rectories contented themselves with Latin dialogues to educate their pupils. These performances were later opened to the public, and it was then that the first admission tickets were sold. Even the medieval christian Market-Place-Play (Marktplatz-Spiel), performed in town squares, apparently never found its way to Berlin. "Real" theater did not arrive on the Berlin scene before the end of the sixteenth century, in the form of German strolling players.

Thereafter, theater history continued to ebb and flow. While the princes' tastes in theater often varied from pure sensational vigor to Italian or French opera, they would also at times prohibit any "plays" altogether. The earliest French court-troupe was not registered until 1706. Thirty-five years earlier,

Translated from the German by Ronald Holloway and Gerhard Kirchhoff.

however, a French troupe had made its first appearance in Germany, 190 miles from Berlin at the court of Hannover. A French troupe had appeared in Dresden six years before it appeared in Berlin, and Berlin is only 120 miles from Dresden.

In terms of theater history, the residence in the Mark Brandenburg, which in 1701 became the kingdom of Prussia, is of interest from only the middle of the eighteenth century. With this in mind one of the forming peculiarities of German theater history should be noted. Berlin, this latecomer in theater, was then part of a Germany belonging to the *Duodezfürsten* (petty princes). This meant not only dependence on the whims and prejudices of a ruling princely lord, but also the lack of any political or cultural German unity.

For the general development of the German theater, these conditions were not a disadvantage. Rather, as a result of these circumstances, which were the base of German theater, a broad, multilayered, court-centered cultural (theatrical) scene came into being. Also incorporated very soon were not only the *Großbürger* (upper middle-class bourgeois) but also the intelligentsia. Despite political power shifts in Germany, no attempt was made to counteract this regionalisation which had originated out of a constantly growing number of court theaters which were opened to the public. Additionally strolling troupes became stationary, at least for a time, in theater buildings they built themselves or which were maintained by well-to-do burghers.

Endeavors of this kind carried a general process of consciousness across Germany. Thus, it was impossible for the first German republic in 1918 not to adopt the existing court theater scene (just as it had gone without saying that, with the birth of a German Imperial State (Deutsches Kaiserreich) in 1871, only regional political march power centers had to give way to Berlin as the new German Imperial capital). Even the centrally oriented National Socialist dictatorship (1933/45) didn't change this structure.

Influenced by the spread of industry, Berlin, the growing, flourishing city, had already also become a theatrically rich center by 1869, when freedom of trade was declared. A special form of popular comedy (the *Alt-Berliner Posse*) had already begun by the 1820s and a culture of popular theater developed. Berlin, the capital of the then German emperors from 1871 on, definitely became the undisputed German theater metropolis as well, with more than fifty stages. Certainly, there was later to be prominent theater work elsewhere in Germany, but Berlin was looked to for comparison and orientation. Here the decisive battles for stylistic trends were fought and here a theater movement on behalf of the common people was pushed through. Here nearly all of the best and most important talents gathered. But this all happened—it should be impressed—within the short span of approximately 75 years, 1871 to 1944! A short period indeed!

As a result of the Second World War, Berlin lost more than its role as the political capital. It did appear for a time that Berlin, the site of early East/West confrontation, could be the German center for those tensions, discussions, and clarifications which often lead to cultural evolution, not the least of which would take place within the theater. But the division of Germany, and the later erection of the wall, which split the city in two, diminished that prospect. As far as the German theater was concerned, this weakening of expectations surely meant a loss but also a gain, because it gave way to the competition of decentralized and differing efforts.

A stronger federalism in the years immediately following 1945, confirmed by the founding of the Federal Republic of Germany in 1949, once again, as the Weimar Republic did, emphasized the historical structure of the German cultural scene by allowing each individual federal state (*Land*) *Kulturhoheit* (cultural sovereignty) to determine its own cultural character. As a result of this decision, diversified theater centers became important throughout the country, and consequently the attraction and the influence which Berlin had doubtlessly exerted on the whole cultural scene of Germany for some 75 years were strongly reduced. A much freer and much more self-conscious feeling permeated the culture, promoting the consciousness and the cultural activities of both West German cities and the regions.

For West Berlin this new situation has presented a challenge, complimenting the city's compulsion to reassert itself politically. As a result of the East/West confrontation the city originated both the *Berlin Festwochen* (Berlin Autumn Arts Festival) and the *Berlinale* (Berlin International Film Festival), both started in 1951. The function of each is the examination of cultural and theatrical achievements on a world-wide scale. Rising to meet its challenge, Berlin set world standards and became a place to go to experience a high calibre of cultural and theatrical performances. Effects on the Berlin scene itself could not fail to appear. Spoken theater, as well as opera, succeeded in renewing themselves by settling for nothing less than celebrated ensemble work recognized beyond Berlin's borders. Important world and German premieres graced the repertoires. All conditions appeared to be met for Berlin to once again claim the role of theatrical leadership, yet this claim came to nought due to the city's environmental conditions! Berlin, as a political island, could no longer entice (as it once could) nearly all of the best and most important talents to settle and to work there. However, in one sense at least, Berlin had not ceased to be *the* German city of theater; it continued (and continues) to boast a high number of theaters as well as visitors, unmatched by any other German city. (According to the latest statistics, the private stages in Berlin embrace one-seventh of all those in the Federal Republic of Germany and account for more than one-fourth of all the private-theater audience. In addition, Berlin's state theaters and theater festivals account for over 10 percent of the overall theater-going public at both state and communal stages in the Federal Republic of Germany.)

A sentimental legend has it that in Berlin you will find the "best public" anywhere, although presumably this is hardly a legend. Even though the ministers of cultural affairs and theater professionals were and are right in proudly raving about the performance standards and the breadth and diversity of the German theater scene, it didn't take very long until the loss dating from 1945 was felt and became conscious: the survey was difficult and the coherence disturbed, since *the* centre as the place for binding orientation no longer existed. The solution was found in 1964. A *Theatertreffen* (Berlin Theater Rally) was organized annually, at which a panel of theater critics chose the most remarkable and trend-setting stage productions on the German speaking scene (including Austria and German-speaking Switzerland;

only the German Democratic Republic refused to participate). This event was enriched by inviting international dance troupes and independent fringe groups in search of new forms for the theater as part of the alternative cultural scene of Berlin. Thus Berlin, despite some disputes on the matter of particular panel decisions, remained for at least these three theater-festival weeks *the* theater capital.

It should perhaps be emphasized once again that even if Berlin might only be *the* theater capital now due to such special events as the *Theatertreffen*, it still remains the leading theater center when compared to the other cities. Berlin's accumulation of theaters surpasses that of any other German city. It receives the comparatively highest state subsidy for state and private stages. Nowhere else can be found such a stock of regular theater audiences. Approximately 100,000 people are registered in "theater-goer" organizations, who annually purchase between 700,000 and 800,000 tickets. This fact alone identifies Berlin as the leading theater center among several others. Furthermore Berlin succeeded on the one hand with the *Deutsche Oper* to thrust forward into the phalanx of internationally recognized music theaters and on the other hand it has firmly established two other theater creations whose

Theater "Schaubühne", Lehniner Platz, Kurfürstendamm 153, ward Charlottenburg/Wilmersdorf.—January 1983. Reproduced with permission of the Landesbildstelle Berlin.

work have achieved world-wide acclaim: the *Schaubühne* which began at Am Halleschen Ufer and now is situated on Lehniner Platz in one of the most modern theaters, and the *Grips Theater* for children and youth. This theater chiefly features original plays of its own, along hilarious comical and

"Grips Theater" for children and adolescents, Altonaerstraße 22, Hansa Viertel (Hansa Quarter), ward Tiergarten.—October 1980. Photograph by Frank Roland Beeneken. Reproduced with permission of the Grips Theater and Frank Roland Beeneken, Berlin.

critical lines that aim to be educational and illuminating. (Most of them are translated into foreign languages and are staged internationally.) Then, in all fairness, I must point out that they are connected to two other stages located on Berlin's renown boulevard Kurfürstendamm: the *Komödie* and the *Theater am Kurfürstendamm*, which in the category of boulevard theater are considered the leading stages in Germany, as well as to the state-financed *Theater des Westens*, the sole theater for revues, musicals, and operettas in the Federal Republic of Germany. Finally, I mention an additional peculiarity in order to keep the record straight within this extensive frame of reference: there are annually between 50 and 75 productions of independent theater groups on the competitive scene, most of which perform on their own premises and many with a modest state subsidy.

Being aware of the function of a German theater metropolis, and that *the* German theater center could not be maintained following the Second World War, who would, on a strictly quantative basis, dispute the city's title of "leading theater center." But, politically and physically, for the time being, nothing more than a half city. There has, for the last couple of years, not reigned an adequate mood for even restricted euphoria. Those most important directors who during the 1950's, 1960's, and 1970's set standards in Berlin's theater life and, at least as guest directors, served as a tie to the other most important theater centers, rarely come to Berlin anymore! And direc-

"Theater des Westens" (Theater of the West), Kantstraße 12, ward Charlottenburg.—
January 1983. Reproduced with permission of the Landesbildstelle Berlin.

tors of the new generation whose talents have matured over the past three
decades and who have made their mark in German theater, they have found
managerial positions and settled elsewhere, working in Berlin only on an
occasional basis. Berlin theater, known over the decades since the war (just
as in its early days of intensity and larger abundance) for its energy and love
of a challenge through creative contact with many highly respected directorial talents, over the recent past has had few opportunities for such important stimulation. As a result of that, the overregional tiffs with other
key centers have also noticeably declined—a fact that, in the last analysis,
is valid for nearly all centers with regard to overregional cooperation.
Furthermore, and almost as confirmation of the overall German theater
scene, it has become evident that, at other centers too, the hopes once set on
the activities of the independent fringe groups materialized only scantily—
just as it happened in Berlin when an Eldorado for independent groups came
into being through a cultural policy aimed at an alternative scene in the
political as well as the experimental theater. But with the loss of social and,
presumably, also cultural points of friction, the inner tension, to a large
extent has been lost. Due to the fact that these independent fringe groups
tend to copy the established theaters, their repertoires are a mishmash of
offerings from yesterday and today. They show as little desire for discovery

(whereby they would appear "alternative" at least in this regard) as do their competitors, the established companies. Stimulation via provocation also seems to be nearly impossible, for the time being.

Berlin's special domain, dating back to the postwar years, to secure a reputation as *the* theater city for discovery and promotion (for example the plays of Beckett and Albee) is today, without any doubt shared by other German theater centers as well. And what had been expected for a couple of years—creative friction and inspiration from the lately more accessible stages in East Berlin, the so-called *Hauptstadt der DDR* (capital of the GDR)—didn't occur at all simply because the most important East German theater directors do not appear very often in their theater capital. Instead, they prefer (if they are allowed) to be guest directors at West German theaters (from where some do not return). Though they are not prepared to work in West Berlin theaters. Moreover, new discoveries are to be found not so much in East Berlin, but in Schwerin, Dresden, Leipzig, and Weimar.

Whether one speaks of West or East Berlin, even when taken together as a common concept, they both appear, above all, to be completely separate theater cities; two individual centers. Should these ever be connected into a single theater center, Berlin would rank as a huge common complex with the opportunity to develop into something much more. What's lacking is not

"Schiller Theater", Bismarckstraße 10, ward Charlottenburg.—January 1983. Reproduced with permission of the Landesbildstelle Berlin.

conceptual thinking on the matter. The East Berlin theater scene, with its accumulation of prominent stages, officially claims to be the center of "Socialist National Theater in the GDR" (even though this claim aesthetically when compared to what is offered, is hardly fulfilled). In West Berlin, the *Schaubühne* once had also established itself as a model for sociopolitical experiment (particularly for a long time under the direction of Peter Stein). Now it has largely developed into a stage of stylistically a esthetic elevation of splendid isolation (though mostly still admired for being just that), where the overriding factor is timelessness, or even flight from time, rather than what could be called a concern with the present, or a look towards the future. Almost as an answer to this development as well as to the East Berlin conception of profile, West Berlin's cultural policy has pondered how to impose upon the *Staatsschauspiel* (Theater of State) with its three stages the character of a German National Theater. Should this effort succeed, we would have, in a different way than before, *the* new theater capital. However, G.E. Lessing (1729–1781) already expressed his doubts concerning the realization of a German National Theater. Today, at this moment in history, it doesn't seem any more likely.

SECTION IV
A Thriving City

CHAPTER 18

Berlin as an Intellectual Center

Karl W. Deutsch

How can I convey to you something about my interests in and my image of Berlin? I first visited this city in 1922, at the ripe age of ten. In 1930, as a student, I hitchhiked there because I felt it was so important to see the great world. Looking at the world from Prague, Berlin was the first piece of the great world, and it was within reach. Later on, I saw Berlin in 1935, bedecked with flags and noisy with parades and loudspeakers, and—after having seen other cities of Germany just rising out of the rubble in 1948—I saw Berlin again in 1963, and I saw both parts of Berlin, West Berlin, and Mr. Khrushchev's visit to East Berlin at that particular time. I went to Berlin again in 1973 when student unrest was still reverberating in the walls of the universities, and again in 1975 and 1976; and from 1976 on, first for a month and then for a half of each year I have been in Berlin, working. Bertolt Brecht once said: it is nice to visit people who invite you into their living-room, but if you really want to feel at home, they will invite you into their kitchen. In Berlin I have been in the kitchen for the last few years, and I have seen that Berlin still is a remarkably good city to work in.

But if I look back at Berlin as an intellectual center, the first thing that strikes me is for how many years Berlin was not the intellectual center of Germany. There have been Germans, who were called Germans, since approximately the year 813. During the time of Charlemagne, first the word *teutiscus*, then the word *deutsch* comes up, meaning 'intelligible', 'language of the people'—but Berlin didn't exist. More than 400 years later, a place

Photographs on p. 228

Friedrich-Wilhelms-University Unter den Linden, ward Mitte, about 1870. A palace for Prince Heinrich, brother of Friedrich the Great, built from 1748 to 1753, with Johann Boumann as architect, probably after a plan by G.W. von Knobelsdorff. From 1809 to 1945 it was Friedrich-Wilhelms-University; it was seriously damaged in 1945; since 1945 it has been Humboldt-University, and it was restored from 1949 to 1967. It is now in East Berlin. Reproduced with permission of the Landesbildstelle Berlin.

Friedrichstraße, ward Mitte; decorated with swastika flags and flags in black, white, and red.—About 1935. Reproduced with permission of the Landesbildstelle Berlin.

called Berlin is founded and mentioned for the first time in the 1230s in a document: the border town Berlin and Cölln. This "Cölln" is the same word as the Slavic word "Kolín," which means a hill surrounded by wet land, by swamp; actually, one hill is Berlin, and the other is Cölln. Today this is of course all one city. Then, it was all a border region; Brandenburg was a march, the Mark Brandenburg; Berlin was a border town. And from Charlemagne to Brandenburg there was always some fighting between the Germans moving East in a moving frontier; somewhat like the Americans did in the seventeeth and eighteenth centuries; and slowly this area became more German, and some of the Sorbes, Abodrites, Lusatians, Slavs, and others stayed around and became Germans, Brandenburgers, and Berliners in the course of time.

It took long for this border town, this off-center region of Germany, to get more or less into the center of things. As late as 1600, there were just 14,000 people in Berlin. During the Thirty Years' War, this population dropped to 6000. By the end of the seventeenth century, the first great infusion came. The French king, Louis XIV, at the suggestion of his mistress, who in turn acted on the suggestion of a father-confessor, revoked the toleration of French Protestants, so some packed up and went to Berlin. At one stage, one-third of the Berliners were French, and there are still many traces of the French influence—even the Berlin "r" is the French "r grassaillé." In the Middle Ages the Germans apparently used to roll their r's as the Czechs and Scotsmen do, but the French changed that in Berlin.

Then people of all kinds came. By the time of Frederick II, the Great, there was not only a court in Berlin but also a china manufacture and a porcelain manufacture as well as textile industries; slowly the city grew. During wars, you had ups and downs. In 1760, Berlin was Russian-occupied, and when the German armies were moving toward Moscow in 1941, the Soviet government broadcast a reminder that they were still keeping the keys to Berlin in the Kremlin, since 1760. The Russians left, back in 1760, and foreign troops probably will not stay there forever unless the Germans want them to stay; and they are not sure whether in the long run Germany and Europe will not be stabilized without garrisons. But at present everybody is still there: again and again, the world has moved into Berlin, and sometimes Berlin has moved into the world. As Berlin grew—by 1820 there were a little less than a quarter million people there, namely 220,000—

Photographs on p. 229

Free University convention meeting (Konventssitzung), Garystraße, ward Zehlendorf/Dahlem, after the demonstration of students at the visit of the Persian imperial couple. During the demonstration, tumults arose and an FU student, Benno Ohnesorg, was shot. At the speaker's desk is Bernhard Wilhelmer and at the left is Wolfgang Lefèvre, president of the FU convention.—June 5, 1967. Reproduced with permission of the Landesbildstelle Berlin.

Science Center Berlin for social research, Reichpietschufer 50, ward Tiergarten; seen from the north-west, Sigismundstraße/corner Hitzigallee.—..........198 ...—WZB/Bavaria aerial photograph, release no. G 16 B 90 A 1 of the Government of Upper Bavaria. Reproduced with permission.

things became more modern. First came the introduction of gaslight through an English company. Then came the first railroad, in 1838, to Potsdam.

And soon the city grew more, it moved up to half a million by 1861. By 1925, there were 4 million people there, and by the 1930s, before World War II, there may have been 4.5 million people in Berlin. And they came from all over the place: I mentioned the French. There were Lusatian Slavs, "Lausitzers," as they were called; there were Poles, both those who could still be counted as Poles—in the 1920s, there were more than 100,000 Polish Poles there—and of course those that had come earlier and were now counted as Germans; all the Wischnewskis and Nowaltnys, all the good German names of today, descended from Poles who had become Germans, often in Berlin. There were Czechs in Berlin; and then came all the South Germans—like Hegel and Einstein. Sometimes they speak of the Swabians as the fifth occupying power, there are so many Swabians in Berlin.

The Jewish people, too, began to move, from Eastern Europe back west again, after they had been driven out of the Rhineland into Eastern Europe during the Crusades in the twelfth and thirteenth centuries. Now their descendants were beginning to move back again in the late nineteenth and early twentieth centuries. They made their contributions to the cultural life of Berlin, and in a competitive society, they aroused the enmity of their competitors when they got some of the desirable posts.

Berlin survived a lot: war, revolution, inflation. Some of the east European immigrants to Berlin came to Berlin in 1919 and 1920 as veterans of inflation in Eastern Europe. They knew how to adjust quickly, thus bringing about the anger of their German neighbors who took longer to get used to the art of surviving in an inflation. But they made their contributions, in literature, in science, in the press, and in many other fields. By the 1920s Berlin was one of the intellectual centers of the world.

With the cooperation of two colleagues, I once tried to make a list of all the major social-science contributions made from 1900 on, up to 1960s. We wanted to find out what the favorable conditions are under which contributions to the social sciences are made, and we found that most of them are made by small teams or by individuals working at great centers. Usually it helps to have more than one university and half a dozen or so of research institutions nearby. It seems that it takes a plurality of places of learning. We found that in the United States, the Chicago area, the Boston–Cambridge area, and the Berkeley–Stanford area were the three great centers of social-science innovation. In Europe it was London and Berlin and, to a lesser degree, Paris, because in those days the Sorbonne was a single university.

Twice in the history of Europe a group of intellectuals succeeded in persuading a ruler to found a great institution of learning. The first time was

Photographs on p. 232

Berlin—a view of the castle and the cathedral; 1922. Reproduced with permission of the Landesbildstelle Berlin.

Hahn-Meitner-Institute for Nuclear Research Berlin, Gliericher Straße 100, at the Wannsee, ward Zehlendorf.—November 1973. Reproduced with permission of the Landesbildstelle Berlin.

early in the sixteenth century, when French intellectuals persuaded King
Francis I of France to found the Collège de France. The second time was
when Wilhelm von Humboldt and others persuaded the Prussian king to
found the University of Berlin. It was one of the great contributions to the
intellectual development of not just Berlin, but of the world. And then, of
course, a famous technical university was founded in Berlin, then called the
"Technische Hochschule Charlottenburg." In America we think of it as the
place where John von Neumann came from, or where the metallurgist
Eugene Orowan of MIT comes from, and many others. Today these institutions are called "Free University" and "Technical University" in West Berlin, and "Humboldt University" in East Berlin. Of these centers of learning
some numbers may be interesting: in 1925, there were about 10,000 students
at the Berlin University and about 5,000 students at the Technical University.

Berlin in the 1920s was, as I said, a great center. It had not only the two
great universities—in quantity, and they were famous in quality—there
were also half a dozen specialized universities, for music, for art, there were
two for physical education, a national one and a Prussian one; altogether
Berlin must have had well over 25,000 students in the 1920s. All the famous
great museums were there, the great picture galleries, 58 theaters, 116 newspapers including 46 local ones. The music from Berlin was world-famous,
and the literature that came out of Berlin was one of the focal points of
German literature. How does it look today?

In the summer of 1982, there were 48,631 students at the Free University,
and 26,906 at the Technical University; in the winter term of 1987/88, there
were 56,515 students enrolled at the Free University, and 29,128 at the Technical University. And, if the students at the University of the Arts (Hoch-
schul der Künste) and those at the institutes of technology are included, the
total number of students in West Berlin surpassed 100,000 for the first time.
In that respect, at least, Berlin has not shrunk, but very much increased.

The universities are bigger, they train many more students, and if anything, they probably do even more research. You cannot discover quantum
physics or the theory of relativity every few years, but you can train a lot
of people in understanding these things and you can expect that more of
the fundamental dicoveries will follow in due time. There are about 26
major scientific institutions in West Berlin alone—I'm thinking of the

---

Photographs on p. 233

*Technical University Berlin (T.U.B.), main building with Auditorium Maximum
(projecting structure); Straße des 17. Juni 135, ward Charlottenburg; view from the
Institute for Architecture.—April 1986. Reproduced with permission of the Landesbildstelle Berlin.*

*Aspen Institute Berlin, institute for humanistic studies, incorporate association, Insel-
straße 10, ward Zehlendorf. Conference on "The Challenges to Public-Service Broadcasting," from June 8 to 11, 1986. From the left: Frank Dahrendorf (Hamburg),
Professor Dr. Shepard Stone (director of the Aspen Institute Berlin), and William
Kobin (Los Angeles).—June 9, 1986. Reproduced with permission of the Landesbildstelle Berlin.*

Hahn-Meitner Institute of Nuclear Physics or the Max Planck Institute of Educational Research, the Heinrich Hertz Institute for Communications Research, the German Institute for Economic Research, and many others. Thanks to an American in Berlin, Shepard Stone, and to the Aspen Institute, the directors of the scientific institutes meet about once every six weeks, so we get to know one another, which is a great step forward from what is traditional in many other places in the world today, where the institutes do not know of each other's work. The theaters are still among the best in Germany, and that means among the best in the world. The Berlin Philharmonic demonstrates what great music still comes out of a Berlin orchestra.

But Berlin was not only then, between the wars, and it is not only now a world city in terms of learning, in terms of culture, in terms of literature, it is also a city of memories: it is haunted by memories. Germany has less a memory of freedom in the nineteenth century than England or France. The great climax of the unsuccessful but important revolution of 1848 took place in Berlin. When in March of 1848 a crowd demonstrated, the soldiers fired into the crowd, and then the dead were put on biers held high above the heads of the crowd and carried to the royal castle, and the king had to bow to show them his respect. The scene is famous through a poem by Freiligrath: it is one of the images of German history, indelibly connected with Berlin. And then once again, at the end of World War I, in the bitterness at the end of the war, in the German revolution, there was an attempt at an extremely radical revolution, partly by an organization called "Spartacus," which later became the Communist party, and partly by spontaneous organizations called the revolutionary shop stewards. That attempt was bloodily suppressed. Two leaders of the Left, Karl Liebknecht and Rosa Luxemburg, were murdered, and their known murderers remained unpunished. Later, when the Nazis took power, they surfaced again and claimed their reward, and got one, in cash, from the Nazi government. All this happened in Berlin and then, when the Nazis succeeded in taking power in Berlin, it was hard— Joseph Goebbels wrote a special book on how hard it was to make the Berliners accept the Nazis—it was harder, he thought, than anywhere else in Germany. But eventually the Nazi terror was at work; this is a German verse: "Berlin, Berlin, thou Athens on the Spree, oh how much bloodshed didst thou see." ("Berlin, Berlin, du Spree-Athen, o wieviel Blut hast du gesehn.")

There are many such memories, but there are also other memories. Berlin television showed a series of interviews with a lot of nice old Berlin ladies: they had hidden persecuted Jewish fellow citizens in the days of the Nazis, and there were 6,000 victims of persecution who had survived with the help of the Berlin population. That too is something worth remembering.

In this city with those many memories—tragic memories and hopeful memories, memories of great achievements—we can ask: what about the quality of people there, what about the quality of the people in general? Goethe, the great poet, formulated it briefly: the Berliners, said he, are a people of temerity—"ein verwegener Menschenschlag." He was right then and he still is right. The Berliners are the least servile people you can meet. If you are nice to them, they may be nice to you. If you try to display authority to them, you won't get far. There are innumerable stories about it. There is, for instance, an almost slanderous story about a Berliner who goes somewhere and says, "How do I get to so-and-so street?" The other fellow says, "Couldn't you ask me a little more politely?" "Oh no, I'd rather lose my way." ("Ach nee, lieber verlauf ick mir"). That is perhaps exaggerated, but there is another story—from the imperial days—of the German emperor who, on his birthday, went on a parade in Berlin and the population was dutifully lined up to watch his majesty appear on his horse; and there was a cobbler's apprentice—and they, the "Berliner Schusterjungen," are famous for their, let us say, economy of respect. The cobbler's apprentice yells out to a journeyman, "When is the old idiot coming?" A policeman appears, pointed helmet and all in those pre–World War I days, and says, "What did you say just now?" "Oh, I was just asking when the foreman was coming." "The foreman? You meant the foreman? Alright," says the policeman and turns away. "Oh, Mr. Policeman," yells the apprentice after him, "Whom were *you* thinking about?" ("An wen dachten *Sie* denn, Herr Schutzmann?")

These are stories of Berlin, but Berlin is a little like that. You cannot make Berliners servile to hierarchical authority from one side or the other. You cannot even make them bow down very much, to any ideology, Western or Eastern. In a certain sense they stay, at least as far as I could see, unmistakably Berliners. You have to get along with them somehow; if you can, so much the better.

What about the individuals there? That is perhaps the most remarkable story about Berlin, the way the city has worked as a magnet for individuals. To begin with, think of the philosophers, Hegel and Schopenhauer, who taught in Berlin. Think of Fichte, all the great minds came; Dilthey is another of the great names of German philosophy. Think of the writers, from Fontane in the nineteenth century to Brecht and Walter Benjamin, Erich Kästner and Kurt Tucholsky; and today, after the Second World War, Günter Grass in West Berlin, Christa Wolf in East Berlin. Some of the greatest names in German literature are living in Berlin, unless they are traveling, which writers like to do. In music, the great conductors, Bruno Walter, Furtwängler, and others, are known from the years between the wars; Karajan is no less a famous conductor today. In the theater, there was the great director Max Reinhardt; and the great actors of today such as Angelika Domröse and Bernhard Minetti are people of the first order in the theater of the world. In psychoanalysis, between the wars there was Franz Alexander, Hans Sachs, Karen Horney. Quite a number of psychoanalysts whose names became household words in America all came out of Berlin. In medicine, there were Virchow and Sauerbruch; in history: Meinecke, Mommsen, Ranke, Treitschke; among the philosophers I have left out, one peculiar one, Max Stirner. Berlin, of all places, gave the world its theories of anarchism, or one of the leading theorists of anarchism. There were the theologians Schleiermacher, Harnack, Dibelius, and even the first theologian to embrace modern anti-Semitism, a court preacher named Stöcker who didn't get very far in those days. There were the great philologists Wilamowitz-Moellendorf and the Brothers Grimm.

There were martyrs in Berlin—I mentioned Rosa Luxemburg, Karl

Liebknecht, but they were not the only ones. It was in Berlin that we were offered a building for our Science Center Berlin which had been the headquarters of the former general staff. And it turned out to be the place where Claus Schenk von Stauffenberg had been shot in the courtyard along with other rebels of the 20th of July, 1944. In Berlin's Plötzensee prison Helmut James von Moltke was murdered by the Nazis. That, too, is Berlin. There is no city in the whole world quite like it.

And what about the contributions, the quality of contributions that came out of Berlin? I mentioned music, and I didn't even mention Arnold Schoenberg and other composers from there. I mentioned Einstein and—with the institutes for research—Otto Hahn. For a time I lived in Berlin one block away from Correns Square, the place where the world's first nuclear chain reaction took place in 1938, in Hahn's laboratory. I mentioned Virchow and I didn't even mention Robert Koch. I didn't mention many others, from the days of Lessing and Moses Mendelssohn and the Berlin salons, over those days of George Grosz and Alfred Döblin up to the nearest past and to today. You may add those whom you remember and who are dear to you. By now, Berlin has been an intellectual center for all fields of human life and letters, for all sciences and arts, a center of scientific and intellectual innovations, and there is an abundance of names and discoveries for illustrating this Berlin reality. There are, as I said, stories too. Berliners like to tell stories about the people who made contributions. One story is about Einstein who, when he was in a coffeehouse in Berlin, ordered another table because he wanted to continue to write down, on the marble top, figures connected with a problem he was thinking about, and he had already completely filled a whole table with figures.

Berlin has been the place where they both created new literature and recast some of the old. How does one translate Friedrich Schiller, the Swabian and Weimar poet, into the language of Berlin? I'll give you a little example. This is a verse by Schiller: "Redet mir nicht, ich bitt' Euch, von der Würde des Menschen, Zu essen gebt ihm, zu wohnen, dann folgt die Würde von selbst." or "Do not speak, I beg you, of the dignity of man, Give him shelter and food and the dignity will follow of itself." So far Schiller. In Berlin it was put more briefly: "Erst kommt das Fressen, dann kommt die Moral," or "First feed the face, then talk of morality." It's the same thought, but it's expressed with Berlin brevity.

Berlin was, in historical times, sometimes a spearhead for the expansion of the Brandenburg and later the Prussian state toward the East. And the Nazis thought they could once more use Berlin for that purpose. After Wold War II, some people thought that Berlin should be a bridge to the East. This didn't quite work out—there is a large wall there and communication across the wall is sparse and difficult. There was a time when Berlin's role was seen as the "front-line city," the city which had to resist pressure from the East, and the West Berliners did resist and, I think, would, if necessary, resist again.

Perhaps the most important role for Berlin is a double one: it is a pledge. Berlin is a symbol of the credit, the economic, the political, and the moral credit of the Western world. If Berlin should in any way decline—and one otherwise very nice Soviet scholar explained to me he was sure West Berlin

Großer Stern (Big Star) with Siegessäule (Triumphal Column), ward Tiergarten.—October 24, 1969. Reproduced with permission of the Landesbildstelle Berlin.

would just shrivel and disappear in the near future—something would happen to the credit of the German Federal Republic; something would happen to the credit and the stability of the country; something would happen to the credit and the stability of Western Europe; something would happen to the credit and the stability of the Western world.

I once had a long conversation with Willy Brandt, who was then the mayor of Berlin and was visiting Harvard. I asked him if he saw any parallels between the situation of Cuba and Berlin. Yes, he said, he did: both were surrounded by the power of another political entity; they were islands, so to speak. Cuba was an island in the sea, West Berlin was a kind of island on dry land, but he thought the importance of Berlin for the West was greater than the importance of Cuba for the East. In a sense he was right. This view is not the monopoly of one party or one statesman.

Berlin is also a pledge, since the Berlin agreements of 1972, of the willingness of the great powers to live somehow, uneasily enough, but together and in peace. And so far this has worked.

If I tried to find a single image of Berlin—I am thinking of it as a city and I am speaking of both Berlins now—I would see Berlin surrounded by the steel jaws of the trap of fate; if the world moves toward war, toward catastrophe, the steel trap may close and Berlin will have another horrible period of suffering and destruction. I have visited Hiroshima, and so I know that what happened to Berlin in World War II might be little compared to what could happen to Berlin if there ever were another world war. But it is also another image that comes to me of Berlin: Berlin is a handful of seed grains, where thought, where art, ideas, literature, where human values have been created and are being created still. Berlin represents a handful of seed grains between millstones and when the millstones start to grind, the seed grain will be in trouble. But when I look at the rocks in the Alps or in any other mountainous landscape, I also remember that there are times and places where seeds are stronger than the rocks.

CHAPTER 19

Berlin—The Cultural Metropolis of Germany?*

Wilhelm A. Kewenig

Everyone will agree: There is no other German city providing a cultural offer comparable to that of Berlin. The numerous museums of the Stiftung Preußischer Kulturbesitz (Foundation for Prussian Cultural Heritage) secure Berlin a position among the most outstanding museum-cities of the world. The orchestra of the Berliner Philharmoniker which, under its chief conductor Herbert von Karajan, in 1982, celebrated its centennial anniversary, is one of the best orchestras worldwide. In a review of the opening night of *Kalldewey* by Botho Strauß at the Schaubühne theater, a critic stated that presently, between New York and Moscow, no other theater could be compared to it. The Opera and the State Theater, now under new direction, again rank among the first of their métier within Germany and even within Europe.

However, Berlin has not only quite a number of internationally renowned cultural institutions which, for friends of culture all over the world, attach an excellent reputation to the name of the city. Besides the "highlights," there is a wide selection of cultural performances satisfying the inhabitants of Berlin as well as its visitors and ranging from the great exhibitions, the boulevard-theaters, and the cabarets to a confusing variety of galleries and studios. But this is not all. We still find a third dimension to complete the image of the cultural metropolis of Berlin: the "off-beat scene," the so-called free groups, the dimension of the hardly countable individual activities in the "Kiez," that is, the city districts of which Kreuzberg, not only in this respect, is the most active and lively one. This "off-scene" is undoubtedly more colourful and more exciting than that of any other German city, and the connections existing between this scene and the officious as well as the official cultural management are frequently closer than anywhere else.

The balance will turn out similarly positive when you have a look at the financial means that Berlin provides for its culture: 296 million D-marks in

---

*Contribution to the periodical *Europa-Archiv*, published in number 23/1982. Almost identical to the contribution to the Boston Symposium in April 1983 of which no manuscript exists. English translation by Ursula Michels-Wenz and Gerhard Kirchhoff

Museum of Musical Instruments of the State Institute for Music Research, Tiergar-tenstraße 1, ward Tiergarten, Stiftung Preußischer Kulturbesitz (Foundation for Prussian Cultural Heritage).—June 1987. Reproduced with permission of the Landes-bildstelle Berlin.

the budget of 1981, 312 million in 1982, 452 million in 1984, 470 million in 1986, and 516 million in 1987. A comparison with Hamburg (1981: 161.1 million, 1982: 173.9 million, 1984: 205 million, 1986: 191.3 million, 1987: 222.7 million), or Munich (1981: 175.4 million, 1982: 177.1 million, 1984: 144 million, 1986: 185 million, 1987: 190 million), or with the respective figures for the Saarland (1981: 14.7 million, 1982: 14.5 million, 1984: 26 million, 1986: 20.3 million, 1987: 21.1 million), Schleswig-Holstein (1981: 51.7 million, 1982: 51.1 million, 1984: 90 million, 1986: 115.2 million, 1987: 138.8 million), or even Rheinland-Pfalz, the Rhineland-Palatinate, (1981: 57.9 million, 1982: 58.6 million, 1984: 136 million, 1986: 151.7 million, 1987: 160.9 million) makes clear how much Berlin really deserves the label of a "cultural metropolis" also in budgetary terms, although the figures listed above do not include the annual means which the *Bund*, that is the federal state, directly raises each year for the Stiftung Preußischer Kulturbesitz (in 1981: 84.335 million D-marks, in 1982: 92.725 million, in 1984: 99.237 million, in 1986: 104.686 million, in 1987: 99.907 million, in 1988: 109.030 million) or for the organization of the Berlin Festival, the Berliner Festspiele GmbH (1981: 10 million D-marks, 1982: 7 million, in 1984: 6.806 million, in 1986: 7.398 million, in 1987: 8.320 million, in 1988: 7.950 million D-marks).

And still, despite of all these undeniable facts and figures, it happens again and again that even declared friends of this city will frown at the idea of Berlin being a cultural metropolis and feel an admittedly negative taste when thinking it over once again.

"Plant for Culture, Sport, and Handicraft registered association" (UFA-Fabrik e.V.),
Viktoriastraße 10, ward Tempelhof; "Café Olé" on the UFA-area.—June 23, 1983.
Reproduced with permission of the Landesbildstelle Berlin.

There are, for instance, those who still have experienced the Berlin of the
twenties or heard of it and now measure the reality of the divided city
against their personal recollection or conception of it. Of course, such comparison will come to a negative conclusion. But does this actually give any
evidence for the importance which today is due to West Berlin as a cultural
center?

However, there are not only reservations which orient themselves according to personal or secondary memories. We also find the rather emotional
reservations preferring Munich, for example, or Hamburg: the cultural life
of these cities is supposed to be "sounder," more strongly embedded and
more firmly anchored in a visible tradition which guarantees continuity. But
reservations are also voiced by those who question the rank of West Berlin
as a cultural metropolis, simply because this city has been reconstructed in a
hardly describable way, because the result of that reconstruction now con-
veys, architecturally as well as in terms of urban design, a predominantly
dull or, at best, insignificant impression. And finally, there is the grave reservation based on the "artificial" character of West Berlin's entire existence
which leads to the allegedly inevitable consequence that Berlin's cultural life
as a whole has something of being superimposed and strained, of being
"parasitical."

These and similar reservations can, by no means, be dismissed as unintelligible or simply injudicious. Berlin does look dull and gray, it is an artificial, morbid and—because of its subsidiary existence—partly paralysed, lonely city, an isolated place left to itself. And yet, I maintain, despite its obvious wounds, its defects and vices, it really is one, is probably *the* cultural metropolis of Germany.

It is worthwhile to think a little more thoroughly about the more or less spontaneous reactions to the question of Berlin's quality as a cultural metropolis. What is it that essentially makes up the quality and rank of a cultural capital? Which are the compulsory conditions, and which are, so to speak, the additional ones? And what kind of quality, what rank does West Berlin represent if these criteria are taken as a measure? Is there a cultural profile of West Berlin that can be considered not only unmistakably unique but also irreplaceable—irreplaceable for the cultural life of Germany?

No doubt, one of the requisites of a cultural metropolis is the critical masses. These do exist in the divided city of Berlin, on both sides of the wall. Furthermore, the state of aggregation of those critical masses is important. Rigid social structures and contentment with the given conditions do not provide a fertile ground for a maximum of cultural first-class performance. In this respect, too, Berlin's conditions are ideal. There is no other German city which can rely on a comparable, similarly open society.

But above all, Berlin has a tremendously curious population—a fact that can always be observed in view of the large numbers of people that attend all kinds of cultural events. Besides this, Berlin has available extensive spiritual and intellectual resources: 90,000 students and their teachers, universities and academies, research institutions and brain-breeding factories, they all add up to a remarkable potential of people who are interested in vivid intellectual discussion and will provoke it. Moreover, Berlin repeatedly succeeds in attracting visitors by arranging great events— such visitors who are willing to contribute to the spiritual and cultural climate of the city and who are able, and indeed manage, with their Berlin counterparts, to create an atmosphere which time and again has been described as particularly stimulating and lively. In addition, the exceptional existence which Berlin has been leading since 1945—so that even by now West Berlin has not yet become a normal big city—and also the ever present burden of its lost function as a capital, have produced a state of tiredness that in many ways certainly causes detrimental effects but, with regard to spiritual and cultural processes, obviously also an increasing productivity.

Altogether, the western part of Berlin will be acknowledged to have that widely extended, tolerant, and generous climate without which hardly any city will be accepted as a cultural center nowadays. But spiritual surroundings and intellectual climate, open society and liberality alone are definitely not sufficient to turn a city into a metropolis. It also needs spiritual impact, originality of acting and thinking, effort to reach perfection and highest accomplishment, and after all: success. Epigonism is not capable of creating any spiritual radiation; and lacking the latter, nobody nor any city will gain, or even only succeed in holding up, the reputation of being of cultural and spiritual importance. West Berlin still has a considerable number of institutions ranking among the first in the world and employing many an internationally-known expert, although it has lost some of its attractions, such as the Theater am Gänsemarkt, the Oper unter den Linden, or the Museumsinsel. But there are also quite a number of high-ranking scientists who now work at Berlin universities even though the scientific reputation of the latter has decreased during the last twenty years because of various events. The same is true, to a still higher degree, for some off-university research institutions which do scientific pioneer work recognized throughout the world—such as the Heinrich-Hertz-Institut, to name only one

Technical University Berlin, Heinrich-Hertz-Institute, institute for vibration research (Schwingungsforschung) Einsteinufer 37, ward Charlottenburg.—August 1975. Reproduced with permission of the Landesbildstelle Berlin.

example. Yet, West Berlin is not merely a city of world-famous institutions, there are also plenty of personalities and individuals who originate or promote the reputation of the city in their respective professional fields, like musicians, writers, sculptors, filmmakers, or painters. The role that Berlin has been playing, for instance, in the world of theater or in the art of painting for some time now is immense. Especially among young artists and intellectuals, you will often hear that they can live only in Berlin, where the challenging atmosphere, the stimulating climate, and also the toughness of the city render the very best conditions for originality and creative imagination. But spiritual climate and originality alone do not suffice . . . to know what is going on is equally necessary in order to be effective and to get "feedback" or interest in return.

Well, one can hardly deny that Berlin is mentioned quite frequently, at least in the German media. However, it is regrettable that during the past decade this has been done by applying a sort of negative trademark to it, particularly by the press, on radio, and on television: Berlin is mainly good for bad news. To be just, it must be added that for the field of the arts in general Berlin has a reputation for variety and quality programs even in the mass media.

On the whole, the radiating power of Berlin and the possibilities of "feedback" in all spheres vastly suffer from the deplorable circumstance that in West Berlin no sophisticated and ambitious daily or weekly newspaper is published that would be noticed beyond Berlin. This lack of a supraregional paper is probably the most perceptible handicap for Berlin's claim to hold a leading, indeed *the* leading, position in Germany as far as the arts and sciences are concerned. The handicap becomes even more evident when you take into consideration that in West Berlin, although it is the address of a multitude of smaller publishers, not a single big and active publishing house has settled, and that for this reason none of the few intellectual periodicals still existing appears in Berlin. So, the natural movements created by the editorial staff of a newspaper or magazine, or by the presence of an important publishing house, do not arise here, a want painfully felt that cannot be compensated by other institutions such as the Akademie der Künste (Academy of Arts) or the Wissenschaftskolleg (College of Science) which has been remarkably active already in its first year.

This deficiency, however, is at least partly counterbalanced in our case by a still maintained and commonly notable "plus" of attention and interest in everything that comes from Berlin, an interest eminent in Germany but even more so in other European countries and abroad. Up to now, the former capital Berlin, the "alte Reichshauptstadt," has continued to be a trademark, the publicity and advertising power of which is rather surprising.

When attempting to summarize this brief review of Berlin's situation, one would not possibly question, for all necessary precaution, that Berlin is one of the few German cultural centres of international rank, in fact—according to my personal impression—Germany's only real metropolis.

That means a lot. But the expectations focussed on Berlin are indeed very high: expectations on the part of politicians who forward considerable allowances out of the federal budget year by year to subsidize Berlin and who have to defend such financial support repeatedly against queries as well as attacks, but expectations, too, on the part of the average citizen who is counting on unmistakable and irreplaceable impulses from Berlin, instead of accepting the negative headlines about his city.

Can Berlin cope with these expectations? Can anybody honestly state that Berlin contributes at least in the cultural and scientific fields to the profile of the Federal Republic of Germany in an unmistakable, nay irreplaceable way?

If you try to answer these questions you will eventually end up with the description of a special feature which is the main characteristic of and the actual reason for the present position of Berlin: this city marks a caesura, it stands for a breaking and turning point in history, in political geography, and in the human and social reality of the presence, respectively.

How much history, especially the most recent German history, becomes evident in Berlin, was demonstrated only a short while ago at the great exhibition on Prussia, in 1981. The Martin-Gropius-Building, formerly Berlin's Arts and Crafts Museum, is located directly at the wall on the ground on which the Prinz-Albrecht-Palais once stood. Anybody entering the building

Kunstgewerbemuseum (arts and crafts museum) Martin Gropius Bau, Stresemann-straße 110, ward Kreuzberg. This building now houses the Berlinische Galerie, the Jewish section of the Berlin Museum, the Werkbund (Work Alliance) archives, museum of the everyday life of the 20th century, . . .—August 1987. Reproduced with permission of the Landesbildstelle Berlin.

with open eyes and glancing out of the window, will feel the German history of the past fifty, even one hundred years, which is immediately revealed to the visitor as a physical experience. At the wall in Kreuzberg, Berlin presents itself not only as a devided city, as a fracture between East and West, it also presents itself like an open wound that more than clearly shows the relativity as well as the transiency of those thirty years just behind us: a diverging development of two German states and an unfortunate and cut-up Berlin, deprived—at least in the western part—of its historical function and *Hinterland*. This existence as a site of fracture—an existence which promptly turns every effort, every progress, every success into a more or less relative matter—is, according to my personal impression, Berlin's basis and threat at the same time, its chance and its danger. Nothing that particularly determines the atmosphere, the mood, and the air of today's Berlin is explicable without this phenomenon, this consciousness of being a site of fracture. The openness of the society, the disposition for the alternative, the liberality in social intercourse, the insular location—which produces quite positive results in the cultural field because of the higher pressure to care for one another—, the decay of the old city and its architecture, the wall, the harsh contrast of freedom and lack of freedom, their mutual influence, which nevertheless was not strong enough to prevent the wall, the joy of living, or even lust of life that always develops where rejections occur, where wounds break open: all these factors, here only indicated, make up Berlin. And all this justifies to state: Berlin indeed represents a unique, an irreplaceable *event* which cannot be "duplicated" by any other German city.

As far as the scientific field is concerned, this unmatched uniqueness will certainly be harder to establish. Of course, research and education can—as we know—be practised also "outdoors" and in "no-man's-land." Yet, scientists and students as well are susceptible to, in fact are dependent on, the atmosphere under which they work and study—and it is almost unanimously accepted that in this respect Berlin offers more than any other academic city in Germany. Obviously, the cultural scope here is so unmistakably singular, as far as atmosphere and living conditions are concerned, and so irreplaceable because nowhere in Germany as much as in Berlin are new ideas stated as courageously and "exported" into the Federal Republic, European, and other foreign countries.

This, however, implies: Berlin is, by no means, just a recipient of fiscal aims financed via taxes as which the city is often perceived and leniently tolerated. Berlin does render an equivalent, although certainly not—at least not yet—in the economical field. That kind of set-off counting each farthing cannot possibly be met by this city and will probably never be met because of its exposed location and situation. But such balance simply uses a wrong scale of measure weighing with inappropriate considerations. Berlin must rather be measured by its creativity, which emanates far beyond the local limits, and by its unequalled vitality which the city proves again and again.

I am aware of the fact that this attempt to describe a phenomenon is bound to be fragmentary and incomplete. Berlin cannot be "captured" and "sold" under a certain label or forced into a palpable verbal corset. What persists, and what is immediately felt even by strangers in this city, is how much Berlin—despite of all its wounds—still continues to be attractive and amazingly manifold in its various forms of appearance.

CHAPTER 20

West Berlin and the International Business Community*

Wolfe J. Frankl

For a place that is one of Europe's largest industrial cities, with a population of almost two million, a GNP half that of Denmark or Austria, and an economy that is an integral part of the Common Market, West Berlin still has to work hard to sell itself to the international business community. Born largely out of ignorance, misinformation, and the memory of the events that engulfed the former German capital after World War II—the division of the city, the airlift, the infamous wall, and the chicanery occasionally experienced in the 1950s and 1960s regarding transport into and out of the city—a negative image has perpetuated itself into the 1980s.

Certainly, Berlin finds itself in an "island" location—but so do Ireland and Taiwan—and, yes, a different ideology prevails in the eastern half of the city, which is the capital of the German Democratic Republic (GDR). However, these potential liabilities are more than offset by the city's many assets.

Current Industrial Status

At the end of World War II, Berlin lay in shambles, and it took longer for the city to recover and rebuild than it did for the rest of West Germany. As a result, Berlin was initially left behind in the German economic miracle of the fifties and sixties. To make matters worse, there was, for a time, an exodus of companies from Berlin to the West. However, after its status was clarified, and especially since the conclusion of the Quadripartite Agreement of 1971 between the United States, the Soviet Union, France, and the United Kingdom, Berlin has evolved into a vital and vibrant city. Industry and commerce thrive in an atmosphere of economic freedom, supported by an educational and scientific infrastructure that is on a par with the best to be found in Europe. In addition, Berlin's cultural facilities, which include von Karajan's world-famous orchestra, first-rate opera and theater, 40 museums, and approximately 70 art galleries, and its natural environment, which features

---

*© 1985 Canon Communications, Inc. Reprinted with permission from *Medical Device and Diagnostic Industry*, May 1985. Revised 1988.

62 square miles of parks, woods, and lakes, guarantee a quality of life as good as any available in western Europe.

Berlin is home to 2300 industrial companies and some 14,000 trading and service enterprises, among them Siemens, AEG, Nixdorf, and Bosch. The city has long been known as a center of electronic and electrotechnical development and manufacturing. Precision tools and instruments and optics are represented by many companies and rank high on the industrial scene. Germany's reputation for excellence in these fields applies as much to Berlin as it does to Munich or Stuttgart.

More than 30 American companies call West Berlin home, some with over 2000 employees. IBM recently celebrated its 50th anniversary in Berlin; others, like the Otis Elevator affiliate of United Technologies, Gillette, ITT, Warner-Lambert, and Philip Morris, also have been there for many years. More recent arrivals are Ford Motor Company, with a 1000-man plastic components plant, and Bausch & Lomb of Rochester, NY, which purchased a Berlin-based pharmaceutical plant.

Financial Incentives

To attract the previously mentioned and many other companies to Berlin and to overcome the perceived location disadvantages, the Berlin government offers a series of financial incentives which, particularly for a capital-intensive, high-technology company, can result in a bottom line unattainable elsewhere in the Common Market. Studies prepared by Arthur Andersen & Company and by the Brussels-based consulting firm Plant Location International bear out this statement. Among the key features of this package are tax-free investment grants averaging 20–25 percent of expenditures for buildings and machinery and equipment, low-interest long-term loans, substantially reduced corporate and personal income taxes, and special depreciation provisions. For example, if investors desire, they can write off 75 percent of the initial investment in year one. These balance-sheet and cash-flow aids enable an investor to start an operation in Berlin with a minimum of equity.

On the profit-and-loss side, and of decisive importance for the ongoing profitability of an enterprise, is Berlin's unique turnover bonus system. Provided by law to all companies operating in West Berlin, the turnover bonus ranges from 3–10 percent of sales, depending on the percentage of value added in Berlin. At the highest level (91 percent value added), the manufacturer is entitled to a 10 percent bonus, i.e., 10 percent of the amount billed to the customer. Customers in turn, provided they are situated in West Germany, receive an additional bonus of 4.2 percent of the purchase price. Most Berlin-based companies sell their entire output to a West German affiliate or sales company, which then bills the ultimate customer; shipment can be made directly from Berlin to the final destination.

Other advantages available in Berlin include special training grants, low-cost rentals of city-owned land or buildings at 3 percent of appraised value annually for up to 50 years, special programs for pioneering enterprises research and development grants, and more. In summary, the business climate in West Berlin can be described as exemplary, with city, state, and federal authorities ready and eager to support and nurture economic activity of all kinds. Especially favored are the new investor, the high-technology manufacturer, and any endeavor in the realm of research and development that has promise of translating innovation into new products and new jobs.

Educational Resources

To intensify its commitment to the entrepreneur, the Berlin government, together with the Technical University of Berlin (TU), has recently launched the Berlin Center for Innovation and New Enterprises, the first of its kind in the Federal Republic. At this center, entrepreneurs are given facilities, expert advice, and infrastructure services at nominal rates to develop their ideas and products from incubation to commercialization. So far, 18 newly founded companies with 55 employees are enjoying this special environment in fields like robotics, hydraulics, software development, and biochemistry. Because the demand for additional space is so great, a technology and research park, patterned on similar parks in the United States, has been established adjacent to the center.

In addition to its involvement in the center, Berlin's educational infrastructure occupies a preeminent position in Germany's research and development activities. TU and the Free University of Berlin together account for some 90,000 students, and there are 16,000 more at other institutions of higher learning in the city. This represents 12 percent of all students at German universities. The TU is considered to rank on a par with such outstanding technical training centers as Aachen and Zurich. It has a close working relationship with the Massachusetts Institute of Technology, which includes the exchange of professors, joint projects, and symposia. An important adjunct is the university's Technology Transfer Center, which encourages and promotes contacts between academia and business and which sponsors many programs benefitting the entrepreneur. The Free University houses Berlin's well-known Medical School and is the focal point of much scientific activity in the fields of chemistry, biochemistry, and pharmacology.

Equally important are Berlin's 185 scientific and research institutes, which have some 35,000 employees—11 percent of the entire research work force in West Germany. Among the better-known facilities are the Max-Planck-Institute, the Hahn-Meitner-Institute, the Fritz-Haber-Institute, the Heinrich-Hertz-Institute, and the Fraunhofer Gesellschaft. BESSY, the new electron storage ring for synchrotron radiation, which is owned partly by the major institutes and partly by Siemens, AEG, and Philips, is available to anyone engaged in basic and applied research. A recent addition is the city-owned Center for Laser Medicine, which has the task of developing new diagnostic and surgical procedures and instruments.

The Work Force

On the manpower front, Berlin, like the other 10 states of the Federal Republic, has an excellent skilled and semiskilled work force. Best of all, as a

Berlin Association of Electron Storage (Berliner Elektronenspeicherring-Gesellschaft) for Synchrotron Radiation, private limited liability company (BESSY), Lentzeallee 100, ward Wilmersdorf.—February 1982. Reproduced with permission of the Landes-bildstelle Berlin.

result of the unions' tacit commitment not to do anything that could harm the city's economy, there are no strikes in West Berlin.

Unemployment is in the 8–9 percent range, so that new companies have little or no difficulty in recruiting personnel. To the extent that certain special skills are not immediately available locally, the city will recruit the required specialists in West Germany and pay for their move to Berlin. Occupational training programs are also available at no cost to the industrial investor. Both the Federal Ministry for Science and Technology and the City of Berlin grant educational allowances for certain specialized skills, as well as for retraining purposes.

Accessibility

Berlin can be reached by air, road, rail, and canal. About 160 flights daily serve Tegel Airport, the city's ultramodern terminal. Flights leave hourly for Frankfurt; these and frequent flights to Hamburg, Munich, and nine other destinations—flights of less than one hour's duration—connect the city tightly with West Germany. Direct service is also available to London, Paris, Zurich, Brussels, and Amsterdam.

Access by road and rail is through part of East Germany, but current controls are perfunctory. Identity papers of transit passengers and the seals on containers and freight cars are checked at the control points. In 1983, 15.2 million tons of goods and 20.2 million travellers used these transit routes to and from West Germany. Since 1971 there has been no interference with traffic in and out of the city, including the free movement of goods in both directions. This is due to the Quadripartite Agreement concluded in that year which guarantees, among many other things, unimpeded access to and egress from West Berlin. The East German authorities have observed this important agreement to the letter.

Another reason why traffic to and from Berlin is without problems has to do with the economic importance attached to West Berlin by the East. To East Germany and its allies, West Berlin is an important window to the West, not unlike Hong Kong has been to China. It is also an important source of hard currency earnings on which the GDR depends to pay for the foodstuffs, machinery, and equipment that it imports from the West. Last, but not least, Berlin is a stage for trade negotiations between the two Germanys and between West and East in general.

Distances from Berlin to the major markets in central Europe are as short as or shorter than distances between major manufacturing centers in the United Kingdom, the Republic of Ireland, and southern Europe. Freight service and passenger schedules are observed with punctuality. West German and other European industrial customers and assemblers know they can rely on tight delivery schedules from the city, and, in many instances, certain items or subassemblies originate only in Berlin. Ford Motor Company Berlin, for example, provides the majority of plastic components required by Ford's assembly plants in West Germany, Belgium, Spain, United Kingdom, and Ireland.

Conclusion

West Berlin is indeed a viable and attractive place in which to set up a manufacturing or research and development activity. Its quasi-isolated location is of little or no consequence, and the financial, cultural, and other advantages are such that a company would be well advised to take a close look at the city before deciding on where to locate or expand in Europe.

CHAPTER 21

Berlin as a Center of Science and Technology: Challenge and Necessity

Jürgen Starnick

Berlin is not like any other metropolis. It is a special city, confronted with situations which do not occur in a comparable way in any other city. Certainly, Berlin's municipal problems are similar not only to those of other German metropolises but of large cities in general. The employment situation, the high percentage of foreigners living in Berlin, the interest of the younger generation in housing, traffic and environmental problems—these are the same topics which are discussed in Berlin as well as in Frankfurt, London, New York, or Chicago, and it is indeed striking that the discussions in Berlin are often more pointed and more hotly debated than in other places. Outside Berlin, these issues are more readily accepted and in many cases are not deemed worthy of such attention.

Berlin has assumed the task of a political seismograph. Situated 180 kilometers east of the so-called Iron Curtain and divided by a wall miles long, Berlin has developed a special sensitivity for political movements in the world. Everything that has to do with crisis or détente between East and West, with securing peace or disarmament is carefully observed and may result in responsive action. But despite all this, people in Berlin do not sleep any worse than their fellow countrymen elsewhere in the Federal Republic. The Quadripartite Agreement has placed a solid roof over our heads that keeps us dry even in spells of bad weather.

The close ties between West Berlin and West Germany, however, should not allow one to forget that Berlin more than any other Western city is confronted with the existence of two German states and thereby with the existence of two political blocs. In Berlin one feels the continuity of Germany's history, not only in its most recent past but also in the period that led up to it. Daily life in Berlin, after all, is the result of a chapter of German history that opened on January 30, 1933. Its conclusion in 1945 was and is in no way satisfactory. The "heritage" of the Third Reich continues to weigh heavily upon the Berliners, both in West Berlin and in East Berlin. The millions of people who live here are confronted daily with the aftermath of that Reich and the Second World War—whereas for western Germany, the

---

*See Notes section at the end of this chapter.

greater parts of western Europe and America, this period from the past belongs to a chapter of history that is closed.

In Berlin the question of national unity is pursued more urgently than anywhere else in Germany. Naturally, in West Germany there is also discussion about what it means to be a nation, to have shared feelings, a common language, culture and history. These and many other concerns are thought about in West Germany and are the object of political and scientific examination. But in Berlin they are always a matter of immediate experience. In their daily lives the people of Berlin feel the inadequacy of the present condition of Germany. Yet in the past they have also shown that, supported by the policies of the Federal government and its allies, especially the United States, Berlin is in a position to resist possible provocations and at the same time to create, beyond its own borders, hope for the people of Germany. Berlin's unique position as a segment of Western Society in the Eastern

Brandenburg Gate with border wall, ward Mitte, East Berlin; border toward East Berlin; photograph taken from the ward Tiergarten, West Berlin, on July 25, 1980.— Text: "ATTENTION you are now leaving West Berlin." Reproduced with permission of the Landesbildstelle Berlin.

territories allows it to make a contribution to interlocking the interests of the Federal Republic with those of the Democratic Republic and thereby to contribute to the gradual normalization and stabilization of the political situation in Europe. Yet, at the same time, Berlin remains a challenge to the surrounding German state. Despite all attempts of the Democratic Republic to hem Berlin in with the help of the wall, the exchange of ideas among people in Germany could not be prevented, and the existence of Germans who are able to live together in a state free from repression could not be obliterated.

I present such general considerations in a chapter about science and technology in Berlin in which I ostensibly want to clarify the present and future role of Berlin as an intellectual center, because the role of Berlin as a focus for scientific endeavor can only be understood correctly in connection with the current situation of the city. Any perspective on Berlin's future is dependent upon the possibilities—and perhaps also the impossibilities—of its horizon for development. And that horizon is essentially determined by the economic situation of the city. In fact, the most difficult problems facing Berlin today are in the area of economics. It has become apparent that Berlin's economic and labour markets are suffering from a lingering gradual decline spurred by the crisis of the AEG (the German General Electric Company). Altogether, the number of available jobs in manufacturing and industry has decreased by 35 percent within ten years. Berlin faces today a challenge to its self-resolution which, to a large degree, is comparable to earlier challenges it faced from external political threats.

In addition to difficulties arising from the viewpoint of the labour market, today's problem in general concerns the capability of Berlin to maintain its place as an industrial city. Until 1945, Berlin was the political capital and the administrative center of Germany. As such it was also a center of commercial predominance, especially for those corporations, businesses, companies, and industrial management firms which were closely connected with the seat of political power. Berlin was, in a certain way, even a special industrial center of Germany, namely, the center of the large corporations that had evolved with the technical advances of time. It was the headquarters for great entrepreneurs with their research and development divisions. Berlin was also the center for typical urban industries: fashion, publishing, and the production of luxury items. All these enterprises, which were at one time the basis of commercial activity, by now appear to have been drained of their life blood little by little. Indeed immediately after the war, one could still consider Berlin to be a capital city in a kind of "provisional retirement," a city which drew its self-image from its special role in German politics and world affairs. Only because of this self-image was it at all possible for Berlin to maintain the enterprises named above. It was only with the construction of the wall, and even more importantly, with the conclusion of a treaty with the East, that Berlin's role was reoriented and Berlin became just another large city.

Those years of brilliant, national, and international economic boom—in which Berlin also participated—veiled the fact that a structural change in Berlin's economy had occured as a result of the new orientation. The general decline of economic conditions, on the scale both of the Federal Republic and of the world, aggravated the negative sides of the development and thereby allowed them to be fully recognized.

Berlin became a so-called extended workbench of specialized manufacture for companies that had their headquarters and their research and development divisions in West Germany. The products of these extended work-

BMW (Bavarian Motor Works) limited company, Am Juliusturm 14, ward Spandau; left: motor assembly line, right: final assembly line.—October 1982. Reproduced with permission of the Landesbildstelle Berlin.

benches were primarily intermediate products. The economic fate of such businesses was dependent upon their "parent firms" even when they were legally independent. Here, too, the crisis of AEG offers a good example. But also Siemens, the second largest manufacturer of electrical appliances, reduced its number of jobs. In an all but symbolic way, this made it clear that those industries which at one time had been the foundation for the rise of Berlin to an industrial metropolis were no longer supporting the city. The economic crisis had unveiled the structural problems of Berlin. A so-called economic summit conference was held. In December 1982 the chancellor of the Federal Republic invited the chairmen and managers of the large corporations in West Germany to Berlin. This was taken even by the general public as a signal "that the clock in Berlin economically—and therefore politically—reads five minutes to midnight." In view of the general condition of the Federal Republic's public budget, there was criticism in the federal parliament about the fact that 53 percent of Berlin's budget comes from grants from the Federal Republic. For this reason the economic summit conference took up the question of the policies constructed in the first years after the war. They determined Berlin's role as a task for the whole nation. But pondering the policies of the past is only the first task.

   The national obligations of Berlin today cannot be sought in international politics, but rather must be defined as a guide to what this city can produce for the Federal Republic—and indeed it must include an economics program which aids and draws upon the scientific and cultural potential of the city as an intellectually and scientifically well-prepared center for the development of new products, new forms and methods of production which use the latest in current technology.

This may be a surprising conclusion; it may even appear a paradox. But it is actually in the fields of innovation where the real chance for the future role of Berlin must be seen. While on the one hand, the economic entities, which indeed at one time formed the basis of the city's vitality, have moved elsewhere, on the other hand, in other areas, especially in cultural and scientific creativity, the city itself is as vital as ever. Berlin is a place of lively cultural events throughout the whole year. There is nothing artificial about its practically ceaseless succession of cultural activities and performances, of unmediated artistic and cultural creativity that is thoroughly independent of any subsidizing bureaucracy—and that is a phenomenon not to be found in any other German city.

The liveliness and vitality of Berlin is often attested—surprisingly above all by foreign visitors who come for only a short visit and then often, contrary to their original plans, remain longer. They praise the variety of milieus to be found in Berlin. They praise the liveliness of the downtown areas at night, and they praise the openness of the cultural environment in general. The opportunities to meet people and exchange ideas, to encounter and experience others are manifold. People love living in Berlin and they say they wouldn't consider living in any other West German city they know. Berlin's theaters offer a variety that is cumbersome to keep in sight. The Stiftung Deutscher Kulturbesitz (the Foundation for the Promotion of Prussian History and Culture) and the Berlin Festival Society offer such a rich variety of exhibitions and excellent museums that one can hardly appreciate them fully. The musical life in Berlin receives its character not only from the Philharmonic Orchestra, but equally from the many-sided European rock scene. Berlin has justifiably earned the appelation "City of Culture" and it was rightly declared the European Metropolis of Culture for 1988.

And now, what is the situation with science and technology in Berlin? Here is a dispassionate citation from the research report written in 1982 by the federal government in its statement of financial aid for the science faculties in Berlin: "With an allotment of 10 percent of the total scientific expenditures for research and development of the Federal Republic and with 11.2 percent of the scientific personnel, Berlin's allotment lies well above the one of the Federal Republic related to the gross internal product of 3.6 percent and to the domestic population of 3.18 percent." In simple words, Berlin has been enabled to spend three times as much for research than other places in Germany. This relation of 3 to 1 finds no parallel in any other federal state.

Two universities, an art school, and six specialized colleges offer around 23,000 jobs; about 7700 of them are for scientific personnel. Outside the university system, there are many institutes and services which form a crucial nexus for scientific research and study.[1] These institutions provide approximately 7900 jobs, of which 2300 are for scientific personnel.

Under the political pressure at the former Friedrich-Wilhelm-University

24th overseas import fair "Partners of Progress," from September 3 to 7, 1986, in the fair halls at the Funkturm (radio tower), ward Charlottenburg. Opening circuit; at the left in the foreground: Eberhard Diepgen (Governing Mayor of Berlin), second row at the right: Elmar Pieroth (Senator for economy and employment). Booth of Senegal.—September 3, 1986. Reproduced with permission of the Landesbildstelle Berlin.

(now in the eastern section of the city and renamed Humboldt-University), academic freedom was no longer granted. Thus, in the western section of the city, the Free University was founded in 1948. Its history is closely tied to the postwar history of Berlin. Its founding itself expressed the will of the people in the Western sectors of Berlin to have self-determination. Even today, Berliners are still thankful for the financial support provided by American endowment funds with which the first building of the Free University was erected. Up to this day, it bears the name "Henry Ford Building." By now, side by side with the University of Munich, the Free University of Berlin is the largest university in Germany with the highest number of academic personnel, current student population of more than 56,000 in the winter term 1987/88, and a budget which in 1982 exceeded 1 billion German mark (more than 400 million dollars). About two-thirds of the students are concentrated in the humanities and social sciences. The remaining third is divided among the natural sciences and medicine.

The second largest university, and at the same time the oldest academic establishment in West Berlin, is the Technical University. It has approx-

Free University Berlin, Henry Ford Building; Garystraße, ward Zehlendorf/Dahlem. Architects: Sobotka and Müller.—July 18, 1956. Reproduced with permission of the Landesbildstelle Berlin.

imately 27,000 students and a budget of 445 million German mark (180 million dollars). The faculty includes about 1800 persons. Its academic concentration in research and education lies in engineering and the natural sciences. About two-thirds of the students major in these courses of study. But the Technical University has a broadly structured curriculum also in the humanities, not only since its reopening in 1945, when it was given its name. From its very beginnings, as the first technical school of higher education in Germany, it has always carried out a broad program to extend instruction in the humanities, cultural, and social sciences in order to promote a deepened, humanistic education even for students of engineering and the natural sciences, and to further research into the complexities of social relations.

In 1879, through the unification of two academies, the Technical University of our days was founded as the Royal Technical School of Higher Education in Berlin. If the history of these academies is included, the history of the Technical University extends back to the beginning of modernization and the later industrialization of the Prussian state.

The two universities of West Berlin are academic institutions of higher education in the traditional sense, having the right to grant degrees and to appoint qualified scholars to faculty standing. Apart from these, however, there are a number of specialized schools in Berlin. These are colleges which offer more scholastically oriented practical instruction. The largest and most important of these colleges is a technical school that offers courses in almost every area of engineering. Others are the School of Economics and the School for Social Work and Social Education as well as the School of Art; the latter is especially noteworthy. It is dedicated to academic inquiry as well as to artistically related questions. It touches especially upon the concerns of the engineering sciences in the area of architecture.

In addition to the universities and specialized schools, Berlin contains a widely differentiated system of different types of research institutions. It is—with all its establishments for higher education—the largest region for education of the Federal Republic, side by side with Munich. Altogether there are over 100,000 students in Berlin, about half of which come from West Germany. A large portion (18 percent of the Technical University's student population) are students from other countries, the great majority of which (15 percent of the student population) are from newly developing countries.

Students come here from West Germany despite the fact that many aspects of the living conditions in Berlin are more difficult than in the immediate areas of their home regions. They come because they are fascinated by the atmosphere Berlin radiates. For Berlin itself, for its economic revitalization, the city's potential in engineering and the natural sciences is of the highest importance. It deserves to be presented in more detail.

The largest aggregation of technological capacities is without doubt exhibited by the Technical University. For years, the development of computerized production methods, automated techniques, and the development of new production processes has had an important position in the research spectrum of the Technical University. In this respect, the Technical University has received support of considerable extent through the centralized promotion of research by the German Research Foundation and by the Federal Ministry of Research and Technology. We set high standards for the promotion in these areas. As a result, this research enjoys high esteem in the Federal Republic. In the last few years, the Technical University has also converted to the use of computer aided design methods in expanding these activities. Those dedicated to this scientific field, come from the areas of machine, ship, and airplane construction, civil engineering, and architecture. Here, too, a large percentage of the research was carried out with the help of financial aid from the federal government and the German Research Foundation. Electrical engineering and computer science are as strongly cultivated at the Technical University as are mechanical and civil engineering. In computer science, we are concerned not only with the question of utilizing available computer systems, but at the same time with the question of promoting fundamental research to develop new generations of computers. This research is being expanded by building up the area of designing and testing of highly-integrated electrical circuitry with the aim of making Berlin a focal point of microelectronics in Germany. Laser research is also intensively carried out at the Technical University. Biotechnology is strongly promoted.

Science Center Berlin, non-profit organization, Griegstraße 5–7, ward Wilmersdorf; with three international instituts in West Berlin.—Reception on the occasion of the visit of Dr. Andreas von Bülow (Federal minister of research and technology) and Günter Gaus (senator of science and research, Berlin). In the middle: Johann Baptist Gradl, MdB (member of the German Federal Diet (Bundestag)); at the right: Professor Dr. Meinolf Dierkes (president of the Science Center Berlin).—March 6, 1981. Reproduced with permission of the Landesbildstelle Berlin.

Although the university has not yet changed over to new methods of genetic engineering, Berlin has joined the scientific community in this area through the construction of a new research institute for gen biology in close connection with the Free University, and partially financed by the Schering Company.

In general, the research potential of the Technical University will be broadened further by numerous research institutes in Berlin, e.g., the Fraunhofer Company and the Heinrich-Hertz-Institute, which cooperate closely with the Technical University. By cooperative agreements, important institutes for social scientific research are also associated with both the Free University and the Technical University. There are the Science Center of Berlin (WZB) that supports numerous research institutes[2] and the Science College of Berlin, a center of advanced study which receives outstanding international scientists from various disciplines as its guests in order that they might pursue research of their own choice for a stipulated period of time. The model for this establishment was the Institute for Advanced Study in Princeton.

Whoever knows the landscape of research institutes in Berlin and can also compare them with those in West Germany will attest that Berlin has at its disposal an eminent accumulation of research establishments in science and technology with which it is able to carry forward the development of newer technology. In addition to that, there also exists an eminent potential of social scientific research establishments which are especially oriented toward finding effective solutions to questions of technological-industrial transformation. Therefore, one can justly say that Berlin is *the* German city of culture and science.

If one compares Berlin as an economic metropolis to Berlin as an intellectual center, it is easy to see that Berlin lives in a paradox. The scientific and cultural capacities are so top-heavy that one might simply say that the whole situation of Berlin is standing on its head. Quite apparently, this is not a natural or stable condition from which something would happen spontaneously. To create a future for Berlin requires concerted, political efforts: one must truly want Berlin to have a future. Naturally, this cannot come merely from blind volition. One must ascertain for oneself what the possibilities and what the limits of those possibilities are. Above all, Berlin must take advantage of the opportunities provided by the uniqueness of its situation. This requires a revitalization of the professional and industrial potential of the city. The locational advantage of Berlin, due to its high concentration of research and educational institutes, must be advertised and used to develop an effective industrial capacity that can advance Berlin to a leading position in modern technology and science. This is especially valid for the production of high-technology products and the establishment of a high-technology industry. It is, however, also valid with regard to the opportunities for developing highly evolved advisory services for businesses in order to aid them in the conversion to the latest technology in administration and management. In addition, the high percentage of foreign students, especially from Third World countries, being as high as the percentage of foreign workers in the city, is another excellent opportunity to be utilized for international economic cooperation.

If, in fact, it were possible to succeed in activating these and other factors of Berlin's present local advantages for the promotion of business and industry, one might arrive at an exemplary contribution to the development of means to solve the general technological and industrial problems of this time. Valid answers to the problems resulting from the paradoxes of Berlin's present situation indicated above, would be of more general—even worldwide—interest.

Whether or not Berlin has a chance of finding solutions to its problems in the way already pointed out in many regards must be left to history, since history occasionally also raises the question of what role might fall to the lot of science from the perspective of the future, and especially what role might be given to the Technical University in Berlin.

There are different meanings one might give to "Germany's unique road" through European history. The most widespread opinion revolves around the concept of "delay": Germany, as the so-called delayed nation, with "delayed industrialization" and "delayed modernisation." The attempt to make up for these delays had a special significance within the German state of Prussia and its capital Berlin. This was true for the process of industrialization in the two periods of industrial development. In both cases, the Technical University of Berlin, by its institutional precursors, was involved to a great degree.

At the beginning of the nineteenth century, immediately after the defeat of Napoleon, but above all after his expulsion, Prussia was the first German state to implement with all its might a decisive policy of industrialization. The primary incentive was the recognition that Germany, compared to England and France, was fundamentally backwards industrially. The response to this situation was, on the one hand, to accept the basic principles of middle-class bourgeois society: the freedom to settle where one wants, the freedom to practice a trade, and, to a certain extent, also the right to free trade. By accepting these principles, the Prussian tradition of national administration was consciously abandoned. On the other hand, however, provisions for the promotion of a national industralization developed in particular through an educational infrastructure whose principal tool was the education of future manufacturers. This education was based above all upon the view of teaching tradesmen how to use technology. For this purpose, the Vocational Institute—one of the two precursors of the present Technical University of Berlin—was founded. According to our current modern understanding, the Vocational Institute became the earliest "agency for the transfer of technology." It endeavored to collect all the latest technological knowledge of the time. It went so far as to use help from industrial spies who were sent to England and France. Machines from over there were reproduced and further developed. Their principles were explained to the manufacturers by exhibitions, or they were simply turned over to them for reproduction. The instructions given at the Vocational Institute were oriented toward practice. Theoretical requests were refused and referred back to the university and consigned solely to it. Like art and handicrafts, practical engineering was not considered a science.

Through this concerted policy of educating a technological intelligentsia and supporting a rapid mediation of technological methods, the Prussians succeeded, by the middle of the nineteenth century, in bringing the general industrial development into the modern technological age. One will probably be correct in stating that, by the beginning of the second phase of German industralization, Germany had at least temporarily succeeded in attaining the summit of industrial progress or, at least, in having made up for its previous delay.

This second phase of industrial development nearly coincided with the founding date of today's Technical University which, in 1879, originated as the Royal Technical School of Higher Education in Berlin through the fusion of the former Vocational Institute with the Building Academy. In 1881, the first electrical train, propelled by a 2-hp motor made by Werner von Siemens, was introduced at a vocational exhibition in Berlin-Moabit. It provided the impetus for the development of high-voltage technology. This

First electrical tramline of the world, opened in May 1881, by Siemens & Halske, limited company; without overhead lead.—May 12, 1881. Reproduced with permission of the Landesbildstelle Berlin.

brought about a revolution in production technology in the whole world, a revolution one could call the second catalyst for the advancement of technology and civilization, the first being the steam engine.

At the same time, the scientific system experienced a particular advancement and an intensive extension in the new technological sciences. The extensive expansion of the Technical University is itself due to this policy. A building was erected in 1884 to house the school. It was called "The Prachtbau (prize building) of the Charlottenburger Chaussee." Its outer form was modelled on that of the Friedrich-Wilhelm-University on Unter den Linden. At this school, for example, the new technologies found their scientific home at the suggestion of Werner von Siemens, e.g., the first professional chair in electrical technology. This model of how a national policy can dynamically further its economic and administrative vitality received attention and was discussed in young industrial nations the world over. It became known simply as the "Charlottenburg model."

Toward the end of the nineteenth century, besides the Technical School for Higher Education, a system of diverse, yet specialized establishments for research in the natural sciences stood out. The most important one was the Imperial Institute for Physics and Technology where Albert Einstein worked temporarily. It was here that he carried out the experiment whose results

Technical University (the "Prachtbau" (prize building)), seen from the east wing, Berliner Straße, ward Charlottenburg. Built from 1878 to 1884; plan by R. Lucae and F.A. Hitzig.—June 6, 1895. Reproduced with permission of the Landesbildstelle Berlin.

later became known as the Einstein–de Haas effect. The foundation of this institute was urged on primarily by the electrical products industry, especially by Siemens, who, to support this institute, donated a part of his private garden as well as considerable funding. For the Kaiser-Wilhelm-Society, industrial support was also of decisive importance. It was founded with the aid of the chemical industry. Under the direction of Otto Hahn, a section of the Kaiser-Wilhelm-Society was devoted to experimentation with radioactivity. And it was here where in 1939, with the help of Fritz Straßmann, the fusion of uranium by neutrons was first discovered. In 1904, when Winslow Taylor's book *The Principles of Scientific Management* appeared in America, Georg Schlesinger, at the then Technical School of Berlin, gave instruction in a new area of speciality: machine tools and factory management. And, in particular after the First World War, Schlesinger became a strong exponent in favour of transferring the perceptions of Taylor to Germany and adopting them critically to the conditions there, including mechanizing German industry.

In history, the attempt to explain anything by the use of a single, causal explanation is bound to fail. This is equally true for the relationship between science and educational systems on the one hand, and industrial and commercial innovation on the other. Nonetheless, this much can be ascertained:

What we may call a delay—taking into account the possibilities offered at that time—results in a lag of technological innovation, and, consequently, in a lag of economic innovation which is based on technological developments. The conditions caused by such a delay, then, necessitate the development of a carefully planned national commerce. An economic renewal which does not develop naturally of itself must be systematically carried out with the help of the state. The state, for its part, reacts to this task by the extension and cultivation of the sciences and the educational system. This has twice been successful. It was successful in the first so-called take-off phase which is thoroughly comparable to the situation one sees in developing countries today. And it was successful yet again in the second phase where the goal was to take our available highly developed technological knowledge and highly developed industrial structure and to concentrate them upon advancing the front lines of technology and industry on a worldwide scale.

The question for Berlin at present is: Can we now profit from this experience? Today Berlin does not have the industries which once not only promoted the research institutes in Berlin, but also partially financed them, and it lacks any administrative or commercial headquarters. But does it really depend upon such headquarters in order to utilize the new technical and industrial possibilities sketched out above? The horizon is open for industrial utilization of the newest development in microprocessing, which is communication's technology in the broadest sense, and in biotechnology. And these are only the most important technologies. Where the development in fact will go, how fast it may move forward, and how extensively the traditional products and their production procedures may change, the future alone can show.

It appears to me that the following point is decisive with regard to the question of whether or not Berlin will succeed in utilizing the chances open to it in technological development in order to prepare for a positive future: its chances depend essentially upon whether society judges the sciences and their ability to effect this development in a positive or in a negative light. In the chances as well as in the risks of technological development, we have to be able to see a task with which we can identify.

At present, dangers lie in a phenomenon which is often described as "the opposition of youth to technological development," a phenomenon which Americans often observe with surprise and that they consider to be a specifically European problem. However, at some point it becomes necessarily unavoidable to recognize that there is no route out of our present artificial living conditions back to a life of simplicity. And furthermore, we must recognize that it *is* possible to overcome the social and cultural damage of our technological-industrial civilization caused by the new technology. This technology is, after all, oriented toward serving the needs of human beings. Only when we recognize these facts will it be possible to heal the injuries of technology, first in the large cities, since it is there that we must first seek to understand the difficulties. That which is valid for cities in general is valid for Berlin in particular. To utilize the opportunity which lies in the tremendous scientific potential of the city requires enormous efforts on its behalf by all those who have responsibility.

Berlin offers the possibility to develop a program by which it could become a "metropolitan center for science and technology" and at the same time a technological focus of the Federal Republic. Some words about the role of the Technical University of Berlin within this process: it is almost trite to say that if the Technical University is going to effect a relevant contribution to the urban problems described above, one prerequisite is that its own self-image must be that of a scientific institution which makes advances toward solving the decisive, scientific questions of our time. In short, it must "attain the heights" of this age. A research profile thus defined is not merely, but especially, a question of concentrating upon the means available to it in its own sphere, where the front lines for the positive extension of the scientific horizon run. With all the skepticism about the future expectations for our planet, first in the face of processes in scientific development which have gone on in the past essentially without careful planning, and second, in consideration of a worldwide shortage of means of subsistence—a shortage which is bound to become substantially more acute in the next few years—we have no alternative but to combine our resources in certain fields of research.

In order to make use of the potential capacity of a university to solve scientific problems for the economic development of a region, it is necessary to develop special instruments of mediation. Exchange programs between universities and companies to serve this goal do not, however, develop naturally by themselves. The pressure to create tools of mediation belongs to the efforts demanded by the situation of Berlin while "standing on its head." There are various tools for "correcting" this position; for instance, an institutional mechanism for the exchange of technology as well as activities to further cooperative work in technology with Third World countries.

The Technical University of Berlin was one of the first German universities that attempted to establish a special agency for the transfer of technology in order to bring its scientific potential into closer contact with Berlin's industry. This kind of agency offers not only general information about the university's scientific potential, but also mediates contacts among scientists from Berlin's higher-educational institutions and firms, as well as other institutions that may be interested in cooperative efforts. It offers advisory services to scientists who wish to found new, scientifically independent enterprises; and finally, it mediates between the graduates of our educational establishment and the Berlin business community.

Because of the large number of foreign students, especially from Third World countries, at the Technical University, various efforts have been made to improve the efficiency in educating this group of students through a special training program with courses including practical experience in business firms as an attempt to facilitate the return of these young academics to their native countries by giving them the added qualification of having relevant experience. In 1981, the Center for Technological Cooperation was established to further develop this program.

We also developed a program for postgraduate or extracurricular scientific work to prepare students to use the scientific experience from their university studies more effectively in general practice, and especially, in a more narrow sense, for business practice.

Such programs are taken for granted at many American universities to-

Institute for machine tools (Werkzeugmaschinen) and manufactoring technic (Ferti-gungstechnik), Fraunhofer Institute for production protection (Produktionsschutz) and construction technic (Konstruktionstechnik), Pascalstraße 13–15, ward Charlot-tenburg, new building.—September 17, 1985. Reproduced with permission of the Landesbildstelle Berlin.

day, but in Germany they are still most unusual. In general, what in reality is accomplished depends on daily, steady work and to a degree upon the imagination, knowledge, and ability contributed by an individual and especially by the weakest links in any cooperative chain. This is just as true for the problem of cooperation between science and other areas of business as for the problem of scientific cooperation outside of the individual institutions or departments and for bringing together capabilities which are often self-reliant. I stress this because effectiveness, and even the desire to be effective, are very divergent in different areas. In many corners of Berlin, there is a trend to give up hope. This attitude is recognized by businessmen who coined the term "the subsidizing mentality" to describe it. And in the public realm it would not be a misunderstanding to say that, in many places, a proliferating bureaucracy grows from the same root. The resulting unstable mood, which one encounters periodically in Berlin, can finally only be overcome when every single individual is challenged to have the courage to try something.

As had already been recognized earlier, the chances for Germany's survival were once bound up with modernization. The graduates of the Vocational Institute at that time were prepared to become the fathers of Berlin's industrial development. The name of August Borsig represents many. I can, naturally, not guarantee whether there are names among today's graduates of the Technical University which in the years to come might perhaps be spoken with a similar weight as Hewlett and Packard, who once started with a new production in a garage not far from a university. What I can say is that

Berlin will succeed today and tomorrow in finding the right answers to the comprehensive problems of cooperative progress. This is the challenge which we must face.

Notes

[1] Three Max-Planck-Institutes (for Educational Research, for Molecular Genetics, and the Fritz-Haber-Institute); the Federal Health Service, the Environmental Office, the Federal Institute of Biology for Agriculture and Forestry, the Federal Laboratories for Material Testing, the Hahn-Meitner-Institute for Atomic Research, the Heinrich-Hertz-Institute, the Federal Institute for Professional Training, the German Archaealogical Institute, and the German Institute for Economic Research, as well as the Fraunhofer Institute for Production Design and Construction Technology

[2] The International Institute for Management and Administration, the International Institute for Environmental and Social Studies, the International Institute for Comparative Social Research

CHAPTER 22

Aims, Work, and Relevancy of Centers for Advanced Study in Transatlantic Dialogue

Wolf Lepenies

My remarks are divided into three parts. I shall begin with a historical reminiscence that links the Institute for Advanced Study in Princeton to the Wissenschaftskolleg in Berlin, and I shall continue with a description of some structural problems of the Kolleg that might be compared to those of other centers for advanced studies. I close with a short comment on interdisciplinarity that shall be confined to the human and the social sciences.

Einstein and Scholem

It is only appropriate to compare the newly established Wissenschaftskolleg to the Institute for Advanced Study in Princeton, New Jersey, that was founded almost exactly fifty years earlier. The deliberately somewhat old-fashioned and politically shrewd name "Wissenschaftskolleg *zu* Berlin" is supplemented by an English subtitle, "Institute for Advanced Study"—hereby referring to an institution that was so successful that its original name could become a generic term. There can be little doubt that the Institute for Advanced Study was founded in a genuinely American spirit. No one influenced Abraham Flexner more than Daniel Coit Gilman, the first president of Johns Hopkins University, "the starting point of higher education, in the modern sense of the term, in the United States." This is a characteristic assigned by Flexner himself who never ceased to admire Gilman's procedure of assembling first-rate minds and subsequently, letting them alone. When Flexner, however, tried to describe the function of an institute for advanced study in the American educational system in more detail, it became obvious at once how important the experience of the German university was to become for the founding of the new institution:

> American universities were, it is true, developing, so that seekers after a Ph.D. degree could obtain admirable opportunities; but nowhere did there exist the untrammeled facilities for easy-going and informal work between men who had passed the Ph.D. stage, had given promise of unusual ability, and who needed now the informal contact with masters which had characterized the German universities during their golden days.

It should not be forgotten that the Institute for Advanced Study was also conceived as a kind of teaching institution, intended for those who taught, as Flexner said, "best by not teaching at all." In this respect, the Institute followed the example of the German university only insofar as it made an important, yet rather concealed structural element manifest for the first time. When the University of Bielefeld was built in the seventies, one of its founding fathers remarked that he would rather like to plan a university with no students. This half-joking remark was received with great bitterness in the wake of the student revolt: I do think, however, that its author, rather than displaying the arrogance traditionally ascribed to the German *ordinarius*, thereby only pointed to a development that was inherent in the German university system yet was never realized. It is not by chance, therefore, that Bielefeld, in the form of its Center for Interdisciplinary Research (ZiF) built the first institution in Germany that could be regarded as resembling an institute for advanced study.

No one has to be reminded that another link exists between Germany and the Institute: the latter is indebted, as Flexner caustically remarked in an article written in 1939, "to Hitler for Einstein, Weyl, and von Neumann in mathematics; for Herzfeld and Panofsky in the field of humanistic studies; and for a host of younger men. . . ." Reading Flexner's autobiography, one cannot help thinking that the Institute for Advanced Study really came to life when, on a cold day in June of 1932, Abraham Flexner visited Potsdam. He saw Albert Einstein and told him about the Institute and invited him to become a member there and finally was bid farewell with the words: "Ich bin Feuer und Flamme dafür". (I am for it heart and soul).

I do not know how Gershom Scholem, born in Berlin, reacted when he was invited to become the first fellow of the Wissenschaftskolleg zu Berlin almost exactly fifty years later, but I think there is no doubt that his acceptance and his presence in Berlin played a similar role for the Kolleg as Einstein had played for the Institute. That the Wissenschaftskolleg had to be modelled after an American institute for advanced study in which the emigrants from Germany assumed such an important role is a legacy of the Nazi period that so deeply affected the German university. Scholem's presence was a constant reminder of this past but it was an act of forgiving as well, a moral legitimation that could not be planned, only hoped for by all those who were engaged in the founding of the Kolleg.

Structural Problems

The Wissenschaftskolleg was founded in 1980. Forty fellows are invited for the academic year. Half of them must be German; in principle, all disciplines are represented among them.

Foundation and Funds

The Institute in Princeton was founded by an act of philanthropy upon which America's institutions of higher learning have so greatly relied. The

Kolleg is financed exclusively by the Federal Republic of Germany and by the Land Berlin, e.g., by the taxpayer. Different forms of funding obviously yield different degrees of expectation and forms of control: philanthropy, cautious and reserved as it may appear in the charter of an institution is, almost by definition characterized by long-term expectations and remote forms of control; direct forms of control and short-term expectations, however, are not only characteristic, but are required by law of public institutions. This may cause a considerable disadvantage as Abraham Flexner anticipated: "Nothing is more likely to defeat itself, nothing is on the whole less productive, in the long run, than immediacy in the realm of research, reflection, and contemplation."

Immediacy of expectations and the need for public visibility favour *performance* at the expense of *competence*. This danger is still present at the Kolleg. A public lecture that attracts a large crowd and is even reviewed in the city's newspapers is more likely to please the administration and to convince it that public funds have been spent adequately than the hidden existence of someone who has "come up to the idea that the fate of his soul depends upon whether or not he makes the correct conjecture at this passage of this manuscript." This is, of course, a quotation from Max Weber's speech on "Science as a Vocation," and it was presented therein as the description of the true scholar. Flexner liked the motto of another scholar from Berlin, Paul Ehrlich, and wanted the Institute's members to follow it: "Work hard and publish little!" (*Viel arbeiten, wenig publizieren*). In a period where the "publish-or–perish" ideology is still prevalent, it would be rather dangerous to use this motto while requiring public funds. One structural problem is thus shared by the Kolleg with all other centers for advanced studies: the increasing difficulty in justifying and financing true scholarship, in defending the "usefulness of useless knowledge" (Abraham Flexner).

Institutionalization

Processes of institutionalization imply acts of refusal: like a new discipline, a newly founded center for advanced studies acquires its identity not only through affirmations but through negations as well. It must not only declare whom it wants to follow but also whom to abandon. For these strategies of intrusion and avoidance, the reputation of similar institutions is of utmost importance.

The founders of the Kolleg made it clear from the beginning that this institution would not and could not be an imitation of the Institute, but that Princeton was the model that should be followed wherever possible. Princeton's "glorious success" let the founders of the Kolleg escape the necessity of justifying an institute for advanced study in principle. What had to be justified was the founding of an additional Institute though it was the first one in Germany, under the present political and historical circumstances.

Like Flexner in the thirties, the founders of the Kolleg fifty years later had to seek legitimation for the building of the Kolleg as an act of compensation. The Institute, in Flexner's words, should be small, informal and plastic, because the universities had become big, overorganized and rigid. Once again,

College of Science, the first "Institute for Advanced Study" on German soil.—June 11, 1981. Reproduced with permission of the Landesbildstelle Berlin.

this was a statement that was familiar in the German context. In 1918 Max Weber said that "inwardly as well as externally, the old university constitution has become fictitious"; and in his fourth lecture "On the Future of our Educational Institutions" (March 5, Basel), Nietzsche had sharply distinguished between "institutions for teaching culture and institutions for teaching how to succeed in life." He was addressing schools as well as universities, but one cannot help, today, thinking of universities on the one, of centers for advanced studies on the other hand, when Nietzsche declared: "What in the latter is permitted, and even freely held out as often as possible, ought to be considered as a criminal offence in the former."

Kolleg and University

Until today, the Institute for Advanced Study has regularly been described in Germany as part of Princeton University. It is hard for the German public to imagine that an institution such as this one can exist in almost complete independence of a university. In Berlin, the Kolleg and the universities are linked through formal contracts of cooperation. Its director is appointed and any future permanent member will have to be appointed professor at one of Berlin's universities. The most difficult structural problem for the Kolleg is perhaps the necessity of distinguishing itself from the university and justifying its existence through the latter's insufficiency while, on the other hand and in sharp contrast to the Institute, remaining dependent from it.

When Max Weber suggested that "democracy should be used only where it is suitable," he was referring to the university as an institution where democracy obviously was out of place. This has changed. The history of the German university in the Weimar Republic and under the Nazi regime led, after a period of restoration and stagnation immediately after the war, to its democratization in the sixties and seventies. The student revolt was an international phenomenon. Yet no other country has preserved its heritage to the extent that Germany has in form of its dramatically changed university structure. On the other hand, there can be no doubt that the German university has considerably suffered from over-democratization. Functioning as a substitute for many other institutions that were hardly changed after the war, the German university has become more democratic for political not for functional reasons. The reform of the German university has been, above all a symptom of a bad conscience.

I do not believe, however, that anyone who speaks out in favour of an institute for advanced study in Germany today, has to defend its internal structure, because it differs considerably from that of our universities. One does not have to accept the view that the university today is basically democratic, while institutions like the Kolleg display an almost aristocratic structure. The difference between the universities and the Kolleg is that of a distinction between two forms of democracy, that of a duty to participate on one side, that of the right to retire into oneself on the other. The university engages its members to participate in scholarly as well as nonscholarly activities. An institution like the Kolleg displays another form of democracy, one that consists, as Flexner put it, of leaving "men of brains alone."

It is exactly because the German university has become an antielitist institution, and understandably so, that institutions like the Kolleg are justified. The anti-elitism of the present German university has often been explained in functional terms, but I think it can only be justified on political grounds, and, more precisely, on those that have not much to do with the university itself; on the other hand, there is no need to procure political arguments in defense of the Wissenschaftskolleg; its internal structure, differing from that of the university, and rightly so, can be justified perfectly not as an ideology but as a functional prerequisite.

Functions

The Institute for Advanced Study still exists, as Flexner described it in 1939, "as a paradise for scholars who, like poets and musicians, have won the right to do as they please and who accomplish most when enabled to do so." It was an educational utopia at its beginning but it has since become an educational reality and a model. The Wissenschaftskolleg zu Berlin is not only an institute for advanced study. Due to the present peculiarities of the German educational system and the specific cultural climate of Berlin, it is at the same time a faculty club—which the universities do not possess; a salon—which hardly exists anywhere in the city; an educational utopia—which has failed in other places—and a testing arena for educational policies of the different political parties.

The Kolleg is often justified on the grounds that it can fulfill all these functions. Divergent functions, however, are responsible for different expectations that more than once collide with one another, even more so since the Kolleg, to paraphrase Wystan Hugh Auden, is still a place where public faces show up quite regularly. It is difficult to fulfill the wishes of those who want to be enlightened by scholarly insights at the same time as the demands of others who want to be entertained in a salonlike atmosphere. A cleansing of functions and a reduction of functional expectations will be required in the near future.

Interdisciplinarity

Finally, I would like to address one topic that plays an important role in any center for advanced studies. I am referring to the problem of interdisciplinarity. Since the times of Nietzsche, Max Weber, and Abraham Flexner, it has been deplored that science, as early as at the beginning of the nineteenth century, entered a phase of specialization that was previously unknown. The resigned tone with which this nostalgic description is still delivered today in regard to the university is matched only by the optimism with which centers for advanced studies are regarded as remedies for the vice of specialization. I should like to subdue this optimism somewhat while at the same time trying to give it a safer ground.

Rather often, interdisciplinarity is trying to be achieved through a cooperation of specialists. Up until now, public funds for conferences and meetings can still be obtained easily, at least in Germany, when one is able to present a list of invitations that is comprised of scholars of the most different orientations and specialties. The results, as a rule, are meager, not least because it is so difficult to find a common language in which these specialists can talk and understand each other. I am not inclined to think of centers for advanced studies as places where interdisciplinary projects of specialists should be particularly promoted.

On the other hand, we should not forget that specialists for interdisciplinarity already exist. I would venture to say that many advances in the human and the social sciences in the last years have not been achieved by projects of groups of specialists but by imaginative ideas of a scholar who had accepted the risk of becoming somewhat alienated from the core of his profession. I like to think of centers for advanced studies as places where, among many others, outsiders of the profession can work, not for the sake of sheer marginality but for the positive consequences this might have for a wide array not only of adjacent but even of rather remote disciplines and areas of inquiry. For these "outsiders," centers of advanced studies should not only be places of freedom but at the same time institutions of control. Professional marginality all too often leads to sectarianism. To prevent this, centers for advanced studies might provide opportunities, by pooling outsiders and specialists, to test ideas that otherwise would have been rejected prematurely or incubated for too long.

However we address our topic, I wish we could do it with some of the laconism that the founder of the Institute for Advanced Study and its most prominent member so marvellously displayed. Einstein described himself as "a horse for single harness, not cut out for tandem or teamwork," and Flexner drew from this and the remarks of others a rather simple conclusion: "Let them alone. No educational administrator can possibly direct the channels in which these or other men shall work." Even if there are not many Einsteins around anymore, I do think that this anti-institutional attitude is the most important prerequisite for an institute for advanced study. After all, such an institute, whether it is located in Princeton or in Berlin, has, as Daniel Coit Gilman and Abraham Flexner said, something in common with Boston: It is not a place but a state of mind.

References

Flexner, Abraham
1939   "The Usefulness of Useless Knowledge," in: *Harper's Magazine*, pp. 544–552.
1952   *Funds and Foundations. Their Policies Past and Present*. With the collaboration of Esther S. Bailey, New York: Harper & Brothers.
1960   *An Autobiography*. New York: Simon & Schuster.
Nietzsche, Friedrich
1964   "The Future of Our Educational Institutions" (1872), in: *The Complete Works*, Vol. 3, New York: Russell & Russell.
Wapnewski, Peter
1982   "Ein Haus der Gelehrsamkeit. Tradition wurde begründet: Das Wissenschaftskolleg zu Berlin nach einem Jahr," in: *Die Zeit*, 24 December 1982.
Weber, Max
1946   "Science as a Vocation," (1918), in: *From Max Weber. Essays in Sociology*. Translated, edited, and with an introduction by H. H. Gerth and C. Wright Mills, pp. 129–156. New York: Oxford University Press.

CHAPTER 23

The Evolution of Berlin's Urban Form Through History, Illustrated by Selected Examples

Wilhelm V. von Moltke

Berlin was built where a trade route from Saxony to the Baltic Sea crosses the Spree River. In its early years, it consisted of the twin settlements of Cölln and Berlin. Cölln, on the left bank of the Spree River, was a settlement of fishermen, huddled around the church of St. Peter, the patron of fishermen. It was first documented in 1237. Berlin, on the opposite bank, first documented in 1244, was a town of traders, grouped around the church of St. Nicholas, the patron of merchants. Archaelogical finds indicate that both settlements existed well before 1237, possibly even as early as the end of the twelfth century, but 1237, the year of the first written evidence of the existence of Cölln, is generally accepted as the year of the birth of Berlin. Both towns were members of the Hanseatic League, when Emperor Sigismund invested in 1417 the Burgrave Friedrich VI of Nürnberg of the House of Hohenzollern who had already been Margrave of Brandenburg since 1415, Elector Friedrich I of Brandenburg; the latter made Berlin the seat of the House of Hohenzollern, which it remained for 500 years.

Friedrich I was an enlightened ruler with political sensitivity, being content with the control of the mint, customs, and jurisdiction of Berlin and Cölln, while he protected the two towns from the robber barons and the Mark Brandenburg from the Poles. After his death in 1440, his son Friedrich II, the Iron Elector, set out to gain control over the twin towns. He built a castle, and, playing one town against the other, he enforced their separation from the Hanseatic League in 1442 and obtained pledges of allegiance from both towns in 1448.

In spite of the geographical advantages of being located on the Spree River, Berlin is not an ideal site for a thriving city because it is surrounded by a sand-covered hinterland devoid of any natural resources. Yet it did become a thriving world city, largely due to the political will of a number of Prussian rulers, beginning with Friedrich Wilhelm, the Great Elector, who ruled from 1640 to 1688.

The Thirty Years' War, 1618 to 1648, affected the economy of central Europe and also that of Berlin. Although the city was never directly involved in this terrible war, the general economic decline and the widespread epidemics took their toll.

The population shrank from 12,000 to 6500. Indeed, at one time abandoning the twin cities of Berlin and Cölln was seriously considered. However, the Great Elector Friedrich Wilhelm did not give in. He promoted the urban and economic development of the city by inviting victims of religious persecution from all parts of Europe to settle in Berlin. In doing so he was motivated by compassion as well as by his desire to attract settlers with much needed skills. They were largely Huguenots who came from France to escape persecution, as well as immigrants from Holland, Switzerland, and Bohemia. Also attracted were Walloons from Flanders and Jews from Austria. By 1688 the population had increased threefold, to 20,000. In 1700, 25 percent of Berlin's population was of French extraction, and the city grew rapidly to 65,300 in 1721, and to 146,500 in 1786.

In 1647 Friedrich Wilhelm planted a 1000-meter-long avenue of linden trees for parades and as a connection to the Tiergarten, the ducal hunting grounds. It became Berlin's future Unter den Linden, the "Via triumphalis," as well as an access to the future suburb of Dorotheenstadt, named after the wife of the Great Elector. Dorotheenstadt, founded in 1673, was largely settled by French immigrants. In 1678, it was included into the modern fortifications which Friedrich Wilhelm had started to build around Berlin in 1658, at the same time enlarging the city by including Friedrichswerder and Neu-Cölln.

In order to stimulate economic development and population growth and to provide decent housing, the Great Elector established enlightened policies which were continued by his successors, the Elector of Brandenburg Friedrich III (who became Friedrich I after his coronation as King of Prussia in 1701) and king Friedrich Wilhelm I, who ruled from 1713 to 1740. Within about seven decades, these rulers provided the urban infrastructure, free building lots, timber, stones, and lime, and tax exemption. In order to ensure a harmonious street-scape the Hohenzollern controlled the design of the facades, and in order to prevent speculation the owner had to complete the construction of the house in a stipulated amount of time and had to occupy the building himself after completion.

In 1688 the Elector Friedrich III started the planning and development of the suburban Friedrichstadt, an area larger than all of Berlin and Cölln within the fortifications. This district is centered on the Friedrichstraße, which bisects Unter den Linden and extends for two kilometers southward. A special feature of the plan for the Friedrichstadt is the vestibulelike squares at the three western gates. The northernmost, at the Brandenburg Gate, allowing access to Unter den Linden, is in the form of a square and was called the "Quarré" (later Pariser Platz); the next, at the Potsdamer Gate in the form of an octagon, was called the "Achteck" (later Leipziger Platz); and the circular southernmost one, at the Hallesches Gate, was called the "Rondell" (later Belle Alliance Square, and after the Second World War Mehring Platz). It is reminiscent of the Piazza del Populo in Rome, with three major avenues converging on this circular space. Another special aspect of the Friedrich-stadt is the Gendarmenmarkt, now Platz der Akademie (Place of the Academy) a three-block square two blocks south of Unter den Linden, bounded in the east by the Markgrafenstraße.

In 1695, Friedrich III began the development of the Charlottenburg Castle as a summer residence for his wife, Sophie Charlotte, with Johann Arnold

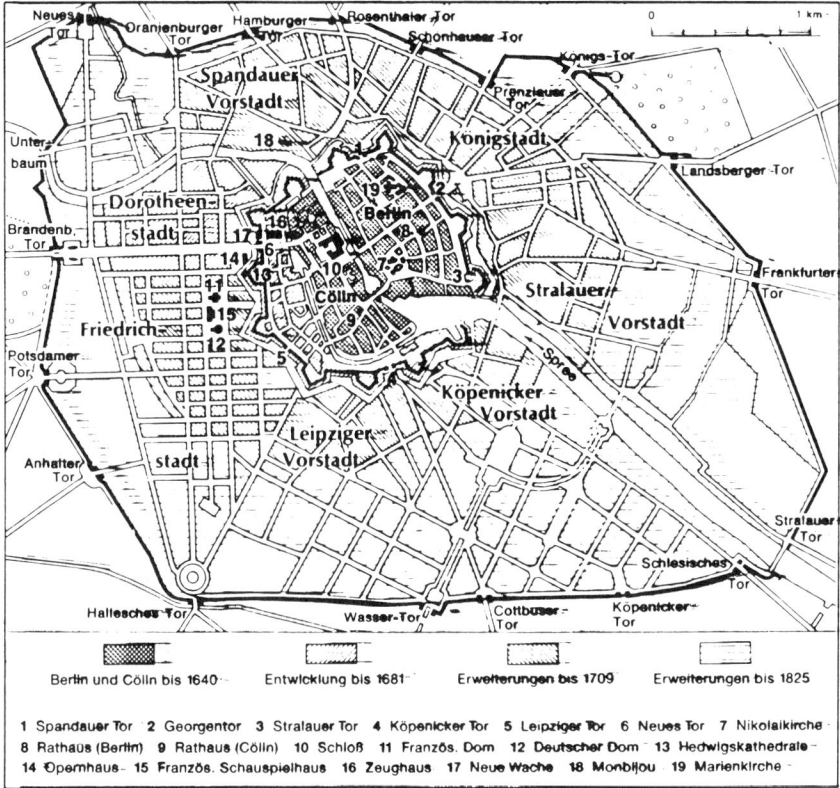

Berlin und Cölln bis 1640   Entwicklung bis 1681   Erweiterungen bis 1709   Erweiterungen bis 1825

1 Spandauer Tor 2 Georgentor 3 Stralauer Tor 4 Köpenicker Tor 5 Leipziger Tor 6 Neues Tor 7 Nikolaikirche
8 Rathaus (Berlin) 9 Rathaus (Cölln) 10 Schloß 11 Französ. Dom 12 Deutscher Dom 13 Hedwigskathedrale
14 Opernhaus 15 Französ. Schauspielhaus 16 Zeughaus 17 Neue Wache 18 Monbijou 19 Marienkirche

Map of Berlin showing its evolution up to 1825.—From Brockhaus Enzyklopädie, *vol. 3, 19th edition, Mannheim 1987. Reproduced with permission of the publishing house F.A. Brockhaus.*

Nering as architect. This palace was later enlarged by Friedrich II, the Great, with Knobelsdorff as architect, and finally completed by Carl Gotthard Langhans, 1788 to 1790, under Friedrich Wilhelm II. The gardens for this five-hundred-meter-long palace were laid out by Siméon Godeau, a student of Le Nôtre.

Around the turn of the eighteenth century, two key buildings on Unter den Linden were completed: the Zeughaus (armory) and the enlarged royal palace at the end of Berlin's "Champs Elysées." The Zeughaus, a Renaissance-inspired building in a pivotal position with regard to Schinkel's Lustgarten (pleasure garden), was built from 1695 to 1706, involving Arnold Nering, Martin Grünberg, Andreas Schlüter, and Jan de Bodt. It aroused the interest of Louis XIV, who sent his architect François Blondel on a diplomatic mission to Berlin. The other key building, the Royal Palace, reminiscent of the Roman Palazo Madama, measures 172 meters by 116 meters by 30 meters. It was begun by Andreas Schlüter in 1698 and completed by Eosander von Göthe in 1707. It terminates visually at Unter den Linden and at the

Charlottenburg Castle (Palace) with monument of the Great Elector.—May 22, 1967. Reproduced with permission of the Landesbildstelle Berlin.

same time serves as a link between the new Frederician city Friedrichstadt and the historic core on the Spree River.

In 1713, Friedrich Wilhelm I, probably the most farsighted planner of the Hohenzollern, came to power. His motto was: "Menschen achte ich vor dem größten Reichtum" ("I respect people more than the greatest treasure"). Friedrich Wilhelm I is known as the Soldier King and the founder of the incorruptible and efficient bureaucracy of Prussia, a man of simple and modest taste who has been referred to as the "Sergeant on the Throne of Prussia." Although he stopped construction on a number of luxurious projects of Friedrich I, he continued to support with vigor the housing policies which were started by his predecessors. He even increased the housing subsidies by paying, in addition to building lot, timber, building stone and lime free of charge and tax exemption a subsidy of 15 percent of the remaining building costs. This support was not even matched by the Weimar Republic 200 years later.

Friedrich Wilhelm I ordered the fortifications of Berlin to be razed in 1732, a mere 50 years after completion. He replaced them by constructing the Zollmauer (customs wall) which was completed in 1736. The area within this wall was adequate to accommodate the population of Berlin for the next

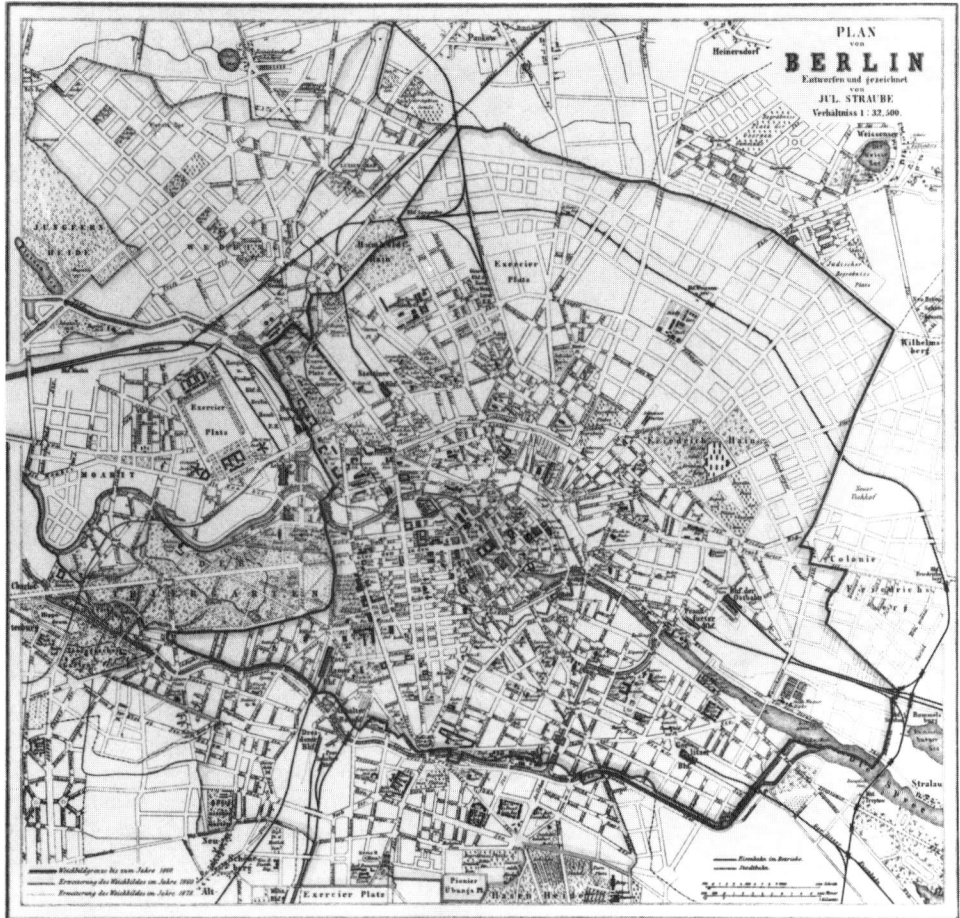

Map of Berlin in 1878, with identifications of the city boundaries before and after 1860 as well as of the expansion of 1878, by Julius Straube.—1878. Reproduced with permission of the Landesbildstelle Berlin.

100 years. The purpose of this wall was to prevent anyone from the garrison, which was stationed in Berlin, from leaving without permission and to ensure that everybody entering or leaving the city had paid customs and taxes. It was finally demolished between 1866 and 1868. By irony of history, a portion of today's wall dividing the city is in exactly the same location.

By 1740, the year of his death, Friedrich Wilhelm I could look back on a number of major accomplishments. Within the twenty-five years of his reign he had razed the fortifications between old Berlin and the newly planned and developed settlements to the west. He had built the Zollmauer, boosted new housing, and attracted new settlers from all parts of Europe. The population of Berlin had grown to 90,000. It is interesting to note that this king spent more on urban development, housing subsidies, and municipal housekeeping than on the army, which was respected throughout Europe for its size, effectiveness, and discipline and which enabled his son Friedrich II, the Great, to establish Prussia as one of the leading powers of Europe.

Friedrich the Great (reigning from 1740 to 1786) was a brilliant and courageous statesman and commander of the army, decisive and at the same time unassuming, a ruler who called himself "the first servant of the State" and who lived up to it, a gifted composer and musician, a sophisticated, well-read francophile whose usual language was French and who asked one of his generals to address his army in his stead because his command of German was inadequate. He continued to plan and build in Berlin, affecting the physical form of the city, although in his later years he was more interested in the development of Potsdam.

In Berlin Friedrich the Great showed interest in the development of two open spaces: the Forum Fredericianum and the Gendarmenmarkt. The Forum Fredericianum was conceived by him before he came to power. It was also the idea of his friend, architect Georg Wenceslaus von Knobelsdorff, whom Friedrich II appointed superintendent of all royal castles, buildings, and gardens, as well as "Directeur en Chef" (principal manager) of all royal buildings in the provinces, until he dismissed him in 1750.

The Forum Fredericianum was to be surrounded by the Royal Palace and buildings housing cultural activities. It was to straddle Unter den Linden just west of the Zeughaus, to include the Markgrafenstraße connecting the Forum with the Gendarmenmarkt to the south, and to terminate in the south at the Collegienhaus (by Phillipp Gerlach, 1735), which is known today as the Berlin Museum. The first building to be constructed as part of this complex was the Opera by Knobelsdorff (1741 to 1743). This fine paladian building of noble proportions was a promising beginning. Soon after its completion in 1747, Knobelsdorff started the development of the Cathedral of St. Hedwig, a Roman Catholic church which was inspired by the Pantheon.

In 1748, Friedrich the Great began the construction of the palace for his brother, Prince Heinrich of Prussia, to the north of Unter den Linden. It has a Court d'honneur flanked by two wings facing Unter den Linden. In 1809, under Friedrich Wilhelm III, this building became the Friedrich Wilhelm University, with Johann Gottlieb Fichte as its first president. In 1949 its name was changed to Humboldt University, after the creator of this institution.

The construction of the Royal Library on the west side of the square in front of the opera began in 1774. The location of this baroque building, based on a design by Erlach von Fischer of Vienna, precluded the possibility of a spatial link between the Forum Fredericianum and the Gendarmenmarkt.

In 1781, the two existing similar churches on the Gendarmenmarkt, the French church for the Huguenot community in the north and the German church in the south, were remodeled by adding domed towers, 76 meters in height, in order to provide two vertical elements which rise from the large square measuring 330 meters by 180 meters. This also provided a relief at this point for Friedrichstadt, which suffered from uniform horizontality. The architect was Karl Phillip von Gontard, a captain in the Prussian Army.

Gendarmenmarkt, ward Mitte, East Berlin; from the front: German cathedral, play house, French cathedral; drawing by Calan, etched in copper by P. Haas in 1795. Reproduced with permission of the Landesbildstelle Berlin.

In addition, he changed the height of the buildings facing the Gendarmenmarkt to a uniform three floors, an expense which was financed by the Royal Treasury. Thus the stage was set for Schinkel's New Theater which was completed in 1821. Friedrich then replaced the Protestant Cathedral at the Schloßfreiheit with one by Johann Boumann east of the Lustgarten (1747 to 50) and added the east wing by Knobelsdorff to the Charlottenburg Palace (1740 to 46) for his own use.

In his later years Friedrich the Great showed greater interest in the development of Potsdam and left important problems in Berlin unattended, in particular those created by the razing of the fortifications, begun by his father. The result was awkward street alignments and discontinuities between the old city and the new districts to the west. This very problem was faced by Karl Friedrich Schinkel in his General Plan of 1817. In all, Friedrich the Great succeeded in making Prussia one of the leading countries of Europe, and Berlin continued to grow to 146,650 inhabitants in 1786, the year of Friedrich's death. This then puts us at the beginning of the French Revolution. Politically, it did not shake Prussia, since the enlightened king had introduced most of the reforms for which the French Revolution was fought. But the architectural revolution, started in Paris in 1770 when Claude Nicholas Ledoux had designed a house in the shape of a globe resting on one point, was a challenge to the Rococo.

Immediately after he came to power, Friedrich Wilhelm II (1786 to 1797) called four master architects to Berlin: Friedrich Wilhelm von Erdmannsdorff, Carl Gotthard Langhans, David Gilly, and Gottfried Schadow.

From 1788 to 1791 Carl Gotthard Langhans built the Brandenburger Tor (Brandenburg Gate), a beautiful structure inspired by the propylaeum at the Acropolis in Athens, the first example of civic architecture in the new classical style on the continent, crowned with the Quadriga by Gottfried Schadow. It completed Unter den Linden, provided a fitting entry to Berlin's "Via Triumphalis" from the west leading to the Royal Palace in the heart of the historic core, and became the symbol of Berlin.

In 1793, David Gilly founded the Berlin School of Building (Bauschule), which became the Bauakademie (the Building Academy) in 1799. For the first years of its existence it was accommodated in the Mint, a revolutionary building designed and built in 1789 by Heinrich Gentz, another architect of great stature who was active in Berlin at that time and who also was a teacher at the Bauakademie.

In 1797, the year in which Friedrich Wilhelm III (1797 to 1840) followed his father as king of Prussia, the 16-year-old Karl Friedrich Schinkel decided "to devote his life to the fine arts and architecture." He had been captured by the work of David Gilly's son Friedrich, who was a genius but unfortunately lived only twenty-eight years. Friedrich Gilly became renowned through his entry into the design competition for a monument for Friedrich den Großen. His concept, which was influenced by the ideas of the French revolutionary architect Boulle, inspired many colleagues and convinced Karl Friedrich Schinkel to become an architect. At the age of eight, the young Schinkel had dropped out of school in 1789 and joined the household and atelier of David and Friedrich Gilly. In 1799 he entered the first class of the newly founded Bauakademie. Seventeen years later, he started to fight for many improvements and decisive developments of the urban form of Berlin. He had done a two-year study tour of Saxony, Austria, Istria, Italy, Sicily, and France, but when he returned to Berlin in 1805, building construction had come to a complete standstill, due to the imminent involvement of Prussia in the Napoleonic wars. Thus Schinkel used the time for painting, drawing, and the designing of panoramas, which were as large as 9 meters in height and 21 meters in width. It was not before 1810 that he, at the age of 29, was charged with reviewing the design of all civic, royal, and religious buildings in Prussia, as well as with the preservation of the historic heritage.

In 1815 Schinkel's most active period began. He developed guidelines for the preservation of historic monuments, designed stage settings for the national theater, prepared redevelopment plans for the center of Berlin, and built many of his best-known buildings. In addition, he published "Standard Designs for Manufacturers and Craftsmen." In 1824 he made his second Italian journey, and two years later traveled to France, England, Scotland, and Wales, met John Nash, commented on society, industry, and town planning, and introduced from England the idea of gas street lighting to Berlin, where it was installed in 1827. By then, Schinkel was widely acclaimed and honored by his contemporaries. He was made an honorary member of the Academies of Fine Arts in Berlin, Munich, Vienna, Rome, Paris, Copenhagen, and St. Petersburg, and of the Royal Institute of British Architects in London.

In the spring of 1816, the king asked Schinkel to design the Neue Wache, the house for the royal guard, on the north side of Unter den Linden, between the Zeughaus and the university, across the street from the Stadt-schloß, the Royal City Palace. This was Schinkel's first commission, and he decided to use it for the improvement of the entire area. His first concept included the proposal to cover a green ditch (a blighting influence for the area), a chestnut grove, statues, and a circular fountain for the royal garden on axis with the guard house to integrate the south side of Unter den Linden into the overall design. The king did not agree. He had developed different concepts, which brought about the revised plan of the autumn of 1816 including only the guard house and the chestnut grove. Thus, Schinkel finally built a very beautiful monument in the Prussian neoclassical style, a building which attracted international attention, but he had lost the opportunity to improve the larger environment. The design process of the Neue Wache shows how Schinkel considered the impact of even a minor building on the larger environment. It also demonstrates his patience and perseverance in the face of lack of appreciation by the king.

In 1817 Schinkel prepared the so called "Bebauungsplan," a master plan for two square kilometers in central Berlin, which would have established a new structure for the city center with a minimum of dislocations and demolition. This plan would have achieved much needed links between Dorotheenstadt and old Berlin as well as a new focus and connecting structure for the Spandauer Vorstadt (suburb); for Unter den Linden an urgently needed eastern terminus appropriate in scale and design; a link between the Gendarmenmarkt and the Schloßplatz, operational efficiencies and economies from the consolidated hospital behind the university; and greater efficiency from the new Packhof and harbor facilities in a more rational location. In preparing his report to the king, Schinkel started by stressing the resulting efficiency and consequently long-term economic gain. But there is no record of even a reply by the king, who apparently lacked the vision or imagination to understand the far-reaching significance of Schinkel's imaginative and yet implementable plan.

After the Nationaltheater (National Theater) by the neoclassicist Carl Gotthard Langhans was gutted by a disastrous fire in 1817, Schinkel was commissioned in 1818 to design a theater, which was completed in 1821. He demanded and received a written guarantee that he, the architect, would be responsible for all design decisions in the urban setting around the Gendarmenmarkt. The Schauspielhaus (theater) formed the central feature of the west side of the plaza, and as mentioned previously, was flanked by two similar churches, to the north and south. The new building was similar to its neighbors in its essentially classical appearance. Freestanding pedimented porticos, a symmetrical balance of masses, and an emphasis on the axis are basic to the design. However, Schinkel's inventive transformation of Grecian and Renaissance elements resulted in a new structure that was distinguishable from the Franco-Italianate character of the two existing churches.

When this new theater was being built, Schinkel was finally also commissioned in 1819 to construct a bridge at the eastern end of Unter den Linden, after having failed to convince the king by his proposals in 1816 in connection with the design of the Neue Wache and in 1817 as part of the proposed master plan for the center of Berlin. This structure was completed in 1823, and thus the much needed appropriate link between Unter den Linden and the Lustgarten was achieved.

In 1822 Schinkel prepared another comprehensive plan for the Lustgarten and its environment which included some of the ideas of his master plan of 1817. This resulted from a request by the king to develop a museum in the existing Akademie. Schinkel was convinced that a new museum terminating the Lustgarten toward the north would be more economical and more satisfactory for the museum itself, and would have a number of environmental advantages. In his report, persuasion is used to convince the ever hesitant king. The advantages begin with the phrase: "An Kosten wird gespart" ("As for expenses, we shall save"). The persuasion of statistics is used very liberally. Schinkel pointed out that the shipping, storage, and transfer of goods—the taxes from which went to the royal treasury—would be facilitated more efficiently and economically by a new complex north of the Lustgarten. The old customs warehouses at Friedrichswerder could be sold or used to build a profitable apartment block. Schinkel also stated that the allocated 700,000 Thaler would be sufficient. In 1823 the king agreed under the condition that the allocated funds had to suffice, including the renovation of the Akademie. Construction was started in 1824 and completed in 1830, and the building was opened to the public in 1831.

Schinkel wanted to build a structure that would serve as a museum and at the same time achieve many of the objectives of his plan of 1817. He intended that the Lustgarten should be closed on the north, that the riverbanks of the Kupfergraben should be embellished with promenades, and that the newly designated site for the customs warehouses and offices, the Packhof, should eliminate disturbing barges and commercial river traffic south of the Lustgarten. In addition, the new Packhof would be more easily accessible for barges arriving mostly from the north, and a new east–west thoroughfare north of the museum would provide the much needed link between Dorotheenstadt, Cölln and old Berlin.

The plan and the composition of the museum were conceived as complementary to the Stadtschloss (the Royal city castle) and the Zeughaus across the Kupfergaben. The cornice levels are approximately the same height, and the relationship to the neighboring buildings was considered of particular importance. The museum is basically a simple rectalinear block with an interior courtyard divided by a central cube containing a circular domed space, similar to the Pantheon in Rome. This domed hall is the focus of the building. The southern elevation, facing the Lustgarten, consists of a *stoa* on a high base (which contains service areas) with 18 columns *in antis*. A very special feature is the central five-bays-wide spacious entrance *loggia*, the main entrance that gives access to both exhibition floors from two sheltered outdoor areas connected by two symmetrical monumental stairs. From the upper level one can enjoy a delightful panorama of the Lustgarten and environs.

For the landscaping of the Lustgarten, Schinkel developed a design in 1828. He proposed to unify the eastern side of this large space through the planting of a wall of trees; only Schinkel's pedimented portico of the Domkirche, or Cathedral, was left visible. On the western side he proposed a corresponding wall of trees with an opening opposite the portico of the Cathedral, thus extending its influence to the area in front of the Zeughaus.

The construction of the Packhof complex to the north of the museum was finally started in 1830 and completed in 1832. The resulting structures added considerably to the improvement of the area and effected greater efficiency. Unfortunately, this complex has been replaced by the former Kaiser-Friedrich-Museum, now the Bode Museum (1897–1903), and the Pergamon Museum (1906–30).

In 1823 Schinkel had designed the neogothic Friedrichswerder church for the Werder market, after his neoclassic design with a free standing campanile had been rejected by the king. The classical design, which Schinkel would have preferred considerably, would have harmonized with the Mint, designed by Heinrich Gentz, which is on the same square. However, the king insisted on a neogothic church and Schinkel complied reluctantly.

Bauakademie (Academy of Building) Schinkelplatz, ward Mitte, East Berlin; built 1832–35; plan by Karl Friedrich Schinkel.—1905. Reproduced with permission of the Landesbildstelle Berlin.

When the king asked Schinkel in 1831 to design and build the Bauakademie, Schinkel created a building that was way ahead of its time. The art historian Goerd Peschken wrote about this structure: "Probably the most important building...built in our country in the last century." But Schinkel had also prepared a new master plan for the Friedrichswerder which included a direct connection between the Französische Straße and the Schloßplatz and included the location of the proposed Bauakademie. When Schinkel presented the plan in 1832, the king approved only the location of the Bauakademie, but the ideas for the improvement of the area were not realized at this time.

The Bauakademie was a complete break with the baroque tradition. The dominating ideas was *not* a sequence of spaces, but rather the purity of structure and the Materialgerechtigkeit (suitability of the material). It was a brick building with terra cotta, sand stone, large windows, ceilings of flat brick arches, and, on the top floor, a wooden roof structure and wood ceilings. This building has four elevations of the same length, with nine pilasters defining eight bays. Consequently, one pilaster is always on axis, something that was unthinkable in the baroque tradition. The building was very much influenced by the brick factories in England, which Schinkel had studied during his English travels in 1826. It is a cubus, skillfully placed into the landscape, an idea which was the precursor of the Garden City movement and of Le Corbusier.

To sum up Schinkel's achievements: He changed the historic core of Berlin. He created the Lustgarten, the climax of Unter den Linden, defined by the Royal Palace, Schinkel's museum, and the walls of trees which he planted. And Schinkel created the links between the old cities of Berlin and Cölln and Dorotheenstadt and, in the appropriate scale, with Unter den Linden. He improved Friedrichswerder by moving the shipping activities, which were previously scattered, to the splendid and efficient Packhof north of the museum. He improved the Werderscher Markt with his neogothic church by building the magnificent Bauakademie on a most appropriate site, and he prepared plans for linking Friedrichstadt and the old city, plans which were not implemented until after his death. He tied the two vertical churches on the Gendarmenmarkt together with his famous National Theater, and he improved the area of the Zeughaus, the university, and the opera with environmental improvements in connection with the new guard house, which, in itself, is an outstanding building in the classical style. Schinkel died in 1841.

Friedrich Wilhelm IV (1840 to 1861), a king with great interest in, knowledge of, and talent for architecture and environmental design, came to power in 1840 when the landscape architect and Royal Director of Gardens, Peter Josef Lenné presented a brilliant, bold, and imaginative plan for a projected landscape design for Berlin and environs. It included a wide sweeping circumferential tree-lined major artery north of the Spree River, ending in the west in a large, formally laid out area, just north of the Tiergarten. In the east it passed the Landsberger Gate. South of the Spree, he laid out a system of canals bordered by tree-lined avenues, accentuated by formal basins. This was an integral part of a lucid geometric system of tree-lined avenues and squares that structured the area called Köpenicker Feld (now largely Kreuzberg). The central system of canals continued in the south-western direction until it flowed into the Landwehr canal, which continued in a westerly direction until it joined the Spree River, just east of Charlottenburg. Of this grand plan, only the south-eastern sector in the Köpenicker Feld was implemented.

During the decade 1850–1860 a period of highly accelerated growth of the population began. Berlin grew to over half a million, and during the following eight decades it grew tenfold, to 4,250,000; this amounts to an average annual growth of 47,000 people. This growth, which was due to industrial development and, after 1871, to the fact that Berlin became the capital of the German empire, had two results: the need to make Berlin the hub of a transportation system, i.e., the focus of the German railroad network, and the need for an overall development plan.

In 1838 the Postsdam railroad was founded, and the Potsdamer station was built. This development was followed by the Anhalter, Frankfurter, and Hamburger rail lines and stations. In 1848 the standardization of the railroads was achieved, and in 1882 twelve lines converged on Berlin. During this time, the Stadtbahn, the Ring-railroad, and the 18-km-long East–West–Central rail line had been completed. (The construction of a north/south link had been the subject of many studies and competitions, but was never accomplished.) This network served the urban, regional, and international transportation needs of people and goods. It was both a response to as well as a stimulant of the city's growth.

Potsdamer Brücke (bridge) with Landwehrkanal, ward Tiergarten.—1899. Reproduced with permission of the Landesbildstelle Berlin.

The growth of Berlin necessitated also the development of an effective plan for the channelling of this vigorous development. The scope of such an undertaking was way beyond the capabilities of the Prussian kings.

In 1858 James Hobrecht began with the development of the overall plan which he completed in 1862. Based on some of the ideas underlying Lennés plan, in particular in the Köpenicker Feld area, he accepted the concept of a Ringstraße (a beltway) and the geometry of the southeastern quadrant. This plan was based on existing building codes. Buildings could be 22 meters high if the street was 15 meters wide. Interior courts had to measure 5.30 meters by 5.30 meters to permit the turning around of a fire engine.

The Hobrecht plan consisted of an approximately 2–3-kilometer-wide band which encompassed the city of 1840. These new areas were laid out in a grid-iron pattern defining sizeable blocks, including a number which measure 250 meters by 350 meters or 750 feet by 1050 feet, which is equivalent in area to six city blocks in Friedrichstadt or to five Manhattan blocks of 250 feet by 600 feet each. This permits very high utilization of the land. It was permitted to use the land in unlimited depth from the street, provided the street front was 20 meters or more in width. There is a complex that was five courtyard in depth from the access street. Through this layout it was possible to achieve densities of 2000 person per ha or 800 per acre and to settle a total of 4,000,000 people in the area included in the unfortunate Hobrecht plan, which was used until 1919. The resulting tenements with only one decent exposure to the street were called "Mietskasernen" ("rentable barracks"). They provided an urban desert of masonry which prompted Werner Hegemann, the architect, historian, city planner, and author to write *Das Steinerne Berlin* ("The Berlin of Stone").

In the courtyards of Ackerstraße 132–133, ward Wedding.—Photograph taken on May 5, 1965. Reproduced with permission of the Landesbildstelle Berlin.

In addition to the enormous density in construction, there was also shocking over-crowding. In 1860, 10 percent of all inhabitants lived in basements and 224,000 people lived at a density of 4.3 persons per room. In 1871, 162,000 persons lived in one-bedroom apartments at a density of 7.3 persons per apartment. This reckless exploitation of the land and of the workers, who flocked to Berlin in search of work, became *the* burning issue in the twenties. Intellectuals and artists were deeply concerned about living conditions in Berlin since the turn of the century. Since the revolution of 1918 it became *the* focus of concern of the architects of the modern movement.

At the same time, suburbs grew, in particular in a westerly direction and preferably along the Berlin-Postsdam railroad. Indeed, one of the most energetic developers, Johann Wilhelm Carsten, evolved a plan for a continuous stretch of suburbs from Berlin to Potsdam. He developed Wilmersdorf, Friedenau, Lichterfelde-Ost, and Lichterfelde-West. In 1912 the "Zweckverband Groß-Berlin" was founded, but it was completely ineffective. The first real reform took place in 1920, after World War I, when outlying districts were annexed to Berlin. In 1925 a new zoning code was enacted, which insured that the inhabitants enjoy air, light, and sun in their dwellings. This was a fundamental change.

There were two buildings in Berlin from the turn of the century, a period that contains the roots for the developments of the twenties, two buildings which had a profound influence on the development of the modern movement. The first was the department store Wertheim by Alfred Messel of 1896 on the Leipziger Straße. Messel built a structure which consisted largely of projecting columns and a recessed glass curtain wall with minimal spandrels. The sheets of glass decreased in size with the higher floors, but the mullions had small profiles and therefore did not diminish the appearance of a continuous glass curtain wall. The three central bays remained open to the street for two floors, making with the recessed wall a very generous entrance porch. This was an extremely bold concept which resulted in a ministerial rule prohibiting such excessive use of glass for a semipublic building. The building was way ahead of its time and had a great influence on the architecture of department stores in the decades to come.

The other building in Berlin, which was widely acclaimed, was the AEG turbine factory of Peter Behrens (1909). Walter Rathenau, president of AEG and in 1922 foreign minister of Germany, was the enlightened client of Behrens. He was anxious to express the nature of production in the building and to show concern for the welfare of the workers. One aspect was the need for good daylight at the working place, hence the large expanse of glass. However, at the gable ends of the building, traditional architectural thinking prevailed. The monumental masonry corners are purely symbolic. Nevertheless, this building had a lasting effect on contemporary architecture.

In addition to that, Hermann Muthesius reformed residential suburban architecture in Berlin. He was one of the founders of the Deutscher Werkbund (German Work Alliance). He was trained as an architect and had practiced architecture in Tokyo and Berlin, and he was attaché for architecture at the German embassy in London. He used this time to study contemporary architecture in England and published *Englische Baukunst der Gegenwart* ("Contempory English Architecture"). After his return to Germany, he introduced the English country house (Landhaus) in Berlin, replacing the traditional formal villa with its main floor about one meter above the level of the garden, access over formal steps, and the rooms arranged symmetrically around the axis of the entry. The Landhaus, on the other hand, has its main floor at the level of the garden, which is regarded as an extension of the

AEG Turbinenfabrik (General Electric Company Turbine Plant Factory), Hutten-
straße, ward Tiergarten/Moabit; built 1909; architect: Peter Behrens. From April 1,
1969: KWU (Power Plant Union limited company).—Around 1912. Reproduced with
permission of the Landesbildstelle Berlin.

house. The floorplan is informal, which—for the various activity areas—
may result in an open plan with a variety of spaces of different dimensions.

The aim of the Werkbund was to promote the cooperation of craftsmen,
artists, industrialists, and merchants in order to improve the visual as well as
the functional quality of German production. The association had conferences, produced publications, and organized exhibitions of industrial products and architecture.

After Emperor Wilhelm II had abdicated at the end of World War I, a new
era began with the formation of a parliamentarian government in Germany.
On August 13, 1919, the Weimar constitution became effective. A new spirit
prevailed in Berlin and in Germany. The working class gained power, and
one of its priorities was decent and healthy housing for persons of low and
moderate income. Beginning in 1919, a number of laws and regulations were
enacted and certain measures were taken to enable the government to insure
the enjoyment of light, sun, and air for each inhabitant at a reasonable cost.

In 1920 the *Reichsheimstättengesetz* (Basic Housing Law) was introduced.
This law allowed the state to control the use of the existing housing stock, in
terms of intensity and of the type of use. Residential units could neither be
converted to offices nor used for other commercial purposes; rent control
and other relevant protection for the user were introduced. In 1922 govern-

Villa Kirchweg 33 "Der Mittelhof" ("The Middle Court"), ward Zehlendorf/ Nikolassee; example of an English country house; built 1914; architect: Hermann Muthesius. Now: place of the historical commission Berlin.—March 26, 1968. Reproduced with permission of the Landesbildstelle Berlin.

ment credits were made available for housing construction. A year later, German inflation was brought under control. In 1924 the housing program was activated, and in 1925 zoning for Berlin was made much more restrictive.

The Weimar Republic lasted from 1919 to 1933. It took five years until the necessary laws and organizations could become effective, resources be mobilized, and runaway inflation be controlled. Consequently, the housing program could not be implemented before 1924, and after 1931 the program had to be terminated due to the Great Depression, which affected the economies of all Western nations. Thus, the Weimar Republic had a mere seven years to meet the enormous housing shortage. In spite of these adverse circumstances, the city of Berlin, in cooperation with a number of mutual benefit corporations, the government, and the private sector, built 135,000 dwelling units for 610,000 people, families with low- to moderate-income, an average of 19,286 units per year. Of these, 61.42 percent were built by cooperatives and 38.58 percent by the private sector. One outstanding example is the so-called Hufeisen Siedlung (horseshoe settlement) or Groß-Siedlung Britz, surrounding a small park with a pond in the center. The units vary in size from 49 square meters to 100 square meters. There is a great

Hufeisensiedling (Horseshoe Settlement), ward Neukölln/Britz; built 1925–1930. Planning and layout by Bruno Taut and Martin Wagner. From left to the right downwards: Fritz Reuter-Allee.—Photograph after 1945. Reproduced with permission of the Landesbildstelle Berlin.

variety of layouts through the curving or bending of streets, the development of open spaces, and the changing of house types. Other outstanding settlements are the Waldsiedlung Zehlendorf and Siemensstadt, adjacent to the factories of the Siemens corporation. Outstanding planners were Bruno Taut, Martin Wagner, Hugo Häring, and Otto Rudolf Salvisberg. For Siemensstadt, the overall planning was undertaken by Hans Scharoun and Martin Wagner. Section A contains 1,678 dwelling units on a site of 16 ha or 40 acres at a density of 42 dwellings per acre. The architects were: Hans Scharoun, Walter Gropius, Hugo Häring, Fred Forbat, Paul Rudolf Henning, and Otto Bartning. Siemensstadt was built from 1929 to 1934. The apartments vary from one room to 4.5 rooms. There are eleven shops, five offices, and three garages within this complex. The settlement enjoyed international acclaim. Like the other two developments, it had the needed social infrastructure and was planned for families of moderate to middle income.

In 1933 the Nazis "legally" usurped the power in the German government, a position they held until 1945. During these 12 years, 102,000 dwellings were built in Berlin, an average of 8500 units per year. I is interesting to realize that the Nazis, in spite of a dictatorship and centralized planning, produced only 44 percent of the number of dwellings per year (19,286) built during the Weimar Republic. The population of Berlin continued to grow. From 1920 to 1944 it increased by 673,000 persons.

The loss of housing stock due to World War II was 40 percent or 612,000 of a total of 1,562,000 dwellings. In the central area of the city, the destruction amounted to 70 percent. The major destruction took place in an area of 25.5 square kilometers. About 500,000 persons died during the bombardments of the war. This was the situation in 1945, at the end of World War II.

During the years from 1945 to 1951 it was necessary to remove the rubble and to repair all dwellings that had suffered minor damages. Fifty-five to sixty million cubic meters of rubble were carted away; about 10,000 damaged dwellings were repaired, and 1500 new apartments were built. This was made possible through a special assessment and donations of building material from the occupying powers, as well as through the Marshall Plan.

Beginning with 1952, after the social market economy, initiated by Dr. Ludwig Erhard, had resulted in a remarkable economic recovery, and after the housing law had been enacted, Berlin produced 338,931 dwellings from 1952 to 1968, of which 80 percent were subsidized as social housing (sozialer Wohnungsbau). This amounted to 21,200 units per year as compared to 19,300 during the Weimar Republic, an increase of about 10 percent. However, the units were smaller, starting with one-room apartments of 22–32 square meters to 2.5-room apartments of 55–65 square meters for the largest units. This is very modest compared with Britz where the apartments range from 46 to 80 square meters. However, speed was of the essence after World War II, since the demand was accentuated by the enormous loss of dwellings during the war.

It is impossible to discuss the great variety of housing types which were developed during that time, but I would like to describe the Märkisches Viertel in the north of Berlin West which has aroused a great deal of interest and notoriety.

The Märkisches Viertel represents an attempt to develop a high-density settlement integrated with large recreational open spaces and existing low-density housing. In laying out the high-density buildings, it was the objective to catch the sun in large interconnected courts open to the south, forming a continuous ridge. The communal and commercial center, which is also connected with a high school, is located in a central position. In the center, an urban, tree-shaded promenade will offer the opportunity to stroll; and it is hoped that the presence of ultimately 18,000 dwellings on a 385-ha area within walking distance of the center with a potential population of 50,000 to 60,000 will insure a lively area which will become not only an administrative and commercial center, but also a social and cultural center for the Märkisches Viertel and its environs. The overall planning was done by Professor Werner Düttmann, George Heinrichs, and Hans Müller. The developer is the De-Ge-Wo, i.e., Deutsche Gesellschaft zur Förderung des Wohnungsbaues, Gemeinnützige Aktiengesellschaft (German Association for the Promotion of Housing, Mutual Benefit Corporation). Construction was started in 1963. It is proposed to develop landscaping of high quality; in this suburban community, all parking areas are to be shaded by trees.

Two world-renowned buildings for cultural pursuits which were built since the war are Scharoun's Philharmonie (1960–63) and the New National

Neue Nationalgalerie (New National Gallery), Potsdamerstraße 50, ward Tiergarten; museum built for the art of the 19th and 20th centuries; built 1965–68; architect: Mies van der Rohe. Behind at the left: St. Matthäi Church at the Matthäi church place (Matthäikirchplatz); right in the background: New Philharmonie.—August 20, 1968. Reproduced with permission of the Landesbildstelle Berlin.

Gallery by Mies van der Rohe (1956–68). Both are on the Mathäikirchplatz. The concert hall of the Philharmonie floats above the foyer, from which exposed stairs rise to the auditorium. The seating is separated into large segments and clustered around the podium. By dividing the 2200 seats into smaller elements, each section is of a comprehensible and human scale. The resulting acoustics are outstanding. One might call the Philharmonie, because of its flowing forms, a building in some way reminiscent of Expressionism; Mies van der Rohe's National Gallery across the square is definitely in the tradition of Prussian neoclassicism. The prominent entrance hall of the National Gallery, a square roof supported by eight soaring steel columns, is a magnificent space sculpture which, however, should not shelter just any art. In my opinion it could house three or five large sculptures in scale with the splendid glass-enclosed space. The main collection is tucked away in the terrace on which the entrance hall stands. This lower floor can be reached over a stair that seems inadequate in relation to the grand entrance hall which could be called an enclosed court d'honneur. The lower floor receives daylight from a sunken area.

We looked at Berlin, the outpost, a city with the tradition of frugality and discipline of a frontier settlement in an infertile province, a history of Protestant ethics, a history of promoted immigration, based on and resulting in an openess to other cultures, and planned and subsidized growth. This city was the result of political will, and without support and guidance it would not have taken off in the middle of the nineteenth century to become a world city. Indeed, the growth was so rapid that it became uncontrollable and within eight decades grew from half a million to about 4.5 million inhabitants, to become the largest city on the European continent.

Three times defeated, first by Napoleon and then in two world wars, and now divided, it has an unbroken vitality, defying conventional wisdom. It also has a future which will be the theme for another chapter on this formidable city.